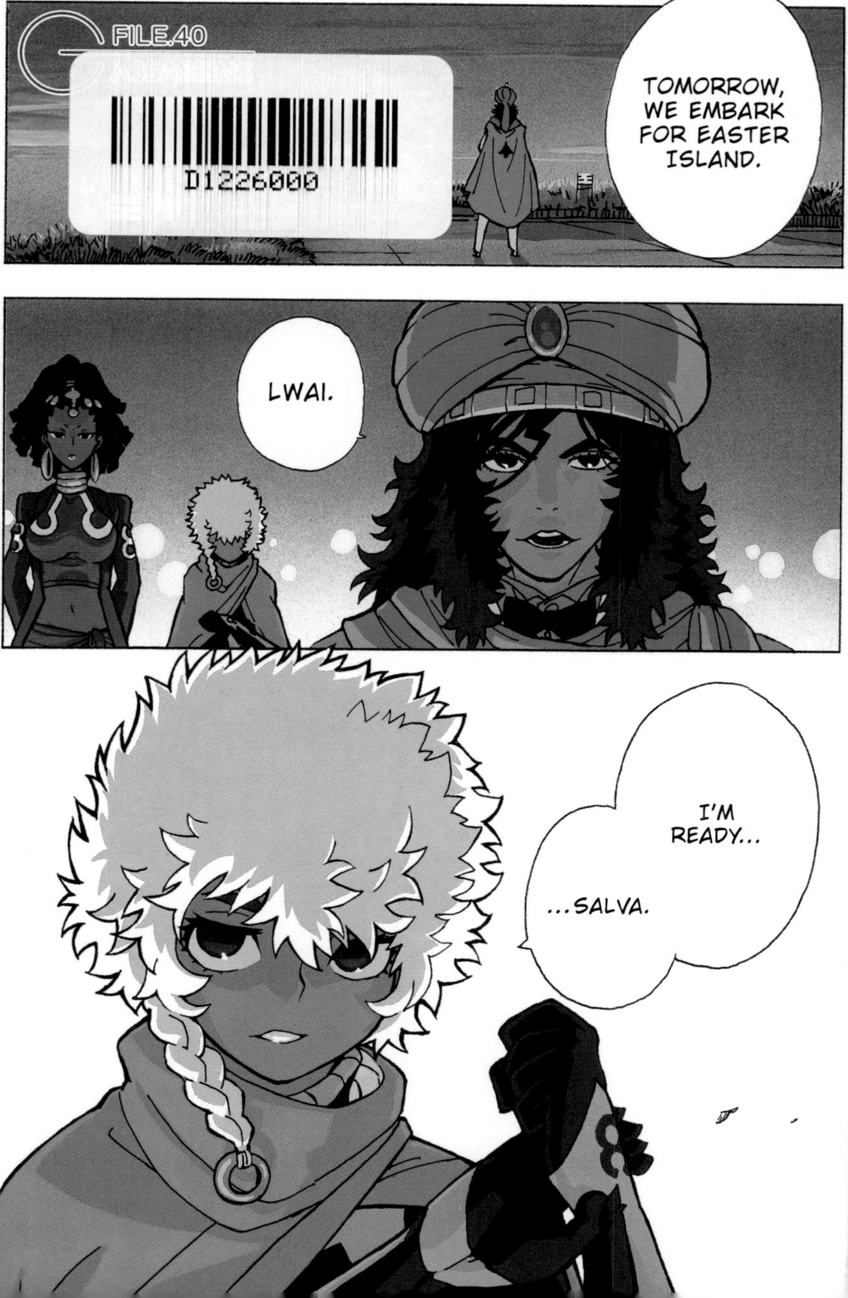
TOMORROW, WE EMBARK FOR EASTER ISLAND.
FILE.40
LWAI.
I'M READY...
...SALVA.

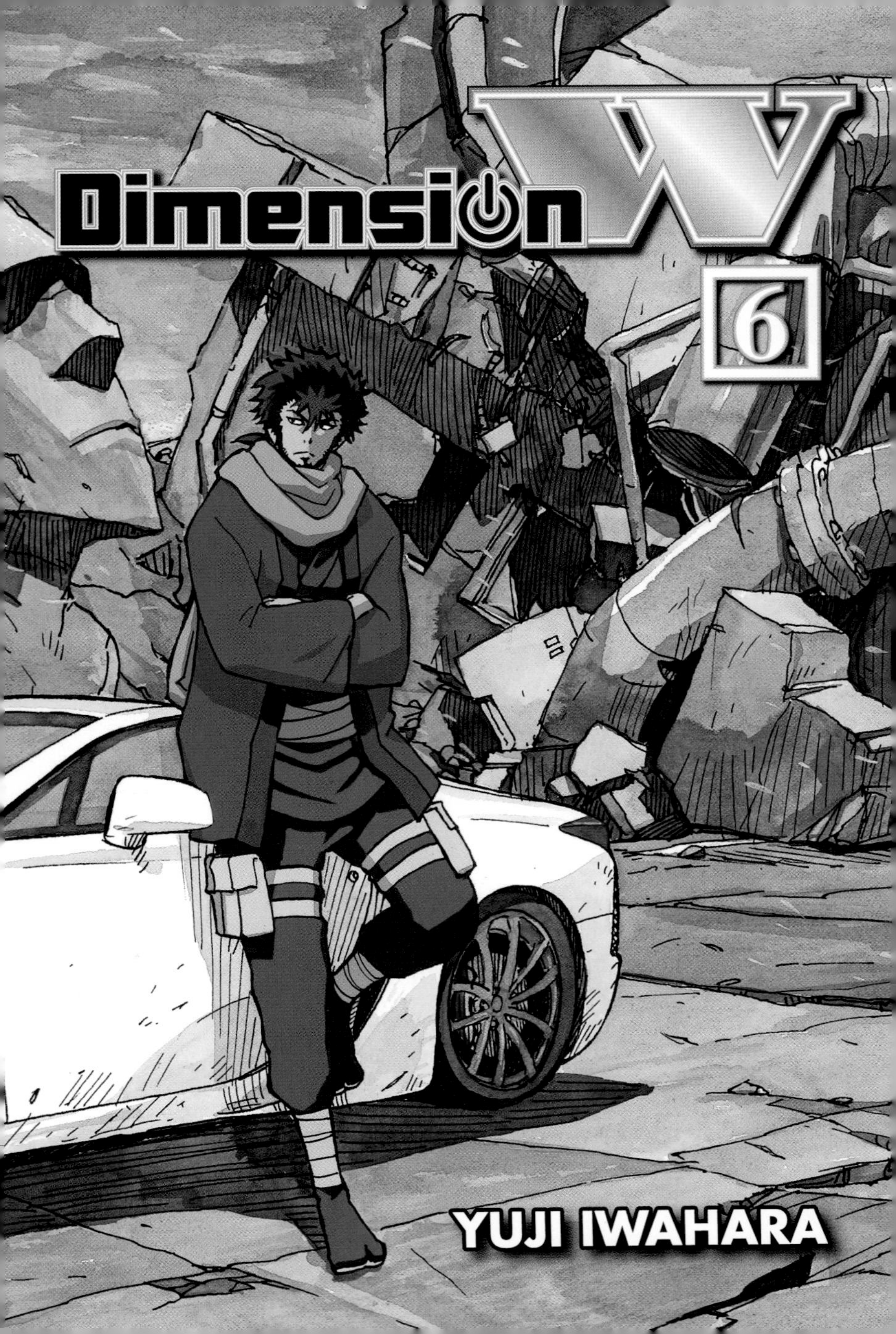
Dimension W
6
YUJI IWAHARA

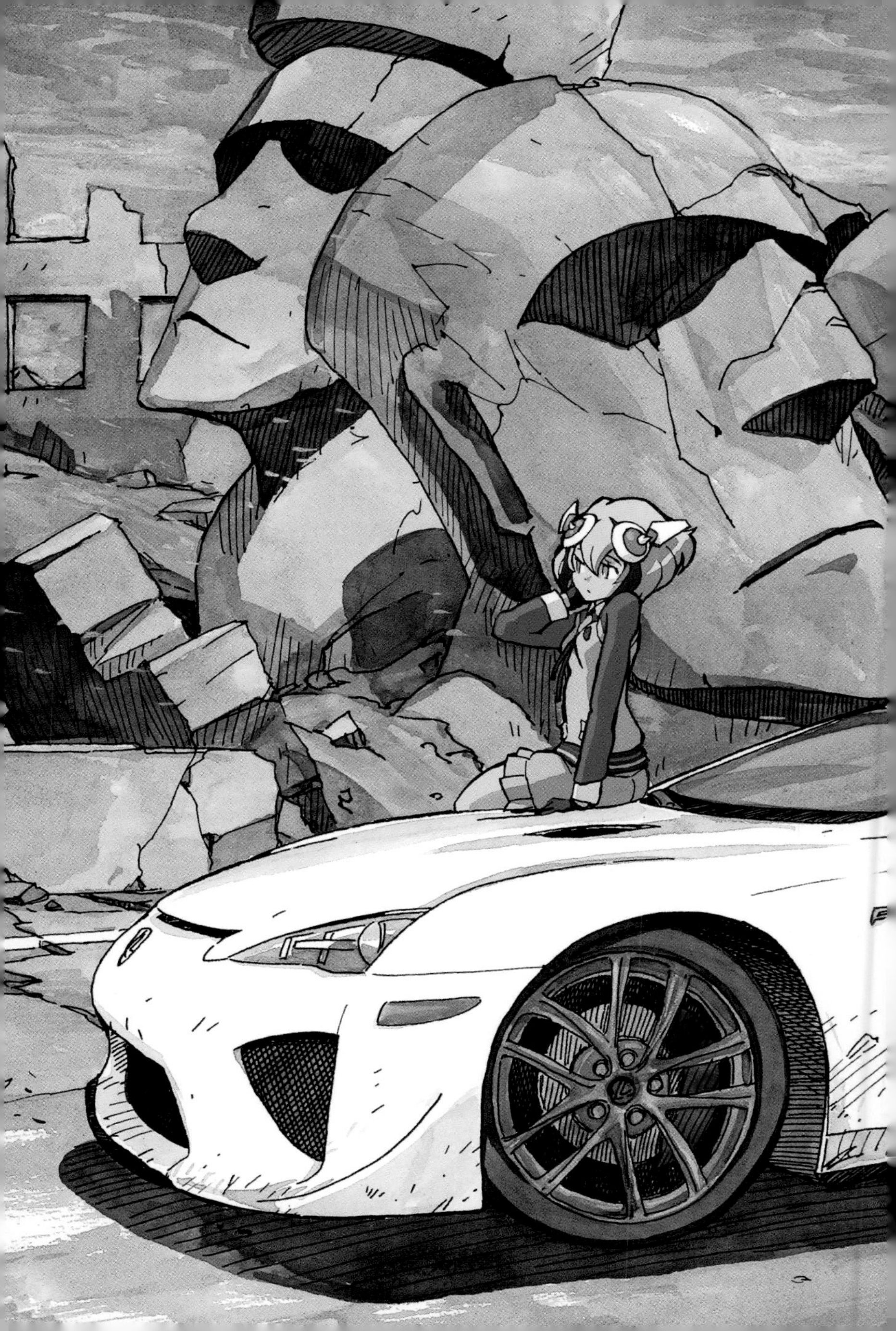

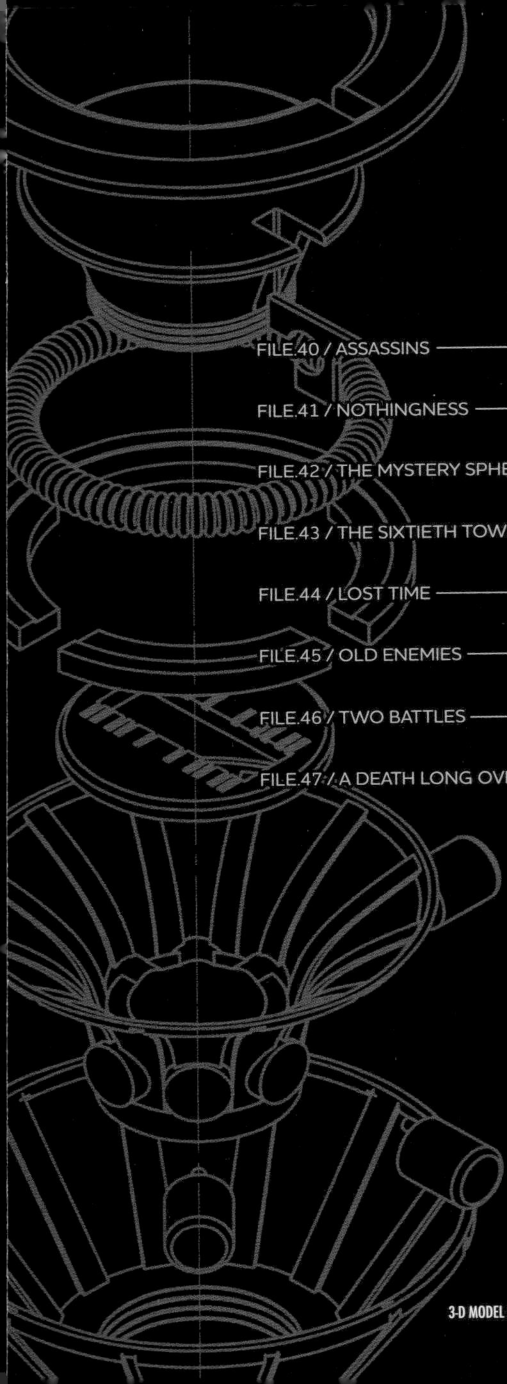

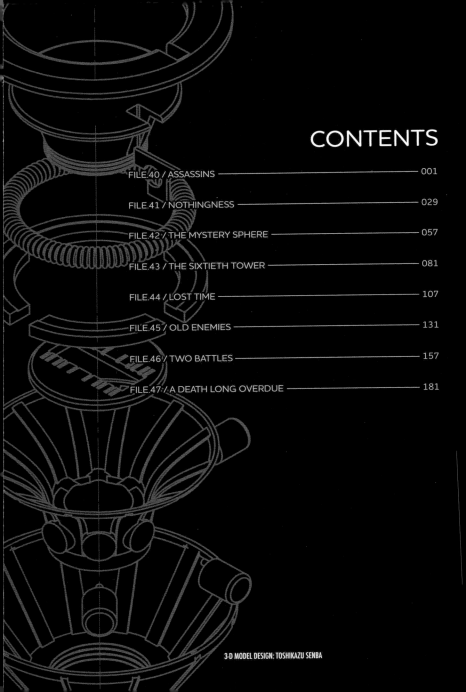

# CONTENTS



3-D MODEL DESIGN: TOSHIKAZU SENBA

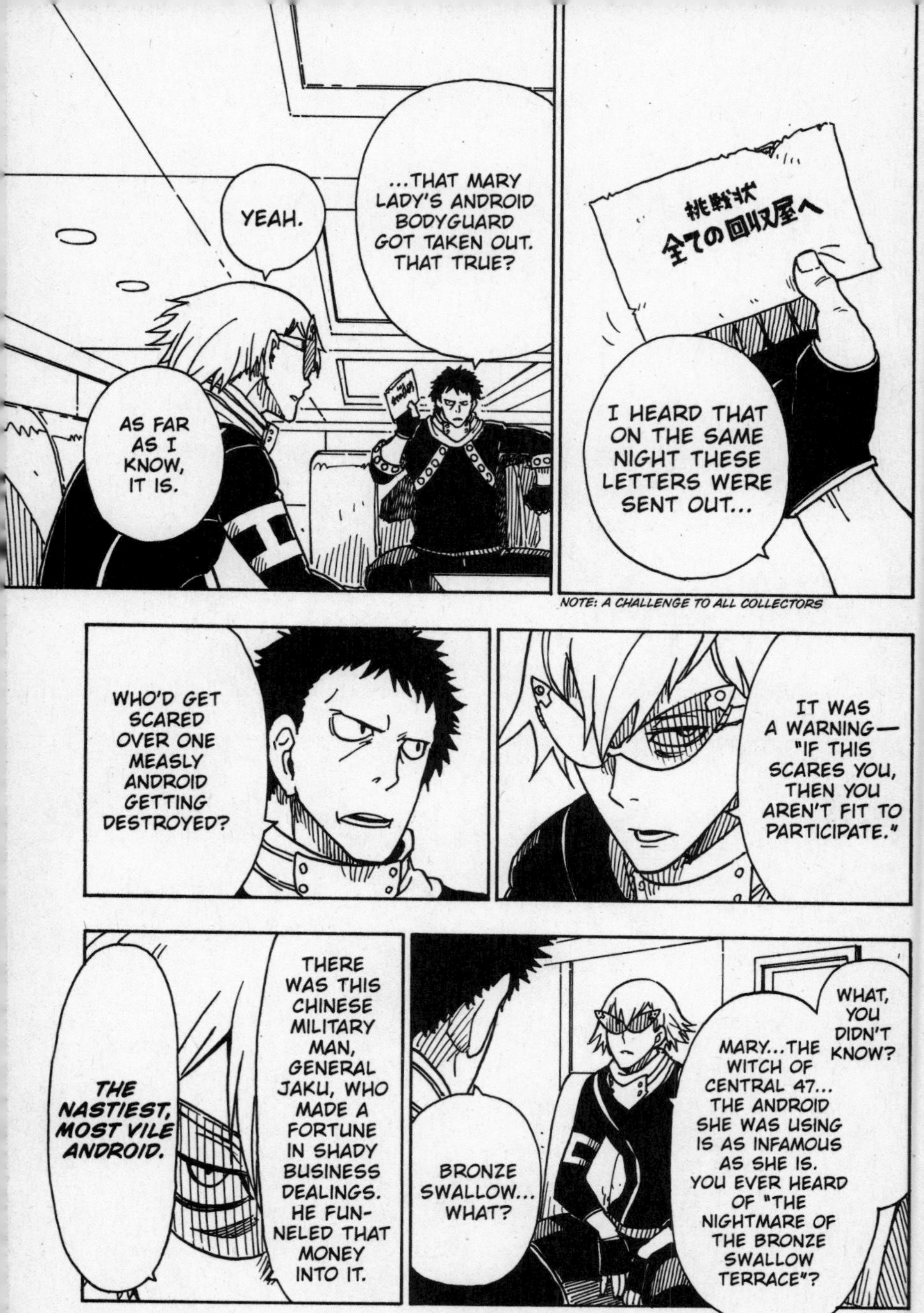
挑戦状
全ての回収屋へ
I HEARD THAT ON THE SAME NIGHT THESE LETTERS WERE SENT OUT...
NOTE: A CHALLENGE TO ALL COLLECTORS
...THAT MARY LADY'S ANDROID BODYGUARD GOT TAKEN OUT. THAT TRUE?
YEAH.
AS FAR AS I KNOW, IT IS.
IT WAS A WARNING—"IF THIS SCARES YOU, THEN YOU AREN'T FIT TO PARTICIPATE."
WHO'D GET SCARED OVER ONE MEASLY ANDROID GETTING DESTROYED?
WHAT, YOU DIDN'T KNOW?
MARY...THE WITCH OF CENTRAL 47... THE ANDROID SHE WAS USING IS AS INFAMOUS AS SHE IS. YOU EVER HEARD OF "THE NIGHTMARE OF THE BRONZE SWALLOW TERRACE"?
BRONZE SWALLOW... WHAT?
THERE WAS THIS CHINESE MILITARY MAN, GENERAL JAKU, WHO MADE A FORTUNE IN SHADY BUSINESS DEALINGS. HE FUN-NELED THAT MONEY INTO IT.
THE NASTIEST, MOST VILE ANDROID.

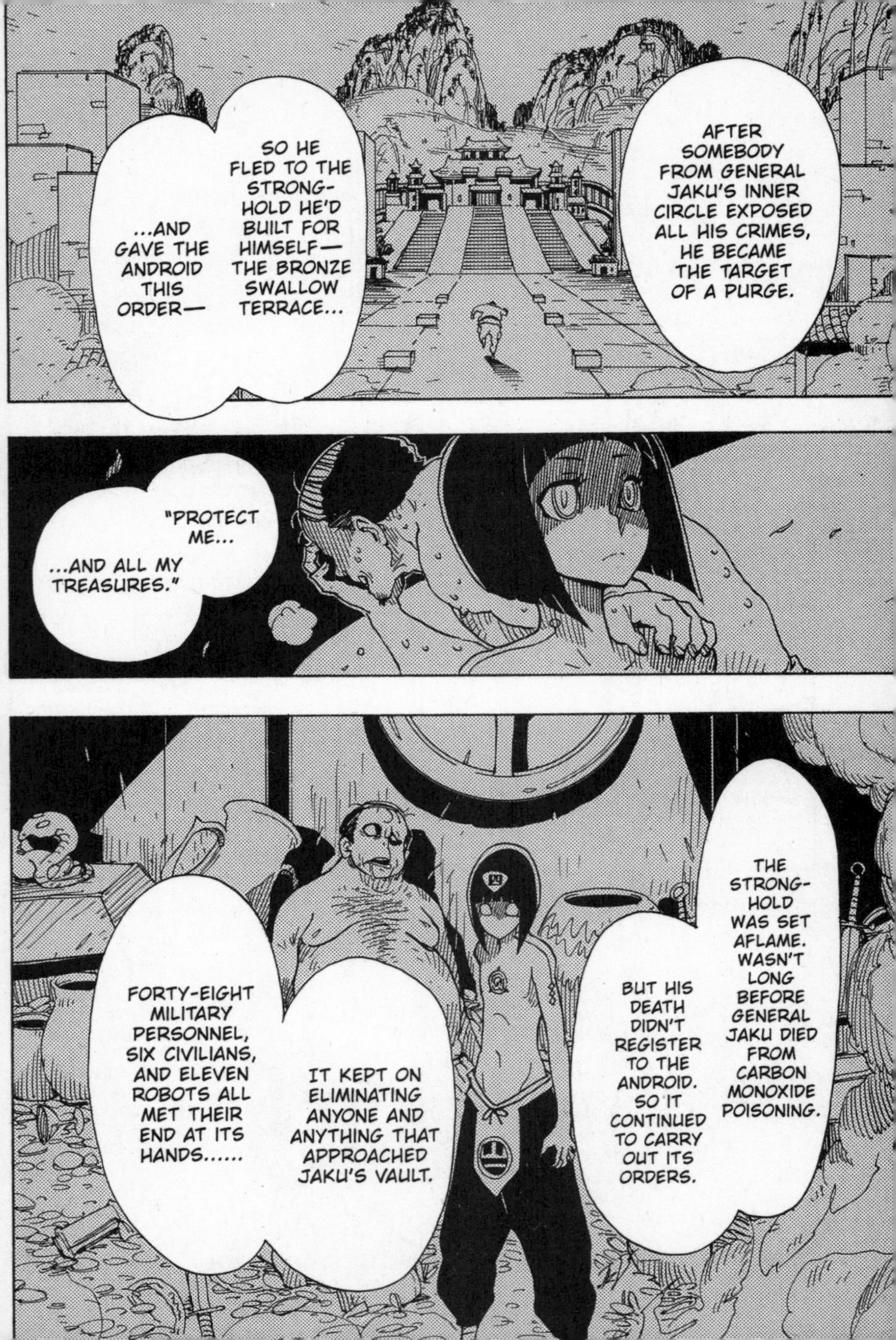
AFTER SOMEBODY FROM GENERAL JAKU'S INNER CIRCLE EXPOSED ALL HIS CRIMES, HE BECAME THE TARGET OF A PURGE.
SO HE FLED TO THE STRONG-HOLD HE'D BUILT FOR HIMSELF—THE BRONZE SWALLOW TERRACE...
...AND GAVE THE ANDROID THIS ORDER—
"PROTECT ME...
...AND ALL MY TREASURES."
THE STRONG-HOLD WAS SET AFLAME. WASN'T LONG BEFORE GENERAL JAKU DIED FROM CARBON MONOXIDE POISONING.
BUT HIS DEATH DIDN'T REGISTER TO THE ANDROID. SO IT CONTINUED TO CARRY OUT ITS ORDERS.
IT KEPT ON ELIMINATING ANYONE AND ANYTHING THAT APPROACHED JAKU'S VAULT.
FORTY-EIGHT MILITARY PERSONNEL, SIX CIVILIANS, AND ELEVEN ROBOTS ALL MET THEIR END AT ITS HANDS......

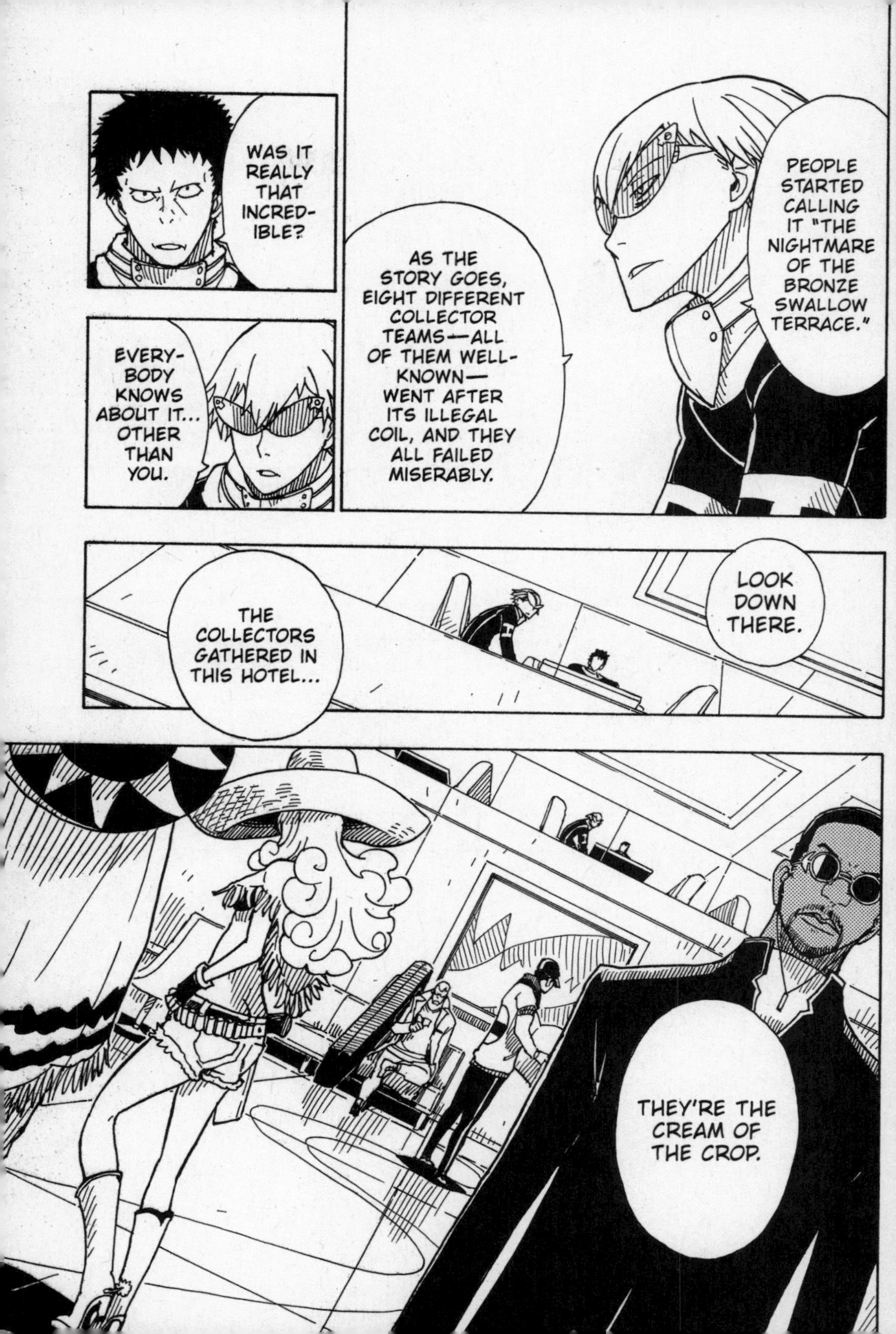
PEOPLE STARTED CALLING IT "THE NIGHTMARE OF THE BRONZE SWALLOW TERRACE."
AS THE STORY GOES, EIGHT DIFFERENT COLLECTOR TEAMS—ALL OF THEM WELL-KNOWN—WENT AFTER ITS ILLEGAL COIL, AND THEY ALL FAILED MISERABLY.
WAS IT REALLY THAT INCRED-IBLE?
EVERY-BODY KNOWS ABOUT IT... OTHER THAN YOU.
LOOK DOWN THERE.
THE COLLECTORS GATHERED IN THIS HOTEL...
THEY'RE THE CREAM OF THE CROP.

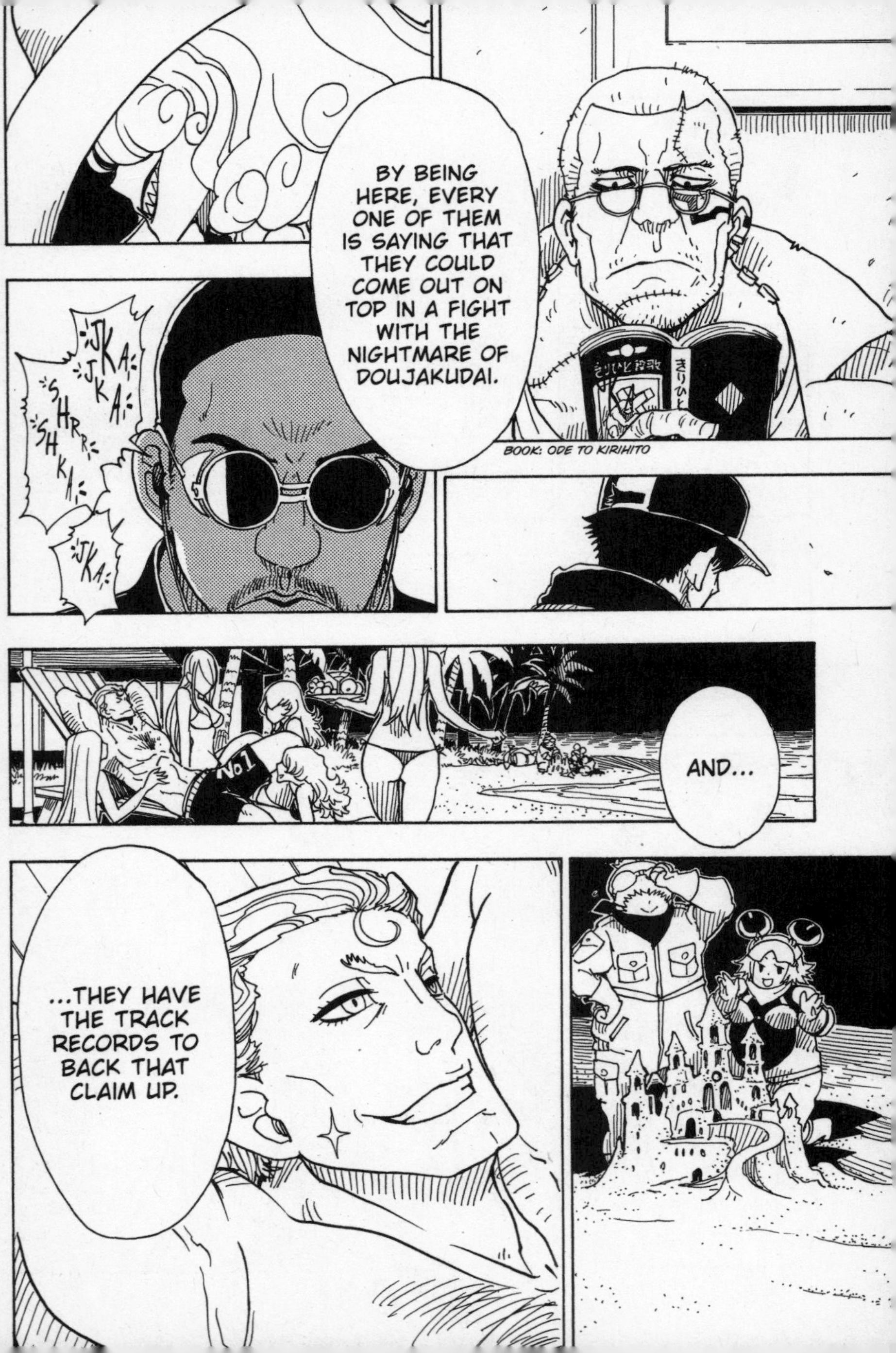

BY BEING HERE, EVERY ONE OF THEM IS SAYING THAT THEY COULD COME OUT ON TOP IN A FIGHT WITH THE NIGHTMARE OF DOUJAKUDAI.
BOOK: ODE TO KIRIHITO
JKA JKA
SHRR
SHKA
JKA
No1
AND...
...THEY HAVE THE TRACK RECORDS TO BACK THAT CLAIM UP.

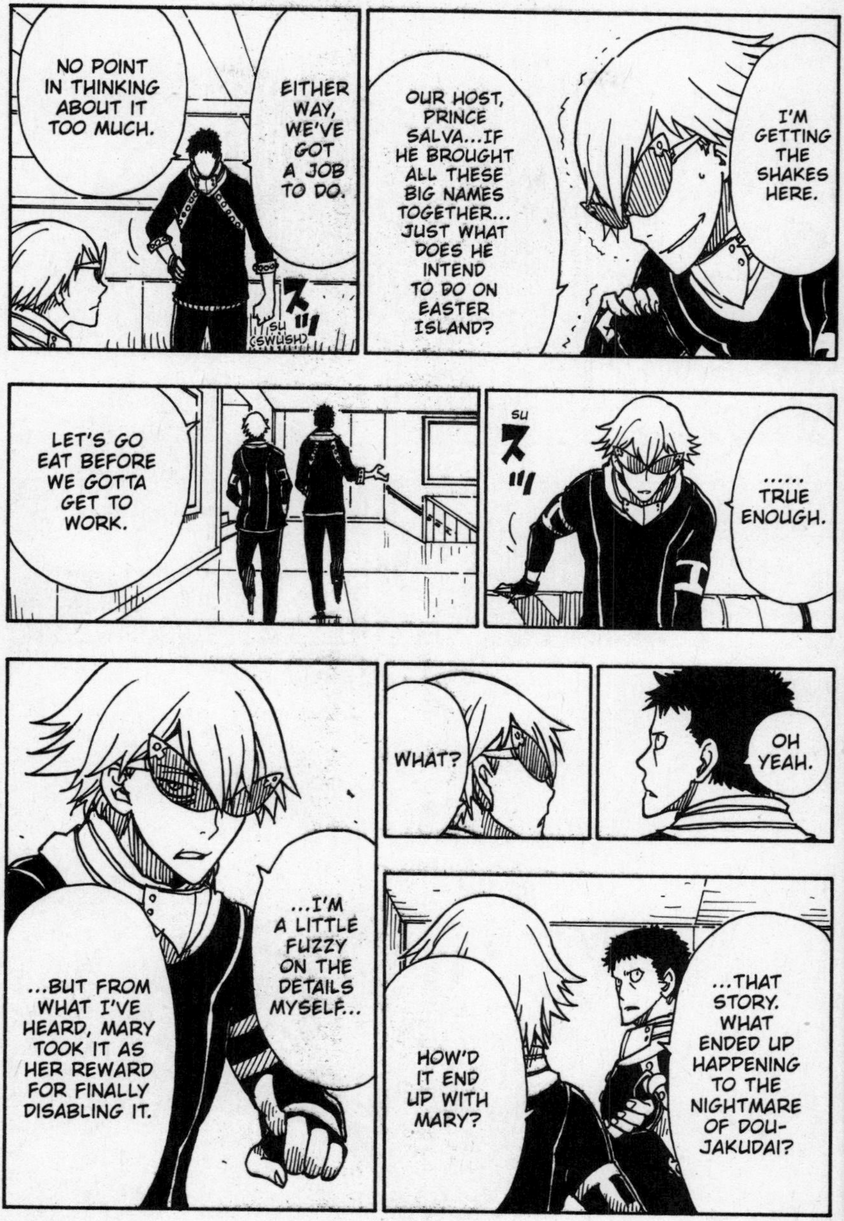
I'M GETTING THE SHAKES HERE.
OUR HOST, PRINCE SALVA...IF HE BROUGHT ALL THESE BIG NAMES TOGETHER... JUST WHAT DOES HE INTEND TO DO ON EASTER ISLAND?
EITHER WAY, WE'VE GOT A JOB TO DO.
NO POINT IN THINKING ABOUT IT TOO MUCH.
スッ
SU (SWUSH)
......TRUE ENOUGH.
SU
スッ
LET'S GO EAT BEFORE WE GOTTA GET TO WORK.
OH YEAH.
WHAT?
...THAT STORY. WHAT ENDED UP HAPPENING TO THE NIGHTMARE OF DOU-JAKUDAI?
HOW'D IT END UP WITH MARY?
...I'M A LITTLE FUZZY ON THE DETAILS MYSELF...
...BUT FROM WHAT I'VE HEARD, MARY TOOK IT AS HER REWARD FOR FINALLY DISABLING IT.

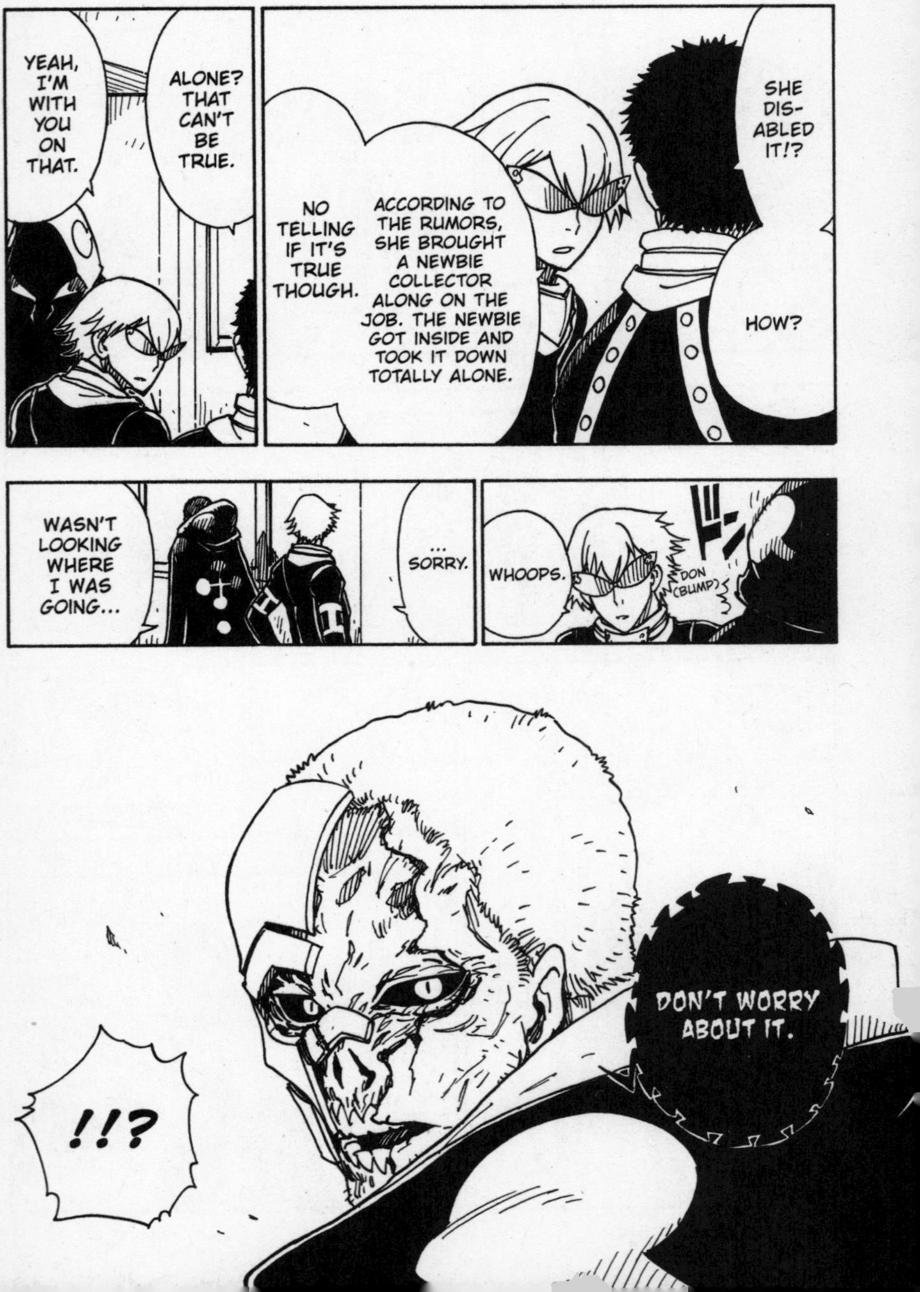
SHE DIS-ABLED IT!?
HOW?
ACCORDING TO THE RUMORS, SHE BROUGHT A NEWBIE COLLECTOR ALONG ON THE JOB. THE NEWBIE GOT INSIDE AND TOOK IT DOWN TOTALLY ALONE.
NO TELLING IF IT'S TRUE THOUGH.
ALONE? THAT CAN'T BE TRUE.
YEAH, I'M WITH YOU ON THAT.
DON (BUMP)
WHOOPS.
... SORRY.
WASN'T LOOKING WHERE I WAS GOING...
DON'T WORRY ABOUT IT.
!!?

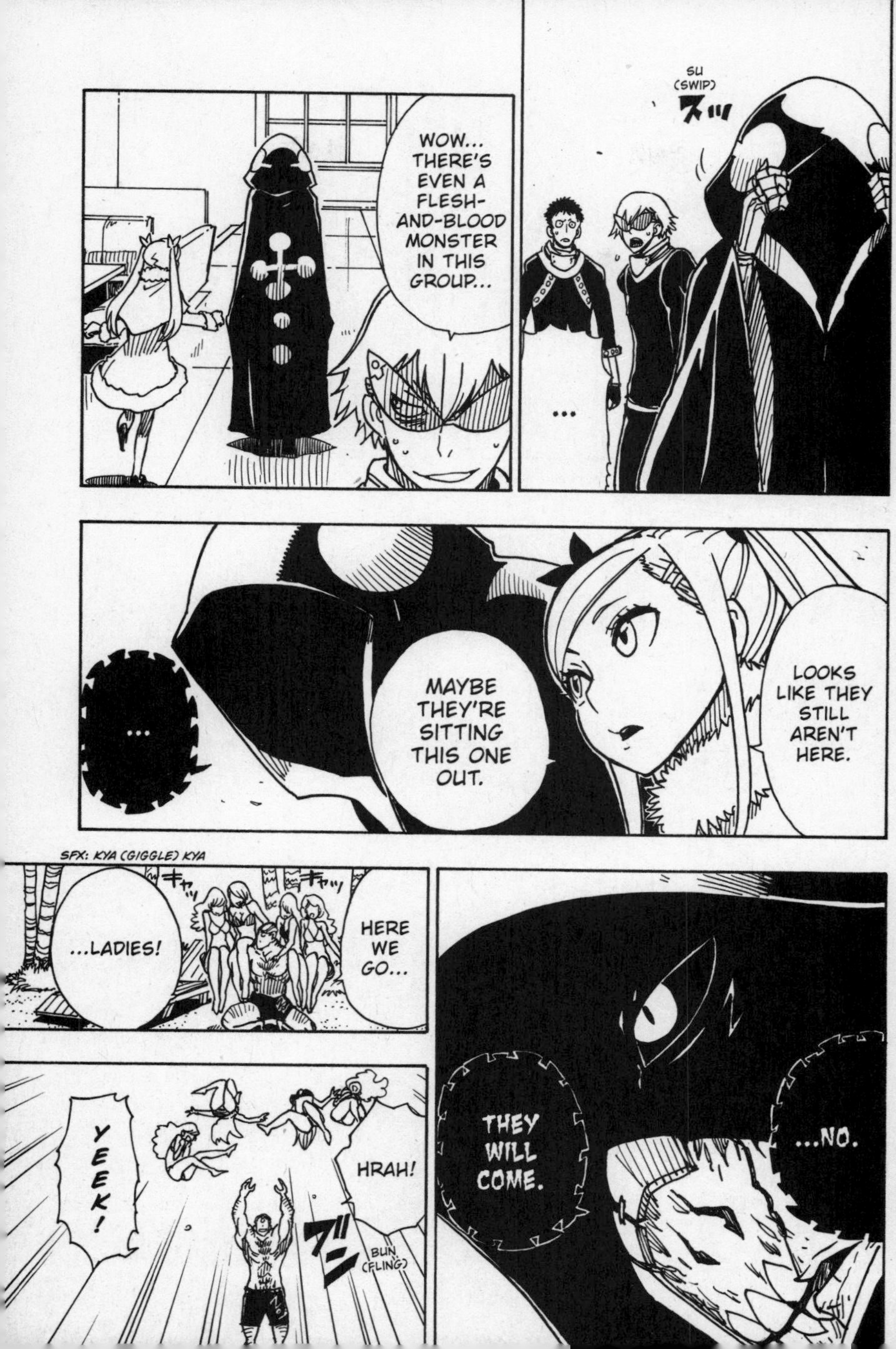
SU (SWIP)
スッ
...
WOW... THERE'S EVEN A FLESH-AND-BLOOD MONSTER IN THIS GROUP...
LOOKS LIKE THEY STILL AREN'T HERE.
MAYBE THEY'RE SITTING THIS ONE OUT.
...
...NO.
THEY WILL COME.
SFX: KYA (GIGGLE) KYA
キャッ
キャッ
HERE WE GO...
...LADIES!
HRAH!
ブン
BUN (FLING)
YEEK!

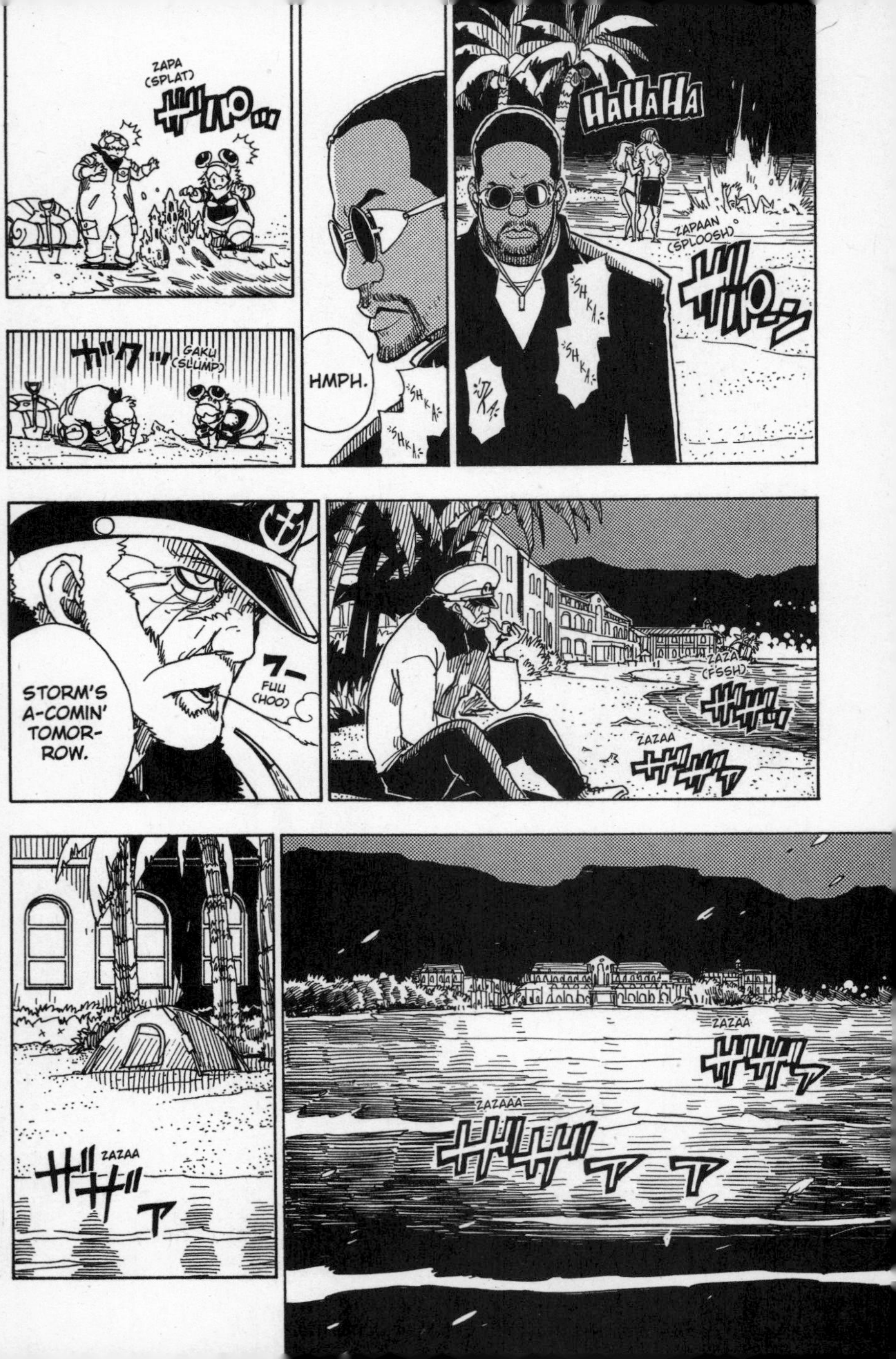
HAHAHA
ZAPAAN (SPLOOSH)
SHKA
SHKA
ZKA
HMPH.
SHKA
SHKA
ZAPA (SPLAT)
GAKU (SLUMP)
ZAZA (FSSH)
ZAZAA
STORM'S A-COMIN' TOMORROW.
FUU (HOO)
ZAZAA
ZAZAAA
ZAZAA

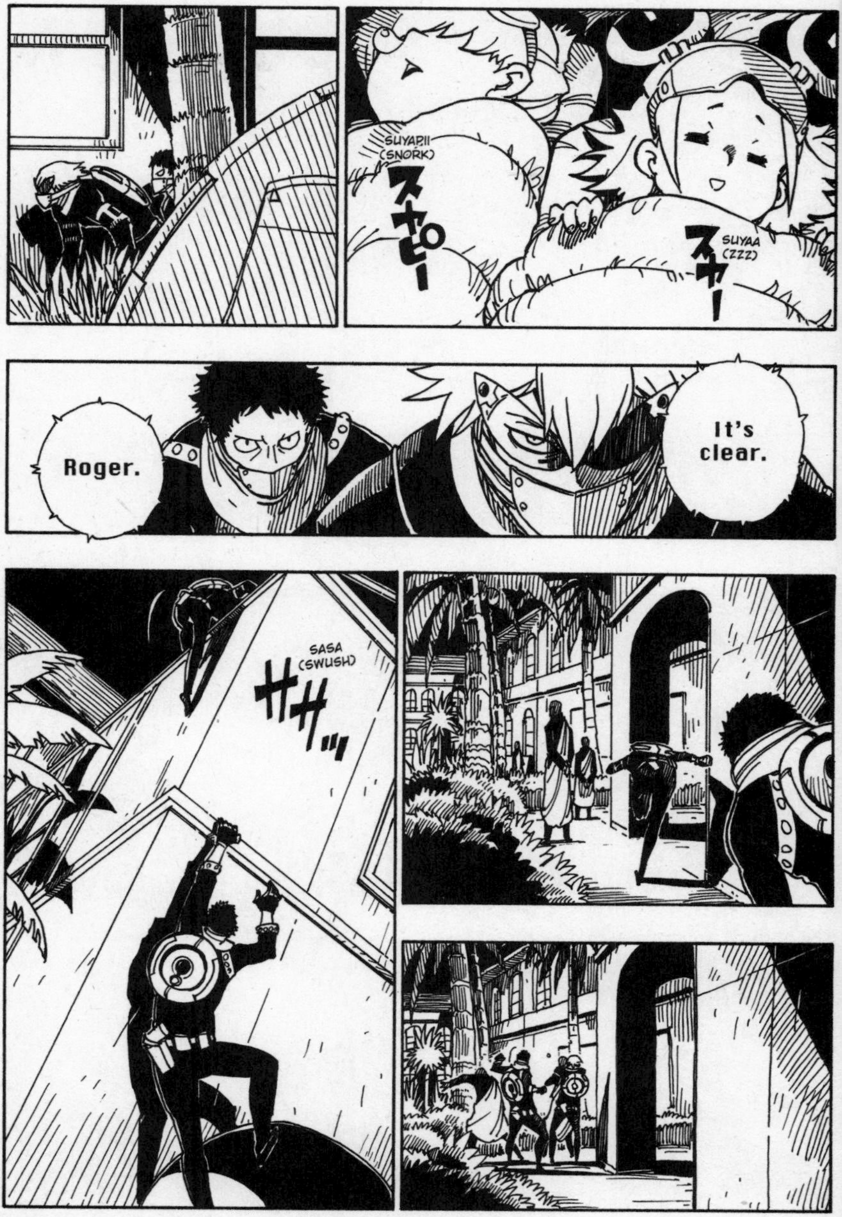
SUYAA (ZZZ)
スヤー
SUYAPII (SNORK)
スヤピー
It's clear.
Roger.
SASA (SWUSH)
ササッ

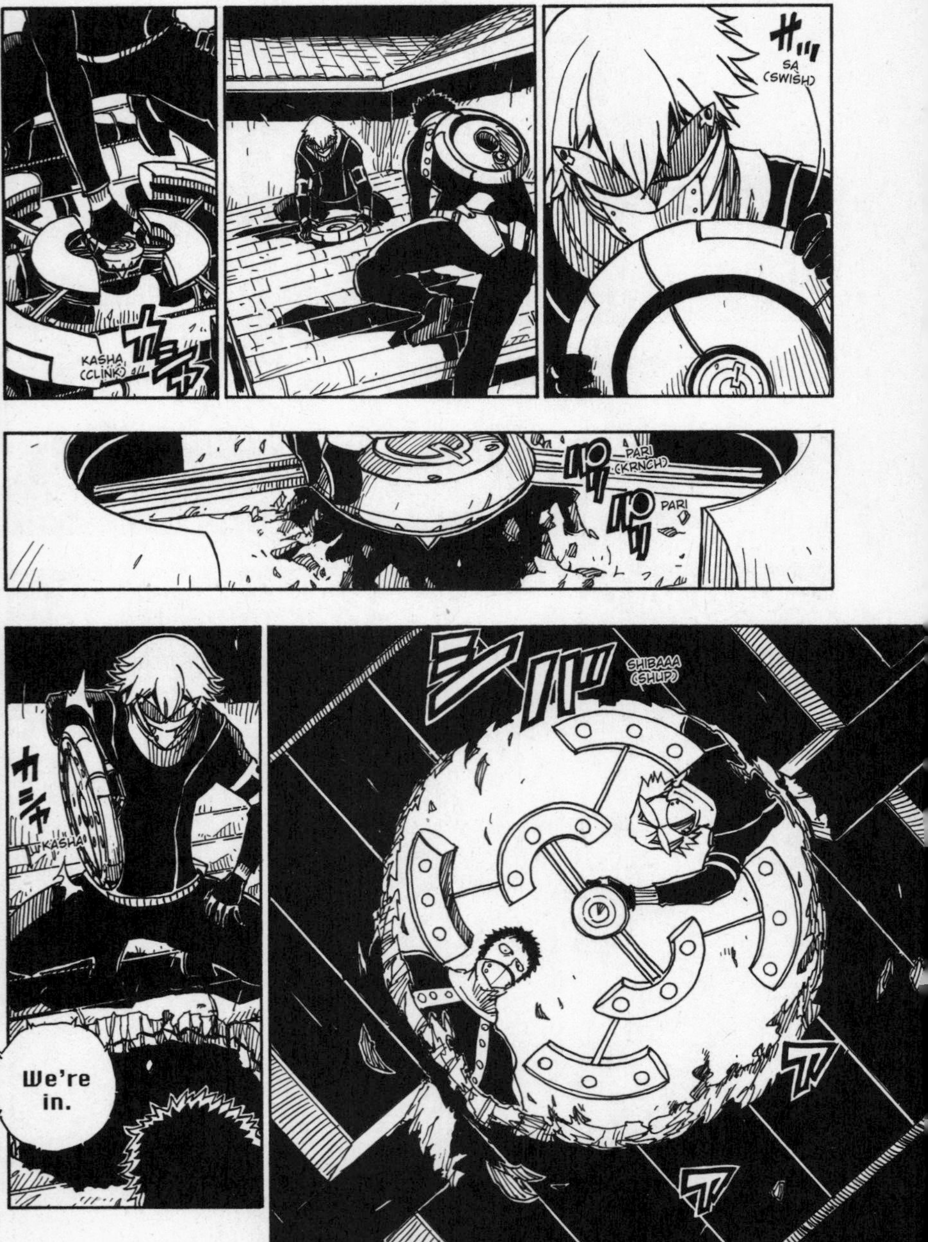
ザッ
SA (SWISH)
カシャ
KASHA (CLINK)
パリ
PARI (KRNCH)
パリ
PARI
シバ
SHIBAAA (SHUP)
カシャ
KASHA
We're in.

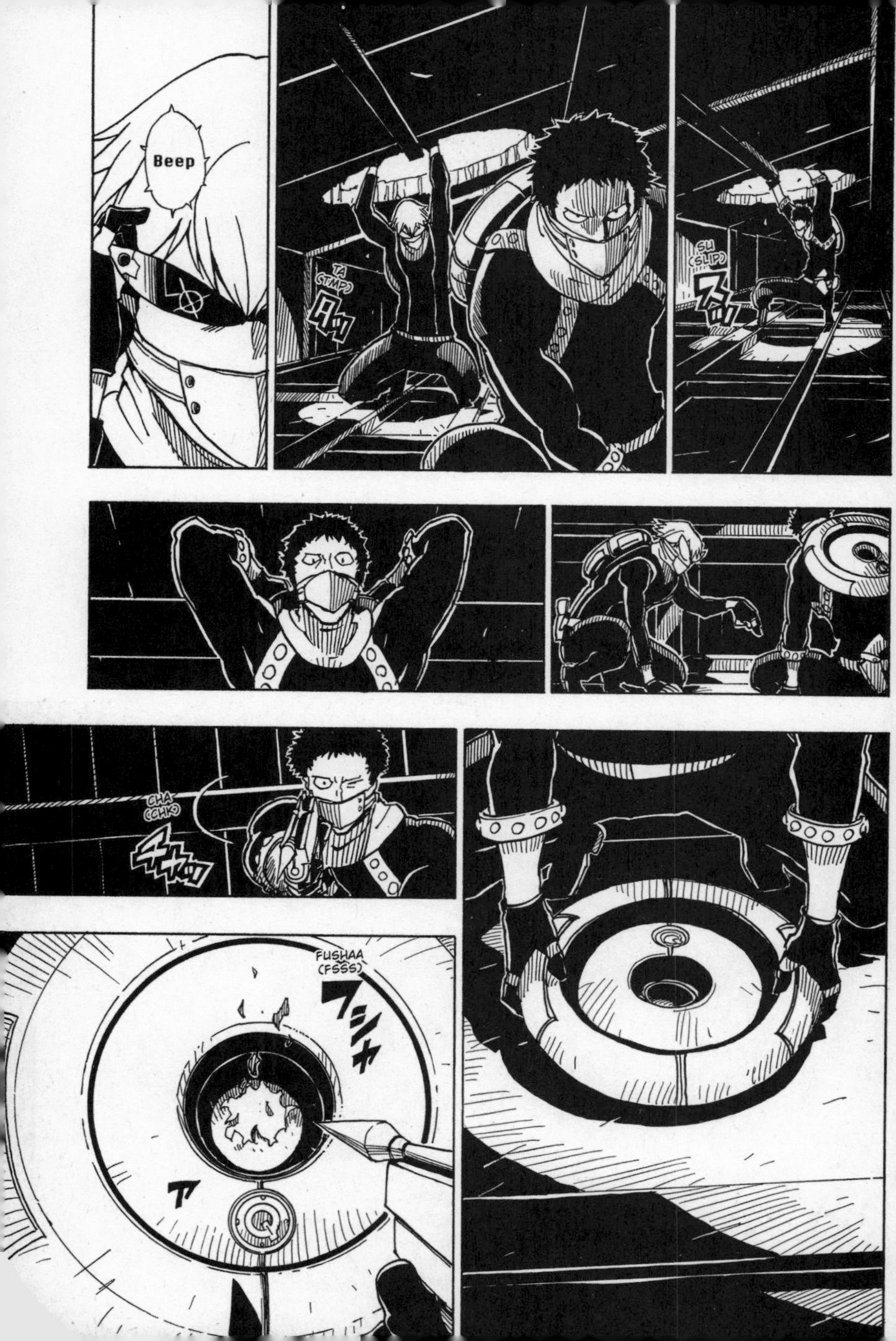
SU (SLIP)
TA (TMP)
Beep
CHA (CHK)
FUSHAA (FSSS)

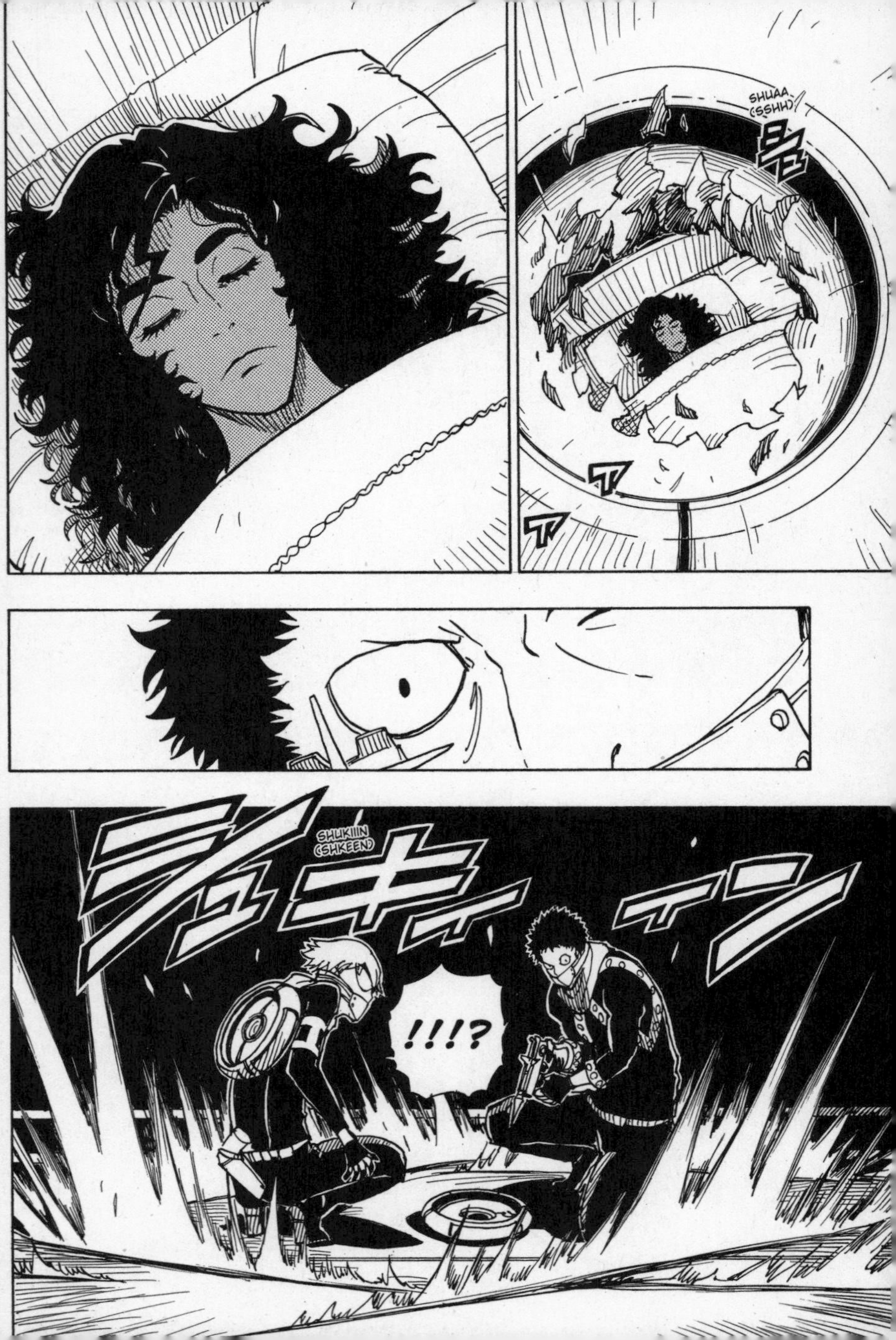
SHUAA (SSHH)
SHUKIIIN (SHKEEN)
!!!?

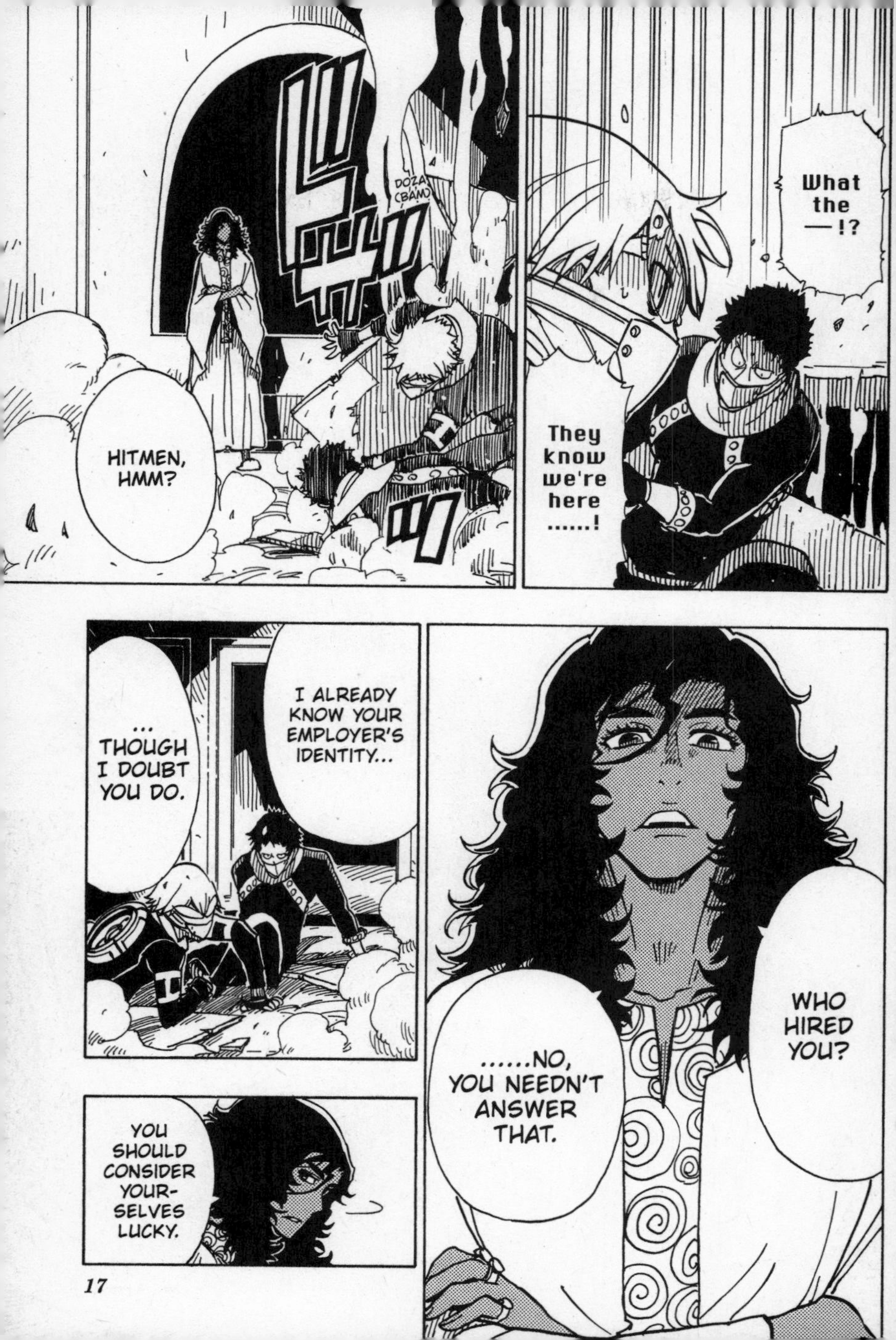
What the—!?
They know we're here......!
DOZA (BAM)
HITMEN, HMM?
WHO HIRED YOU?
......NO, YOU NEEDN'T ANSWER THAT.
I ALREADY KNOW YOUR EMPLOYER'S IDENTITY...
...THOUGH I DOUBT YOU DO.
YOU SHOULD CONSIDER YOURSELVES LUCKY.

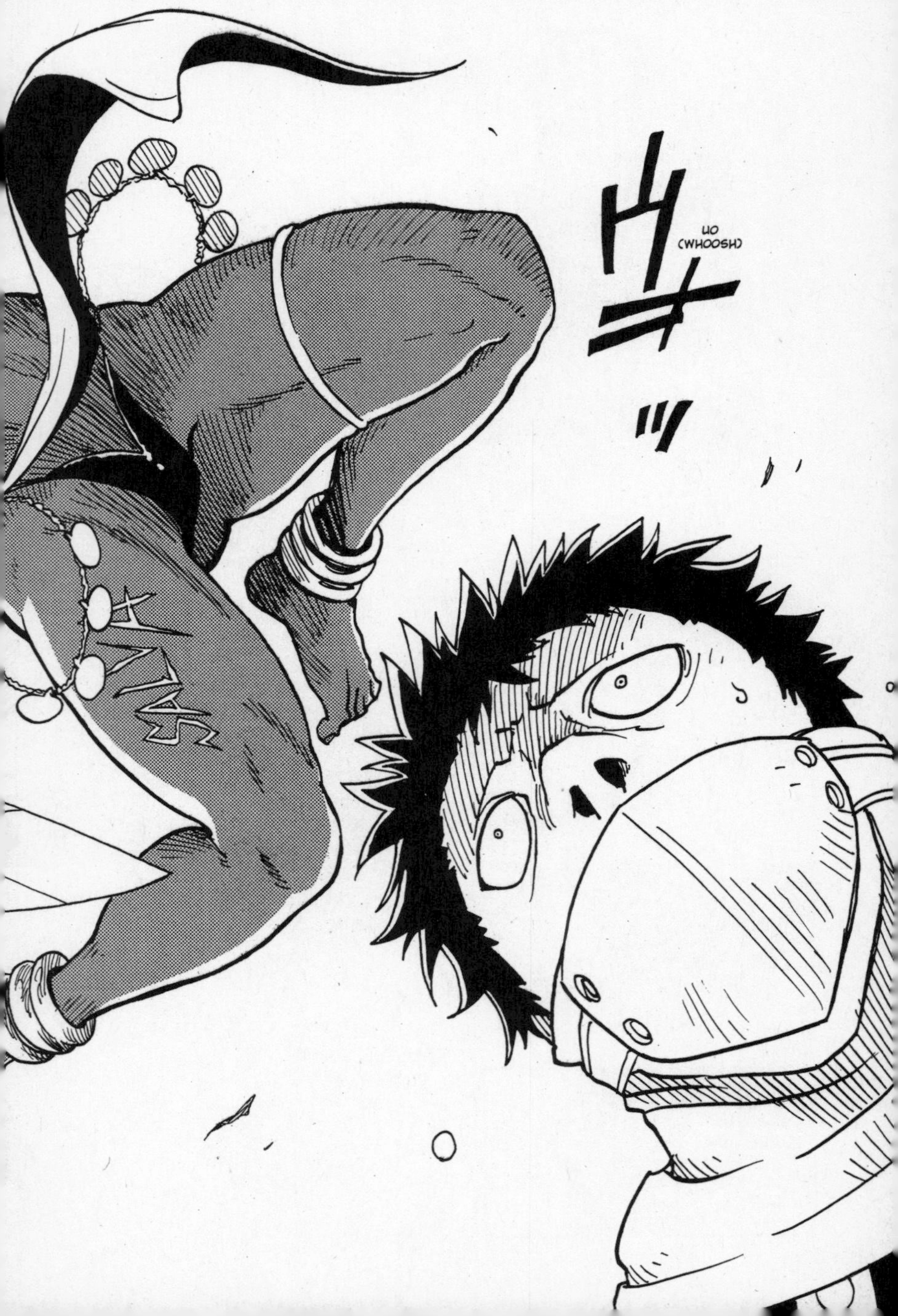

UO
(WHOOSH)

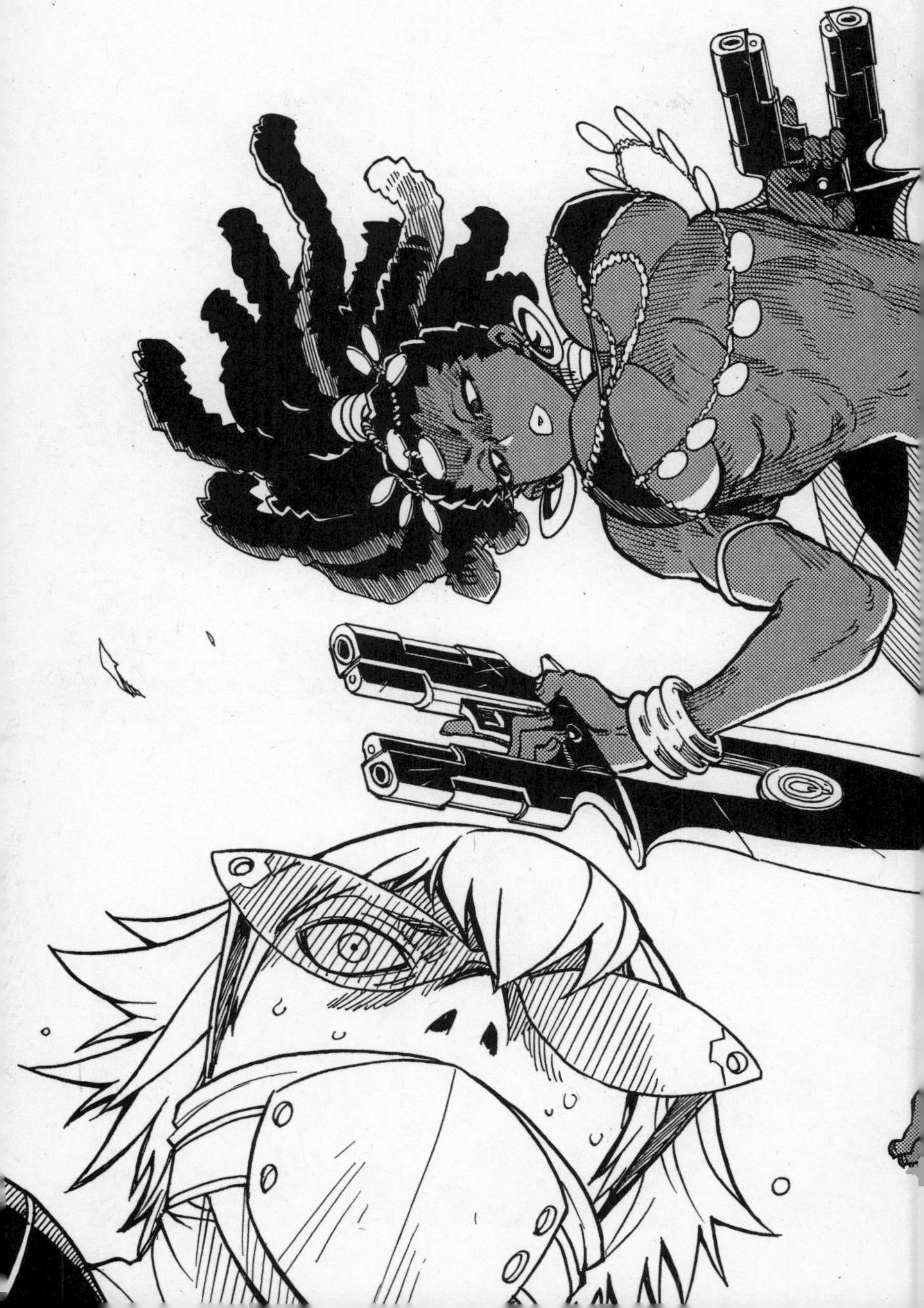

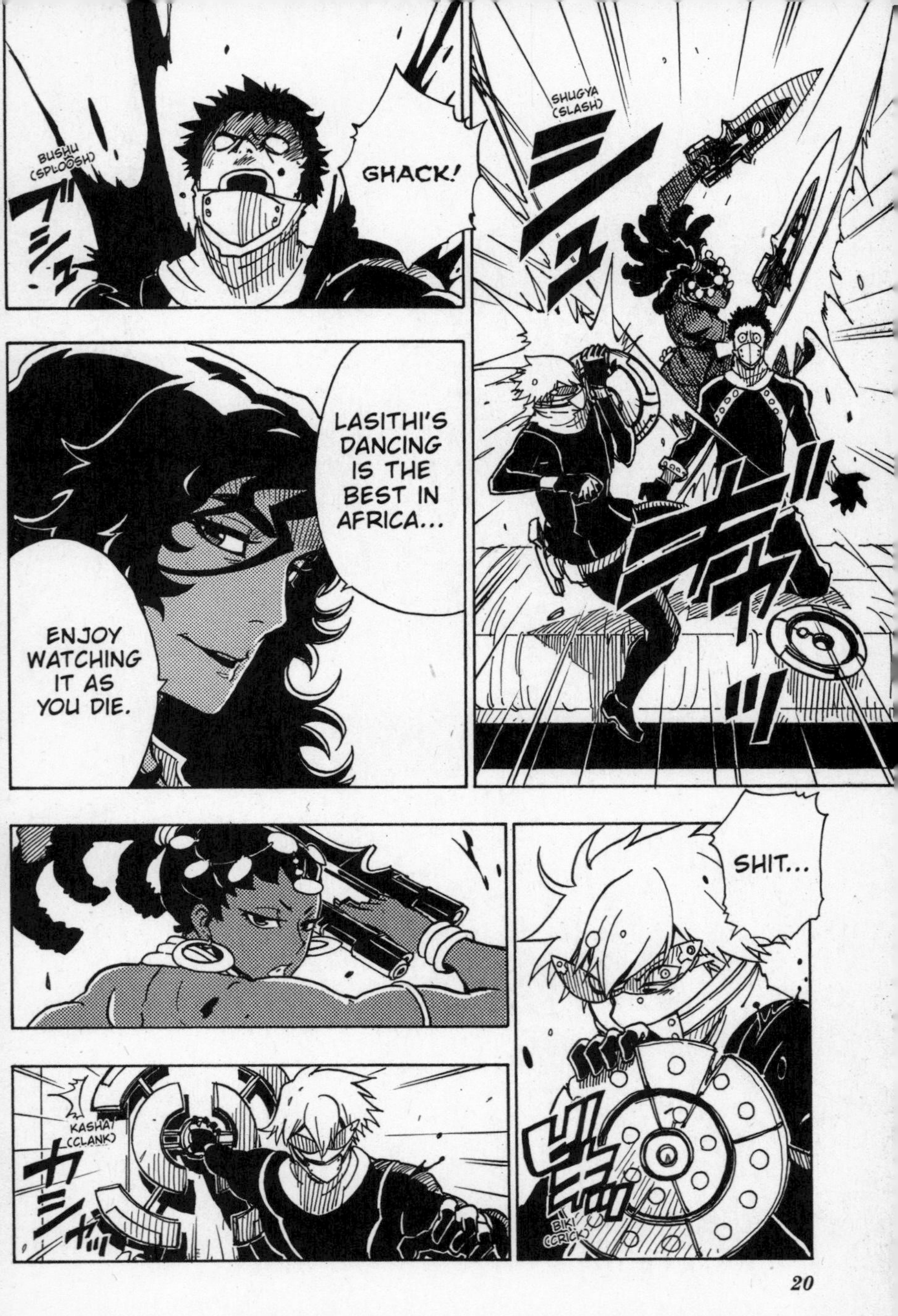
SHUGYA (SLASH)
BUSHU (SPLOOSH)
GHACK!
LASITHI'S DANCING IS THE BEST IN AFRICA...
ENJOY WATCHING IT AS YOU DIE.
SHIT...
BIKI (CRICK)
KASHA (CLANK)

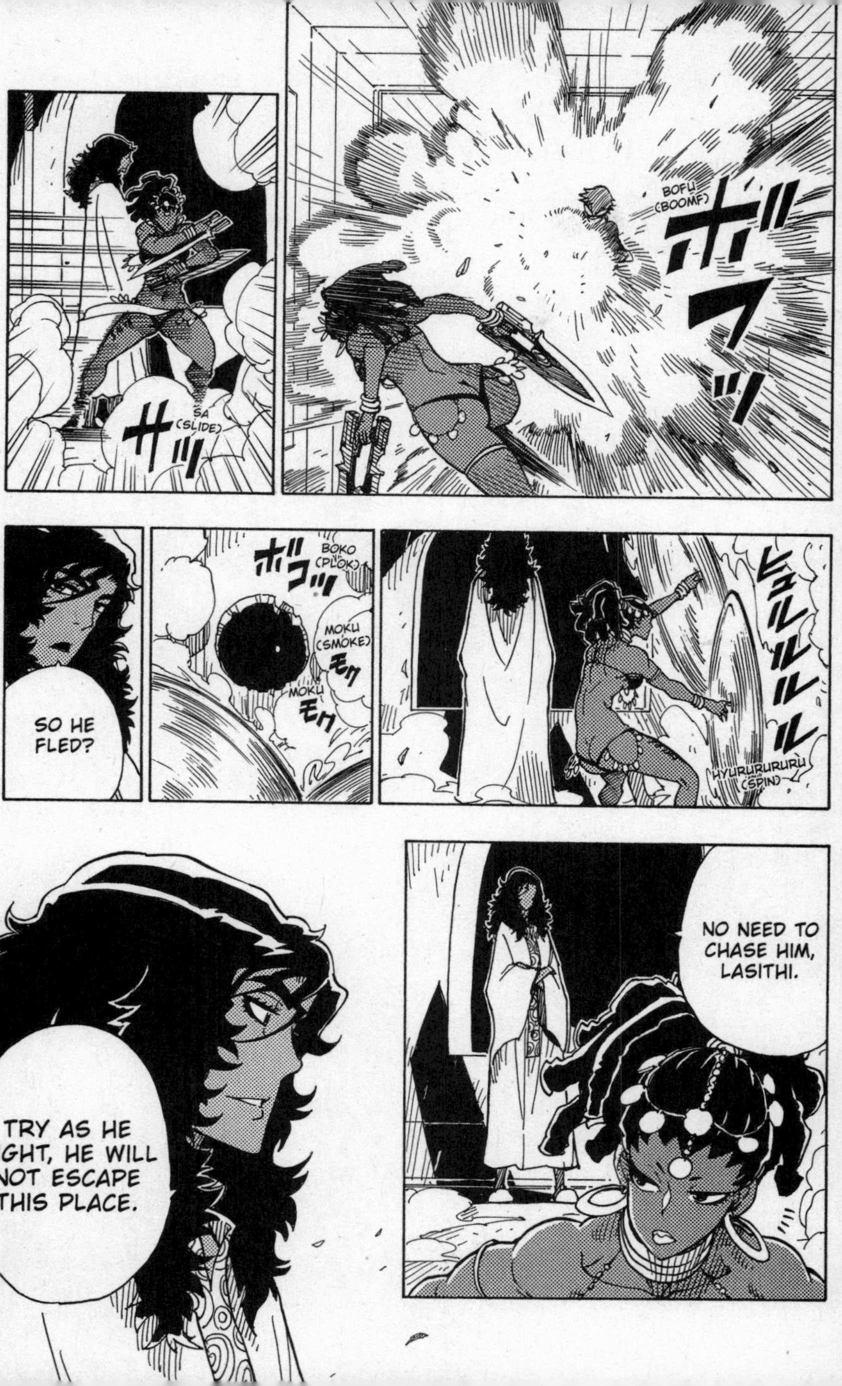
BOFU (BOOMF)
ボフッ
SA (SLIDE)
サッ
ヒュルルルル
HYURURURURU (SPIN)
BOKO (PLOK)
ボコッ
MOKU (SMOKE)
モク
MOKU
モク
SO HE FLED?
NO NEED TO CHASE HIM, LASITHI.
TRY AS HE MIGHT, HE WILL NOT ESCAPE THIS PLACE.

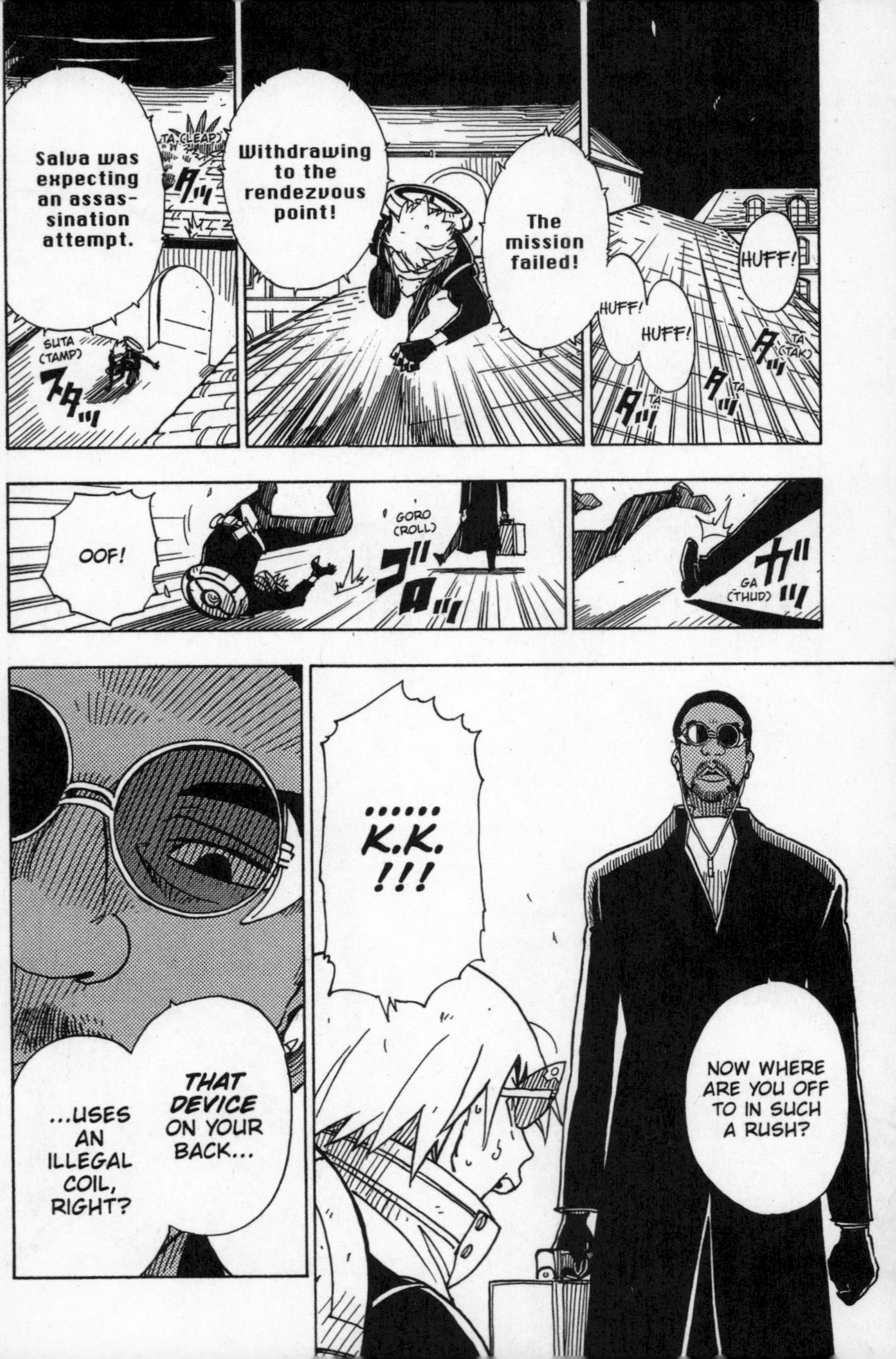

The mission failed!
HUFF!
HUFF!
HUFF!
TA (TAK)
TA
TA
Withdrawing to the rendezvous point!
Salva was expecting an assas- sination attempt.
TA (LEAP)
SUTA (TAMP)
GA (THUD)
GORO (ROLL)
OOF!
NOW WHERE ARE YOU OFF TO IN SUCH A RUSH?
......K.K. !!!
THAT DEVICE ON YOUR BACK...
...USES AN ILLEGAL COIL, RIGHT?

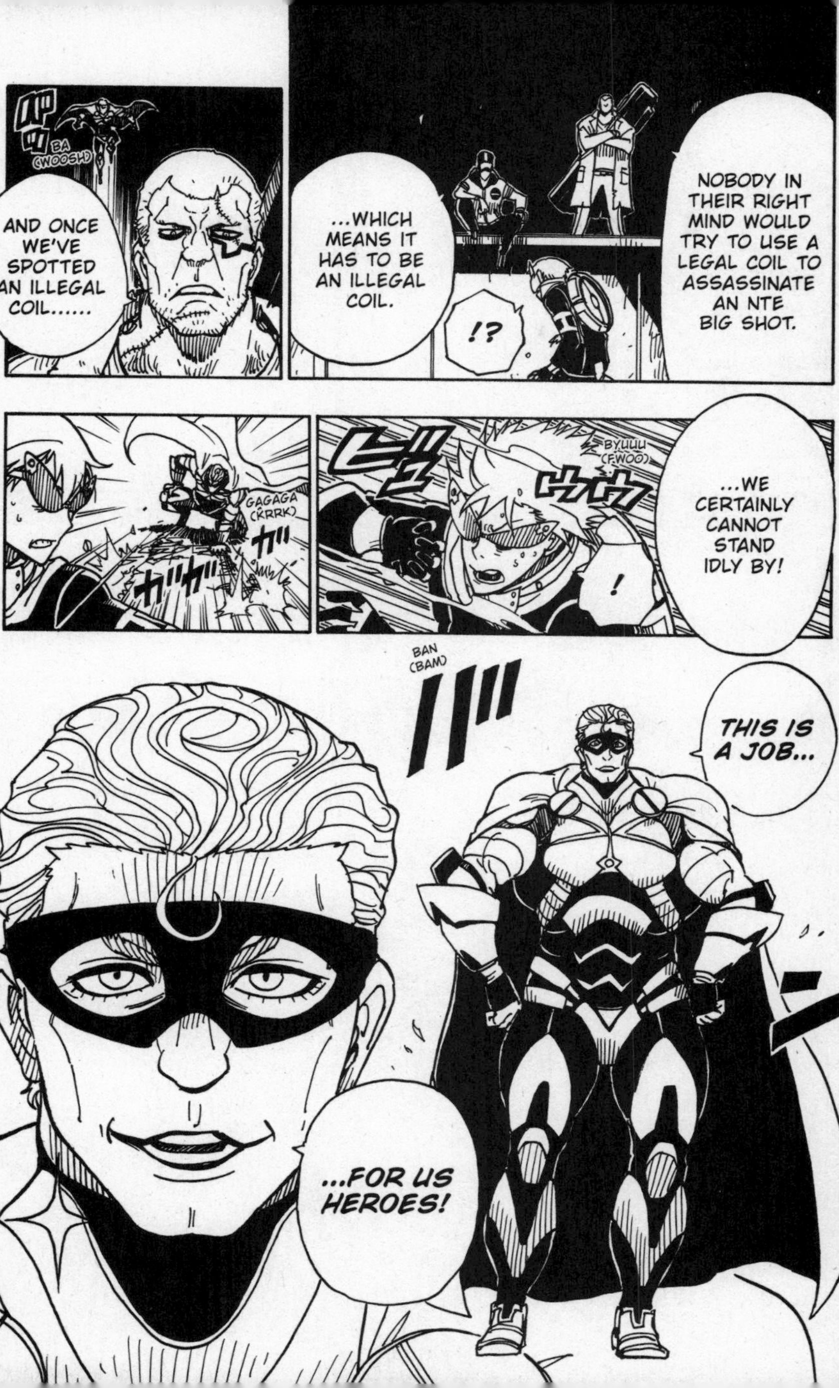
NOBODY IN THEIR RIGHT MIND WOULD TRY TO USE A LEGAL COIL TO ASSASSINATE AN NTE BIG SHOT.
!?
...WHICH MEANS IT HAS TO BE AN ILLEGAL COIL.
BA (WOOSH)
AND ONCE WE'VE SPOTTED AN ILLEGAL COIL......
...WE CERTAINLY CANNOT STAND IDLY BY!
BYUUU (FWOO)
!
GAGAGA (KRRK)
BAN (BAM)
THIS IS A JOB...
...FOR US HEROES!

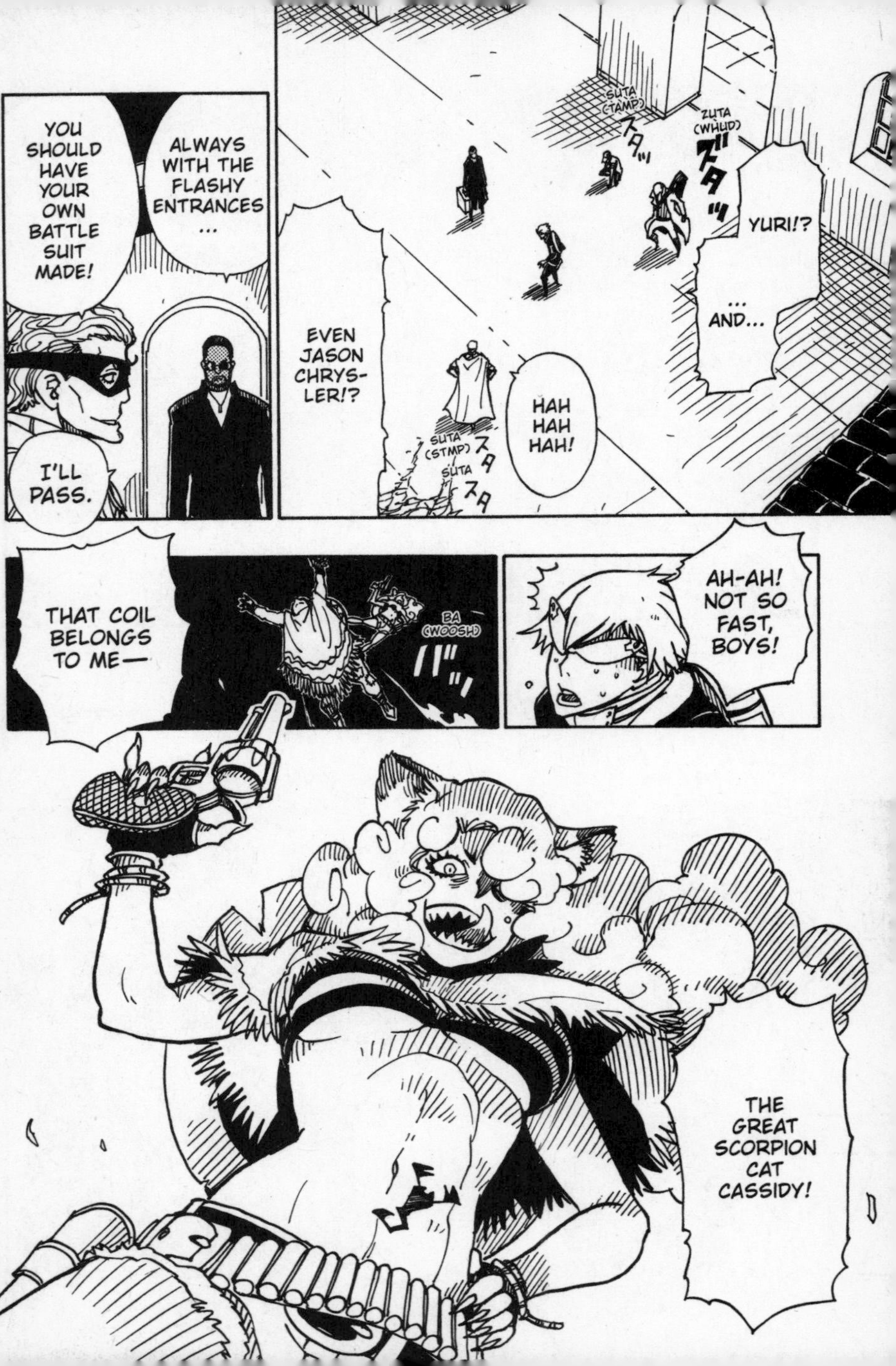
SUTA (TAMP)
スタッ
ZUTA (WHUD)
ズタッ
YURI!?
... AND...
HAH HAH HAH!
EVEN JASON CHRYS-LER!?
SUTA (STMP)
スタ
SUTA
スタ
ALWAYS WITH THE FLASHY ENTRANCES ...
YOU SHOULD HAVE YOUR OWN BATTLE SUIT MADE!
I'LL PASS.
AH-AH! NOT SO FAST, BOYS!
BA (WOOSH)
バッ
THAT COIL BELONGS TO ME—
THE GREAT SCORPION CAT CASSIDY!

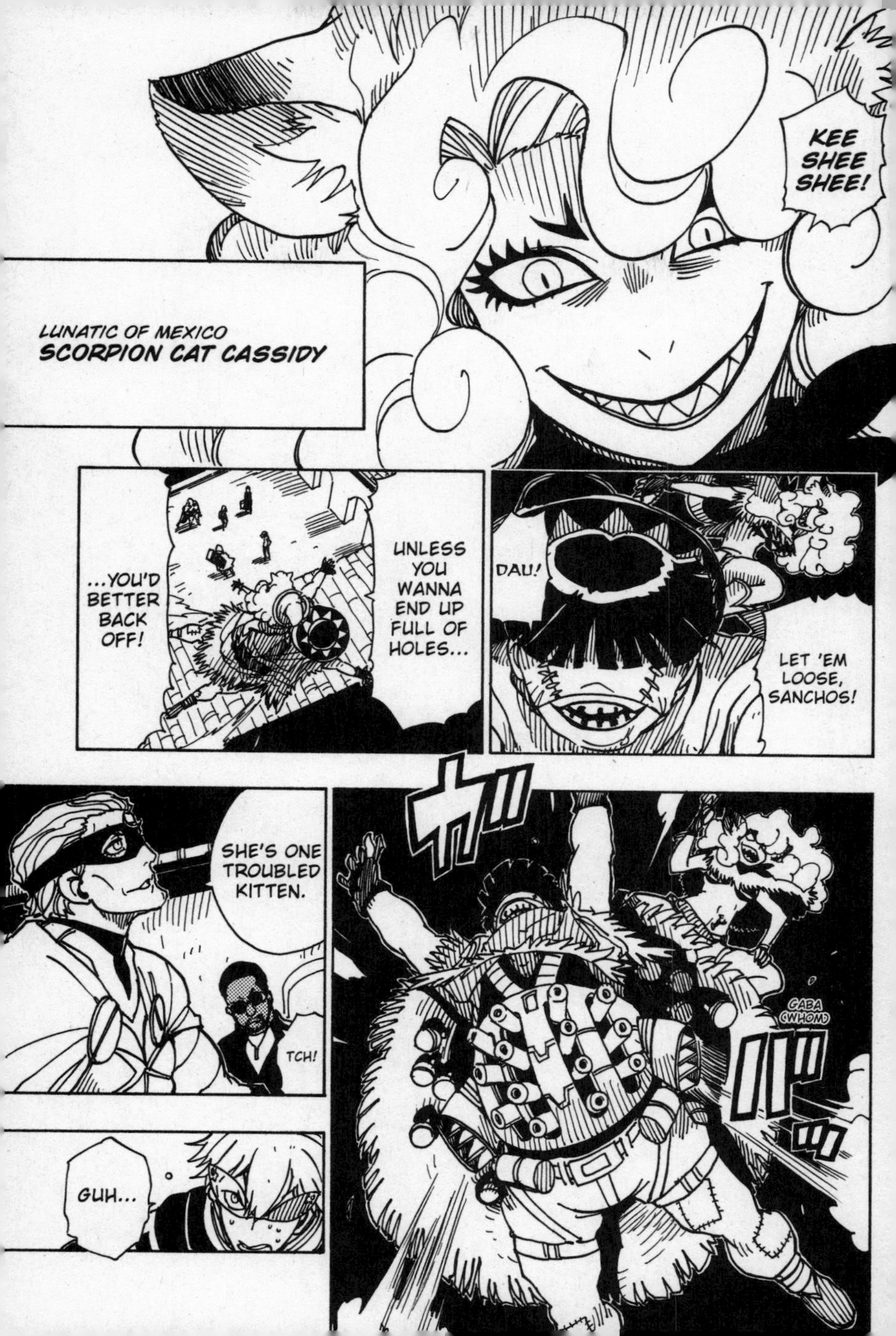
KEE SHEE SHEE!
LUNATIC OF MEXICO
SCORPION CAT CASSIDY
DAU!
LET 'EM LOOSE, SANCHOS!
UNLESS YOU WANNA END UP FULL OF HOLES...
...YOU'D BETTER BACK OFF!
GABA (WHOM)
SHE'S ONE TROUBLED KITTEN.
TCH!
GUH...

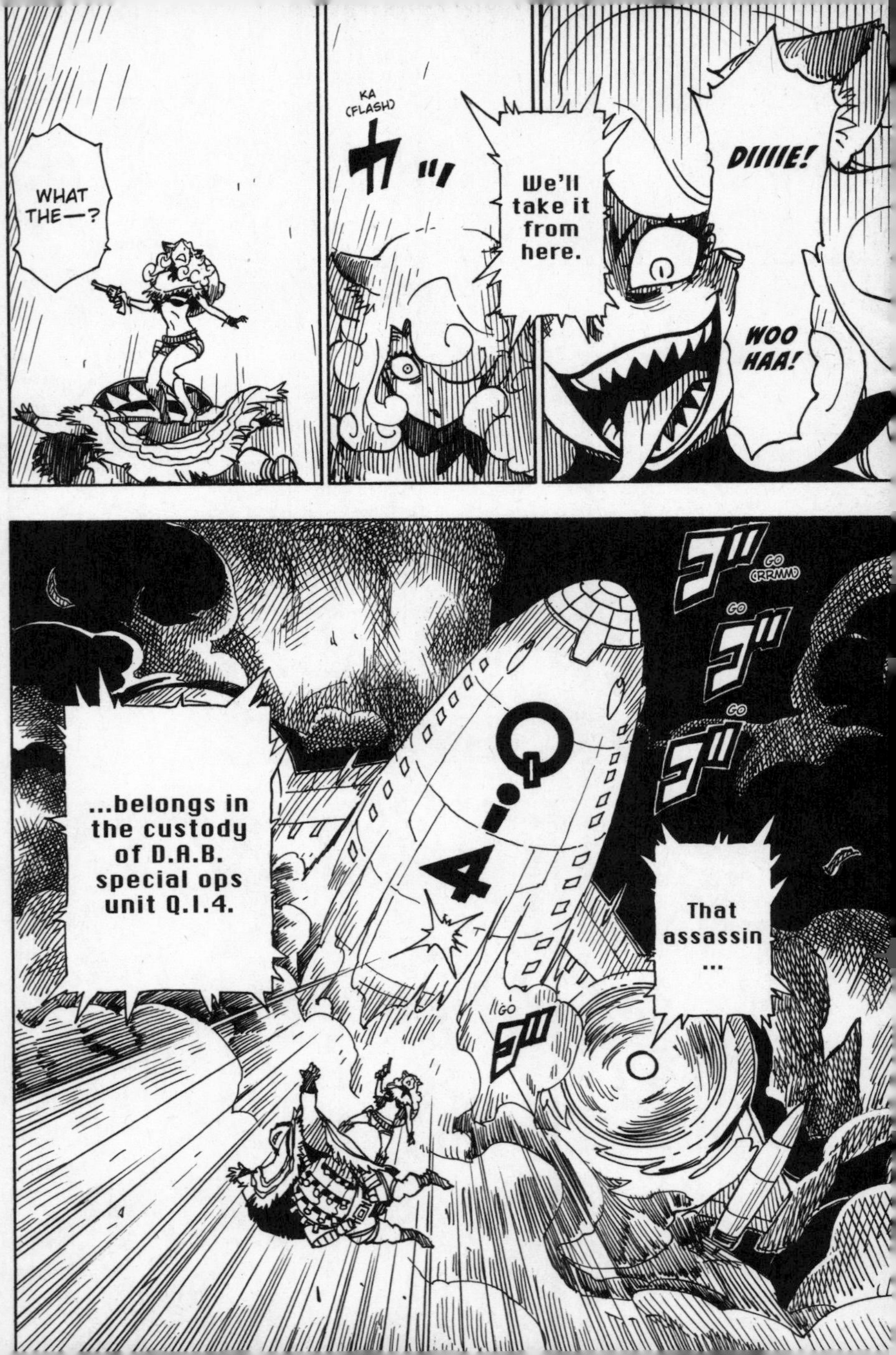
DIIIIE!
WOO HAA!
KA (FLASH)
We'll take it from here.
WHAT THE—?
GO (RRMM)
GO
GO
That assassin ...
...belongs in the custody of D.A.B. special ops unit Q.I.4.
GO

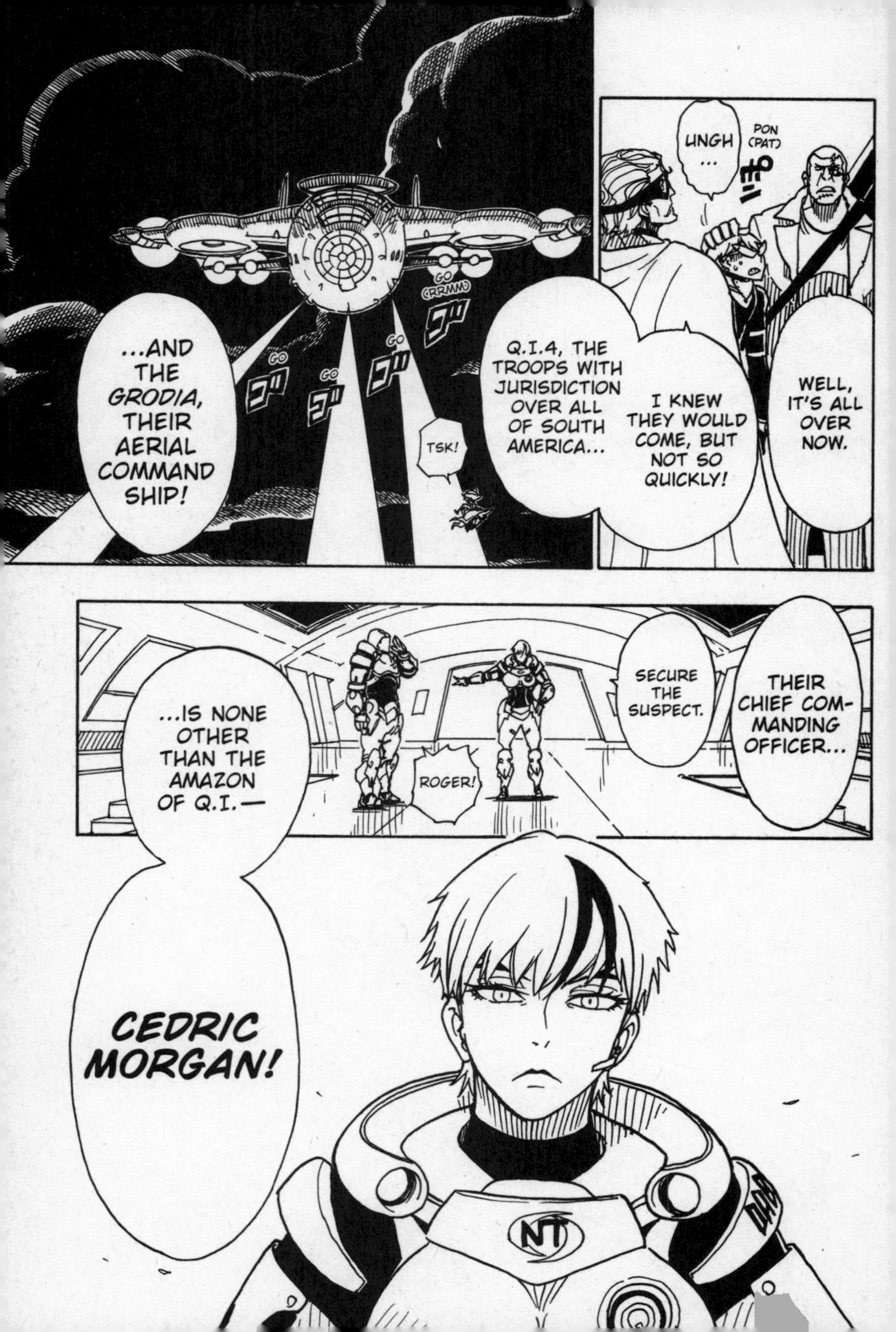
PON (PAT)
UNGH ...
WELL, IT'S ALL OVER NOW.
I KNEW THEY WOULD COME, BUT NOT SO QUICKLY!
GO (RRMM)
Q.I.4, THE TROOPS WITH JURISDICTION OVER ALL OF SOUTH AMERICA...
GO
TSK!
GO
GO
...AND THE *GRODIA*, THEIR AERIAL COMMAND SHIP!
THEIR CHIEF COMMANDING OFFICER...
SECURE THE SUSPECT.
ROGER!
...IS NONE OTHER THAN THE AMAZON OF Q.I.—
CEDRIC MORGAN!

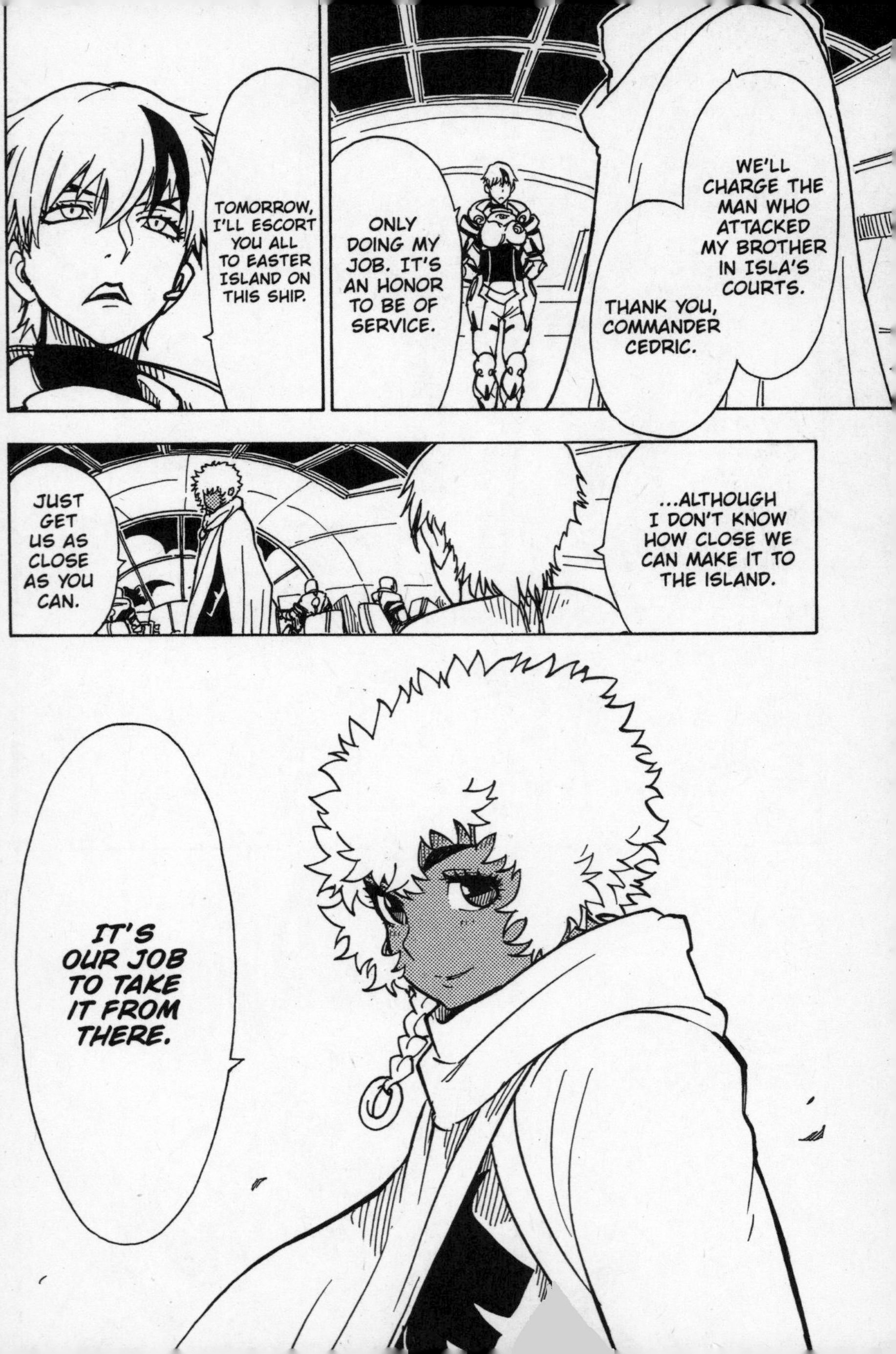
WE'LL CHARGE THE MAN WHO ATTACKED MY BROTHER IN ISLA'S COURTS.
THANK YOU, COMMANDER CEDRIC.
ONLY DOING MY JOB. IT'S AN HONOR TO BE OF SERVICE.
TOMORROW, I'LL ESCORT YOU ALL TO EASTER ISLAND ON THIS SHIP.
...ALTHOUGH I DON'T KNOW HOW CLOSE WE CAN MAKE IT TO THE ISLAND.
JUST GET US AS CLOSE AS YOU CAN.
IT'S OUR JOB TO TAKE IT FROM THERE.

# FILE.41
# NOTHINGNESS

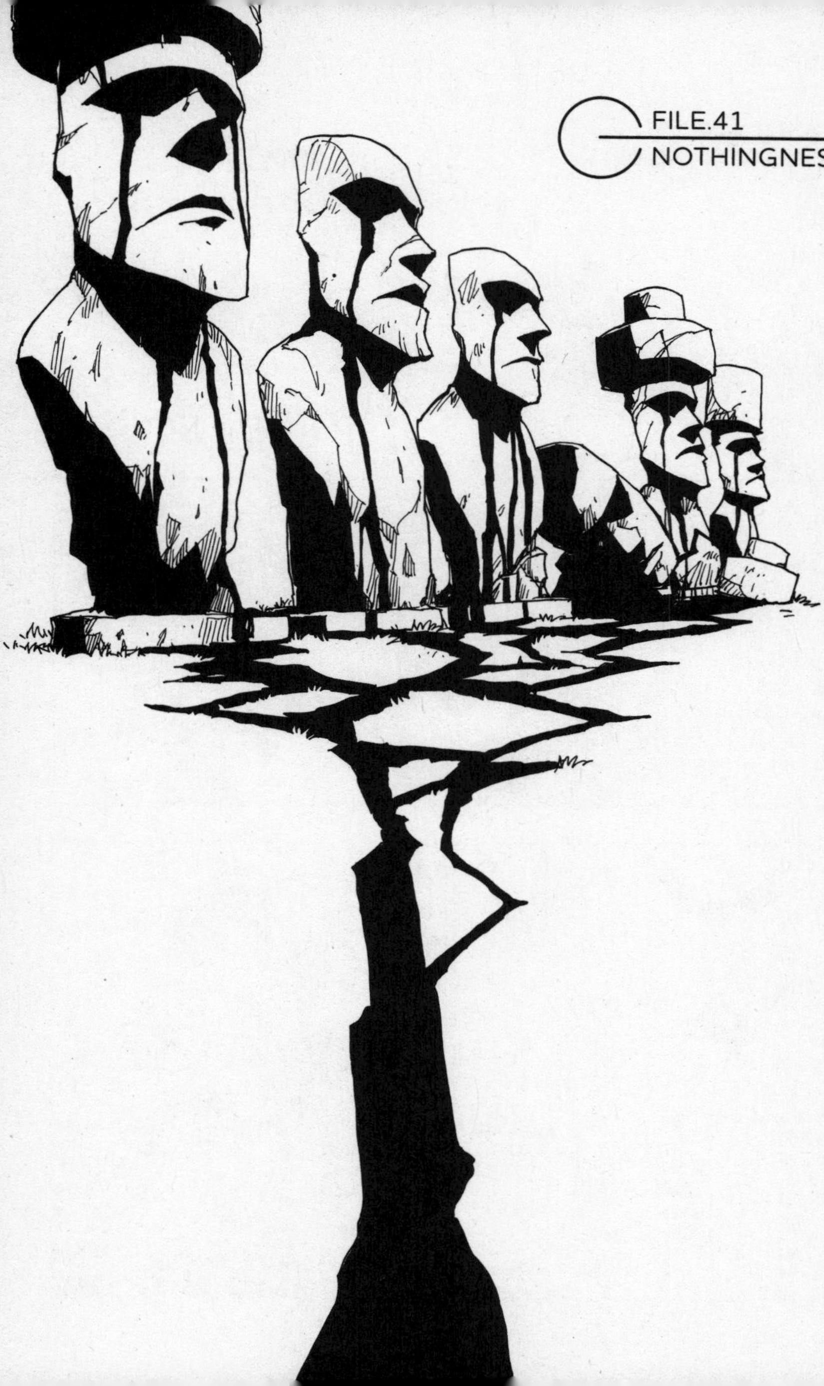

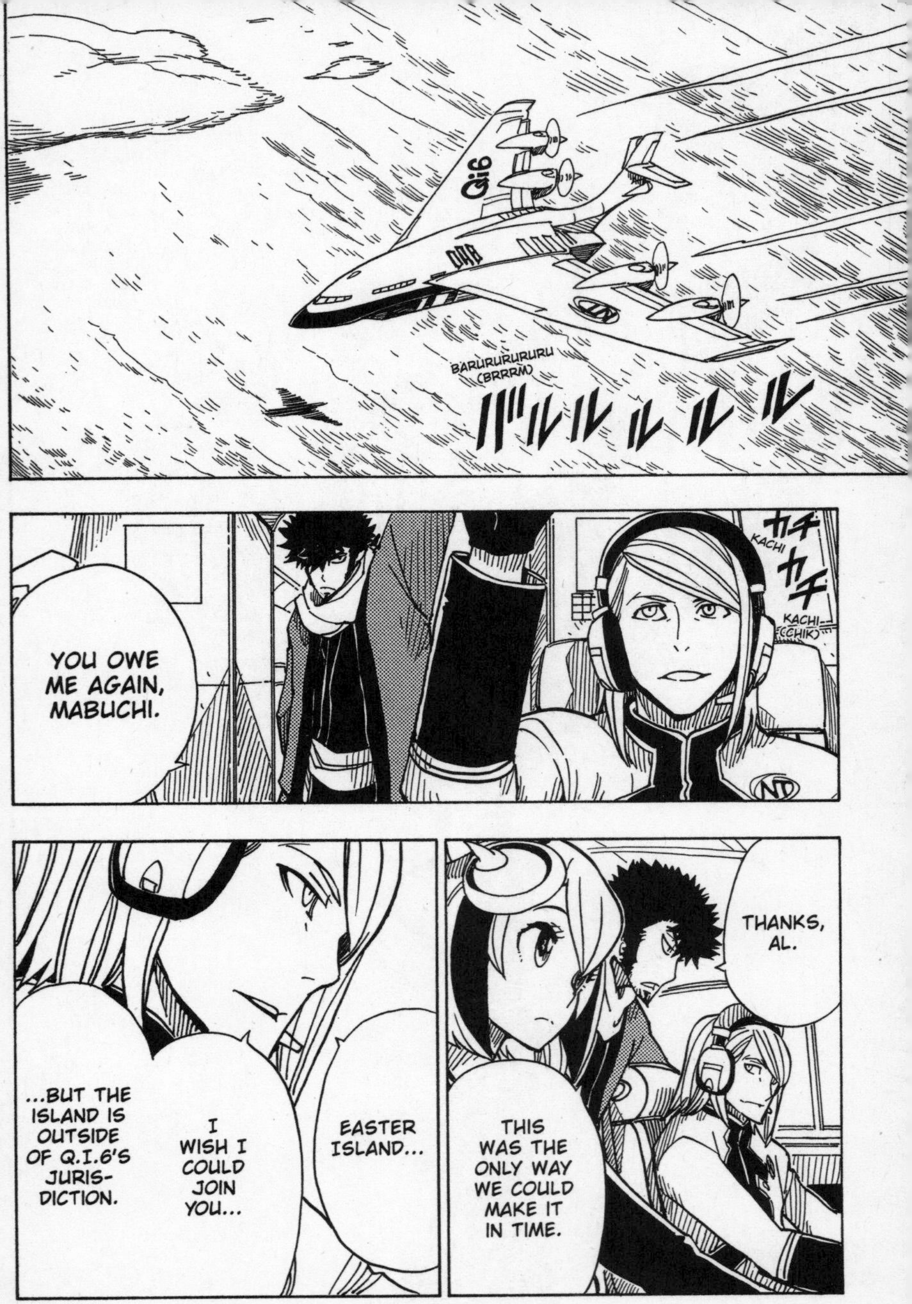
バルルルルル
BARURURURURU (BRRRM)
カチカチ
KACHI KACHI (CHIK)
YOU OWE ME AGAIN, MABUCHI.
THANKS, AL.
THIS WAS THE ONLY WAY WE COULD MAKE IT IN TIME.
EASTER ISLAND...
I WISH I COULD JOIN YOU...
...BUT THE ISLAND IS OUTSIDE OF Q.I.6'S JURIS-DICTION.

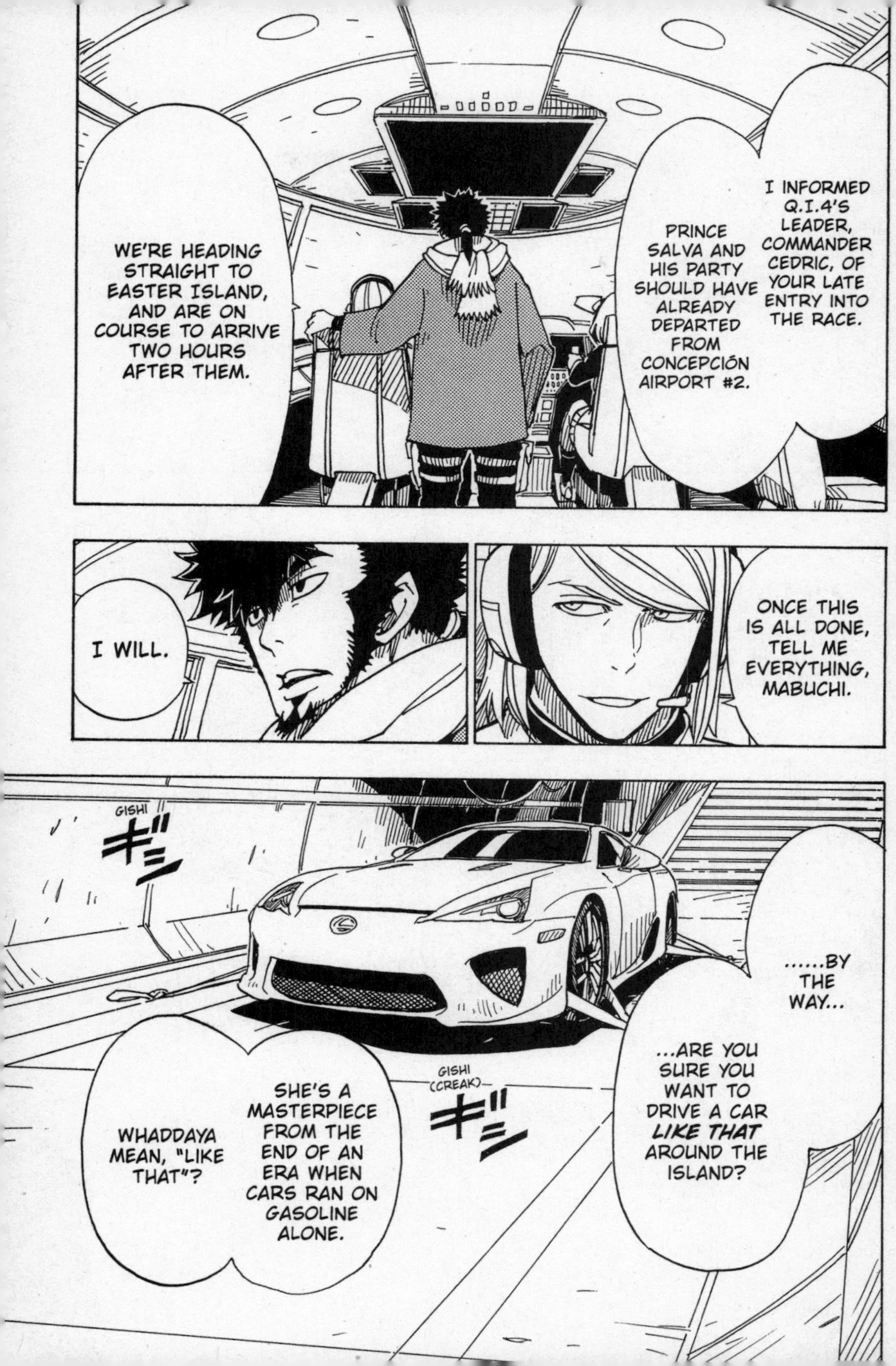
I INFORMED Q.I.4'S LEADER, COMMANDER CEDRIC, OF YOUR LATE ENTRY INTO THE RACE.
PRINCE SALVA AND HIS PARTY SHOULD HAVE ALREADY DEPARTED FROM CONCEPCIÓN AIRPORT #2.
WE'RE HEADING STRAIGHT TO EASTER ISLAND, AND ARE ON COURSE TO ARRIVE TWO HOURS AFTER THEM.
ONCE THIS IS ALL DONE, TELL ME EVERYTHING, MABUCHI.
I WILL.
......BY THE WAY...
...ARE YOU SURE YOU WANT TO DRIVE A CAR *LIKE THAT* AROUND THE ISLAND?
GISHI (CREAK)
SHE'S A MASTERPIECE FROM THE END OF AN ERA WHEN CARS RAN ON GASOLINE ALONE.
WHADDAYA MEAN, "LIKE THAT"?
GISHI

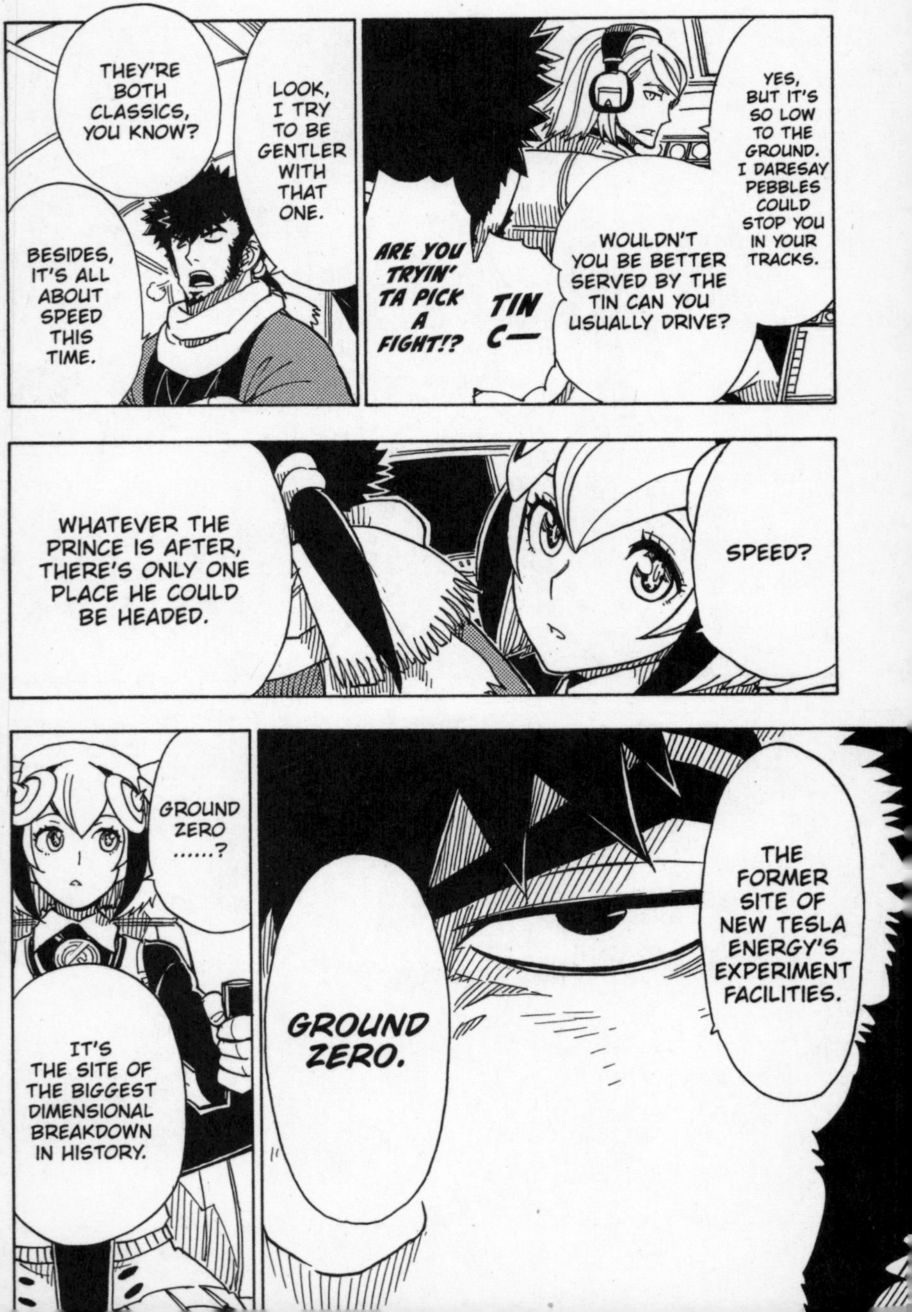
YES, BUT IT'S SO LOW TO THE GROUND. I DARESAY PEBBLES COULD STOP YOU IN YOUR TRACKS.
WOULDN'T YOU BE BETTER SERVED BY THE TIN CAN YOU USUALLY DRIVE?
TIN C—
ARE YOU TRYIN' TA PICK A FIGHT!?
LOOK, I TRY TO BE GENTLER WITH THAT ONE.
THEY'RE BOTH CLASSICS, YOU KNOW?
BESIDES, IT'S ALL ABOUT SPEED THIS TIME.
SPEED?
WHATEVER THE PRINCE IS AFTER, THERE'S ONLY ONE PLACE HE COULD BE HEADED.
THE FORMER SITE OF NEW TESLA ENERGY'S EXPERIMENT FACILITIES.
GROUND ZERO.
GROUND ZERO ......?
IT'S THE SITE OF THE BIGGEST DIMENSIONAL BREAKDOWN IN HISTORY.

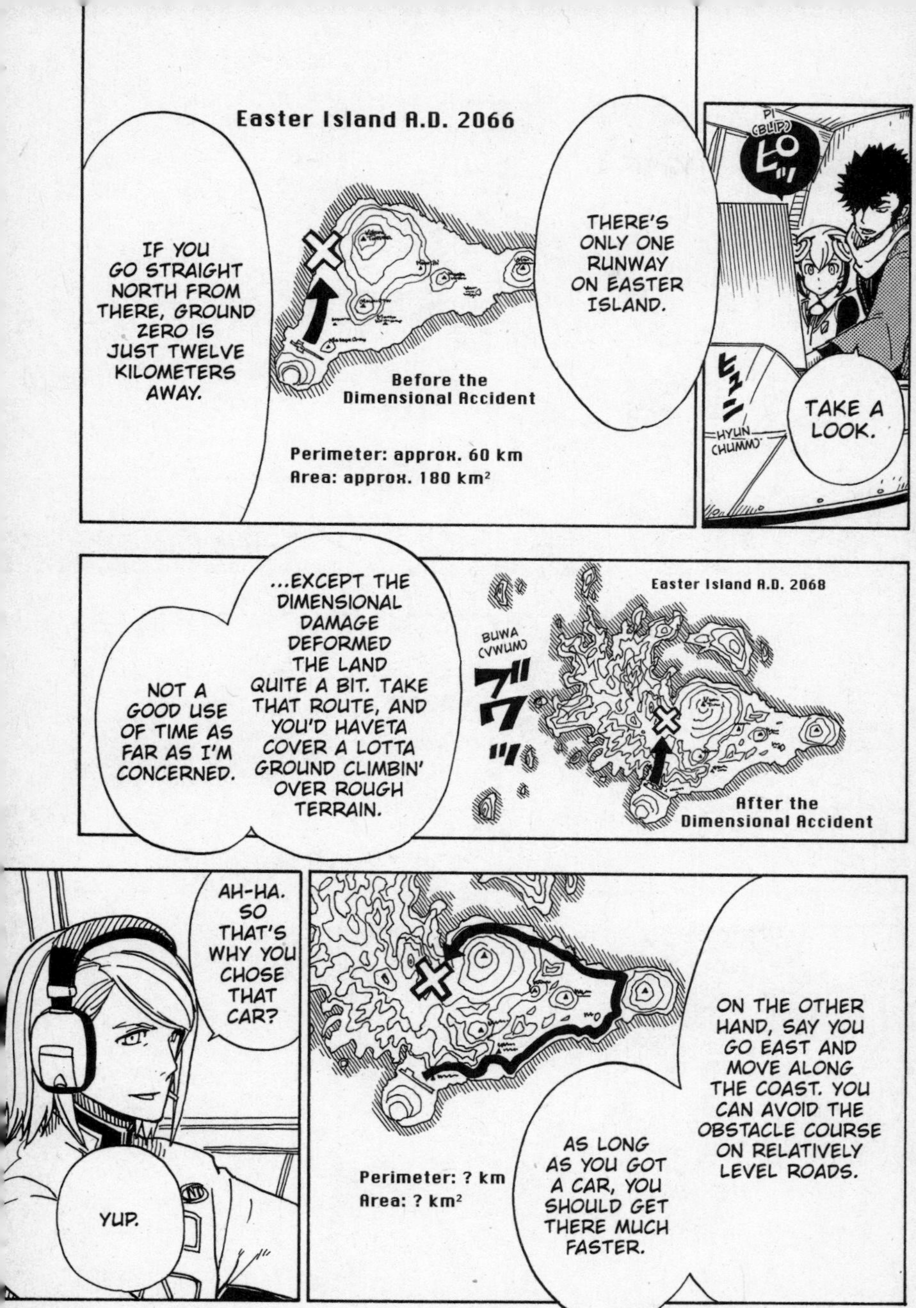
PI (BLIP)
HYUN (CHUMM)
TAKE A LOOK.
Easter Island A.D. 2066
THERE'S ONLY ONE RUNWAY ON EASTER ISLAND.
IF YOU GO STRAIGHT NORTH FROM THERE, GROUND ZERO IS JUST TWELVE KILOMETERS AWAY.
Before the Dimensional Accident
Perimeter: approx. 60 km
Area: approx. 180 km²
Easter Island A.D. 2068
BUWA (VWUM)
After the Dimensional Accident
...EXCEPT THE DIMENSIONAL DAMAGE DEFORMED THE LAND QUITE A BIT. TAKE THAT ROUTE, AND YOU'D HAVETA COVER A LOTTA GROUND CLIMBIN' OVER ROUGH TERRAIN.
NOT A GOOD USE OF TIME AS FAR AS I'M CONCERNED.
ON THE OTHER HAND, SAY YOU GO EAST AND MOVE ALONG THE COAST. YOU CAN AVOID THE OBSTACLE COURSE ON RELATIVELY LEVEL ROADS.
AS LONG AS YOU GOT A CAR, YOU SHOULD GET THERE MUCH FASTER.
Perimeter: ? km
Area: ? km²
AH-HA. SO THAT'S WHY YOU CHOSE THAT CAR?
YUP.

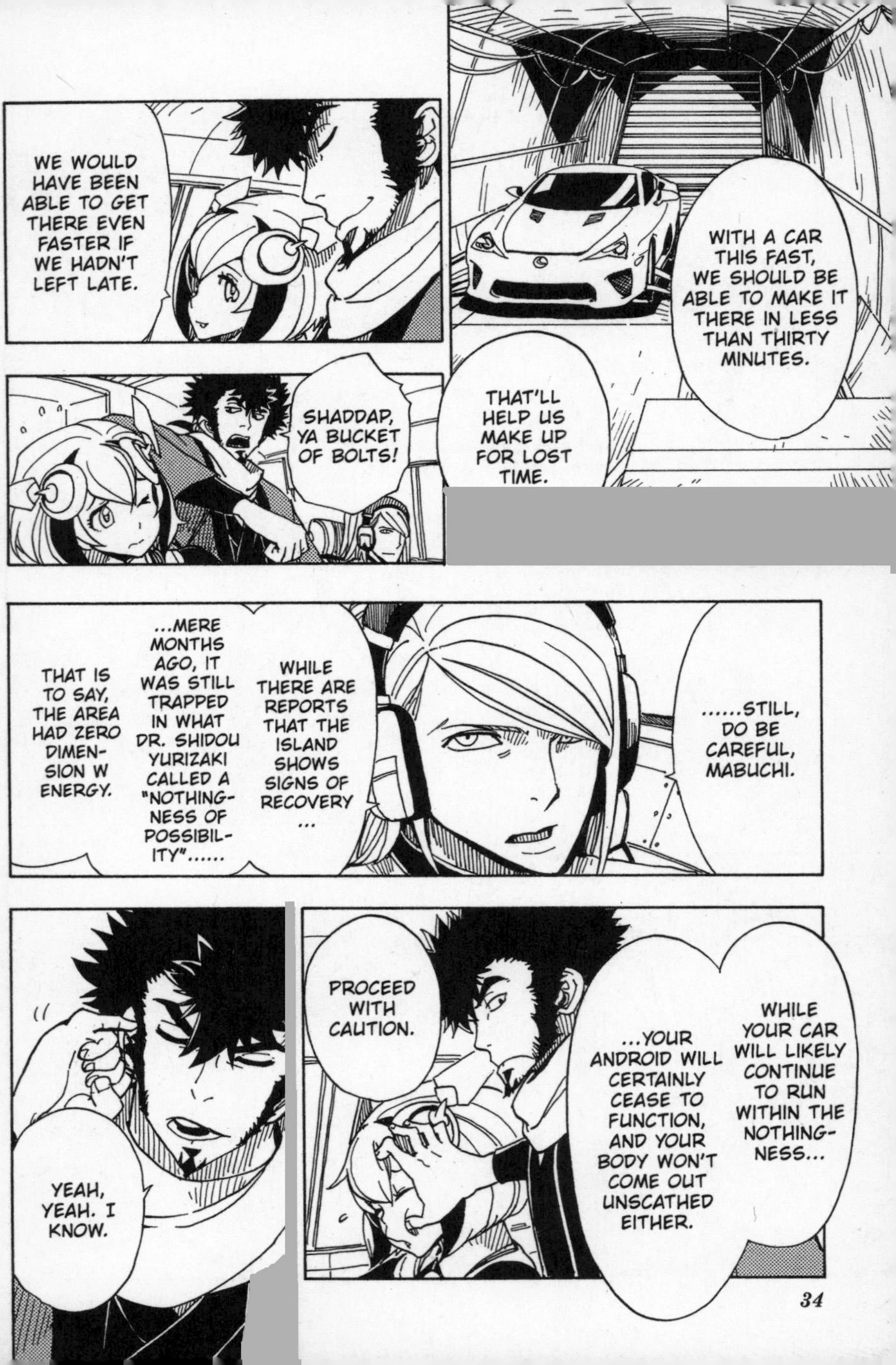

WITH A CAR THIS FAST, WE SHOULD BE ABLE TO MAKE IT THERE IN LESS THAN THIRTY MINUTES.
THAT'LL HELP US MAKE UP FOR LOST TIME.
WE WOULD HAVE BEEN ABLE TO GET THERE EVEN FASTER IF WE HADN'T LEFT LATE.
SHADDAP, YA BUCKET OF BOLTS!
......STILL, DO BE CAREFUL, MABUCHI.
WHILE THERE ARE REPORTS THAT THE ISLAND SHOWS SIGNS OF RECOVERY ...
...MERE MONTHS AGO, IT WAS STILL TRAPPED IN WHAT DR. SHIDOU YURIZAKI CALLED A "NOTHINGNESS OF POSSIBILITY"......
THAT IS TO SAY, THE AREA HAD ZERO DIMENSION W ENERGY.
WHILE YOUR CAR WILL LIKELY CONTINUE TO RUN WITHIN THE NOTHINGNESS...
...YOUR ANDROID WILL CERTAINLY CEASE TO FUNCTION, AND YOUR BODY WON'T COME OUT UNSCATHED EITHER.
PROCEED WITH CAUTION.
YEAH, YEAH. I KNOW.

I AIN'T EXPECTIN' THIS TO END SO EASILY.

GOOD.

HOLD ON TIGHT!

WE'RE ABOUT TO FLY INTO A STORM.

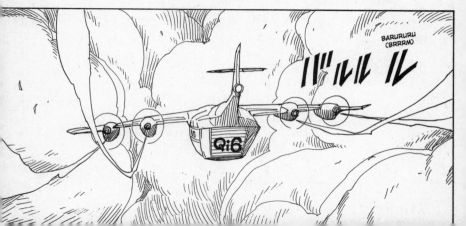

BARURURU (BRRRM)

Qi6

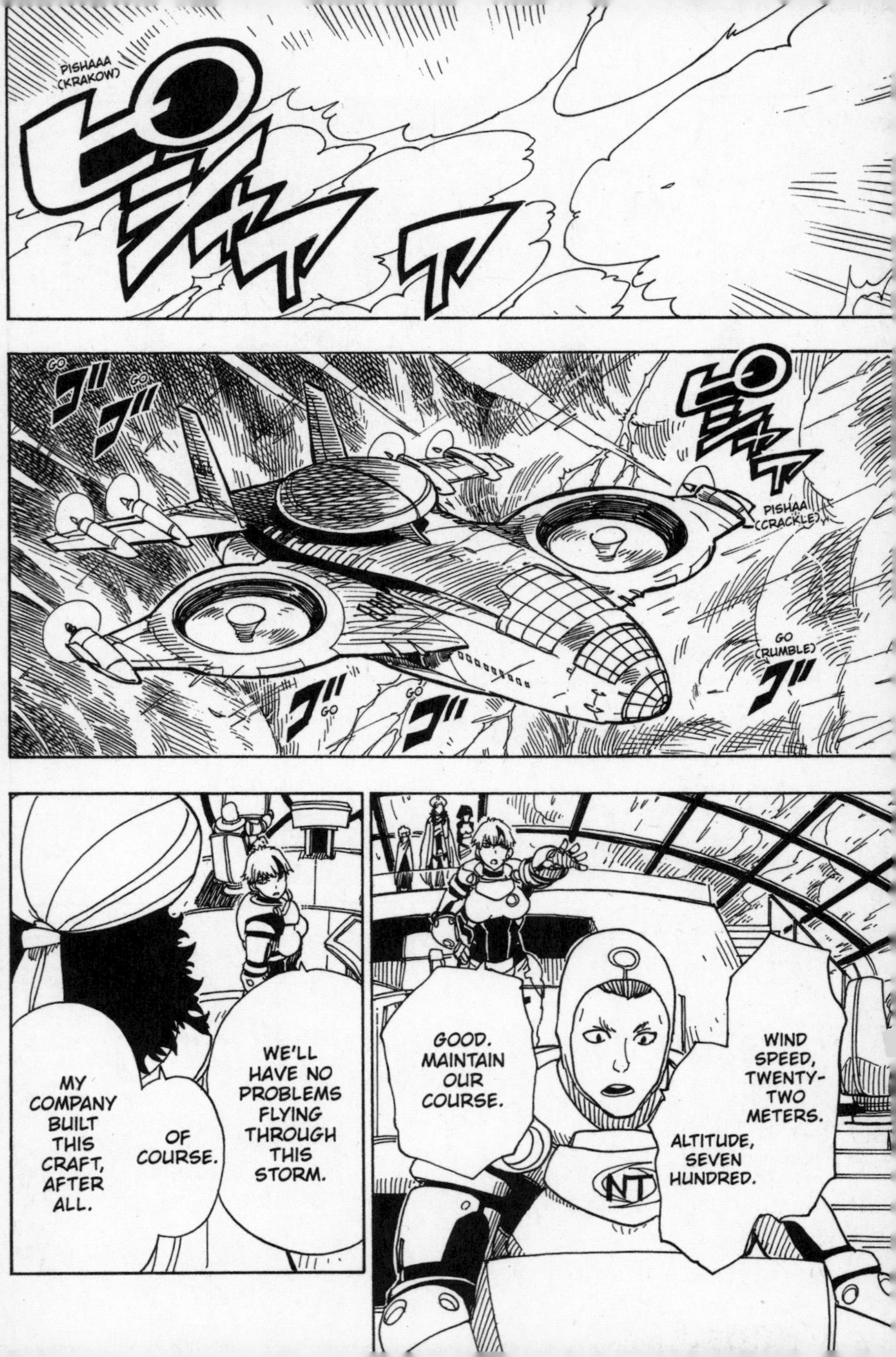

PISHAAA (KRAKOW)
PISHAA (CRACKLE)
GO (RUMBLE)
GO
GO
GO
GO
WIND SPEED, TWENTY-TWO METERS.
ALTITUDE, SEVEN HUNDRED.
GOOD. MAINTAIN OUR COURSE.
WE'LL HAVE NO PROBLEMS FLYING THROUGH THIS STORM.
OF COURSE.
MY COMPANY BUILT THIS CRAFT, AFTER ALL.
NT

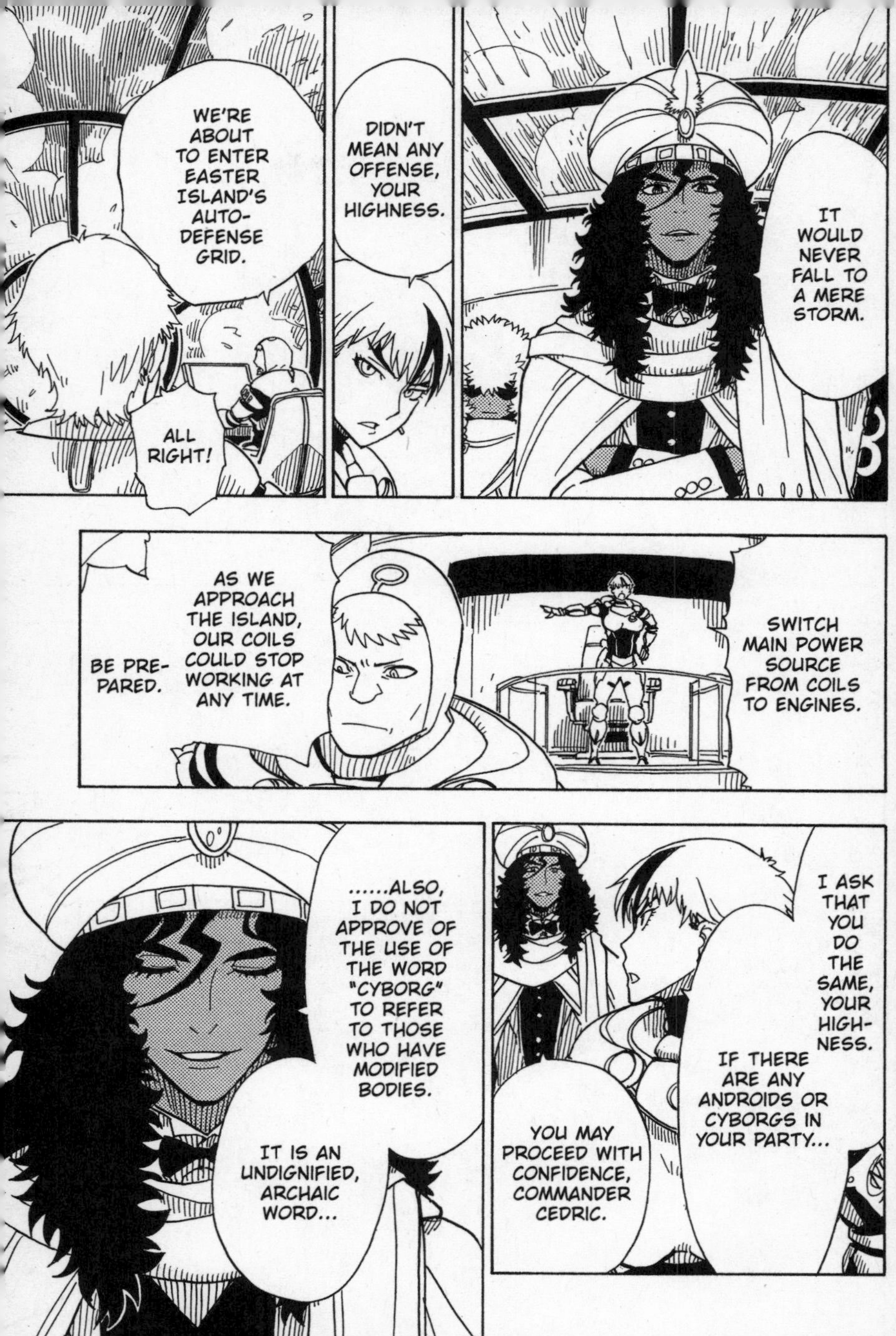
IT WOULD NEVER FALL TO A MERE STORM.
DIDN'T MEAN ANY OFFENSE, YOUR HIGHNESS.
WE'RE ABOUT TO ENTER EASTER ISLAND'S AUTO-DEFENSE GRID.
ALL RIGHT!
SWITCH MAIN POWER SOURCE FROM COILS TO ENGINES.
AS WE APPROACH THE ISLAND, OUR COILS COULD STOP WORKING AT ANY TIME.
BE PRE-PARED.
I ASK THAT YOU DO THE SAME, YOUR HIGH-NESS.
IF THERE ARE ANY ANDROIDS OR CYBORGS IN YOUR PARTY...
YOU MAY PROCEED WITH CONFIDENCE, COMMANDER CEDRIC.
......ALSO, I DO NOT APPROVE OF THE USE OF THE WORD "CYBORG" TO REFER TO THOSE WHO HAVE MODIFIED BODIES.
IT IS AN UNDIGNIFIED, ARCHAIC WORD...

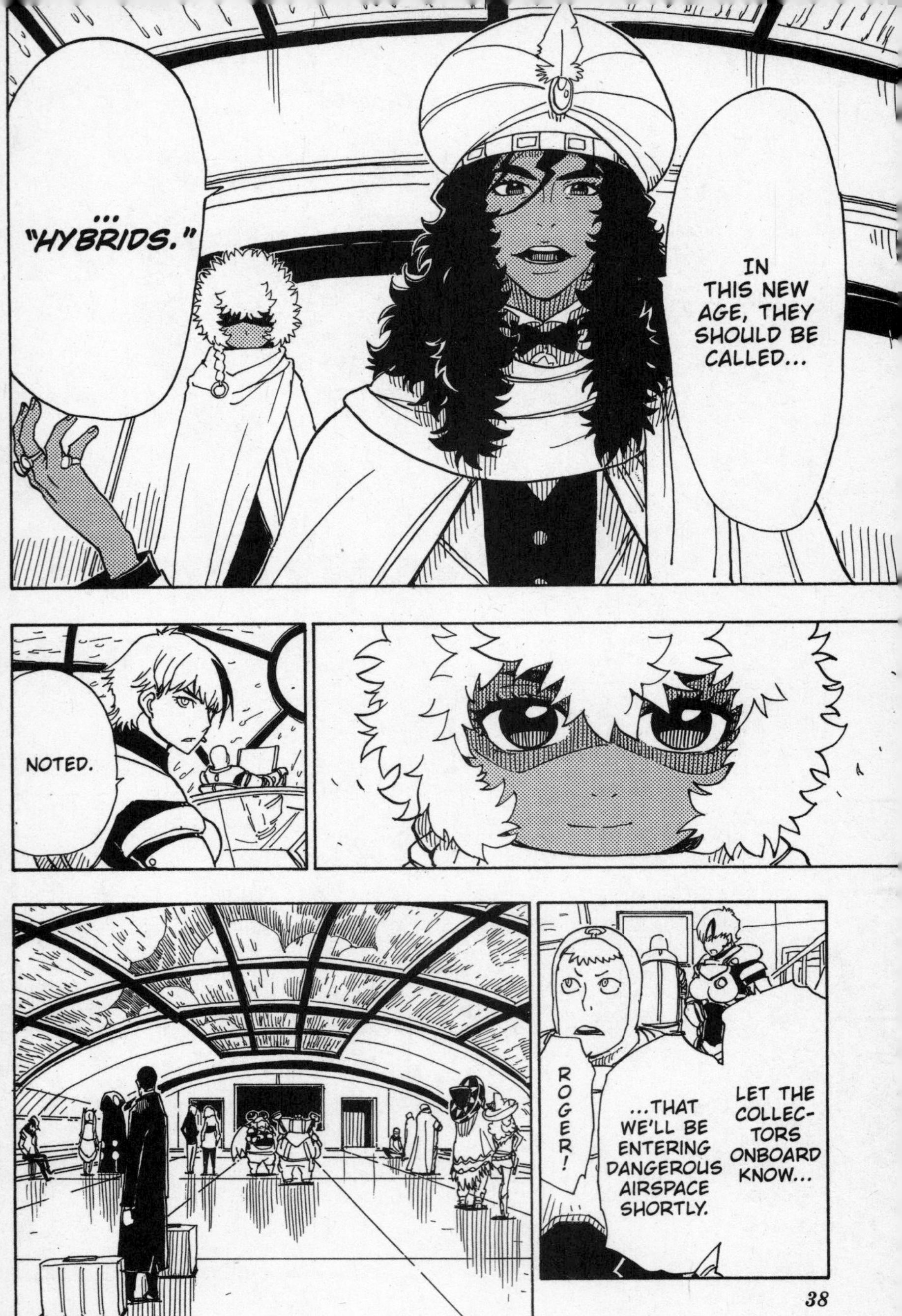
IN THIS NEW AGE, THEY SHOULD BE CALLED...
... "HYBRIDS."
NOTED.
LET THE COLLECTORS ONBOARD KNOW...
...THAT WE'LL BE ENTERING DANGEROUS AIRSPACE SHORTLY.
ROGER!

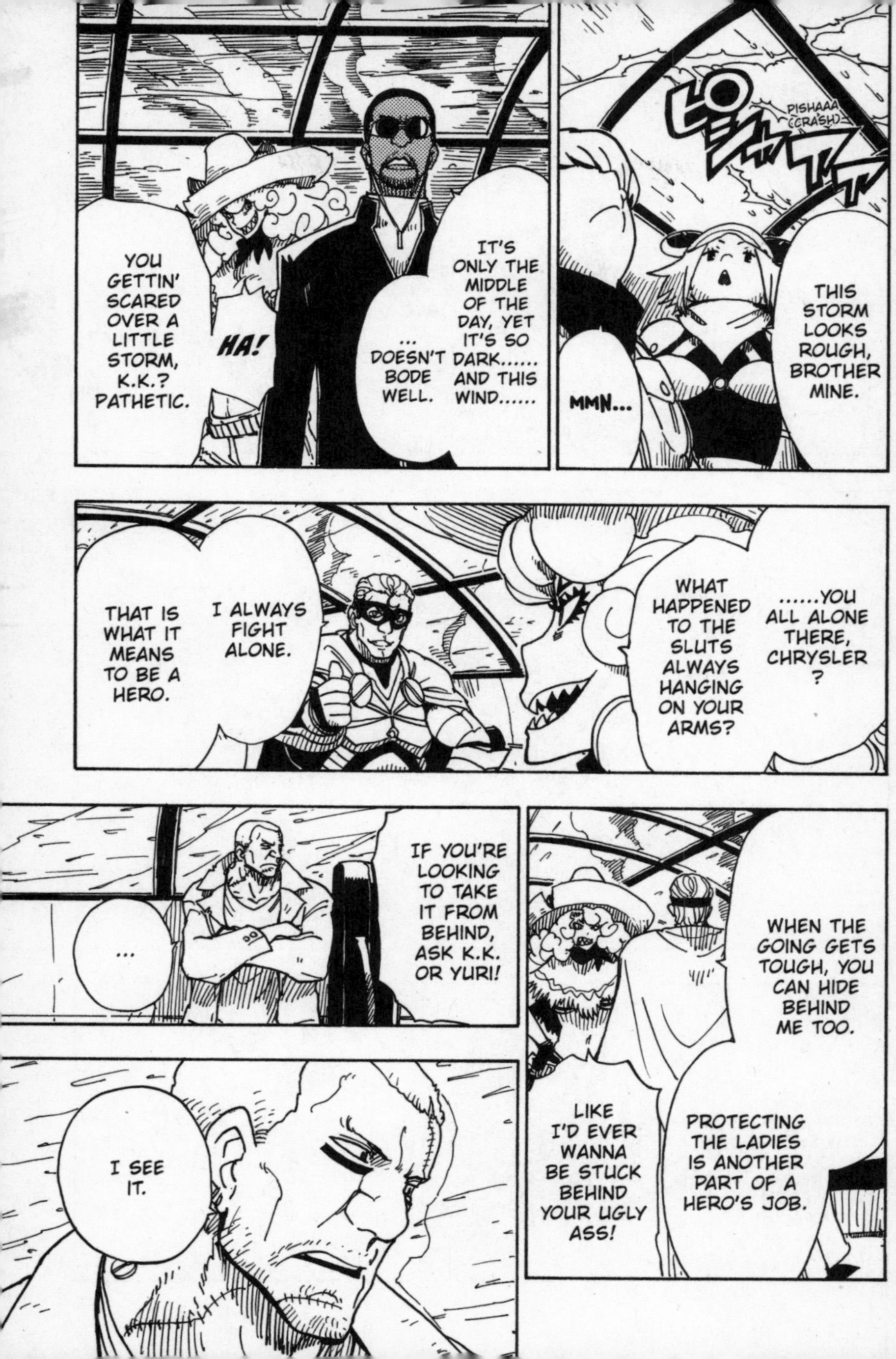
PISHAAA (CRASH)
THIS STORM LOOKS ROUGH, BROTHER MINE.
MMN...
IT'S ONLY THE MIDDLE OF THE DAY, YET IT'S SO DARK...... AND THIS WIND......
... DOESN'T BODE WELL.
HA!
YOU GETTIN' SCARED OVER A LITTLE STORM, K.K.? PATHETIC.
......YOU ALL ALONE THERE, CHRYSLER?
WHAT HAPPENED TO THE SLUTS ALWAYS HANGING ON YOUR ARMS?
I ALWAYS FIGHT ALONE.
THAT IS WHAT IT MEANS TO BE A HERO.
WHEN THE GOING GETS TOUGH, YOU CAN HIDE BEHIND ME TOO.
PROTECTING THE LADIES IS ANOTHER PART OF A HERO'S JOB.
LIKE I'D EVER WANNA BE STUCK BEHIND YOUR UGLY ASS!
IF YOU'RE LOOKING TO TAKE IT FROM BEHIND, ASK K.K. OR YURI!
...
I SEE IT.

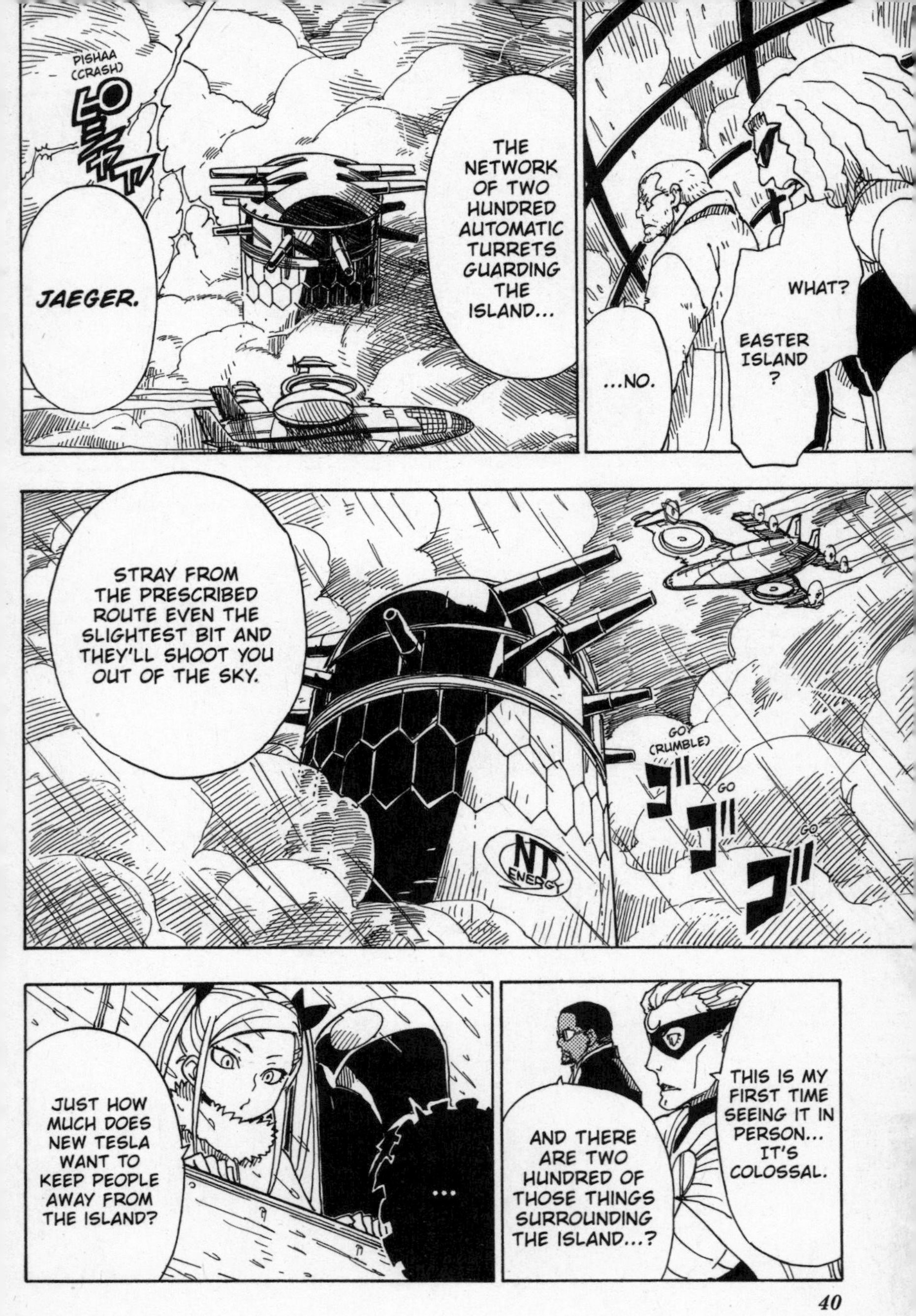
WHAT?
EASTER ISLAND ?
...NO.
THE NETWORK OF TWO HUNDRED AUTOMATIC TURRETS GUARDING THE ISLAND...
PISHAA (CRASH)
JAEGER.
STRAY FROM THE PRESCRIBED ROUTE EVEN THE SLIGHTEST BIT AND THEY'LL SHOOT YOU OUT OF THE SKY.
GO (RUMBLE)
GO
GO
NT ENERGY
THIS IS MY FIRST TIME SEEING IT IN PERSON... IT'S COLOSSAL.
AND THERE ARE TWO HUNDRED OF THOSE THINGS SURROUNDING THE ISLAND...?
JUST HOW MUCH DOES NEW TESLA WANT TO KEEP PEOPLE AWAY FROM THE ISLAND?
...

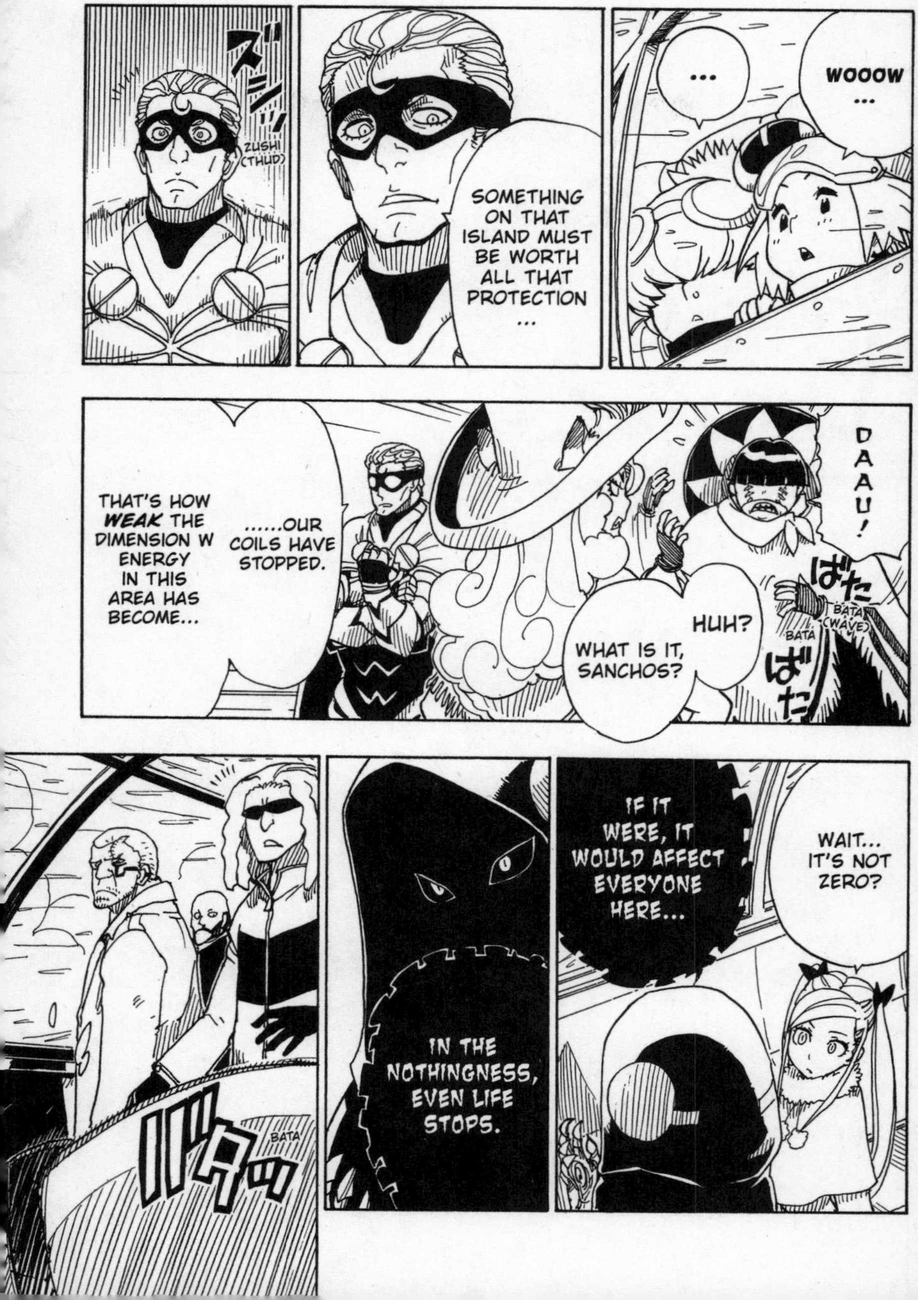
...
WOOOW ...
SOMETHING ON THAT ISLAND MUST BE WORTH ALL THAT PROTECTION ...
ズシ
ZUSHI (THUD)
DAAU!
ばた
BATA (WAVE)
BATA
ばた
HUH?
WHAT IS IT, SANCHOS?
......OUR COILS HAVE STOPPED.
THAT'S HOW ***WEAK*** THE DIMENSION W ENERGY IN THIS AREA HAS BECOME...
WAIT... IT'S NOT ZERO?
IF IT WERE, IT WOULD AFFECT EVERYONE HERE...
IN THE NOTHINGNESS, EVEN LIFE STOPS.
バタッ
BATA

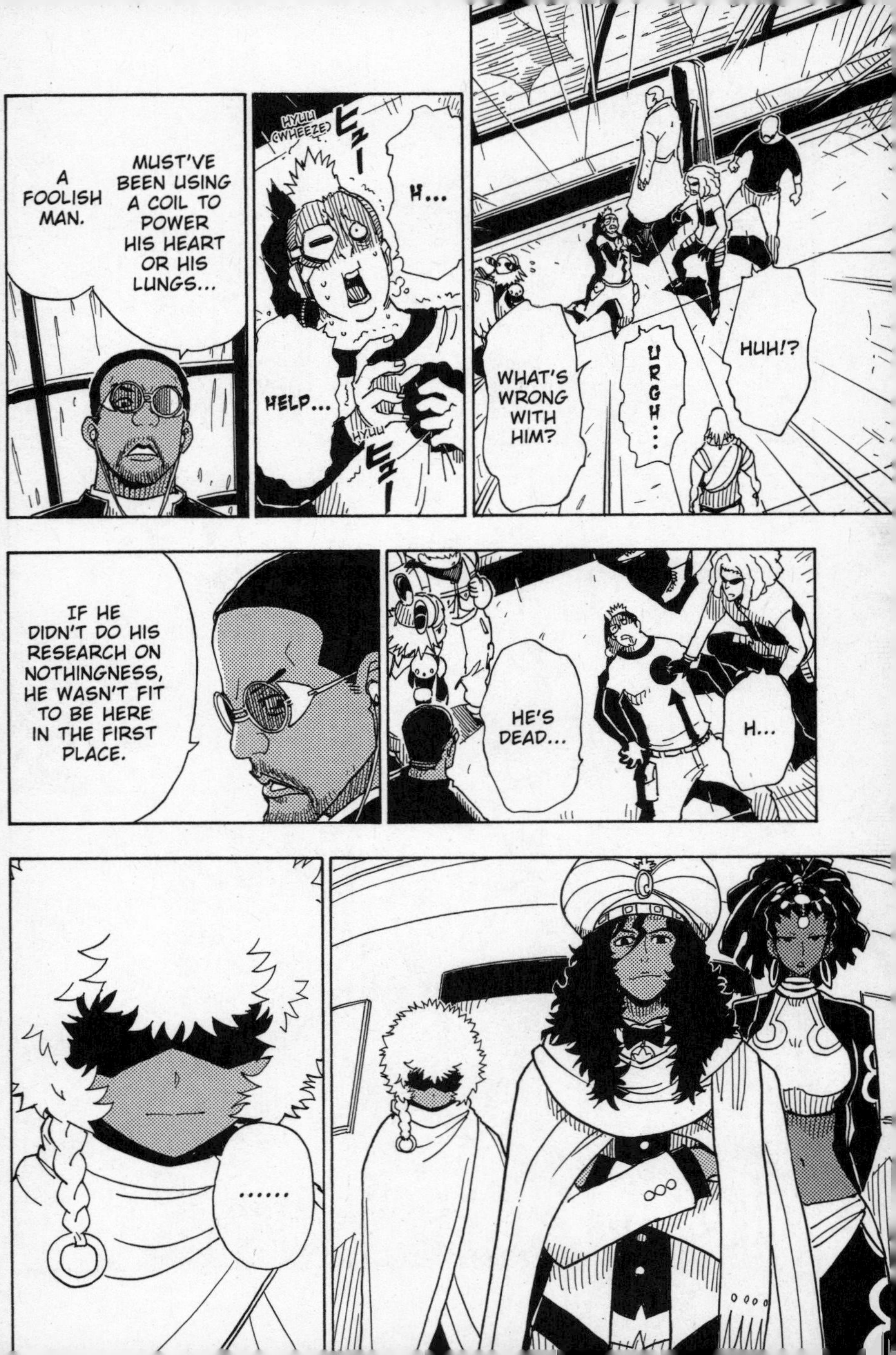
HUH!?
URGH...
WHAT'S WRONG WITH HIM?
HYUU (WHEEZE)
ヒュー
H...
HELP...
HYUU
ヒュー
MUST'VE BEEN USING A COIL TO POWER HIS HEART OR HIS LUNGS...
A FOOLISH MAN.
H...
HE'S DEAD...
IF HE DIDN'T DO HIS RESEARCH ON NOTHINGNESS, HE WASN'T FIT TO BE HERE IN THE FIRST PLACE.
......

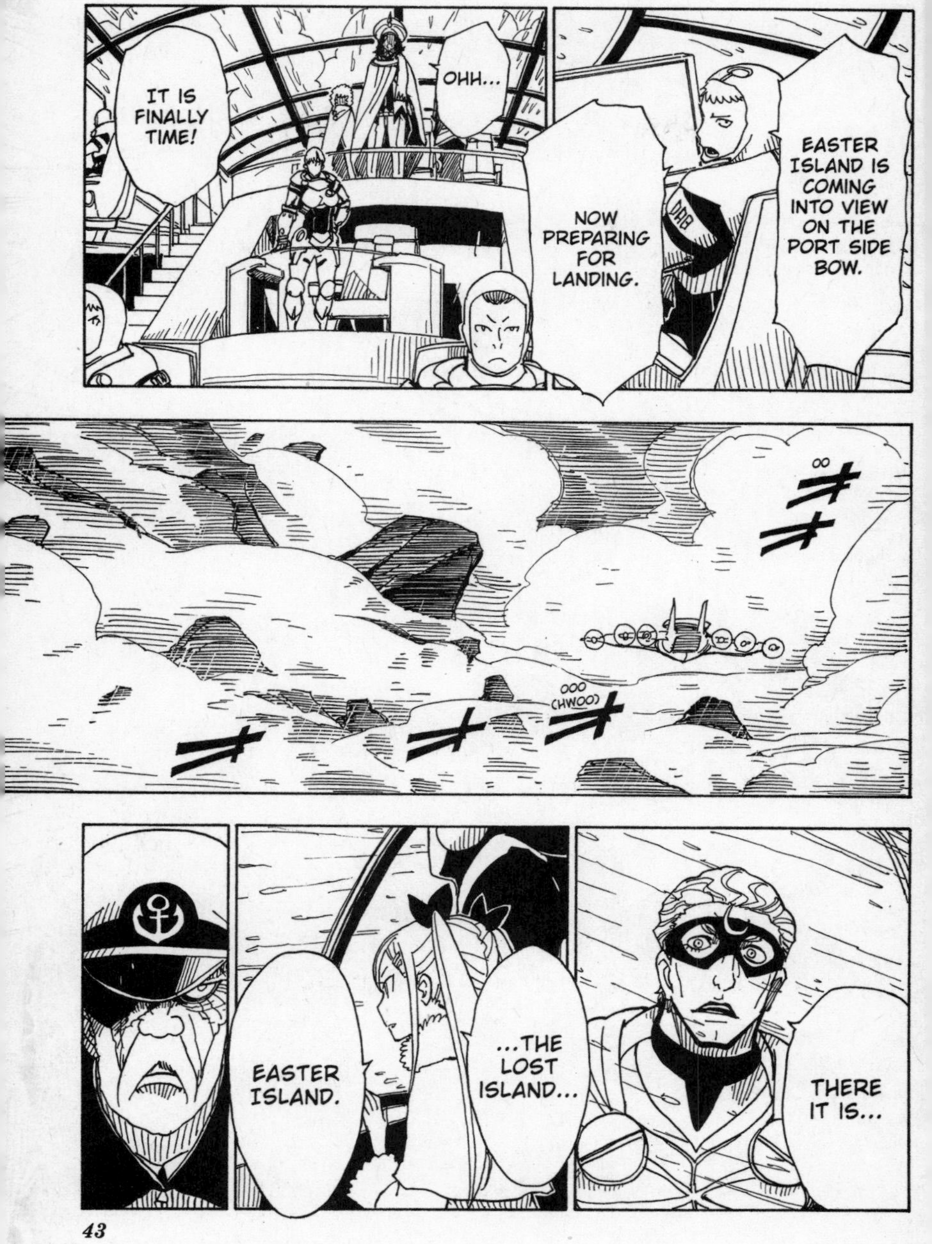
EASTER ISLAND IS COMING INTO VIEW ON THE PORT SIDE BOW.
NOW PREPARING FOR LANDING.
OHH...
IT IS FINALLY TIME!
OOO (HWOO)
THERE IT IS...
...THE LOST ISLAND...
EASTER ISLAND.

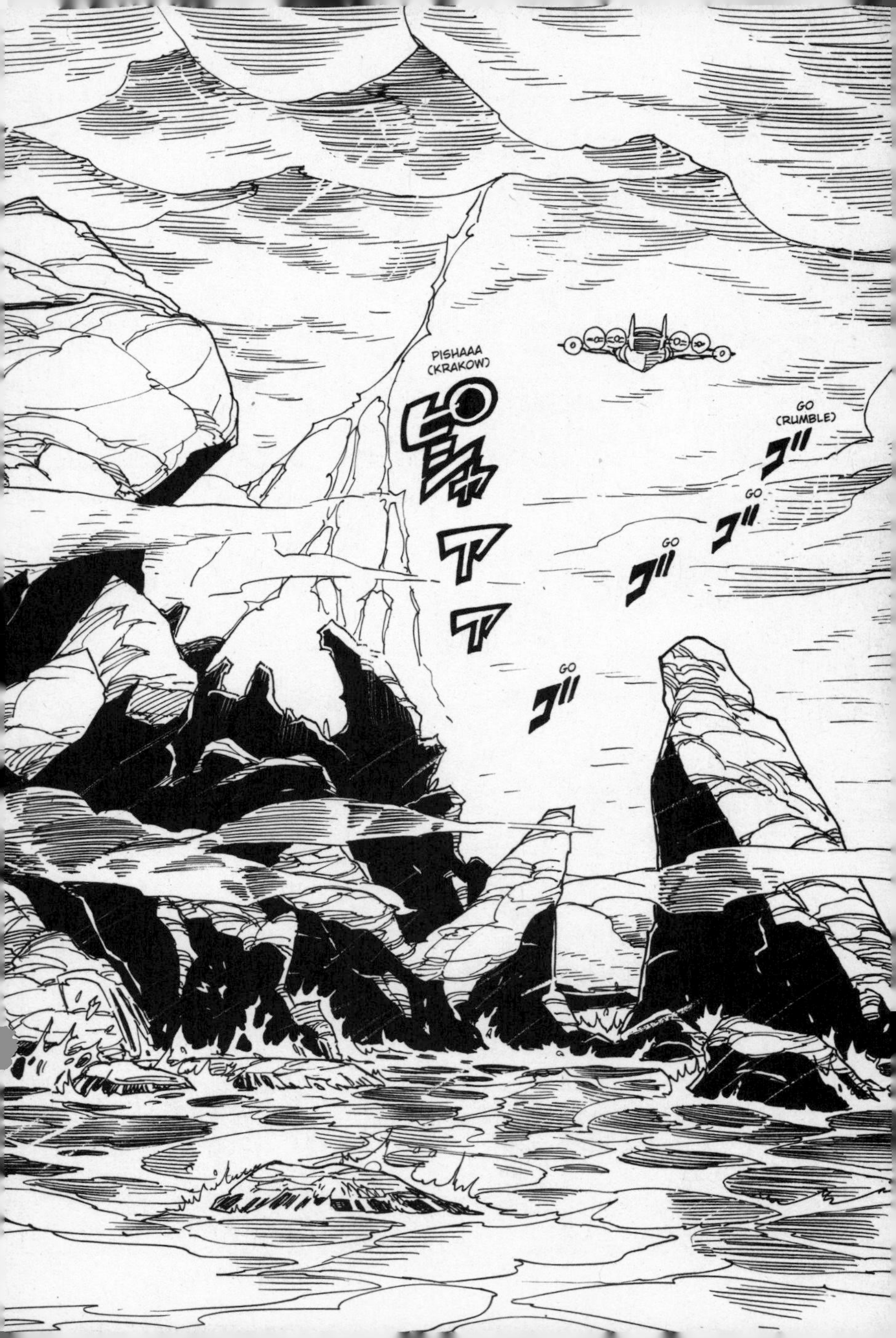

GO
(RUMBLE)
ゴ
GO
ゴ
GO
ゴ
PISHAAA
(KRAKOW)
ピシャアア
GO
ゴ

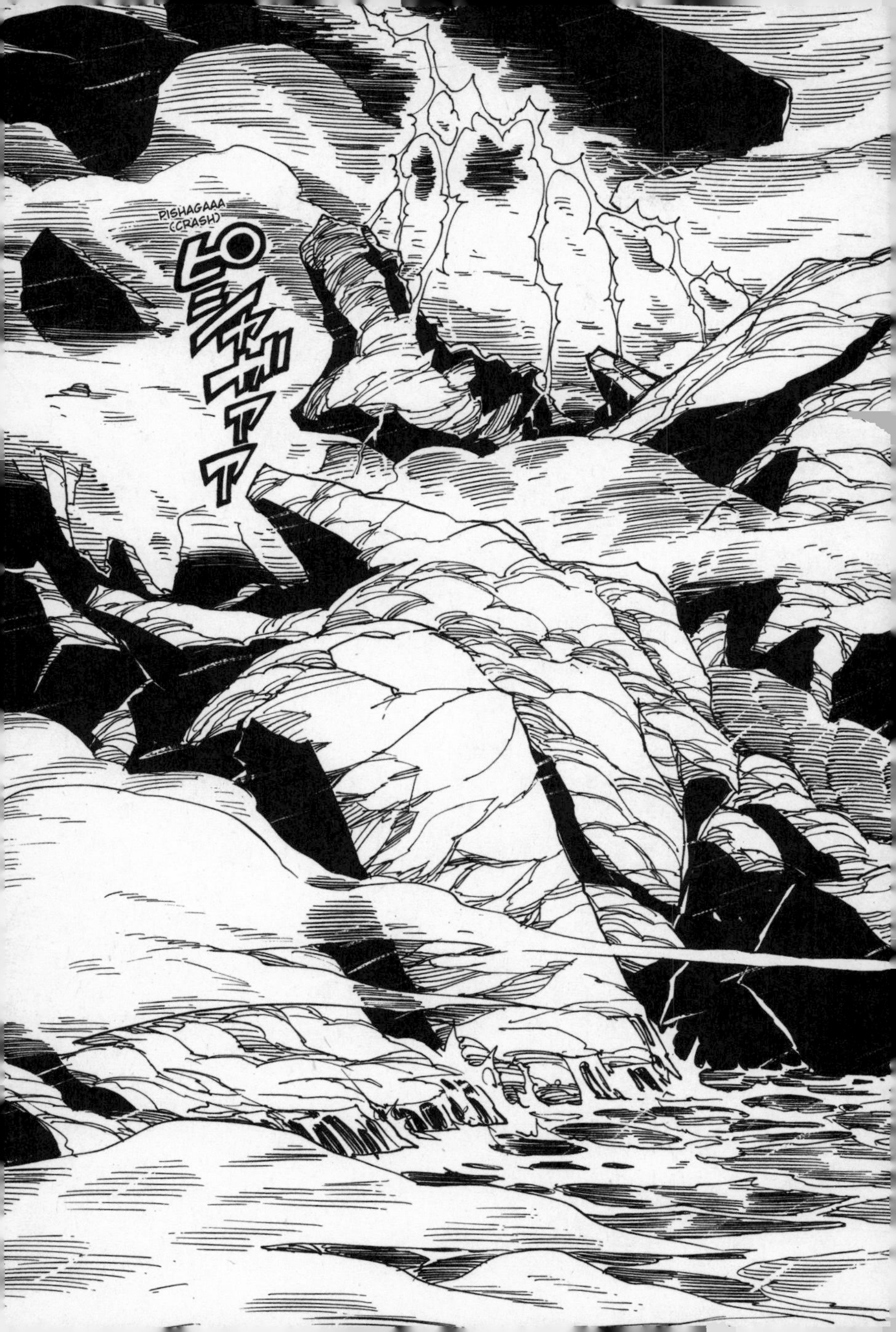
PISHAGAAA
(CRASH)
ピシャアア

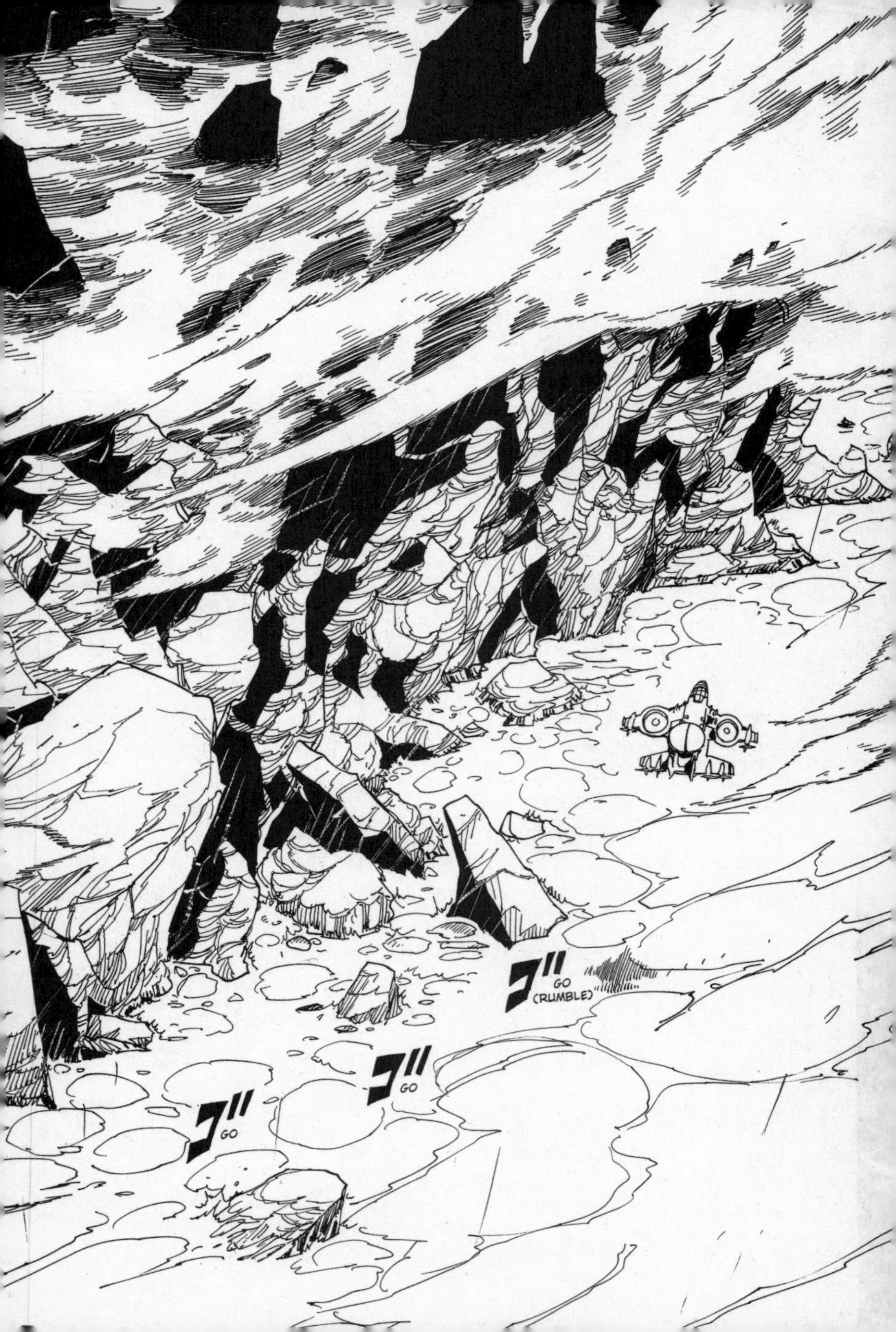
ゴ GO (RUMBLE)
ゴ GO
ゴ GO

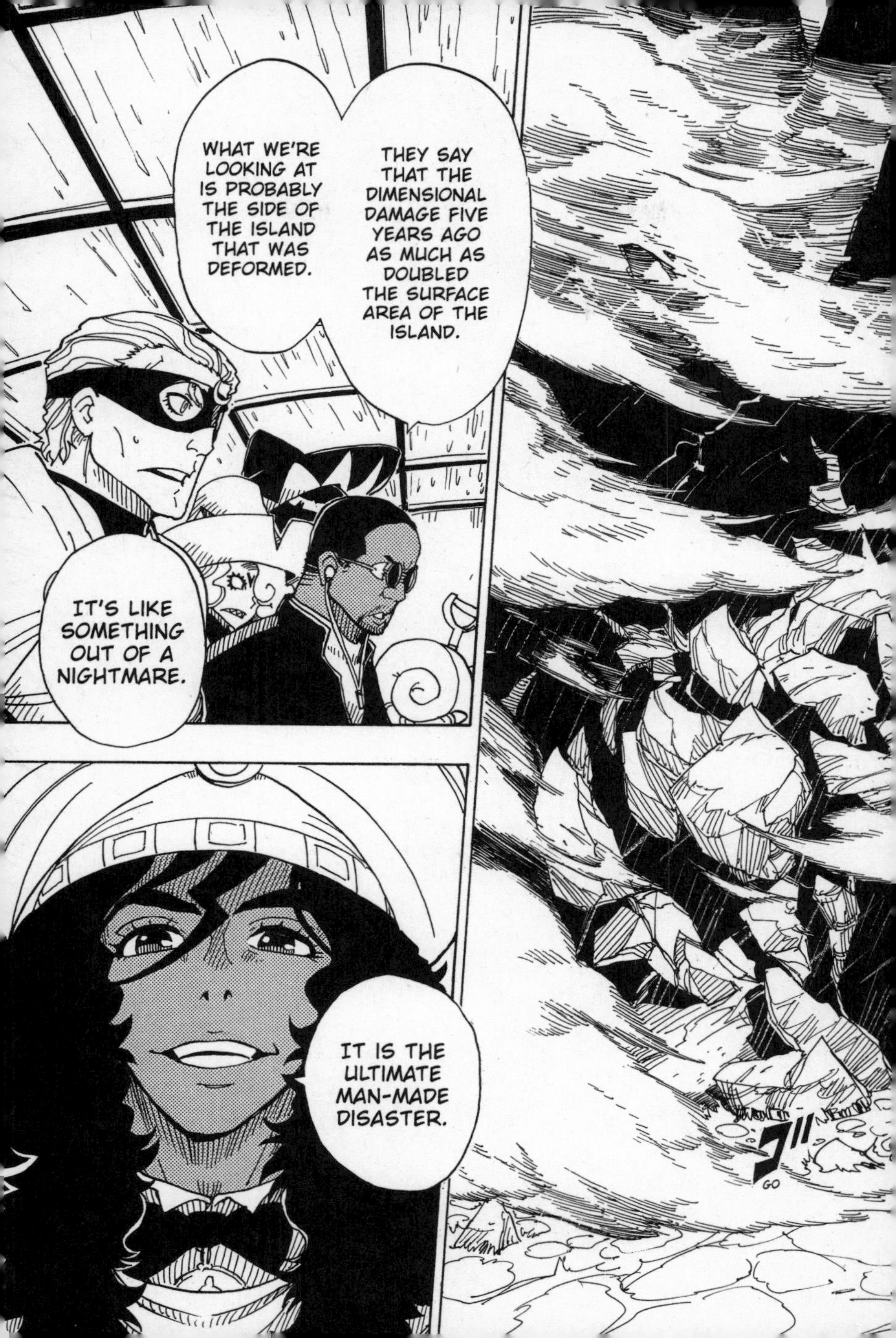
GO
THEY SAY THAT THE DIMENSIONAL DAMAGE FIVE YEARS AGO AS MUCH AS DOUBLED THE SURFACE AREA OF THE ISLAND.
WHAT WE'RE LOOKING AT IS PROBABLY THE SIDE OF THE ISLAND THAT WAS DEFORMED.
IT'S LIKE SOMETHING OUT OF A NIGHTMARE.
IT IS THE ULTIMATE MAN-MADE DISASTER.

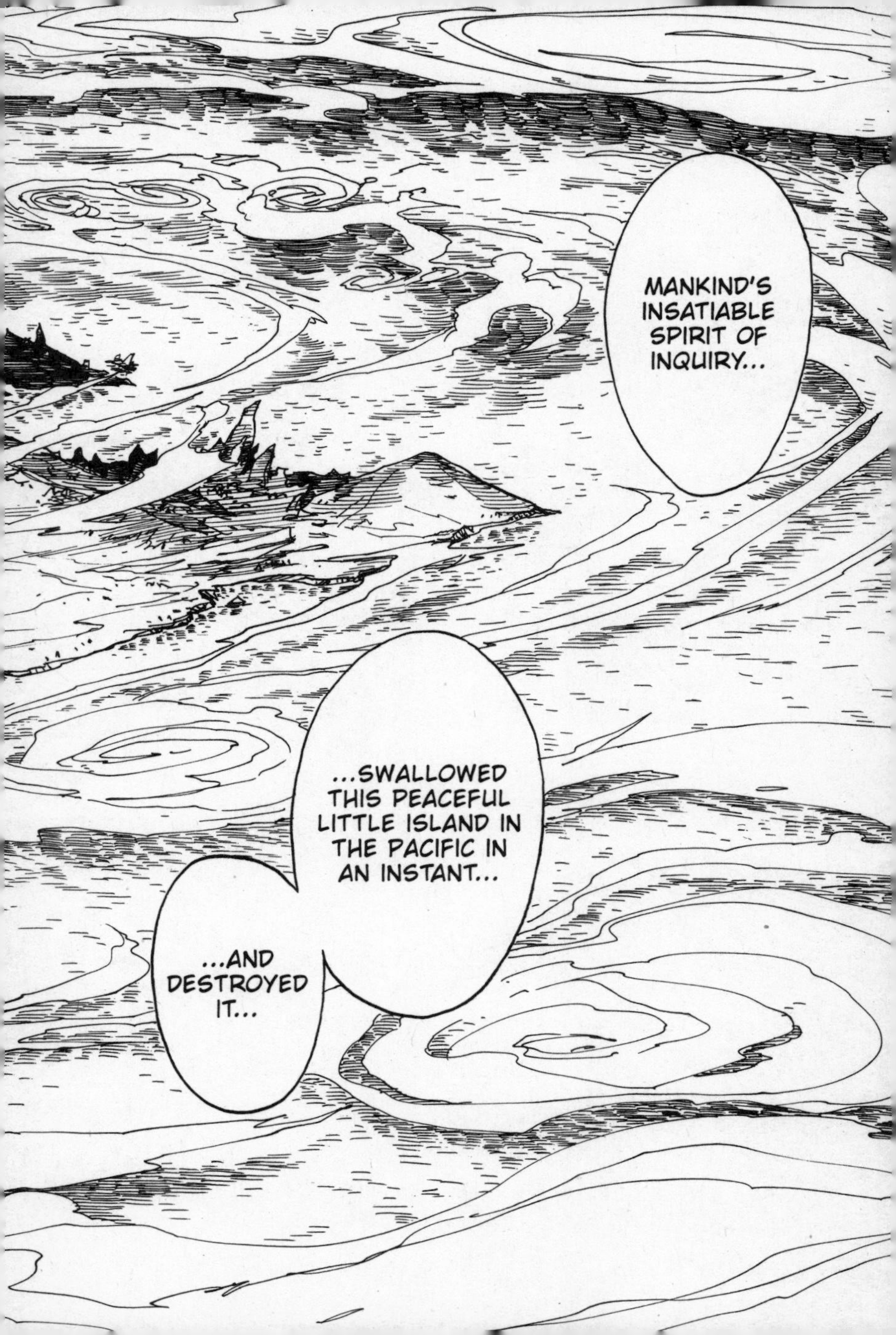
MANKIND'S INSATIABLE SPIRIT OF INQUIRY...
...SWALLOWED THIS PEACEFUL LITTLE ISLAND IN THE PACIFIC IN AN INSTANT...
...AND DESTROYED IT...

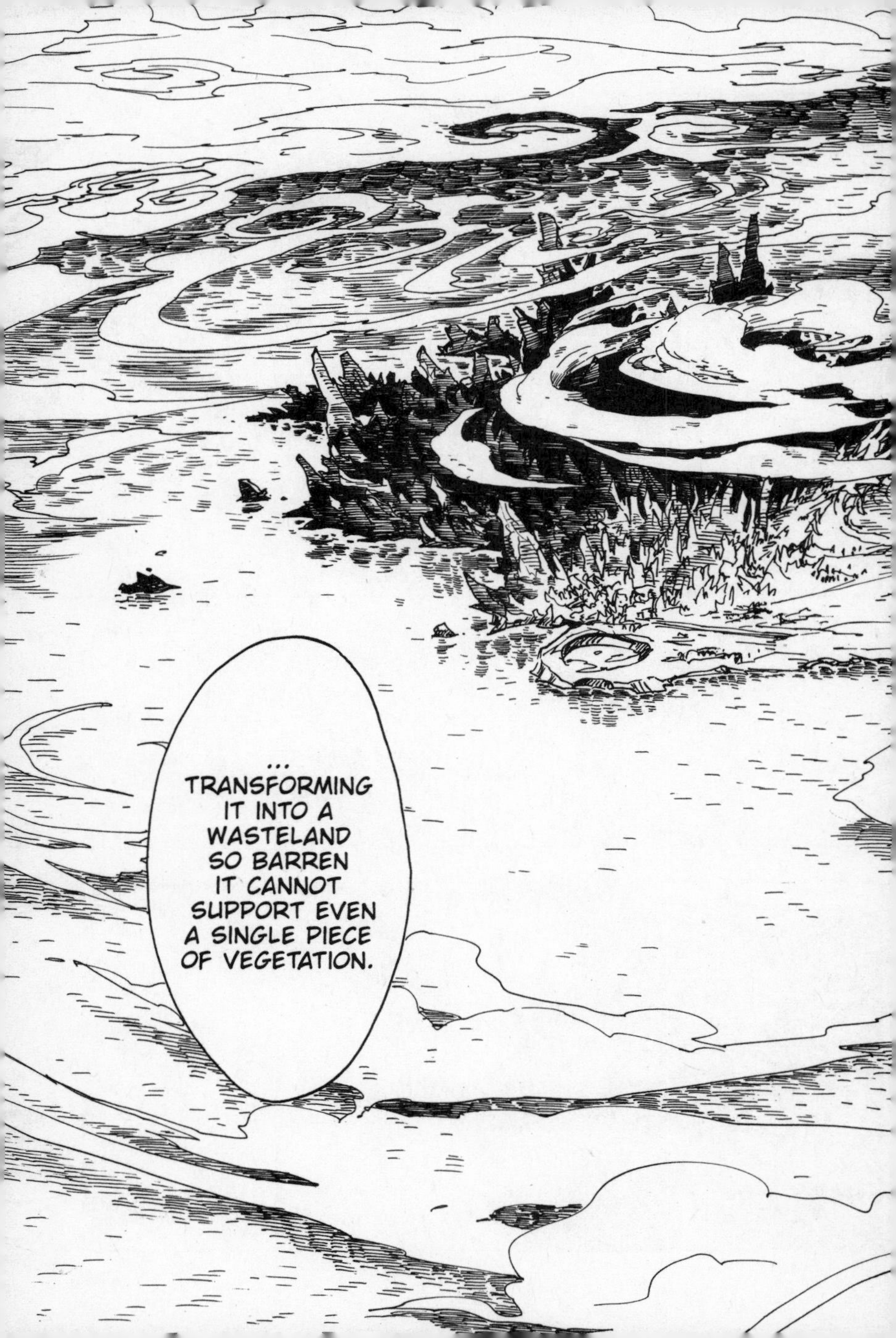
... TRANSFORMING IT INTO A WASTELAND SO BARREN IT CANNOT SUPPORT EVEN A SINGLE PIECE OF VEGETATION.

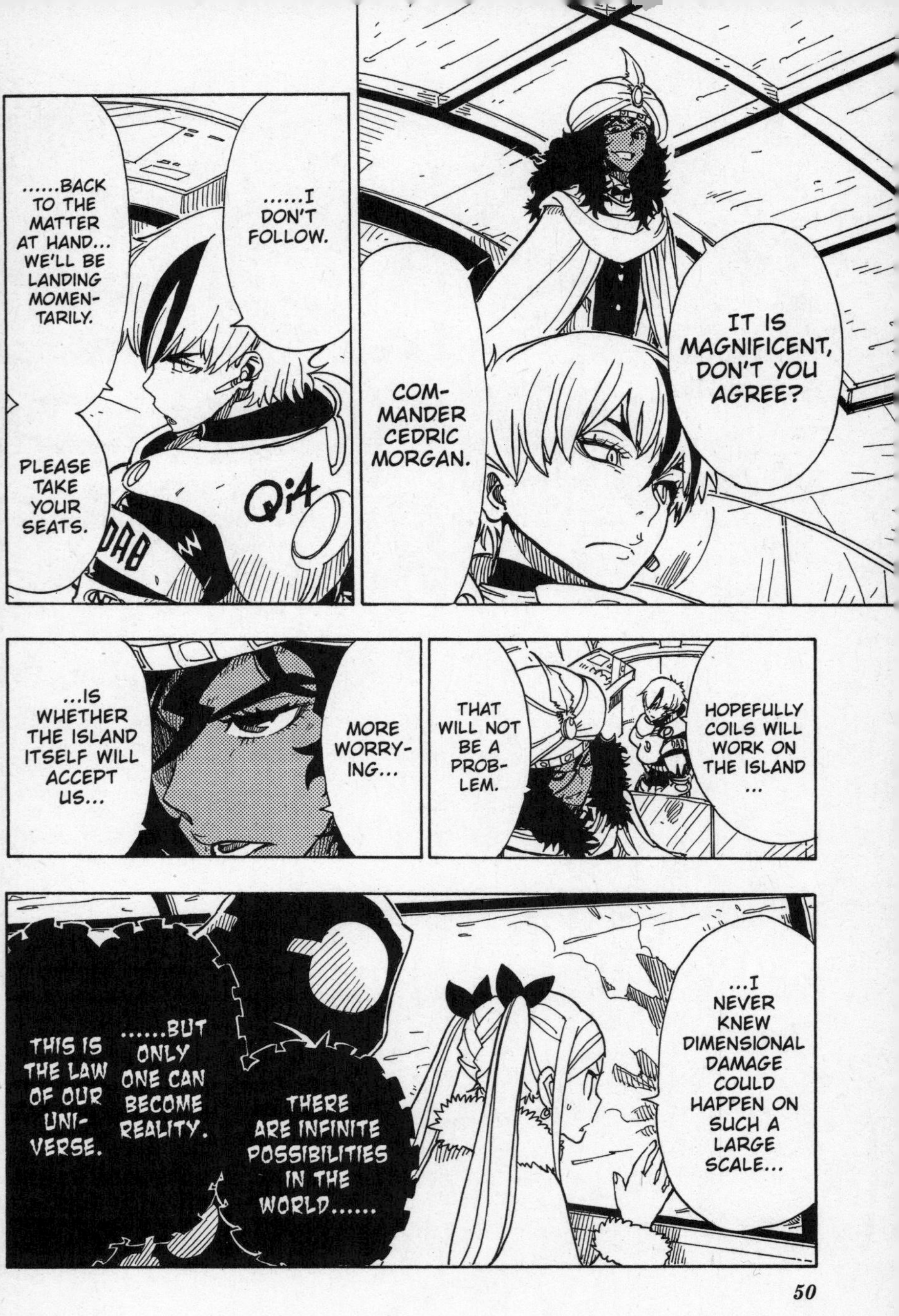
IT IS MAGNIFICENT, DON'T YOU AGREE?
COMMANDER CEDRIC MORGAN.
......I DON'T FOLLOW.
......BACK TO THE MATTER AT HAND... WE'LL BE LANDING MOMENTARILY.
PLEASE TAKE YOUR SEATS.
HOPEFULLY COILS WILL WORK ON THE ISLAND ...
THAT WILL NOT BE A PROBLEM.
MORE WORRYING...
...IS WHETHER THE ISLAND ITSELF WILL ACCEPT US...
...I NEVER KNEW DIMENSIONAL DAMAGE COULD HAPPEN ON SUCH A LARGE SCALE...
THERE ARE INFINITE POSSIBILITIES IN THE WORLD......
......BUT ONLY ONE CAN BECOME REALITY.
THIS IS THE LAW OF OUR UNIVERSE.

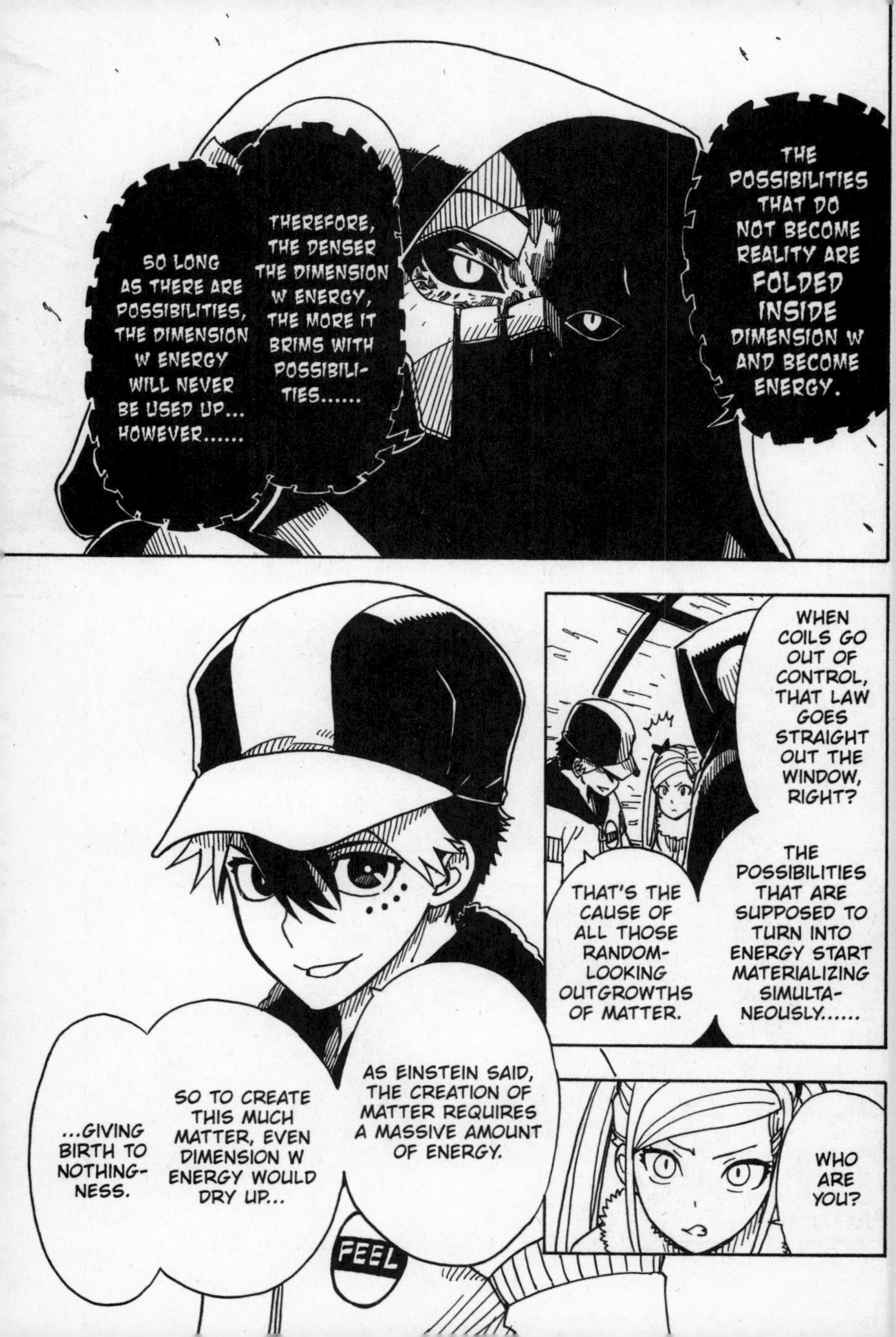
THE POSSIBILITIES THAT DO NOT BECOME REALITY ARE FOLDED INSIDE DIMENSION W AND BECOME ENERGY.
THEREFORE, THE DENSER THE DIMENSION W ENERGY, THE MORE IT BRIMS WITH POSSIBILI-TIES......
SO LONG AS THERE ARE POSSIBILITIES, THE DIMENSION W ENERGY WILL NEVER BE USED UP... HOWEVER......
WHEN COILS GO OUT OF CONTROL, THAT LAW GOES STRAIGHT OUT THE WINDOW, RIGHT?
THE POSSIBILITIES THAT ARE SUPPOSED TO TURN INTO ENERGY START MATERIALIZING SIMULTA-NEOUSLY......
THAT'S THE CAUSE OF ALL THOSE RANDOM-LOOKING OUTGROWTHS OF MATTER.
WHO ARE YOU?
AS EINSTEIN SAID, THE CREATION OF MATTER REQUIRES A MASSIVE AMOUNT OF ENERGY.
SO TO CREATE THIS MUCH MATTER, EVEN DIMENSION W ENERGY WOULD DRY UP...
...GIVING BIRTH TO NOTHING-NESS.
FEEL

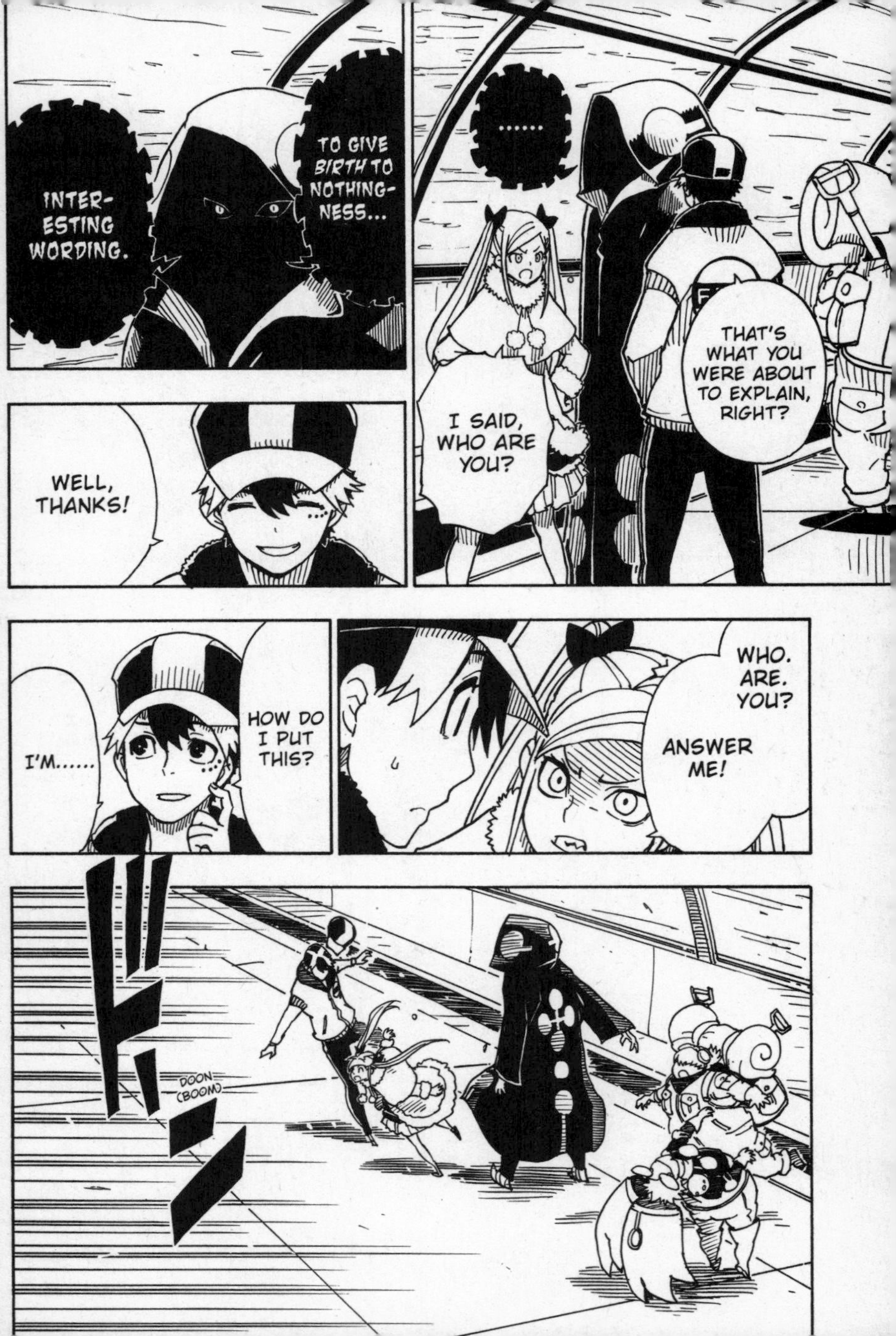
......
THAT'S WHAT YOU WERE ABOUT TO EXPLAIN, RIGHT?
I SAID, WHO ARE YOU?
TO GIVE BIRTH TO NOTHINGNESS...
INTERESTING WORDING.
WELL, THANKS!
WHO. ARE. YOU?
ANSWER ME!
HOW DO I PUT THIS?
I'M......
DOON (BOOM)

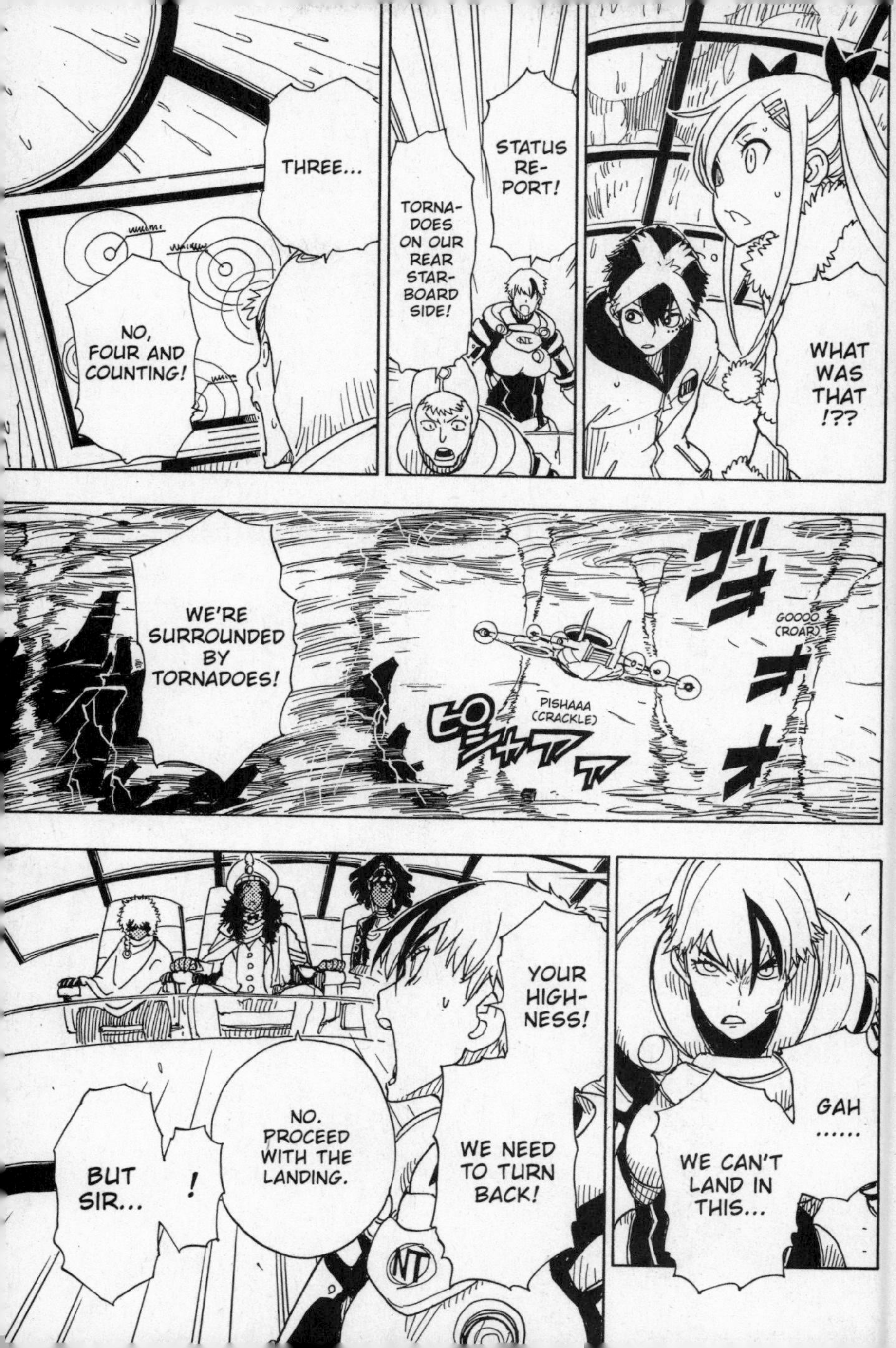
WHAT WAS THAT !??
STATUS RE-PORT!
TORNA-DOES ON OUR REAR STAR-BOARD SIDE!
THREE...
NO, FOUR AND COUNTING!
GOOOO (ROAR)
WE'RE SURROUNDED BY TORNADOES!
PISHAAA (CRACKLE)
GAH ......
WE CAN'T LAND IN THIS...
YOUR HIGH-NESS!
WE NEED TO TURN BACK!
NO. PROCEED WITH THE LANDING.
!
BUT SIR...

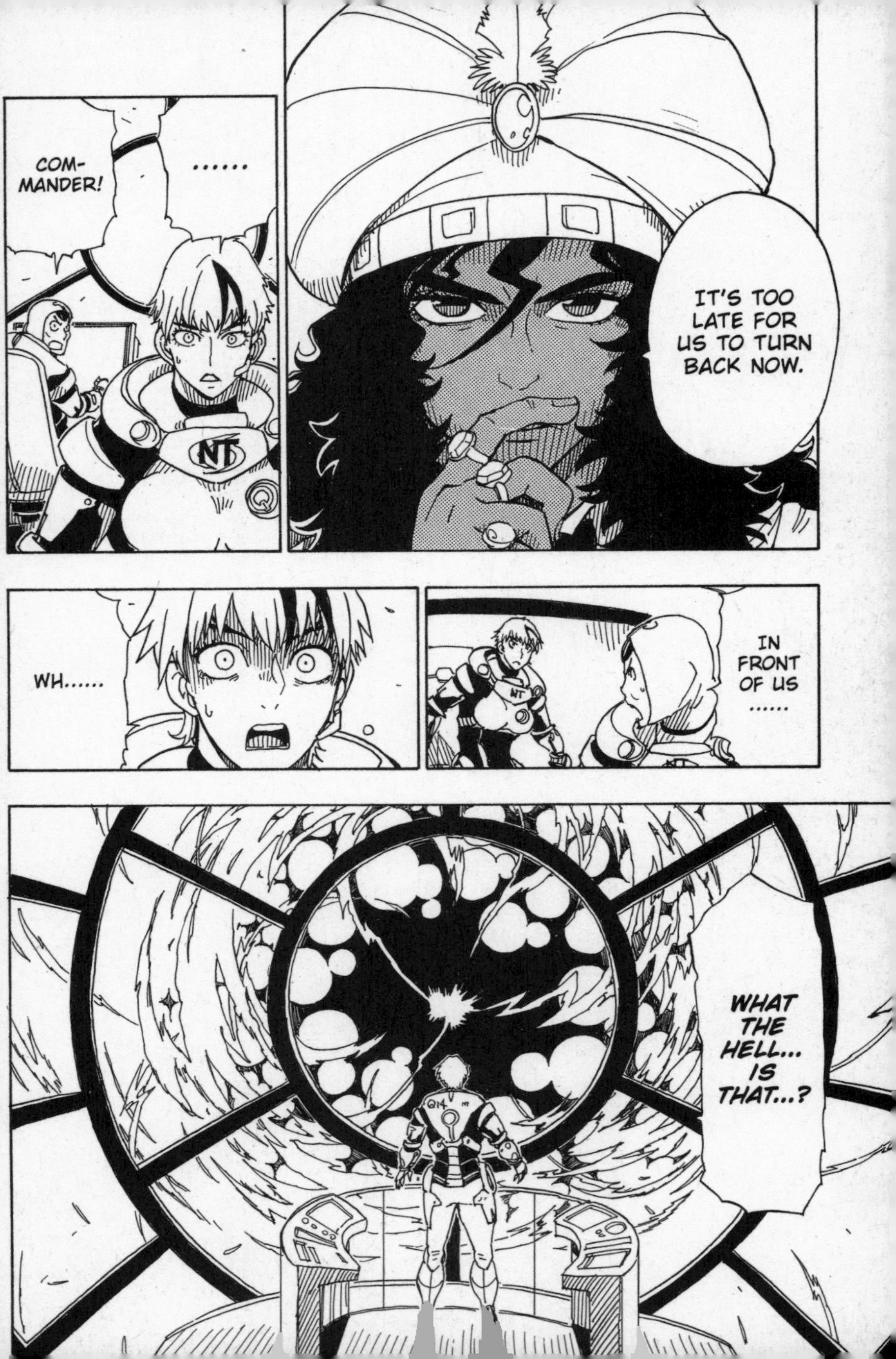
IT'S TOO LATE FOR US TO TURN BACK NOW.
......
COM-MANDER!
IN FRONT OF US ......
WH......
WHAT THE HELL... IS THAT...?

Dimension W

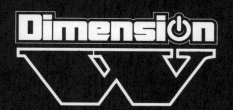

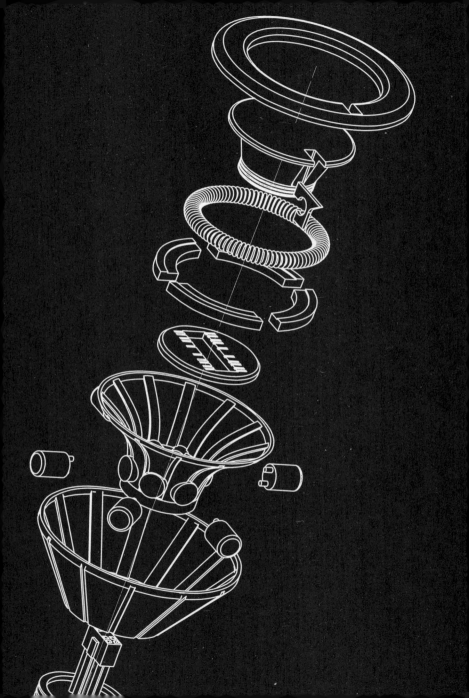

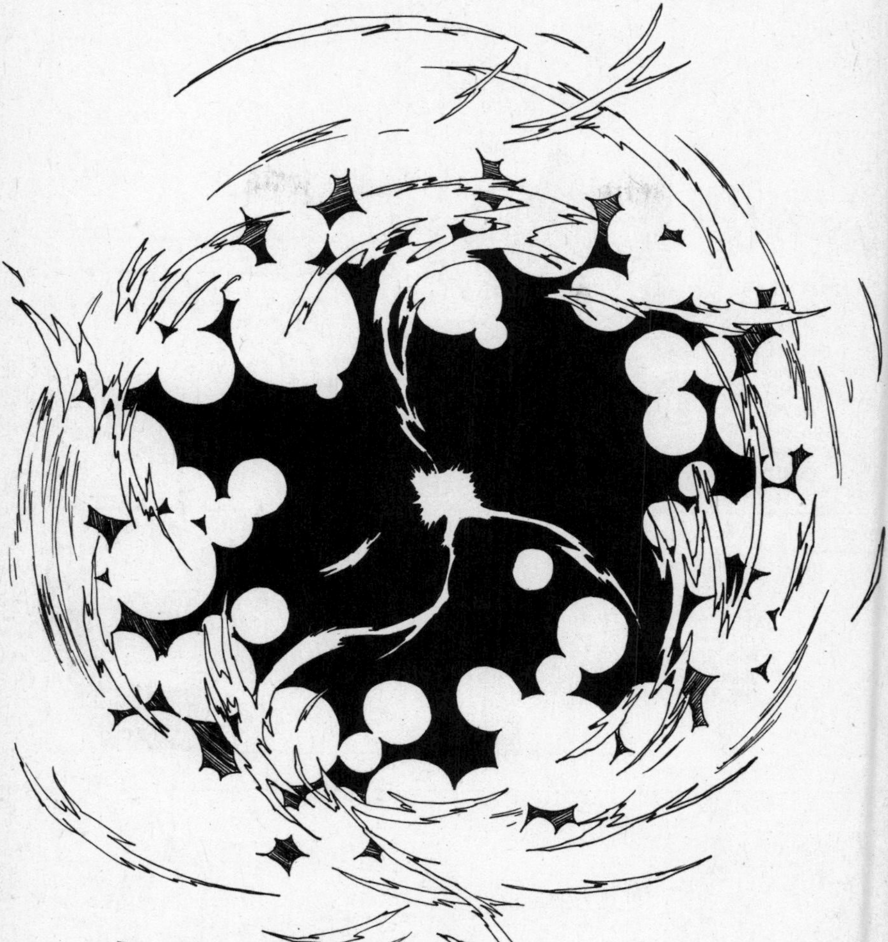

## FILE.42
## THE MYSTERY SPHERE

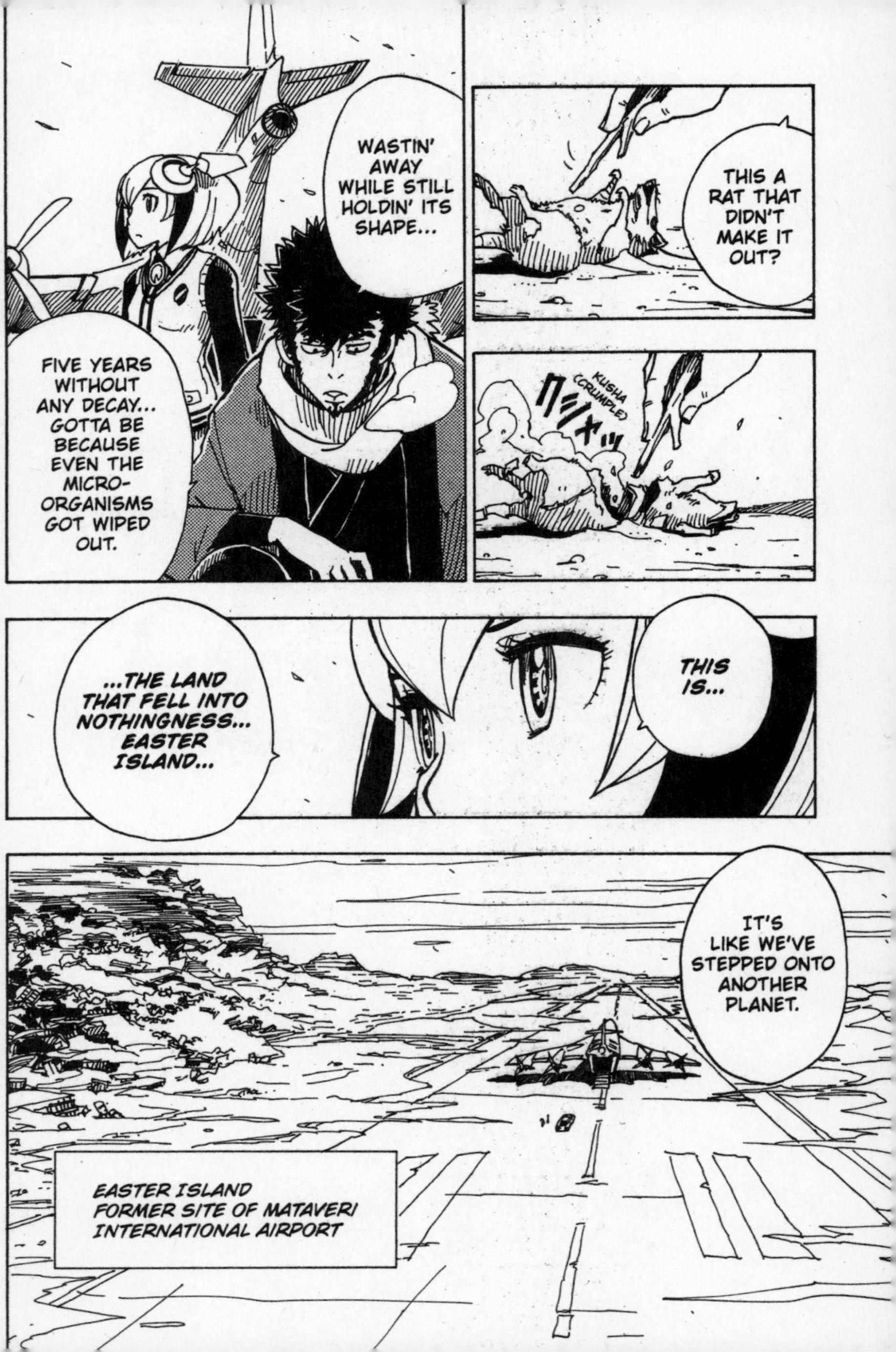
THIS A RAT THAT DIDN'T MAKE IT OUT?
クシャッ KUSHA (CRUMPLE)
WASTIN' AWAY WHILE STILL HOLDIN' ITS SHAPE...
FIVE YEARS WITHOUT ANY DECAY... GOTTA BE BECAUSE EVEN THE MICRO-ORGANISMS GOT WIPED OUT.
THIS IS...
...THE LAND THAT FELL INTO NOTHINGNESS... EASTER ISLAND...
IT'S LIKE WE'VE STEPPED ONTO ANOTHER PLANET.
EASTER ISLAND FORMER SITE OF MATAVERI INTERNATIONAL AIRPORT

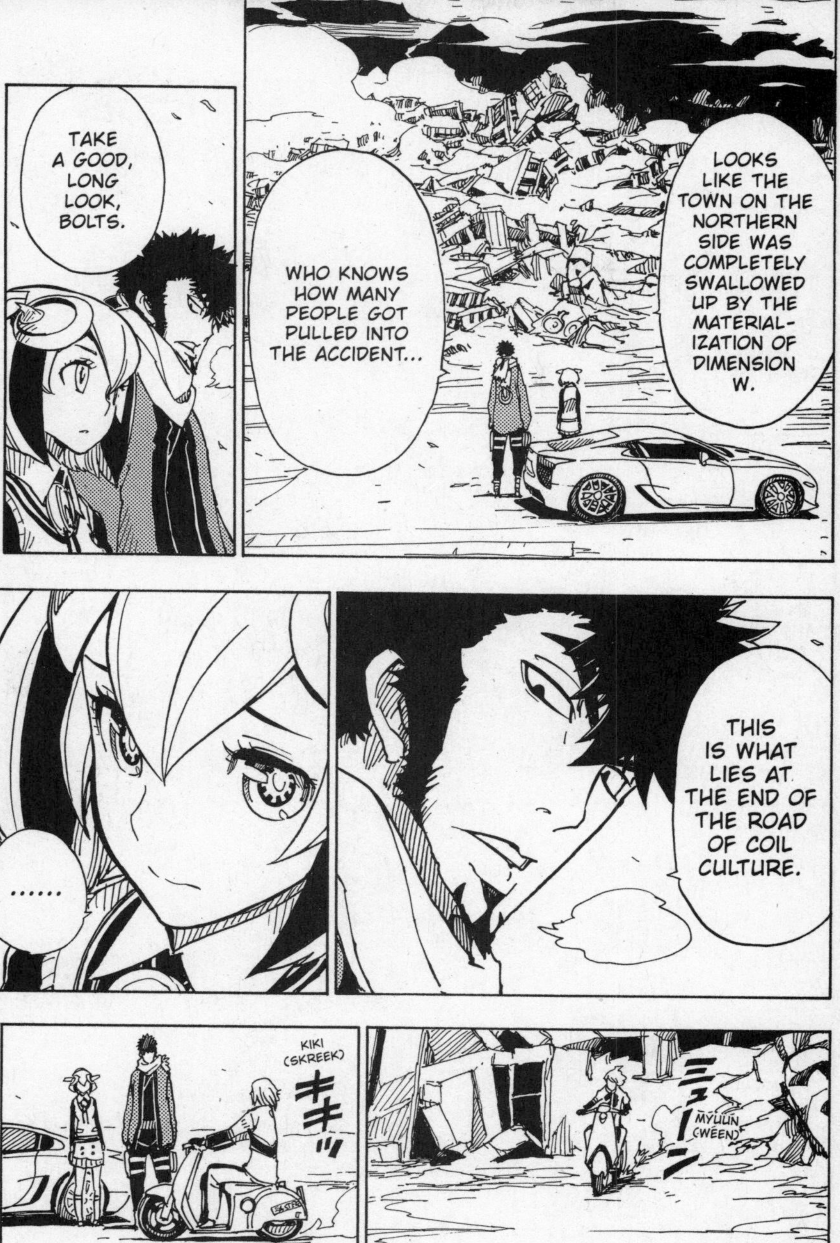
LOOKS LIKE THE TOWN ON THE NORTHERN SIDE WAS COMPLETELY SWALLOWED UP BY THE MATERIAL-IZATION OF DIMENSION W.
WHO KNOWS HOW MANY PEOPLE GOT PULLED INTO THE ACCIDENT...
TAKE A GOOD, LONG LOOK, BOLTS.
THIS IS WHAT LIES AT THE END OF THE ROAD OF COIL CULTURE.
......
MYUUN (WEEN)
KIKI (SKREEK)
キキッ

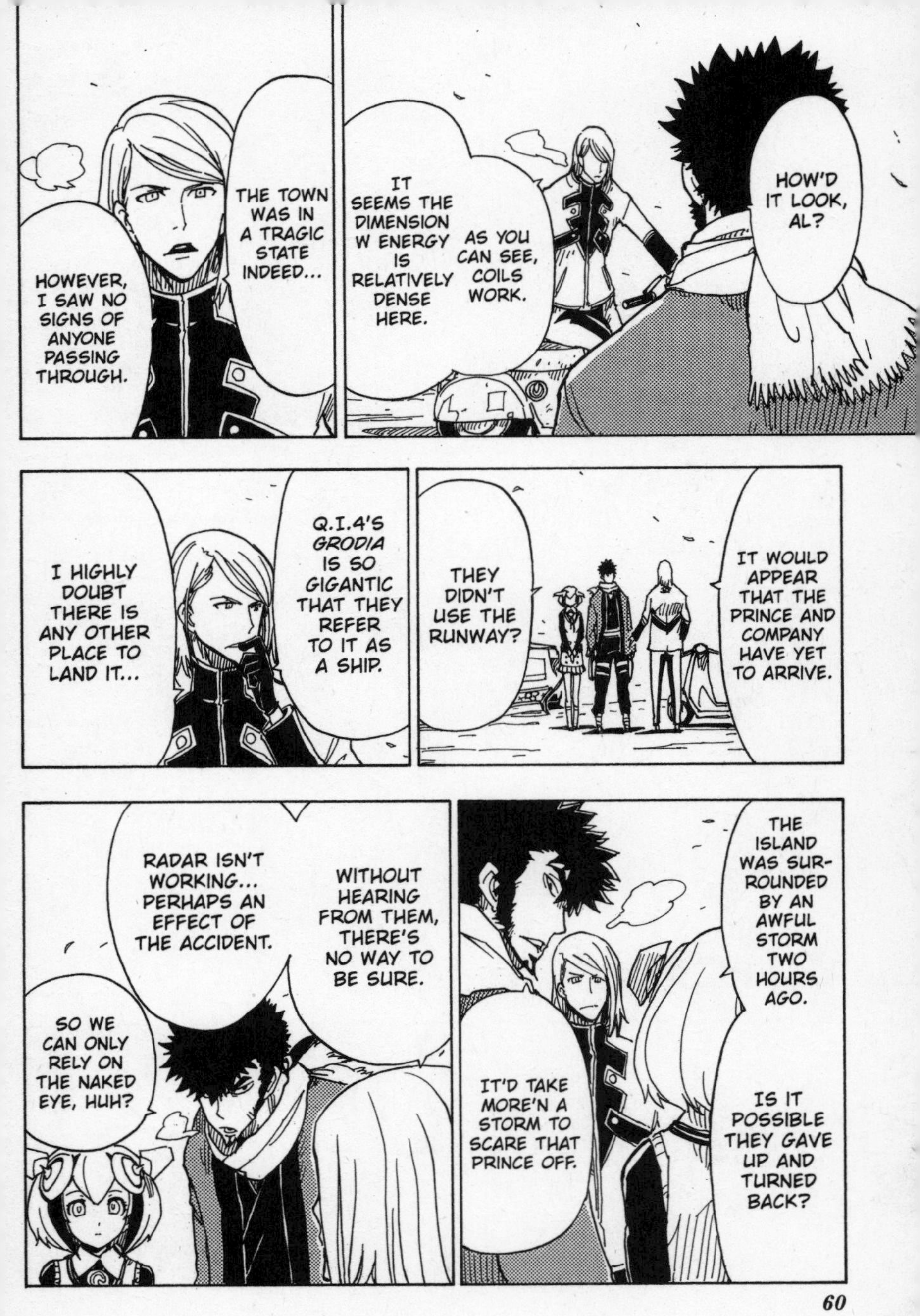
HOW'D IT LOOK, AL?
AS YOU CAN SEE, COILS WORK.
IT SEEMS THE DIMENSION W ENERGY IS RELATIVELY DENSE HERE.
THE TOWN WAS IN A TRAGIC STATE INDEED...
HOWEVER, I SAW NO SIGNS OF ANYONE PASSING THROUGH.
IT WOULD APPEAR THAT THE PRINCE AND COMPANY HAVE YET TO ARRIVE.
THEY DIDN'T USE THE RUNWAY?
Q.I.4'S *GRODIA* IS SO GIGANTIC THAT THEY REFER TO IT AS A SHIP.
I HIGHLY DOUBT THERE IS ANY OTHER PLACE TO LAND IT...
THE ISLAND WAS SURROUNDED BY AN AWFUL STORM TWO HOURS AGO.
IS IT POSSIBLE THEY GAVE UP AND TURNED BACK?
IT'D TAKE MORE'N A STORM TO SCARE THAT PRINCE OFF.
WITHOUT HEARING FROM THEM, THERE'S NO WAY TO BE SURE.
RADAR ISN'T WORKING... PERHAPS AN EFFECT OF THE ACCIDENT.
SO WE CAN ONLY RELY ON THE NAKED EYE, HUH?

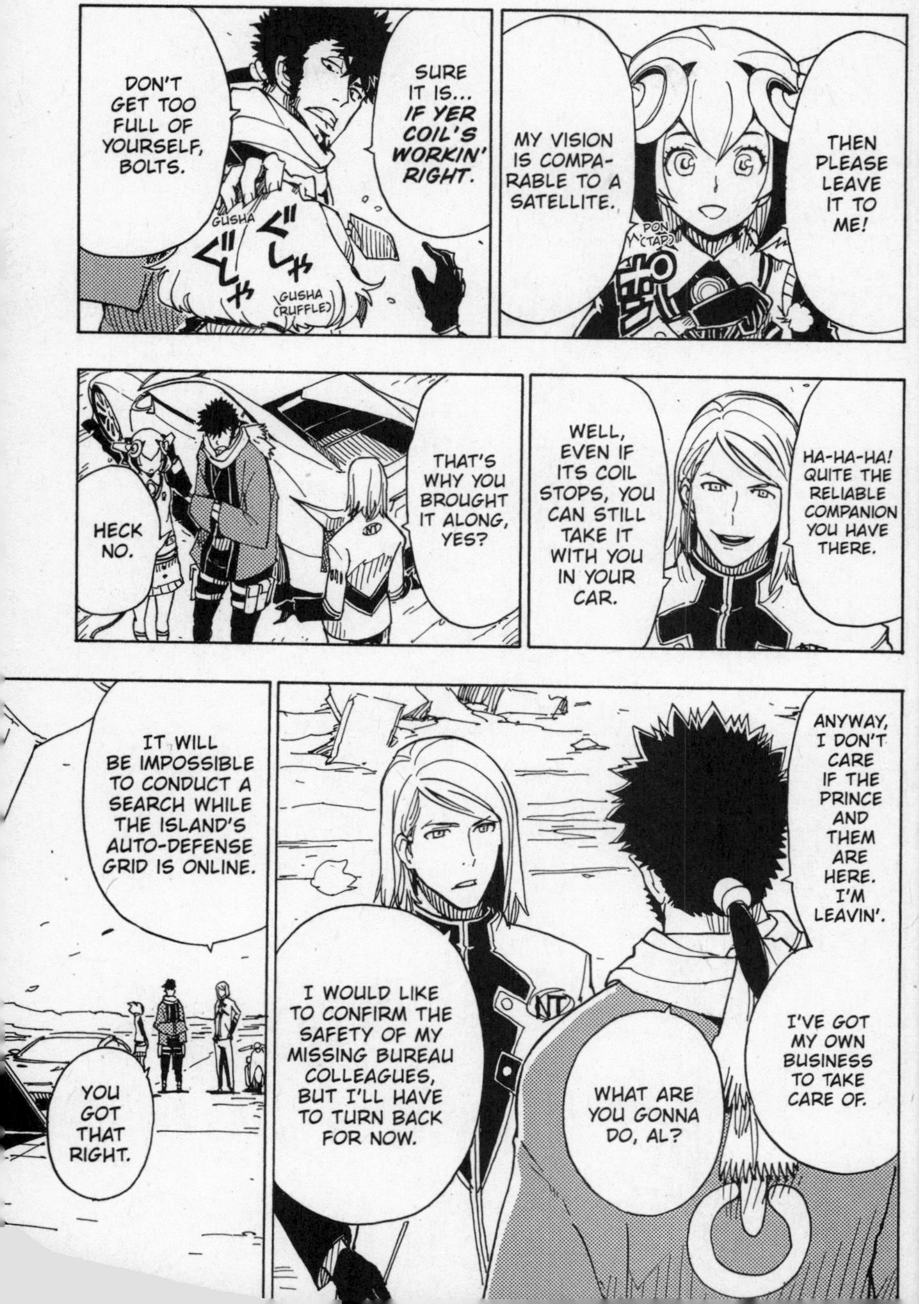
THEN PLEASE LEAVE IT TO ME!
MY VISION IS COMPA-RABLE TO A SATELLITE.
PON (TAP)
SURE IT IS... IF YER COIL'S WORKIN' RIGHT.
DON'T GET TOO FULL OF YOURSELF, BOLTS.
GUSHA
GUSHA (RUFFLE)
HA-HA-HA! QUITE THE RELIABLE COMPANION YOU HAVE THERE.
WELL, EVEN IF ITS COIL STOPS, YOU CAN STILL TAKE IT WITH YOU IN YOUR CAR.
THAT'S WHY YOU BROUGHT IT ALONG, YES?
HECK NO.
ANYWAY, I DON'T CARE IF THE PRINCE AND THEM ARE HERE. I'M LEAVIN'.
I'VE GOT MY OWN BUSINESS TO TAKE CARE OF.
WHAT ARE YOU GONNA DO, AL?
I WOULD LIKE TO CONFIRM THE SAFETY OF MY MISSING BUREAU COLLEAGUES, BUT I'LL HAVE TO TURN BACK FOR NOW.
IT WILL BE IMPOSSIBLE TO CONDUCT A SEARCH WHILE THE ISLAND'S AUTO-DEFENSE GRID IS ONLINE.
YOU GOT THAT RIGHT.

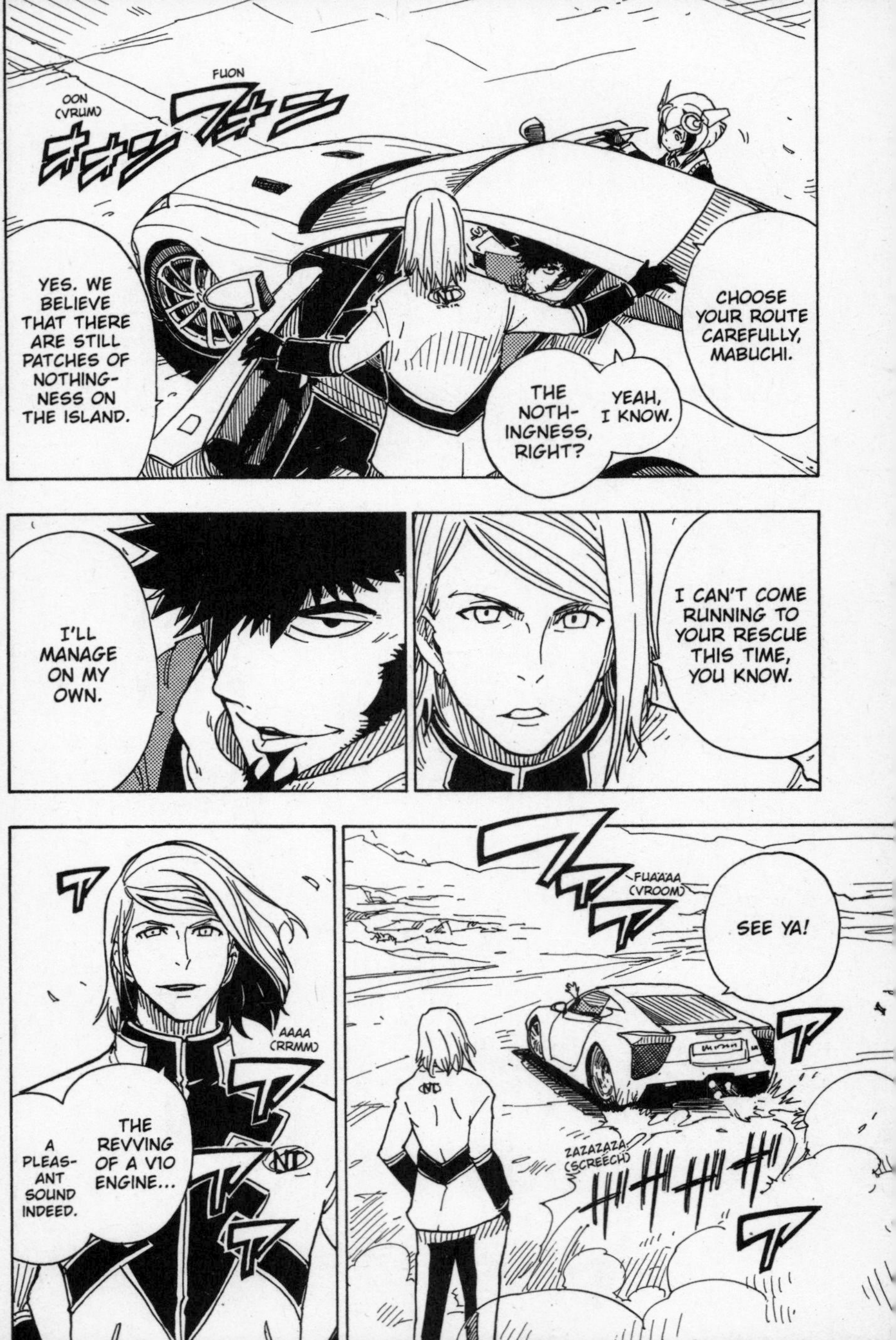
FUON
OON (VRUM)
CHOOSE YOUR ROUTE CAREFULLY, MABUCHI.
YEAH, I KNOW.
THE NOTHINGNESS, RIGHT?
YES. WE BELIEVE THAT THERE ARE STILL PATCHES OF NOTHINGNESS ON THE ISLAND.
I CAN'T COME RUNNING TO YOUR RESCUE THIS TIME, YOU KNOW.
I'LL MANAGE ON MY OWN.
FUAAAA (VROOM)
SEE YA!
ZAZAZAZA (SCREECH)
AAAA (RRMM)
THE REVVING OF A V10 ENGINE...
A PLEASANT SOUND INDEED.

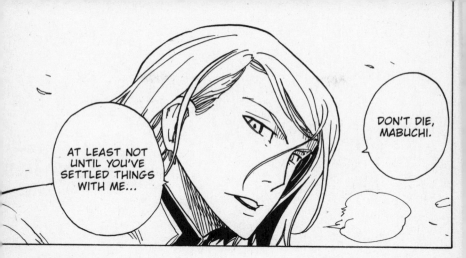

DON'T DIE, MABUCHI.
AT LEAST NOT UNTIL YOU'VE SETTLED THINGS WITH ME...
AAA
Easter Island Current Locations
Ground Zero
Former Site of Mataveri International Airport
MIRA
KYOUMA
ALBERT
Easter Island Protrusions Areas
New Island a-01
a-01 Eastern Coast

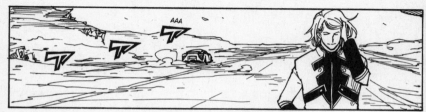

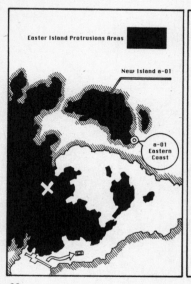

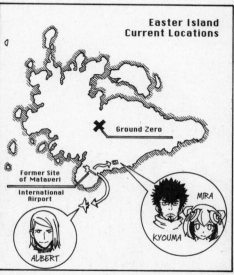

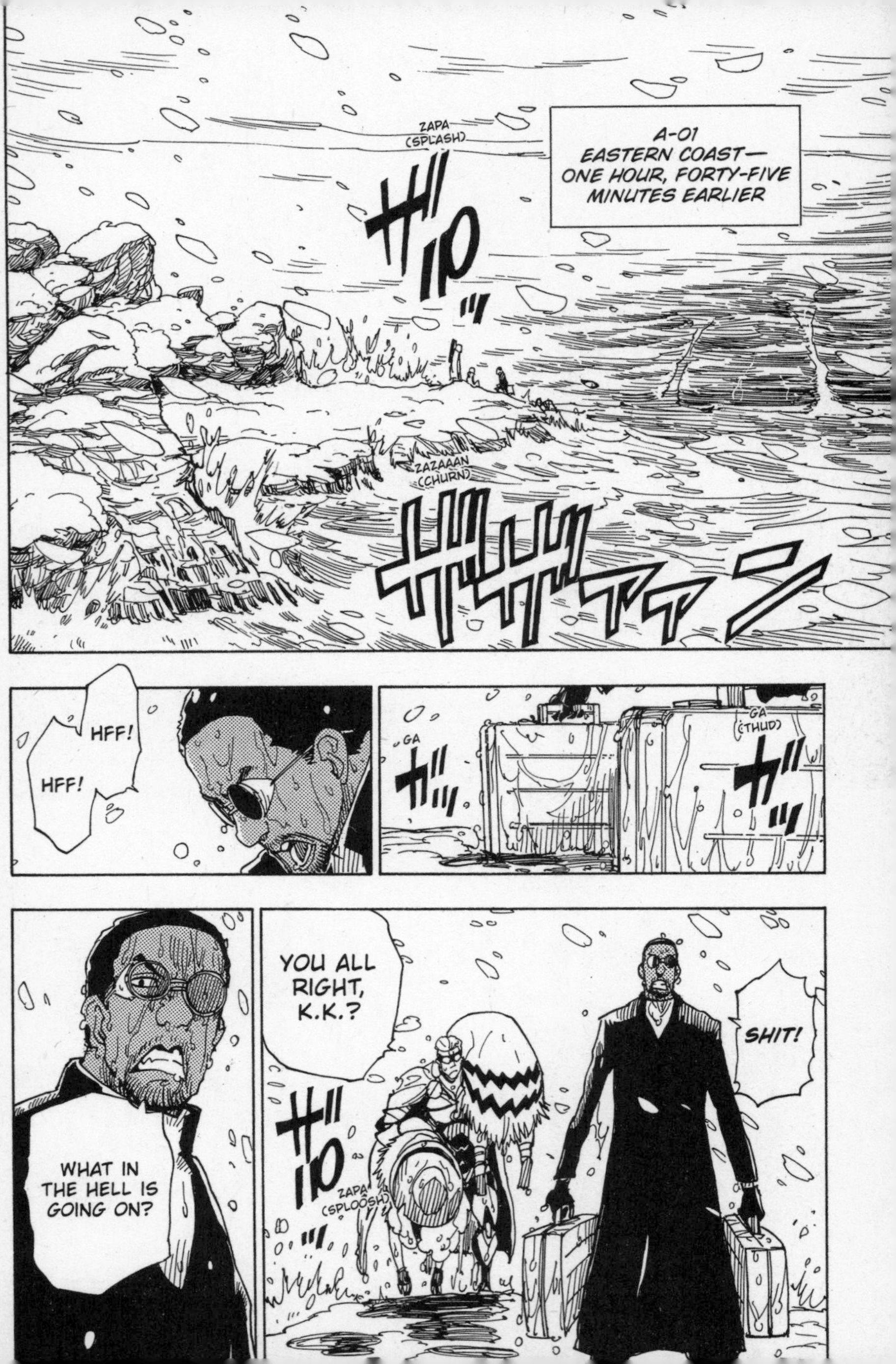
A-01 EASTERN COAST— ONE HOUR, FORTY-FIVE MINUTES EARLIER
ZAPA (SPLASH)
ZAZAAAN (CHURN)
GA (THUD)
GA
HFF!
HFF!
SHIT!
YOU ALL RIGHT, K.K.?
ZAPA (SPLOOSH)
WHAT IN THE HELL IS GOING ON?

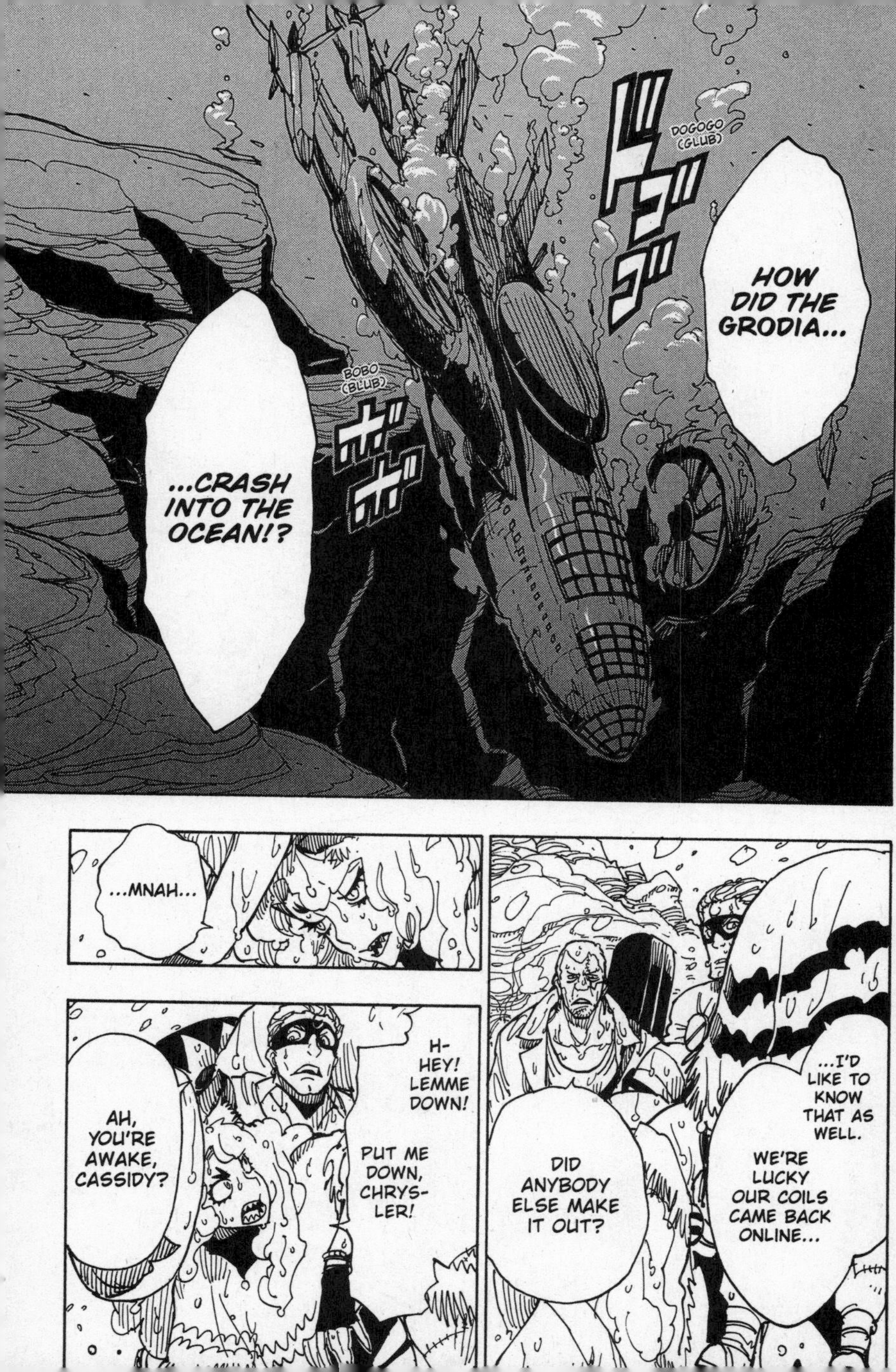
DOGOGO (GLUB)
HOW DID THE GRODIA...
BOBO (BLUB)
...CRASH INTO THE OCEAN!?
...I'D LIKE TO KNOW THAT AS WELL.
WE'RE LUCKY OUR COILS CAME BACK ONLINE...
DID ANYBODY ELSE MAKE IT OUT?
...MNAH...
H-HEY! LEMME DOWN!
PUT ME DOWN, CHRYS-LER!
AH, YOU'RE AWAKE, CASSIDY?

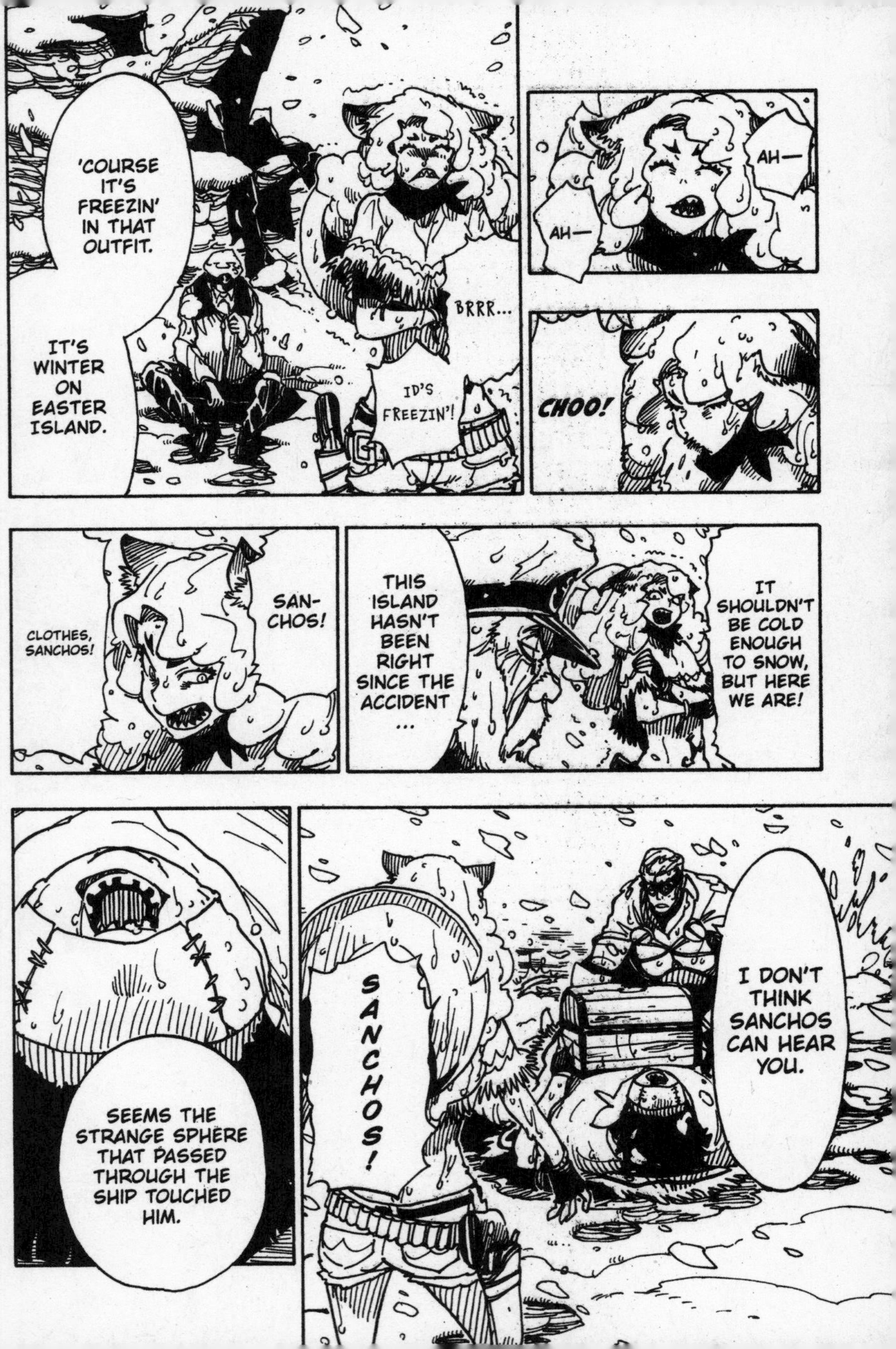
AH—
AH—
CHOO!
BRRR...
ID'S FREEZIN'!
'COURSE IT'S FREEZIN' IN THAT OUTFIT.
IT'S WINTER ON EASTER ISLAND.
IT SHOULDN'T BE COLD ENOUGH TO SNOW, BUT HERE WE ARE!
THIS ISLAND HASN'T BEEN RIGHT SINCE THE ACCIDENT ...
SAN-CHOS!
CLOTHES, SANCHOS!
SANCHOS!
I DON'T THINK SANCHOS CAN HEAR YOU.
SEEMS THE STRANGE SPHERE THAT PASSED THROUGH THE SHIP TOUCHED HIM.

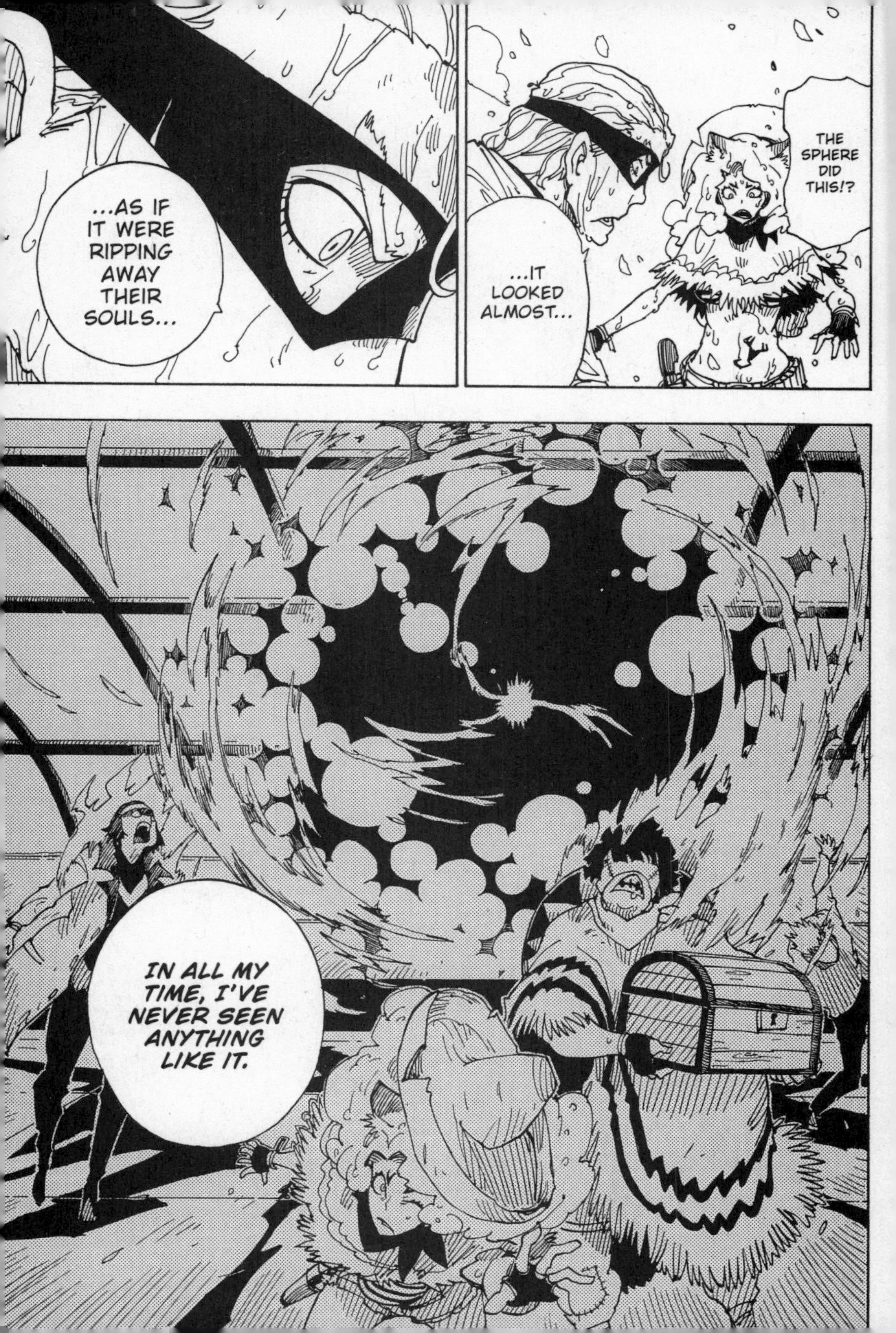
THE SPHERE DID THIS!?
...IT LOOKED ALMOST...
...AS IF IT WERE RIPPING AWAY THEIR SOULS...
IN ALL MY TIME, I'VE NEVER SEEN ANYTHING LIKE IT.

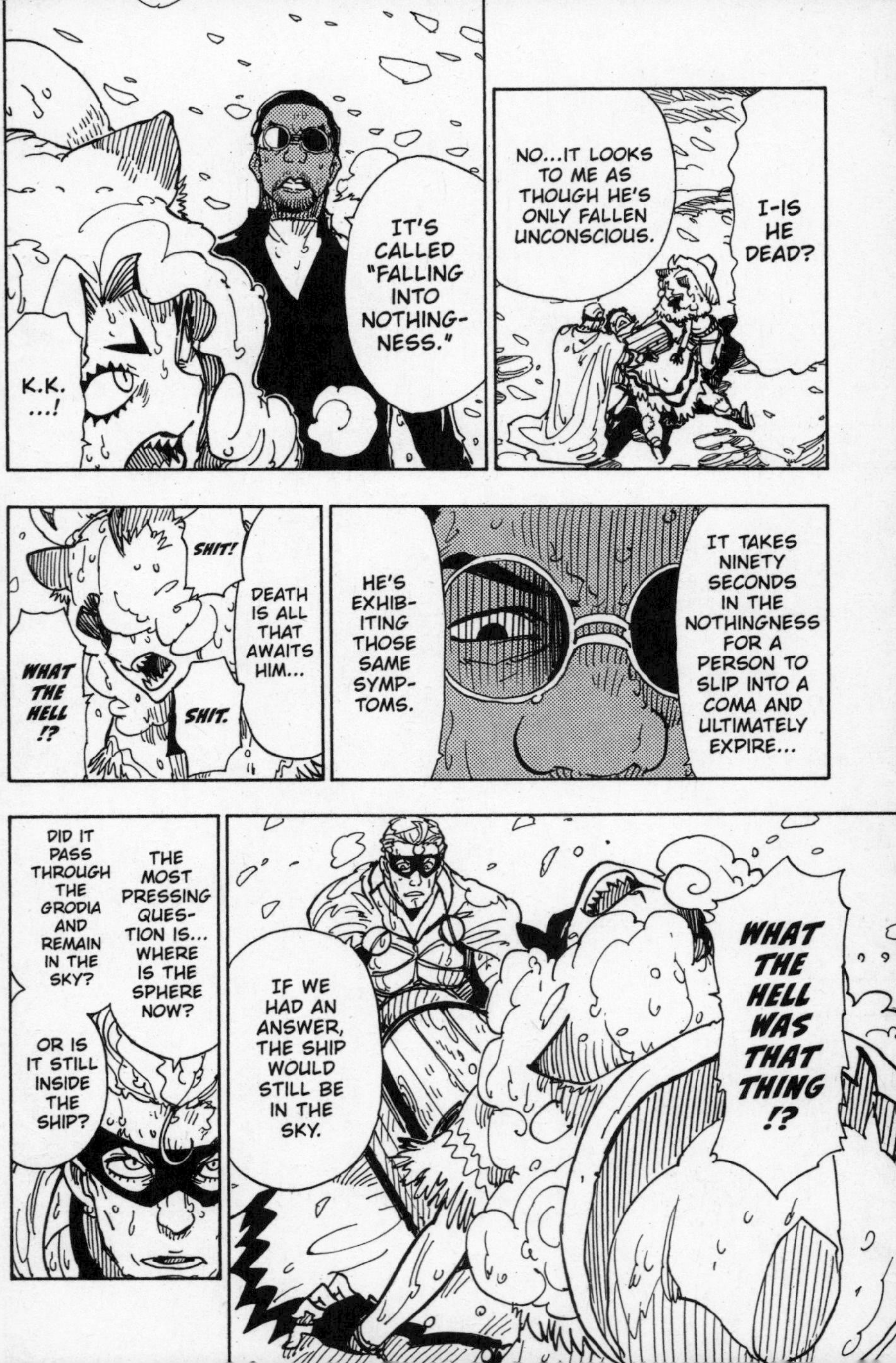
I-IS HE DEAD?
NO...IT LOOKS TO ME AS THOUGH HE'S ONLY FALLEN UNCONSCIOUS.
IT'S CALLED "FALLING INTO NOTHINGNESS."
K.K. ...!
IT TAKES NINETY SECONDS IN THE NOTHINGNESS FOR A PERSON TO SLIP INTO A COMA AND ULTIMATELY EXPIRE...
HE'S EXHIBITING THOSE SAME SYMPTOMS.
DEATH IS ALL THAT AWAITS HIM...
SHIT!
SHIT.
WHAT THE HELL !?
WHAT THE HELL WAS THAT THING !?
IF WE HAD AN ANSWER, THE SHIP WOULD STILL BE IN THE SKY.
THE MOST PRESSING QUESTION IS... WHERE IS THE SPHERE NOW?
DID IT PASS THROUGH THE GRODIA AND REMAIN IN THE SKY?
OR IS IT STILL INSIDE THE SHIP?

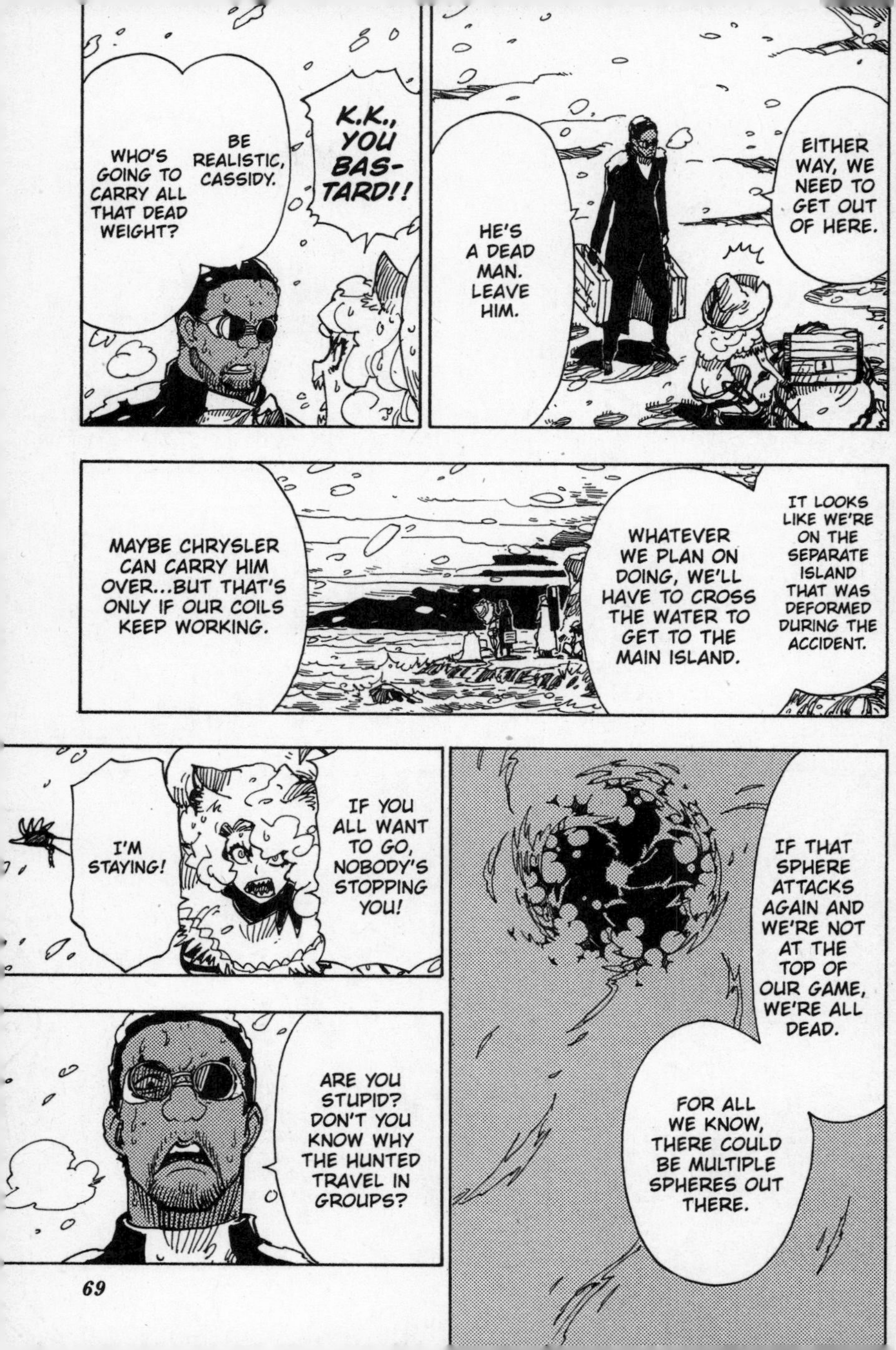
EITHER WAY, WE NEED TO GET OUT OF HERE.
HE'S A DEAD MAN. LEAVE HIM.
K.K., YOU BAS-TARD!!
BE REALISTIC, CASSIDY.
WHO'S GOING TO CARRY ALL THAT DEAD WEIGHT?
IT LOOKS LIKE WE'RE ON THE SEPARATE ISLAND THAT WAS DEFORMED DURING THE ACCIDENT.
WHATEVER WE PLAN ON DOING, WE'LL HAVE TO CROSS THE WATER TO GET TO THE MAIN ISLAND.
MAYBE CHRYSLER CAN CARRY HIM OVER...BUT THAT'S ONLY IF OUR COILS KEEP WORKING.
IF THAT SPHERE ATTACKS AGAIN AND WE'RE NOT AT THE TOP OF OUR GAME, WE'RE ALL DEAD.
FOR ALL WE KNOW, THERE COULD BE MULTIPLE SPHERES OUT THERE.
IF YOU ALL WANT TO GO, NOBODY'S STOPPING YOU!
I'M STAYING!
ARE YOU STUPID? DON'T YOU KNOW WHY THE HUNTED TRAVEL IN GROUPS?

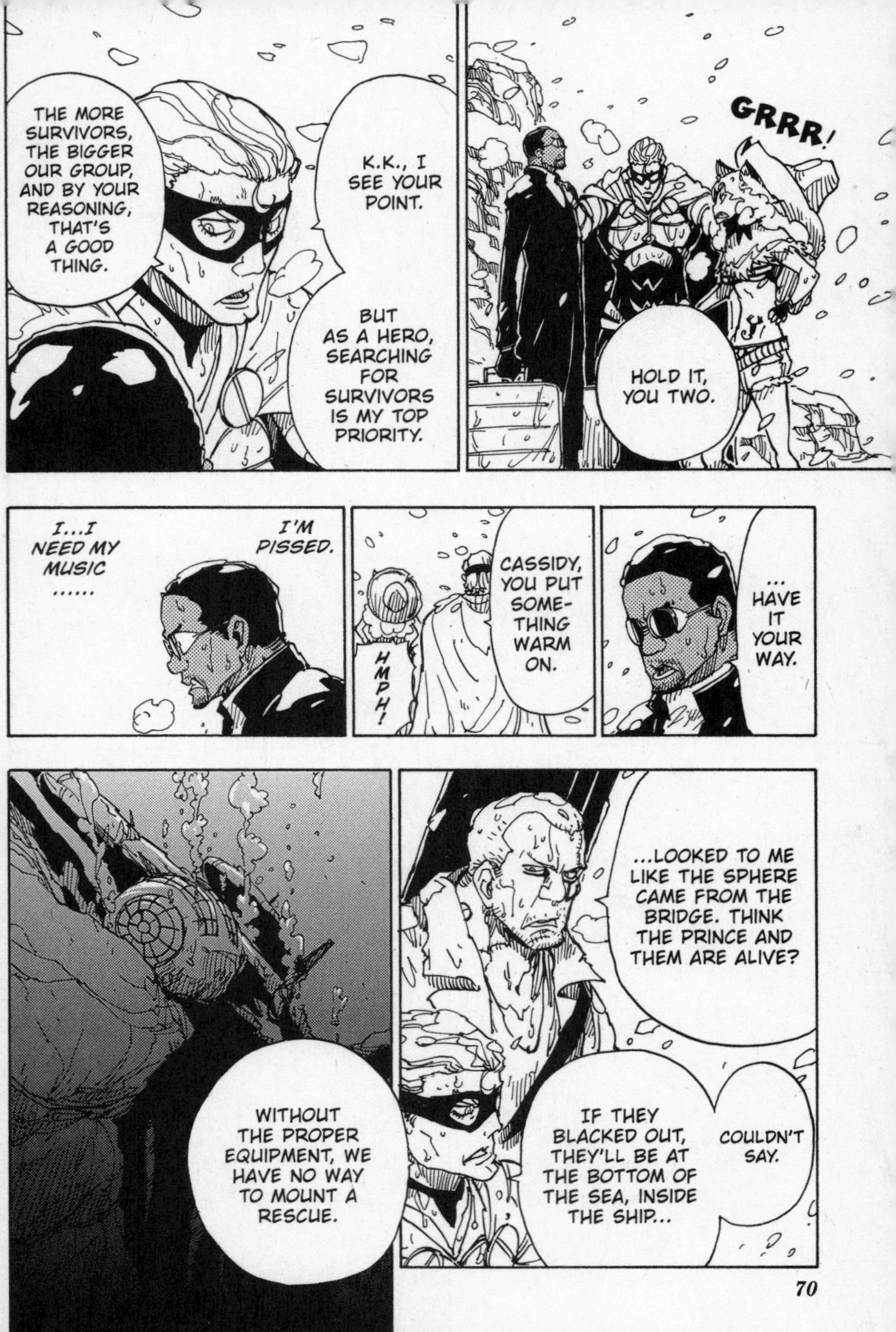
GRRR!
HOLD IT, YOU TWO.
THE MORE SURVIVORS, THE BIGGER OUR GROUP, AND BY YOUR REASONING, THAT'S A GOOD THING.
K.K., I SEE YOUR POINT.
BUT AS A HERO, SEARCHING FOR SURVIVORS IS MY TOP PRIORITY.
...HAVE IT YOUR WAY.
CASSIDY, YOU PUT SOME-THING WARM ON.
HMPH!
I'M PISSED.
I...I NEED MY MUSIC ......
...LOOKED TO ME LIKE THE SPHERE CAME FROM THE BRIDGE. THINK THE PRINCE AND THEM ARE ALIVE?
COULDN'T SAY.
IF THEY BLACKED OUT, THEY'LL BE AT THE BOTTOM OF THE SEA, INSIDE THE SHIP...
WITHOUT THE PROPER EQUIPMENT, WE HAVE NO WAY TO MOUNT A RESCUE.

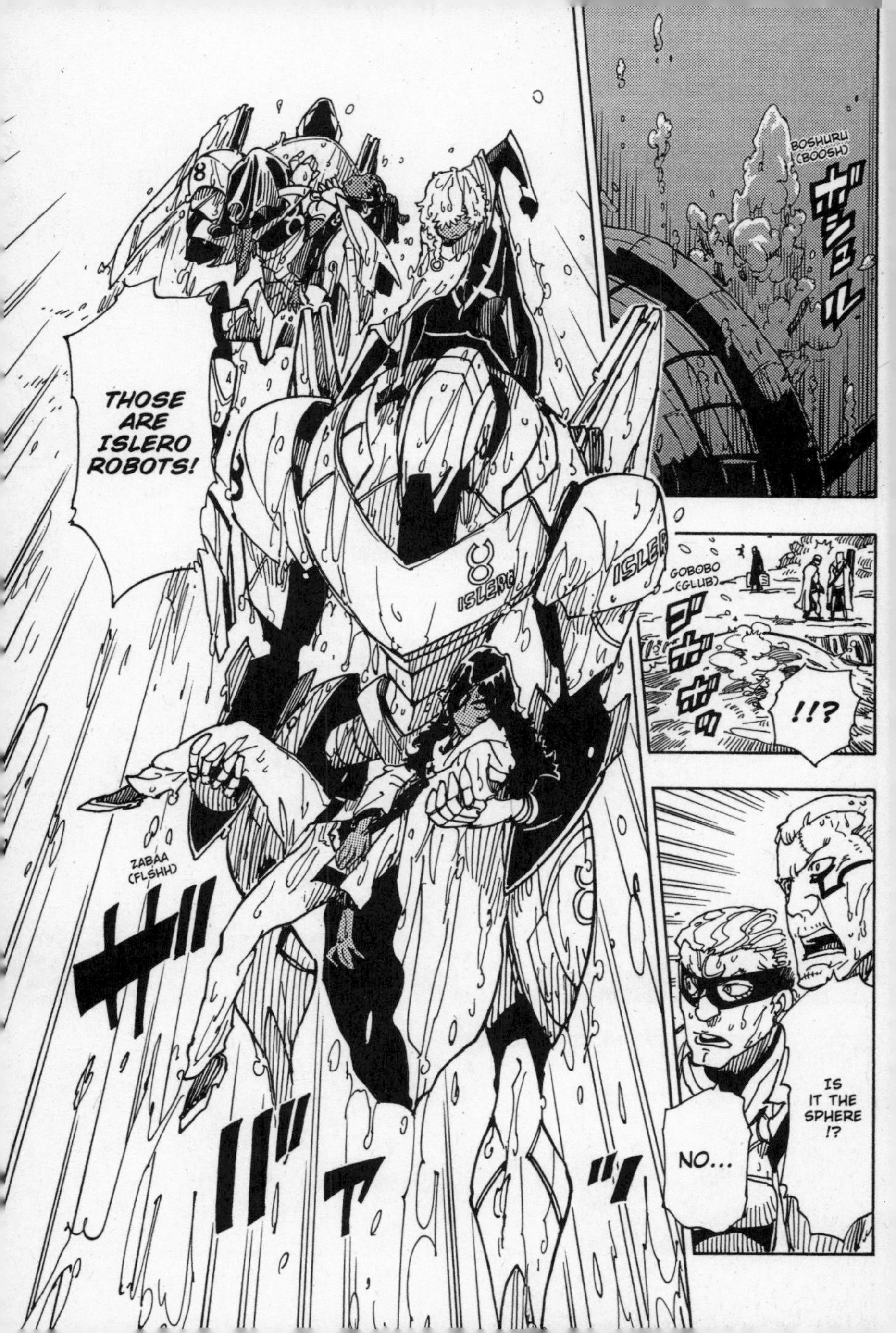
BOSHURU (BOOSH)
GOBOBO (GLUB)
!!?
IS IT THE SPHERE !?
NO...
THOSE ARE ISLERO ROBOTS!
ISLERO
ISLERO
ZABAA (FLSHH)

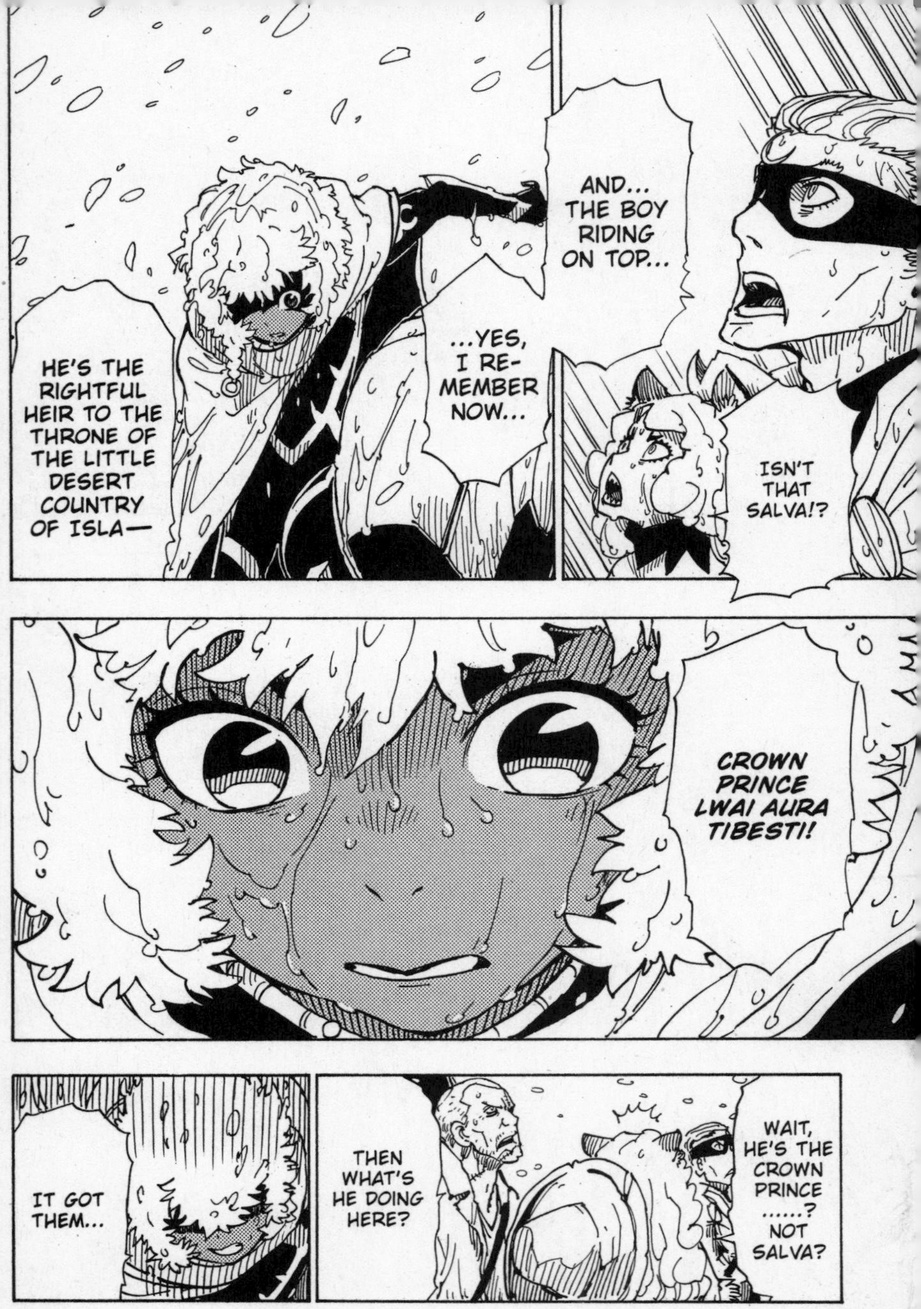
AND... THE BOY RIDING ON TOP...
ISN'T THAT SALVA!?
...YES, I RE-MEMBER NOW...
HE'S THE RIGHTFUL HEIR TO THE THRONE OF THE LITTLE DESERT COUNTRY OF ISLA—
CROWN PRINCE LWAI AURA TIBESTI!
WAIT, HE'S THE CROWN PRINCE ......? NOT SALVA?
THEN WHAT'S HE DOING HERE?
IT GOT THEM...

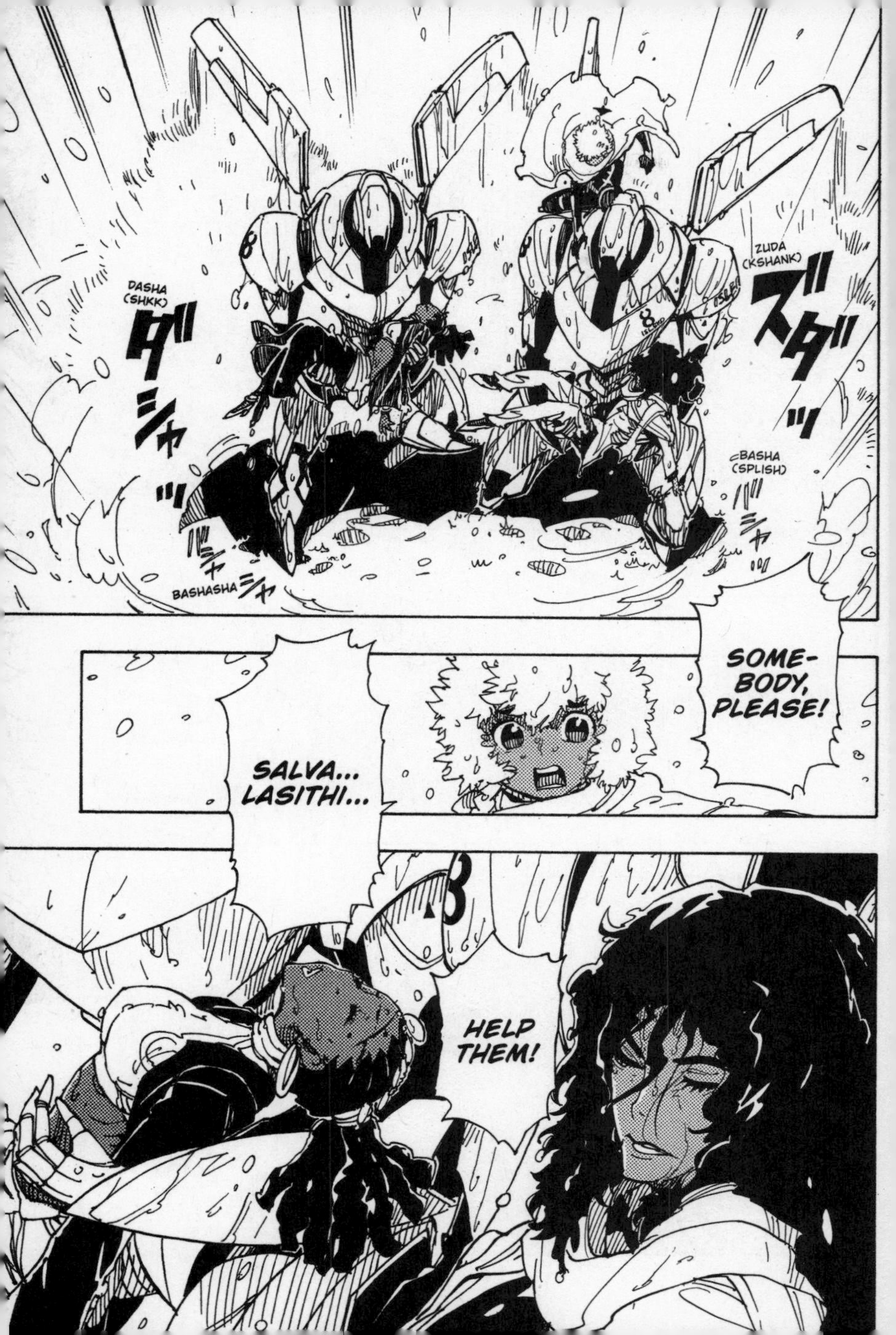
ZUDA (KSHANK)
ズダッ
BASHA (SPLISH)
バシャ
DASHA (SHKK)
ダシャッ
BASHASHA
バシャシャ
SOME-BODY, PLEASE!
SALVA... LASITHI...
HELP THEM!

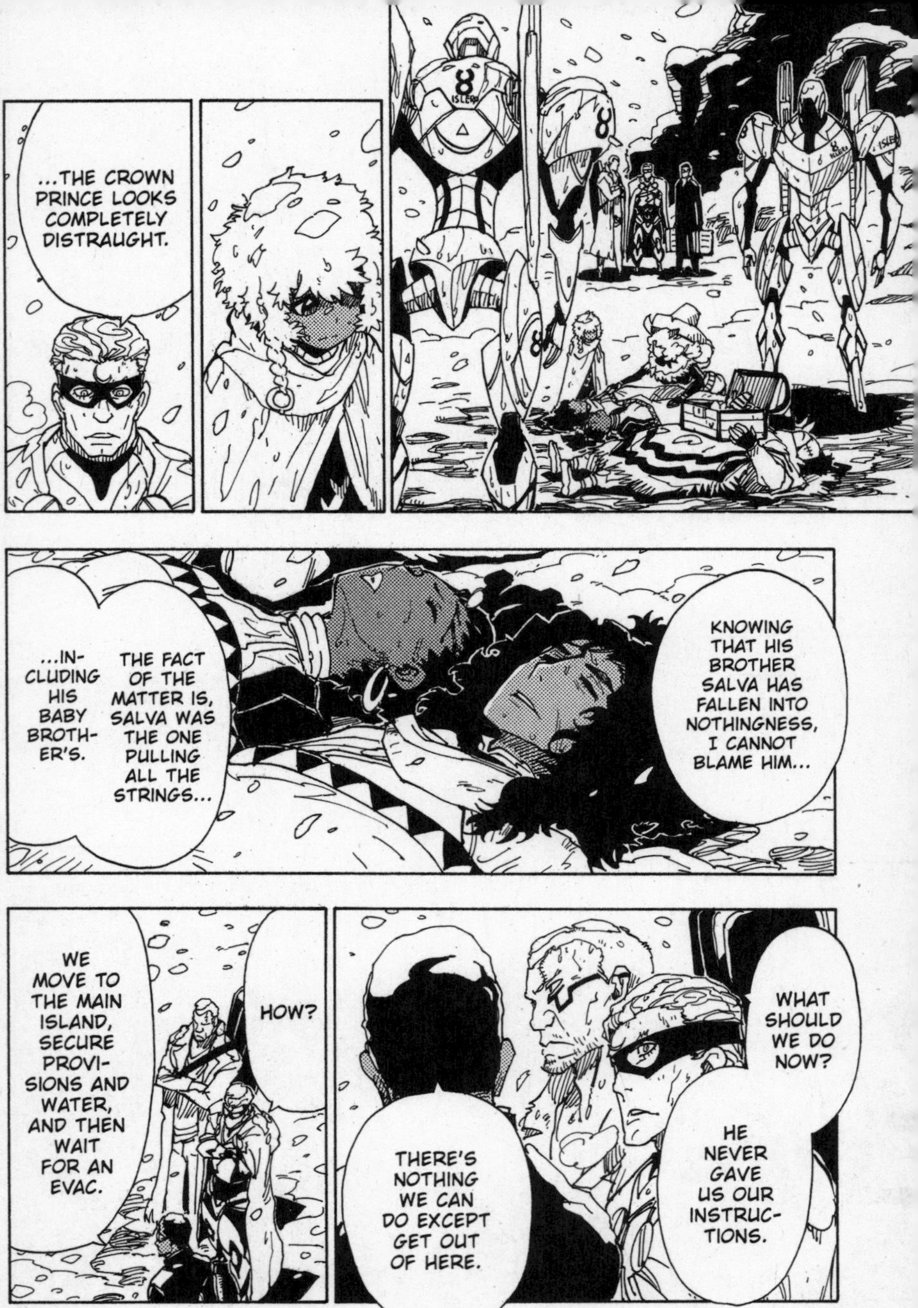
...THE CROWN PRINCE LOOKS COMPLETELY DISTRAUGHT.
KNOWING THAT HIS BROTHER SALVA HAS FALLEN INTO NOTHINGNESS, I CANNOT BLAME HIM...
THE FACT OF THE MATTER IS, SALVA WAS THE ONE PULLING ALL THE STRINGS...
...INCLUDING HIS BABY BROTHER'S.
WHAT SHOULD WE DO NOW?
HE NEVER GAVE US OUR INSTRUCTIONS.
THERE'S NOTHING WE CAN DO EXCEPT GET OUT OF HERE.
HOW?
WE MOVE TO THE MAIN ISLAND, SECURE PROVISIONS AND WATER, AND THEN WAIT FOR AN EVAC.

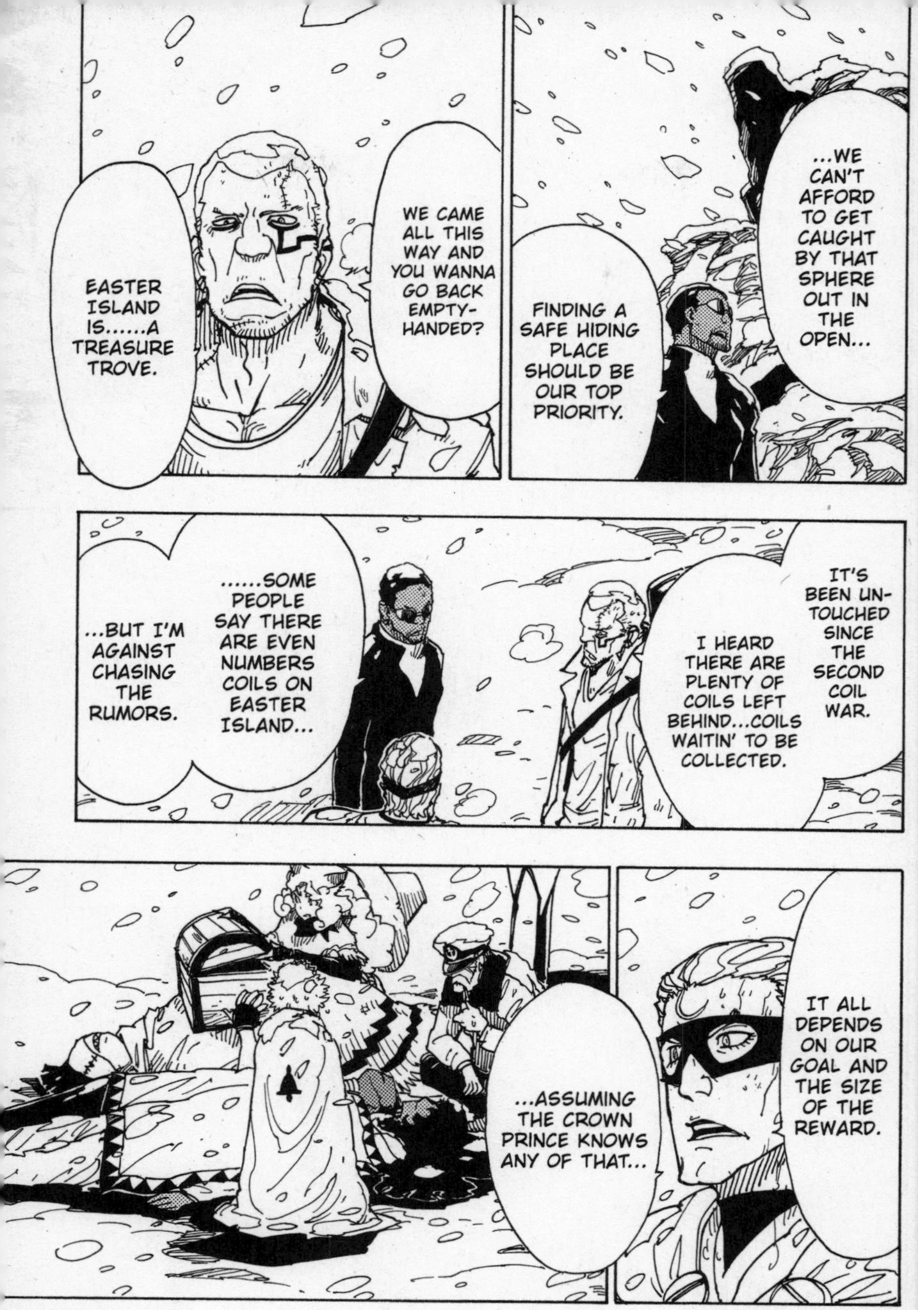
...WE CAN'T AFFORD TO GET CAUGHT BY THAT SPHERE OUT IN THE OPEN...
FINDING A SAFE HIDING PLACE SHOULD BE OUR TOP PRIORITY.
WE CAME ALL THIS WAY AND YOU WANNA GO BACK EMPTY-HANDED?
EASTER ISLAND IS......A TREASURE TROVE.
IT'S BEEN UNTOUCHED SINCE THE SECOND COIL WAR.
I HEARD THERE ARE PLENTY OF COILS LEFT BEHIND...COILS WAITIN' TO BE COLLECTED.
......SOME PEOPLE SAY THERE ARE EVEN NUMBERS COILS ON EASTER ISLAND...
...BUT I'M AGAINST CHASING THE RUMORS.
IT ALL DEPENDS ON OUR GOAL AND THE SIZE OF THE REWARD.
...ASSUMING THE CROWN PRINCE KNOWS ANY OF THAT...

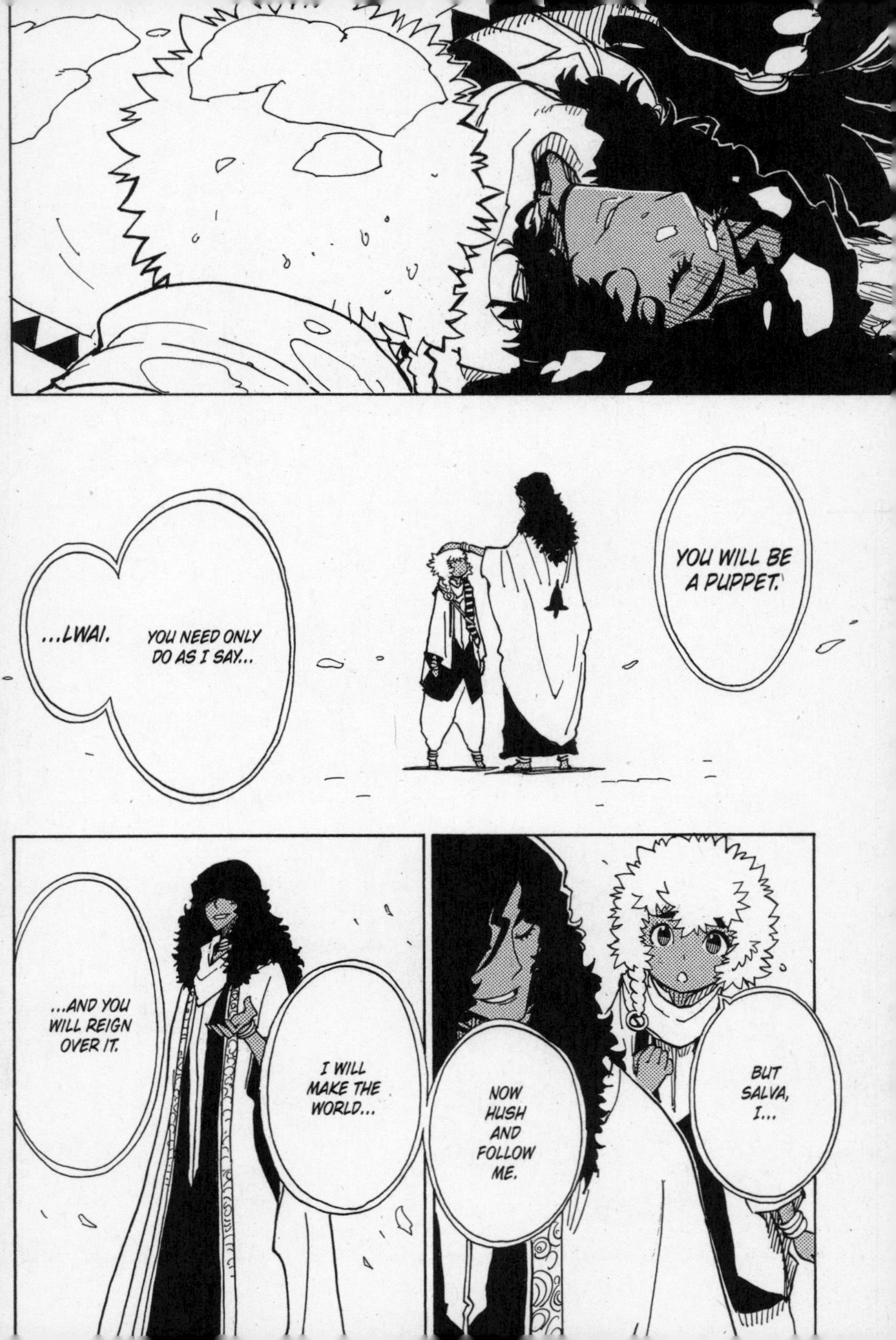
YOU WILL BE A PUPPET.
...LWAI.
YOU NEED ONLY DO AS I SAY...
BUT SALVA, I...
NOW HUSH AND FOLLOW ME.
I WILL MAKE THE WORLD...
...AND YOU WILL REIGN OVER IT.

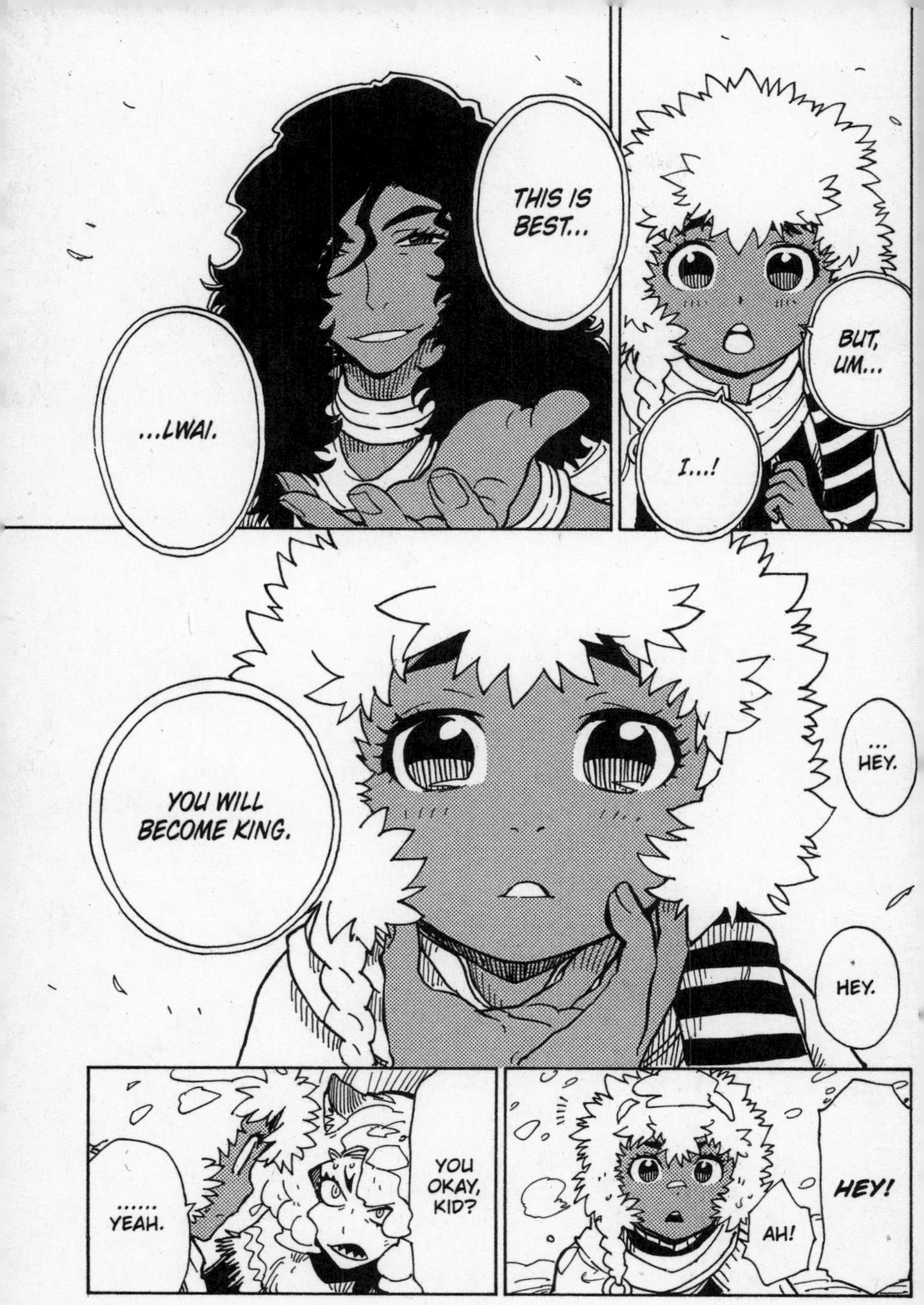
BUT, UM...
I...!
THIS IS BEST...
...LWAI.
YOU WILL BECOME KING.
... HEY.
HEY.
HEY!
AH!
YOU OKAY, KID?
...... YEAH.

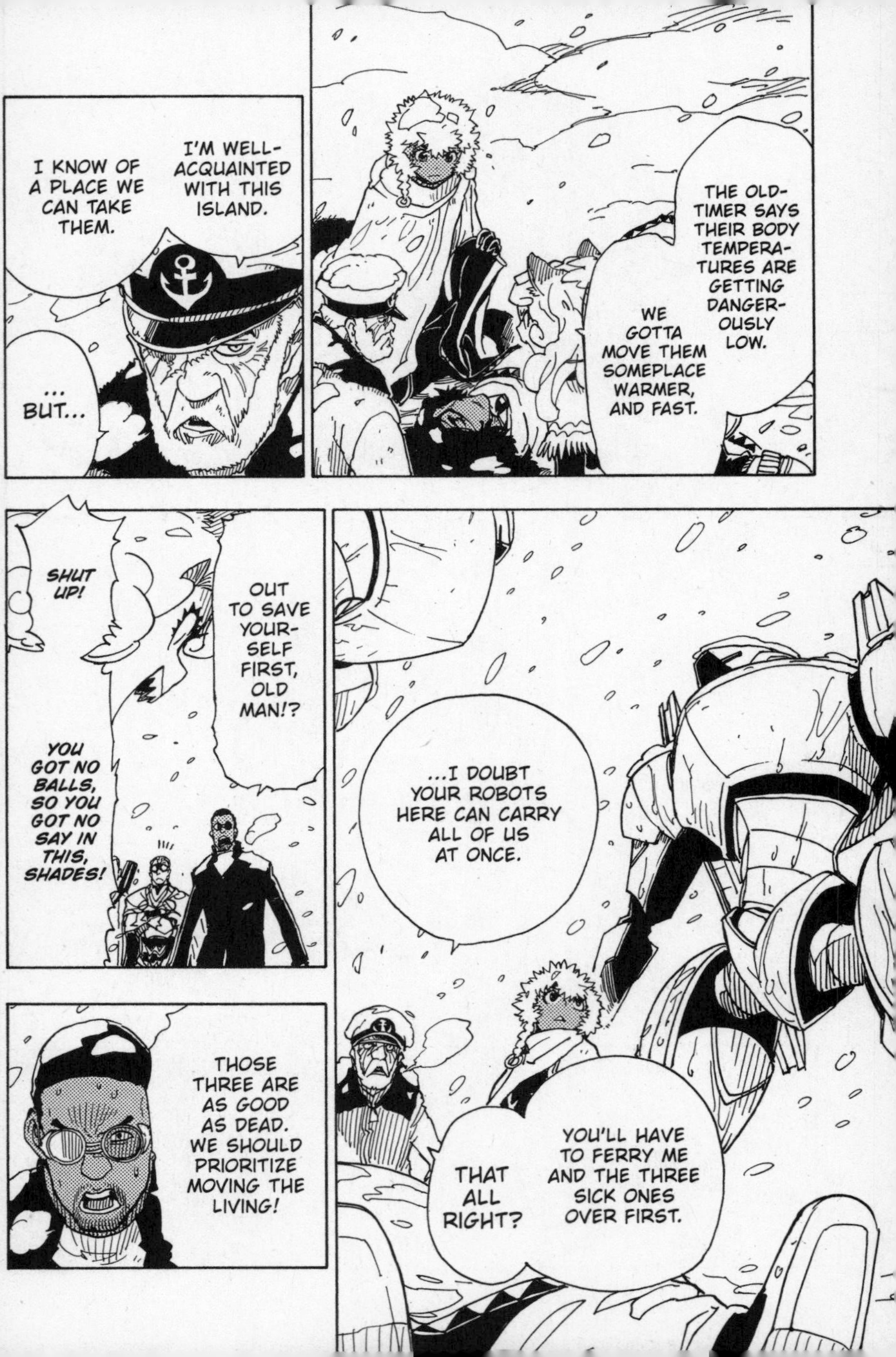
THE OLD-TIMER SAYS THEIR BODY TEMPERATURES ARE GETTING DANGEROUSLY LOW.
WE GOTTA MOVE THEM SOMEPLACE WARMER, AND FAST.
I'M WELL-ACQUAINTED WITH THIS ISLAND.
I KNOW OF A PLACE WE CAN TAKE THEM.
... BUT...
...I DOUBT YOUR ROBOTS HERE CAN CARRY ALL OF US AT ONCE.
YOU'LL HAVE TO FERRY ME AND THE THREE SICK ONES OVER FIRST.
THAT ALL RIGHT?
OUT TO SAVE YOURSELF FIRST, OLD MAN!?
SHUT UP!
YOU GOT NO BALLS, SO YOU GOT NO SAY IN THIS, SHADES!
THOSE THREE ARE AS GOOD AS DEAD. WE SHOULD PRIORITIZE MOVING THE LIVING!

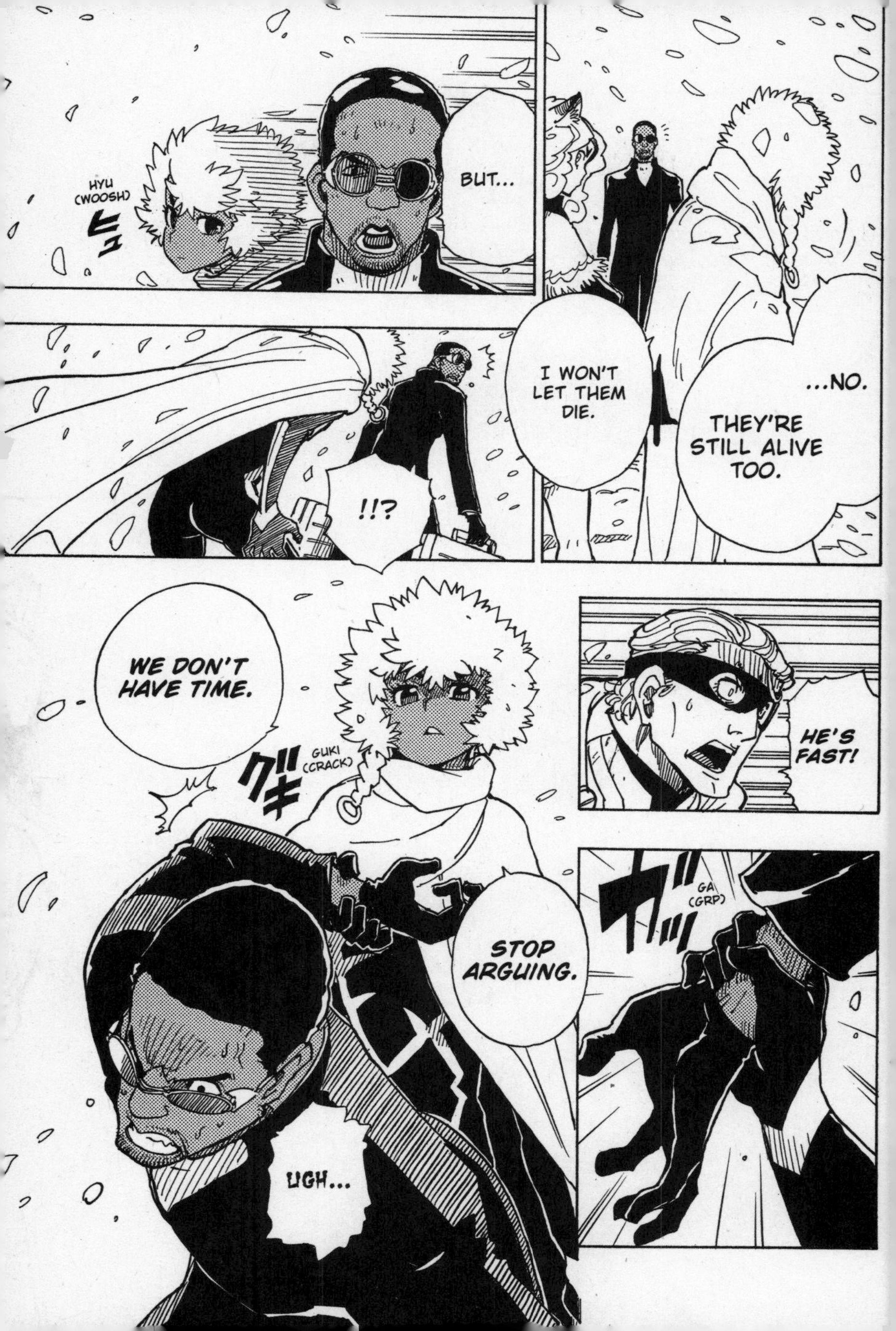
...NO.
THEY'RE STILL ALIVE TOO.
I WON'T LET THEM DIE.
BUT...
HYU (WOOSH)
ヒュ
!!?
HE'S FAST!
GA (GRP)
ガッ
WE DON'T HAVE TIME.
GUKI (CRACK)
グキ
STOP ARGUING.
UGH...

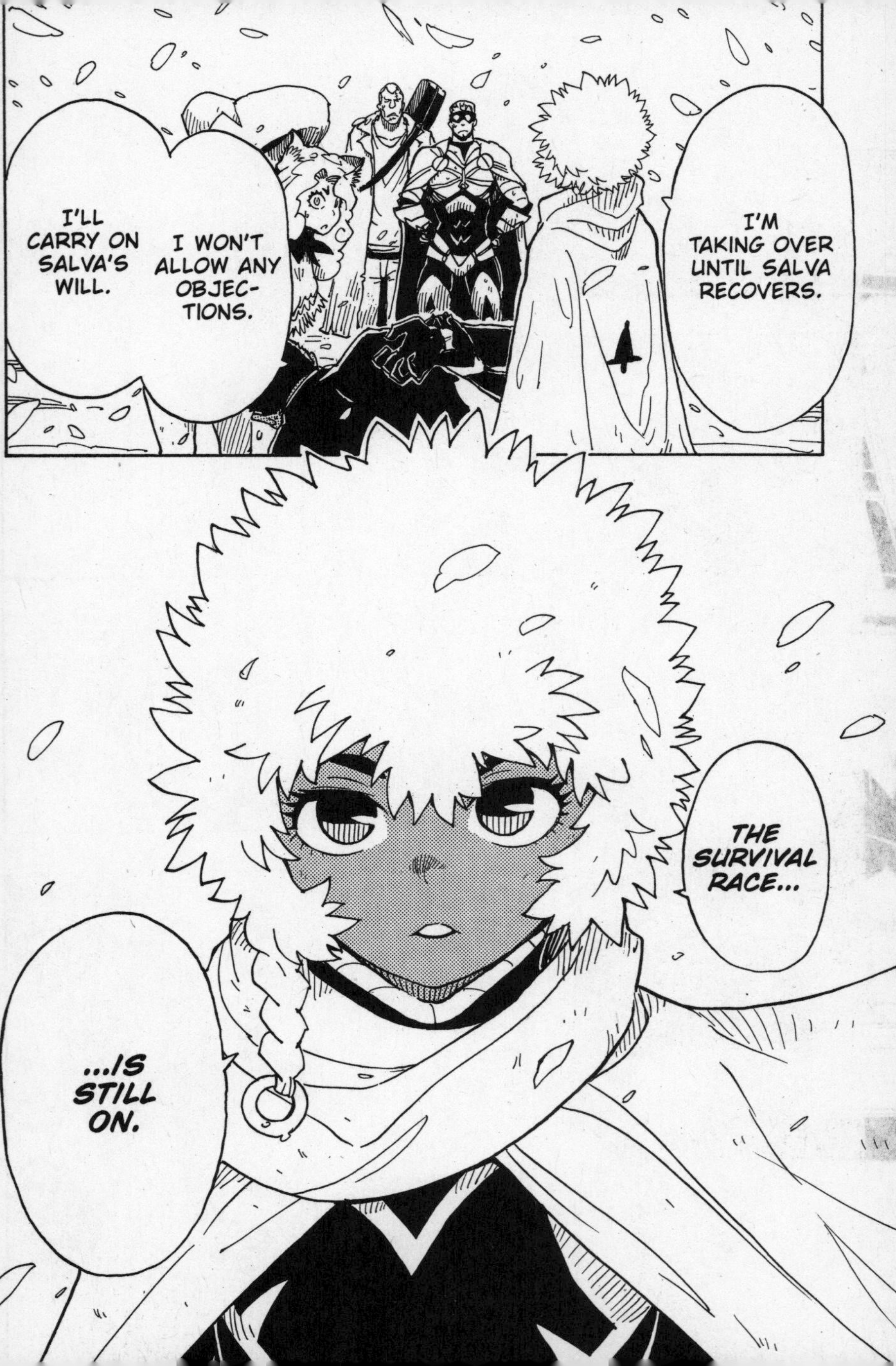
I'M TAKING OVER UNTIL SALVA RECOVERS.
I WON'T ALLOW ANY OBJECTIONS.
I'LL CARRY ON SALVA'S WILL.
THE SURVIVAL RACE...
...IS STILL ON.

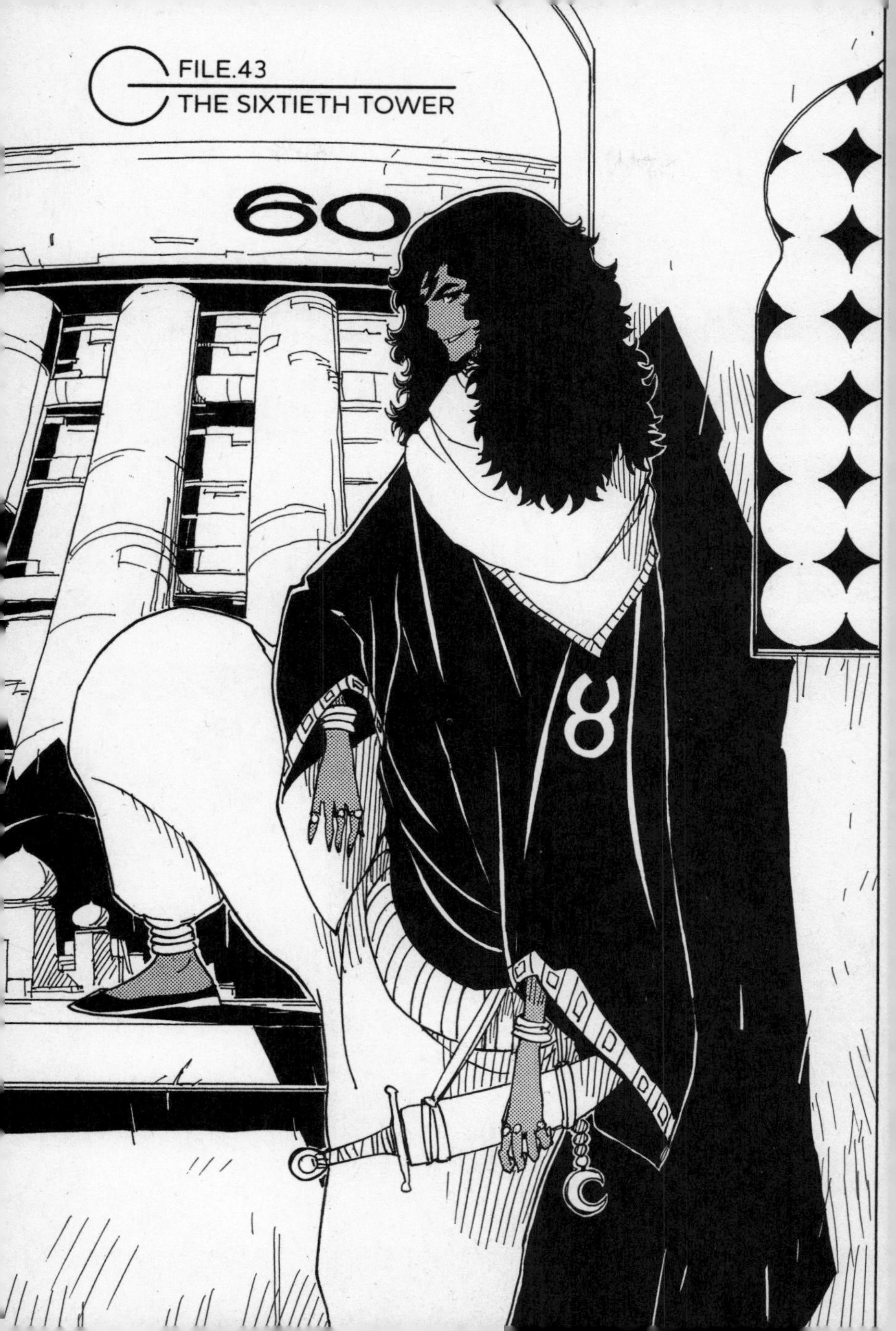
FILE.43
THE SIXTIETH TOWER
60

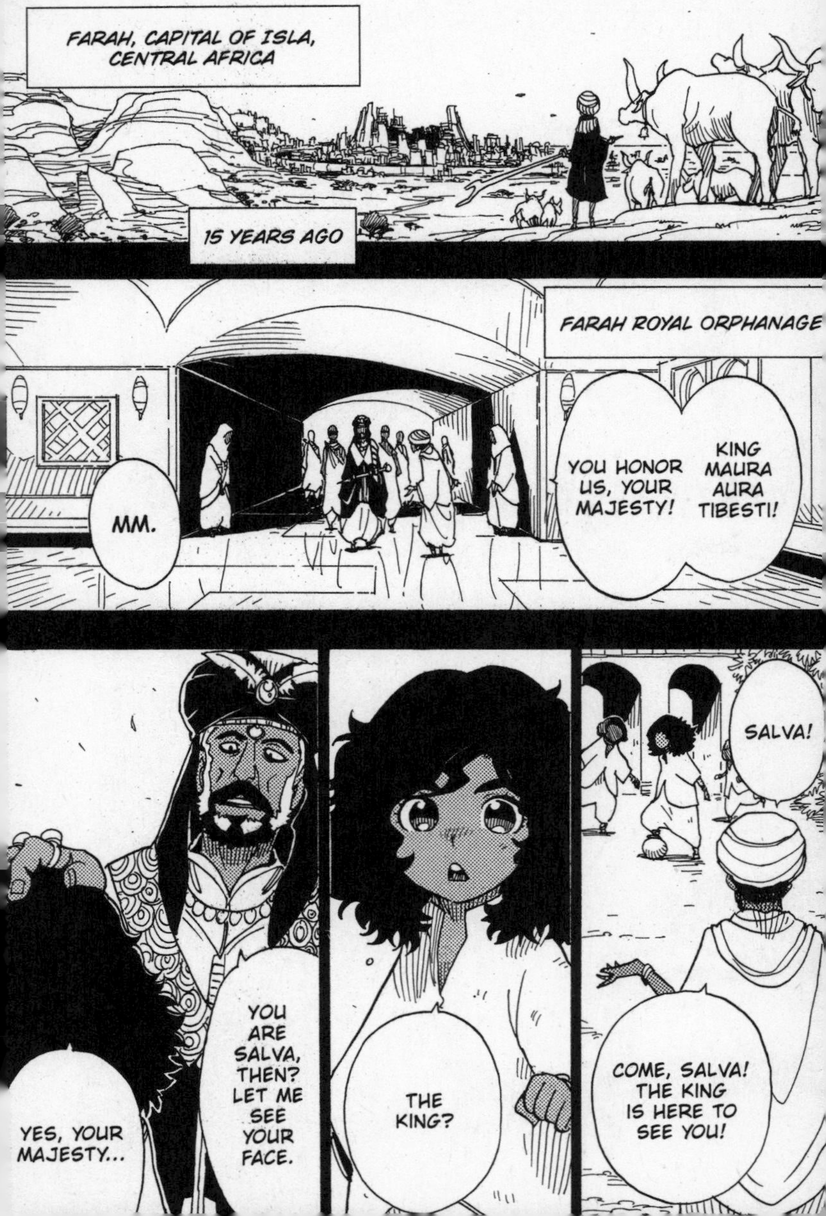
FARAH, CAPITAL OF ISLA, CENTRAL AFRICA
15 YEARS AGO
FARAH ROYAL ORPHANAGE
KING MAURA AURA TIBESTI!
YOU HONOR US, YOUR MAJESTY!
MM.
SALVA!
COME, SALVA! THE KING IS HERE TO SEE YOU!
THE KING?
YOU ARE SALVA, THEN? LET ME SEE YOUR FACE.
YES, YOUR MAJESTY...

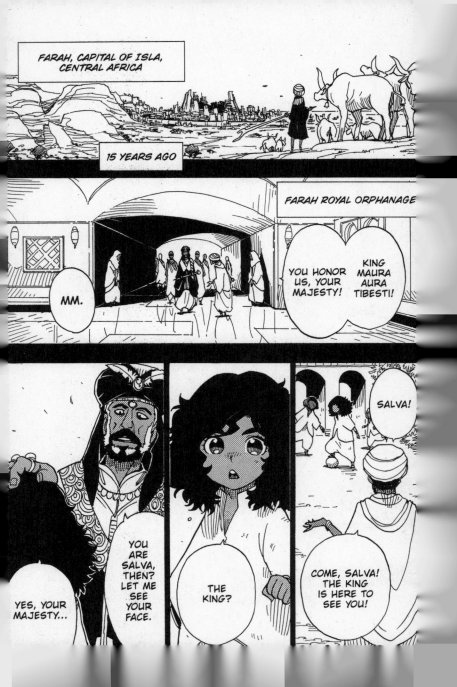

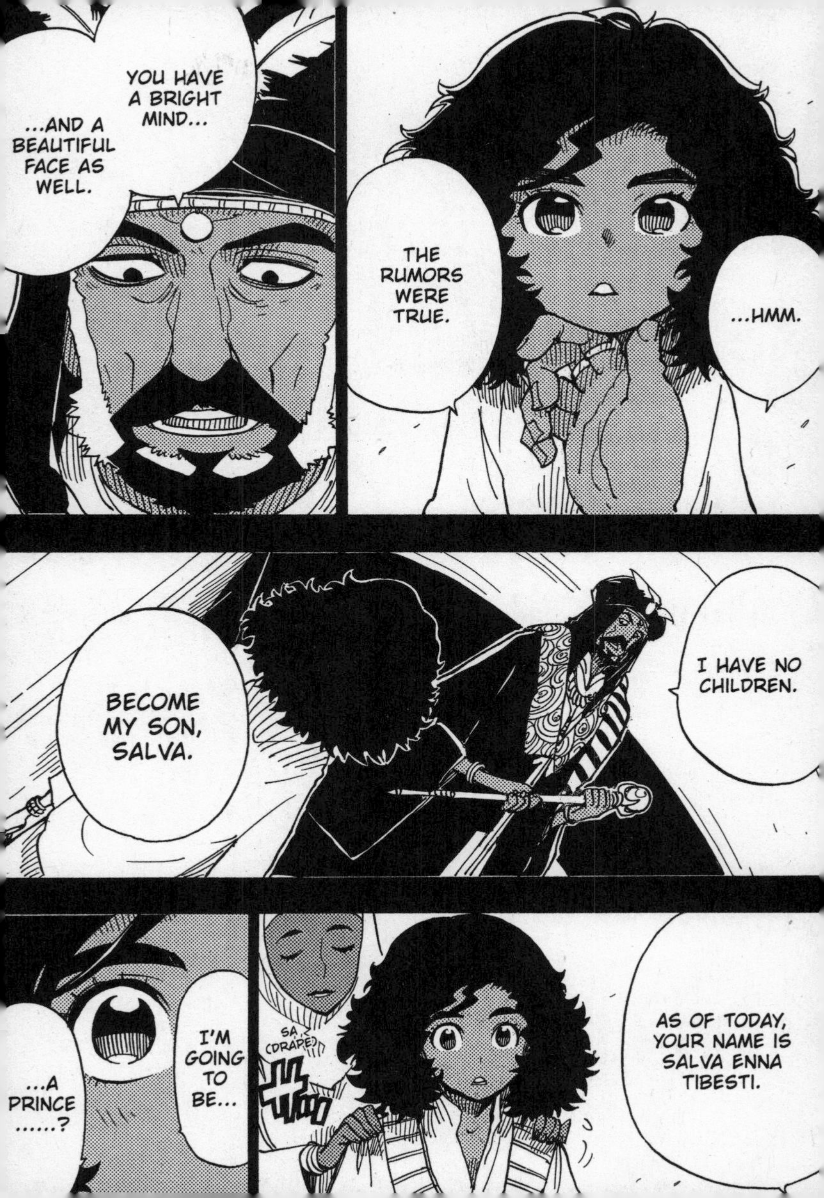
...HMM.
THE RUMORS WERE TRUE.
YOU HAVE A BRIGHT MIND...
...AND A BEAUTIFUL FACE AS WELL.
I HAVE NO CHILDREN.
BECOME MY SON, SALVA.
AS OF TODAY, YOUR NAME IS SALVA ENNA TIBESTI.
SA (DRAPE)
I'M GOING TO BE...
...A PRINCE ......?

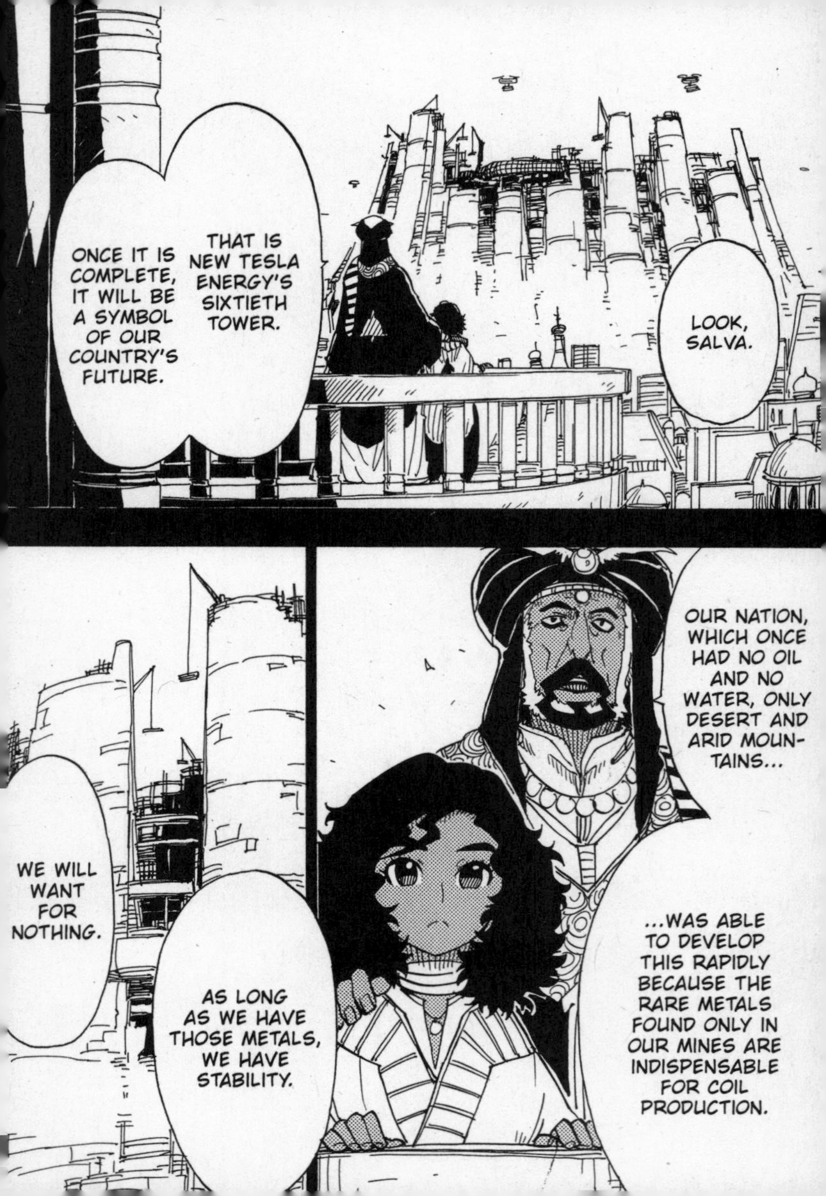
LOOK, SALVA.
THAT IS NEW TESLA ENERGY'S SIXTIETH TOWER.
ONCE IT IS COMPLETE, IT WILL BE A SYMBOL OF OUR COUNTRY'S FUTURE.
OUR NATION, WHICH ONCE HAD NO OIL AND NO WATER, ONLY DESERT AND ARID MOUN-TAINS...
...WAS ABLE TO DEVELOP THIS RAPIDLY BECAUSE THE RARE METALS FOUND ONLY IN OUR MINES ARE INDISPENSABLE FOR COIL PRODUCTION.
AS LONG AS WE HAVE THOSE METALS, WE HAVE STABILITY.
WE WILL WANT FOR NOTHING.

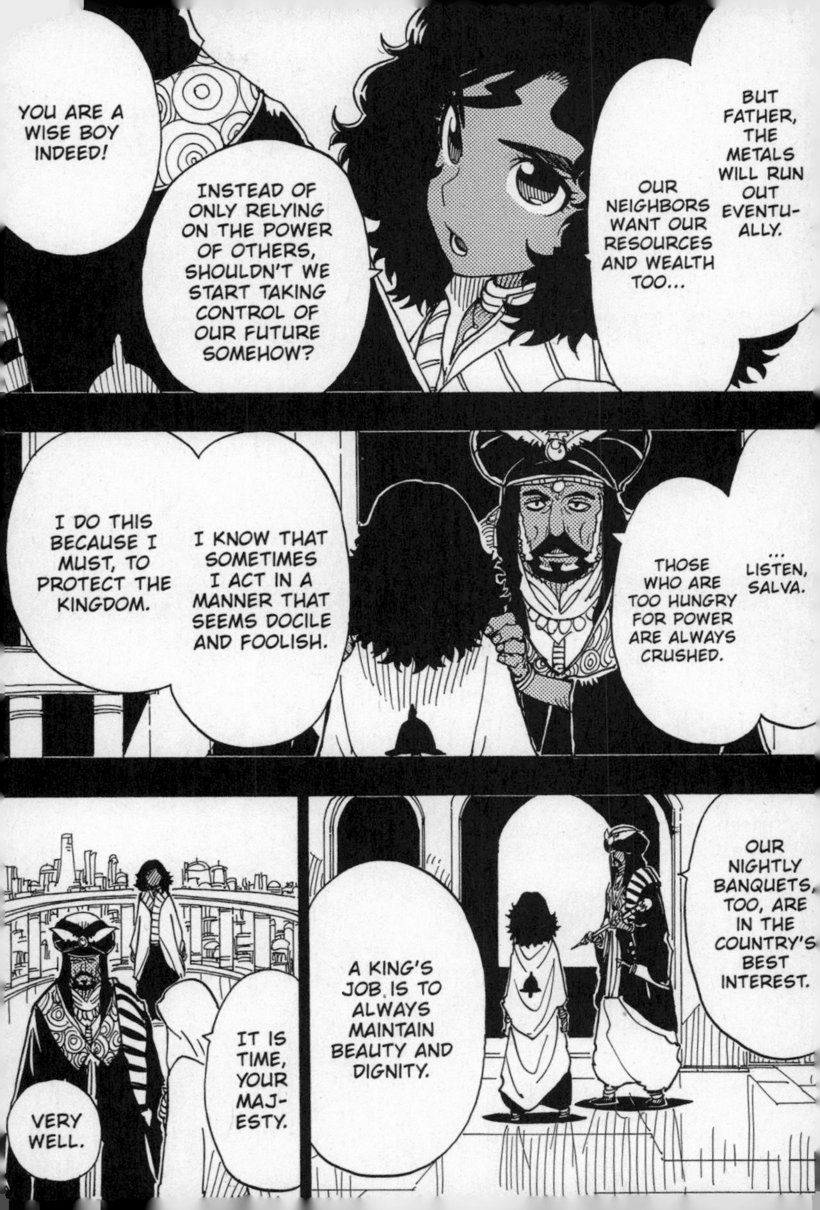
BUT FATHER, THE METALS WILL RUN OUT EVENTU-ALLY.
OUR NEIGHBORS WANT OUR RESOURCES AND WEALTH TOO...
INSTEAD OF ONLY RELYING ON THE POWER OF OTHERS, SHOULDN'T WE START TAKING CONTROL OF OUR FUTURE SOMEHOW?
YOU ARE A WISE BOY INDEED!
... LISTEN, SALVA.
THOSE WHO ARE TOO HUNGRY FOR POWER ARE ALWAYS CRUSHED.
I KNOW THAT SOMETIMES I ACT IN A MANNER THAT SEEMS DOCILE AND FOOLISH.
I DO THIS BECAUSE I MUST, TO PROTECT THE KINGDOM.
OUR NIGHTLY BANQUETS, TOO, ARE IN THE COUNTRY'S BEST INTEREST.
A KING'S JOB IS TO ALWAYS MAINTAIN BEAUTY AND DIGNITY.
IT IS TIME, YOUR MAJ-ESTY.
VERY WELL.

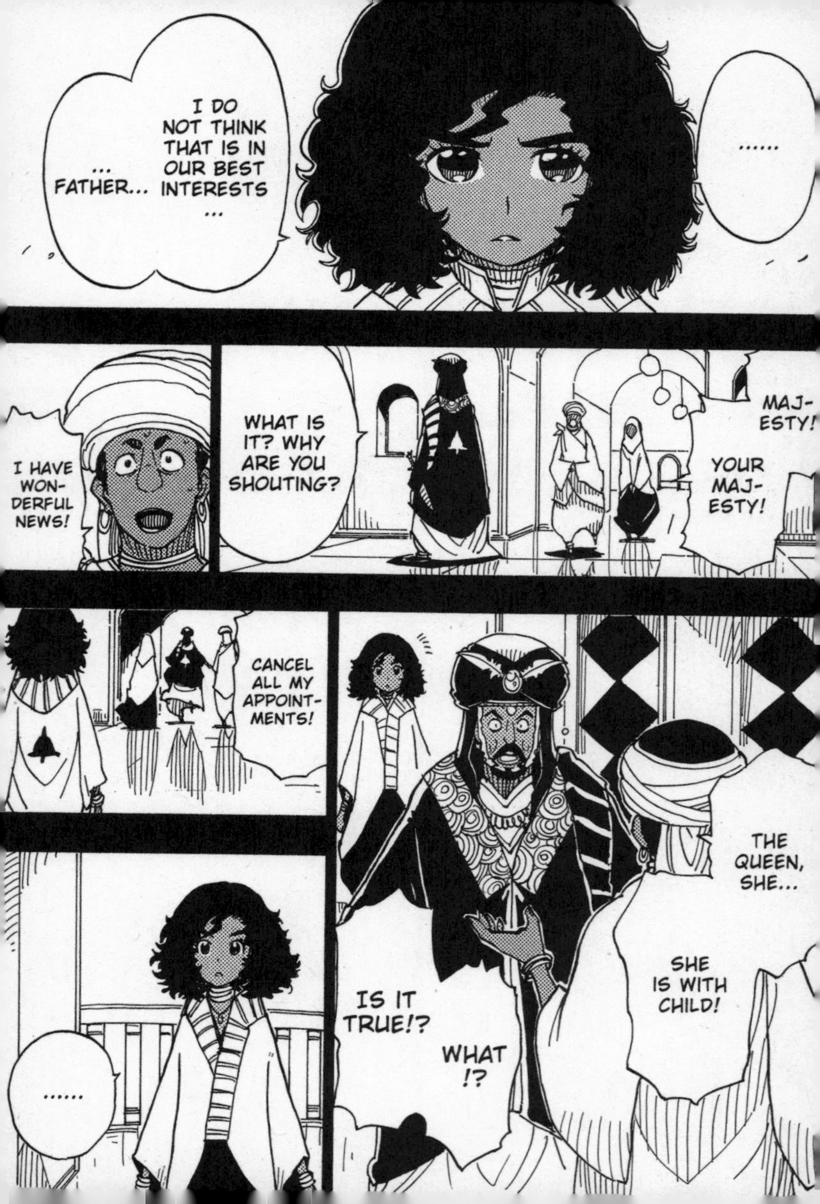
......
I DO NOT THINK THAT IS IN OUR BEST INTERESTS ... ... FATHER...
MAJ-ESTY!
YOUR MAJ-ESTY!
WHAT IS IT? WHY ARE YOU SHOUTING?
I HAVE WON-DERFUL NEWS!
THE QUEEN, SHE...
SHE IS WITH CHILD!
WHAT !?
IS IT TRUE!?
CANCEL ALL MY APPOINT-MENTS!
......

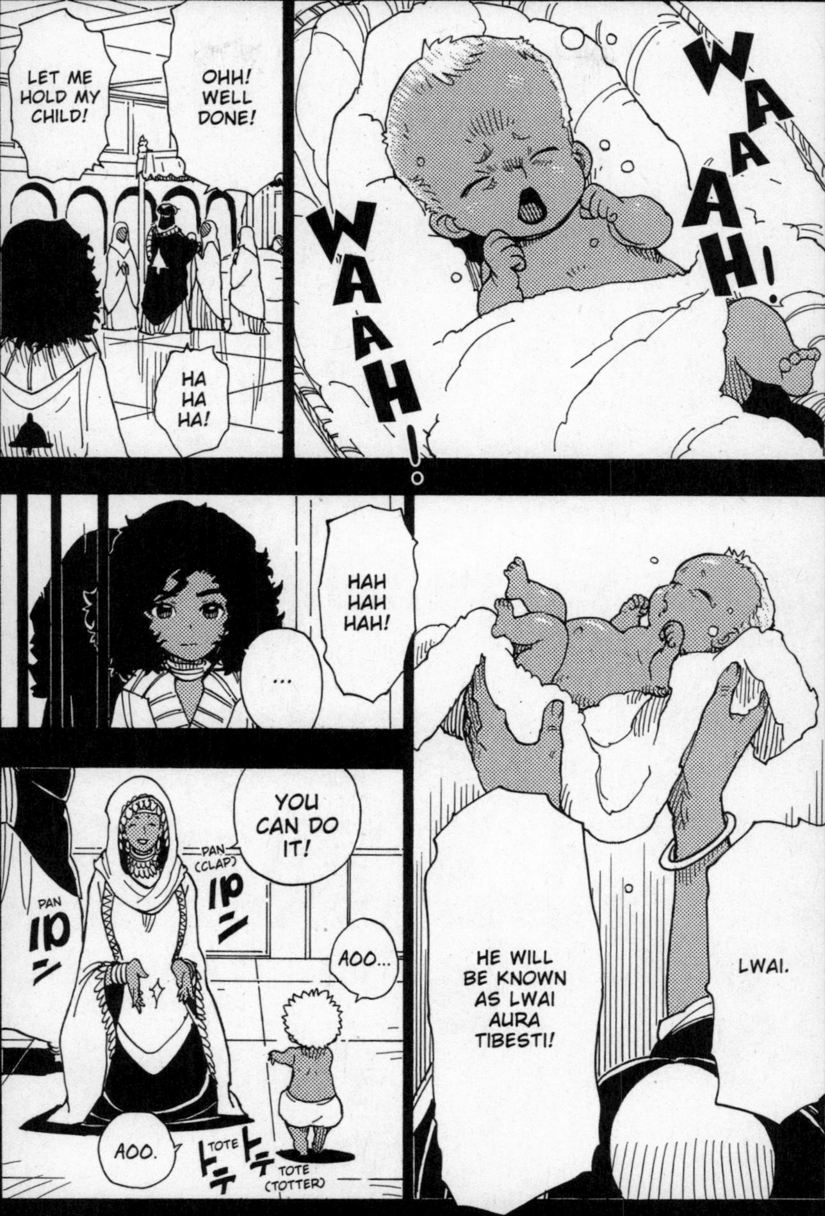
WAAAH!
WAAH!
OHH! WELL DONE!
LET ME HOLD MY CHILD!
HA HA HA!
LWAI.
HE WILL BE KNOWN AS LWAI AURA TIBESTI!
HAH HAH HAH!
...
YOU CAN DO IT!
PAN (CLAP)
PAN
AOO...
TOTE
TOTE (TOTTER)
AOO.

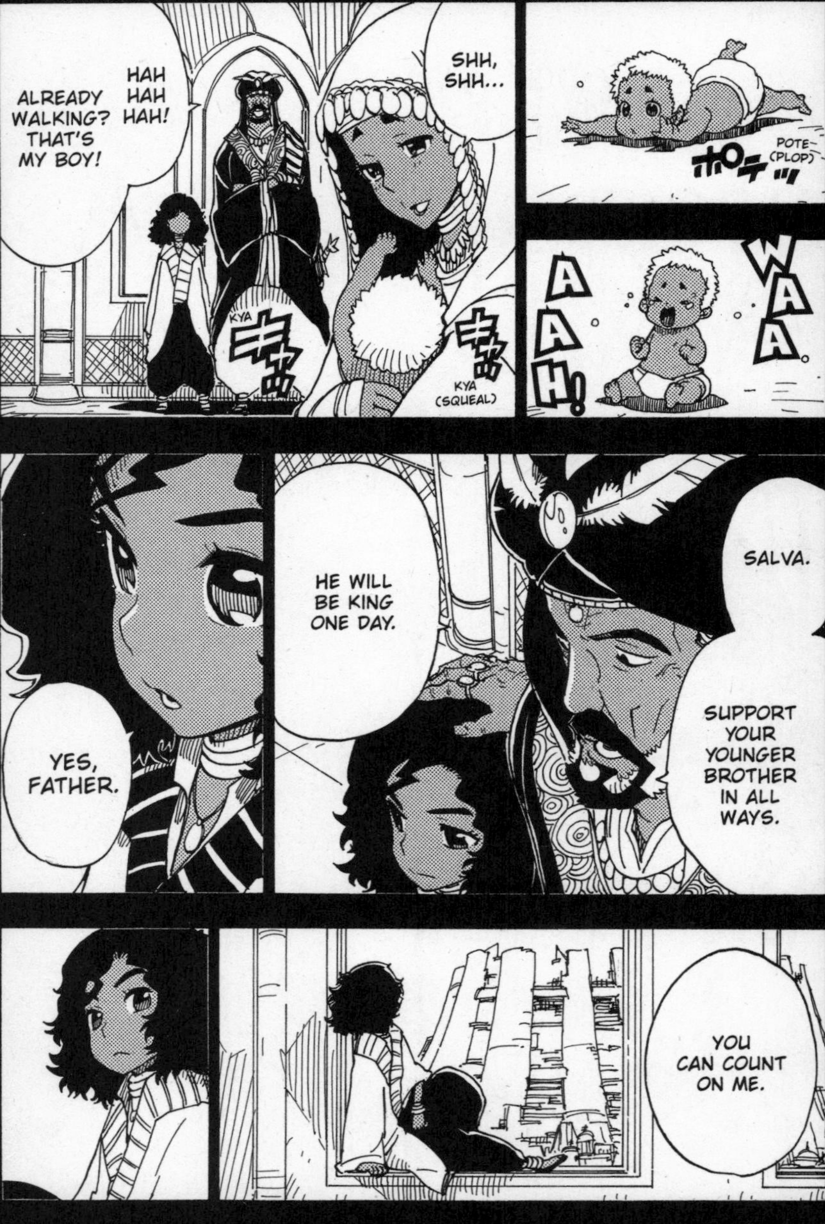
POTE (PLOP)
WAAA.
AAAH!
SHH, SHH...
HAH HAH HAH!
ALREADY WALKING? THAT'S MY BOY!
KYA (SQUEAL)
KYA
SALVA.
SUPPORT YOUR YOUNGER BROTHER IN ALL WAYS.
HE WILL BE KING ONE DAY.
YES, FATHER.
YOU CAN COUNT ON ME.

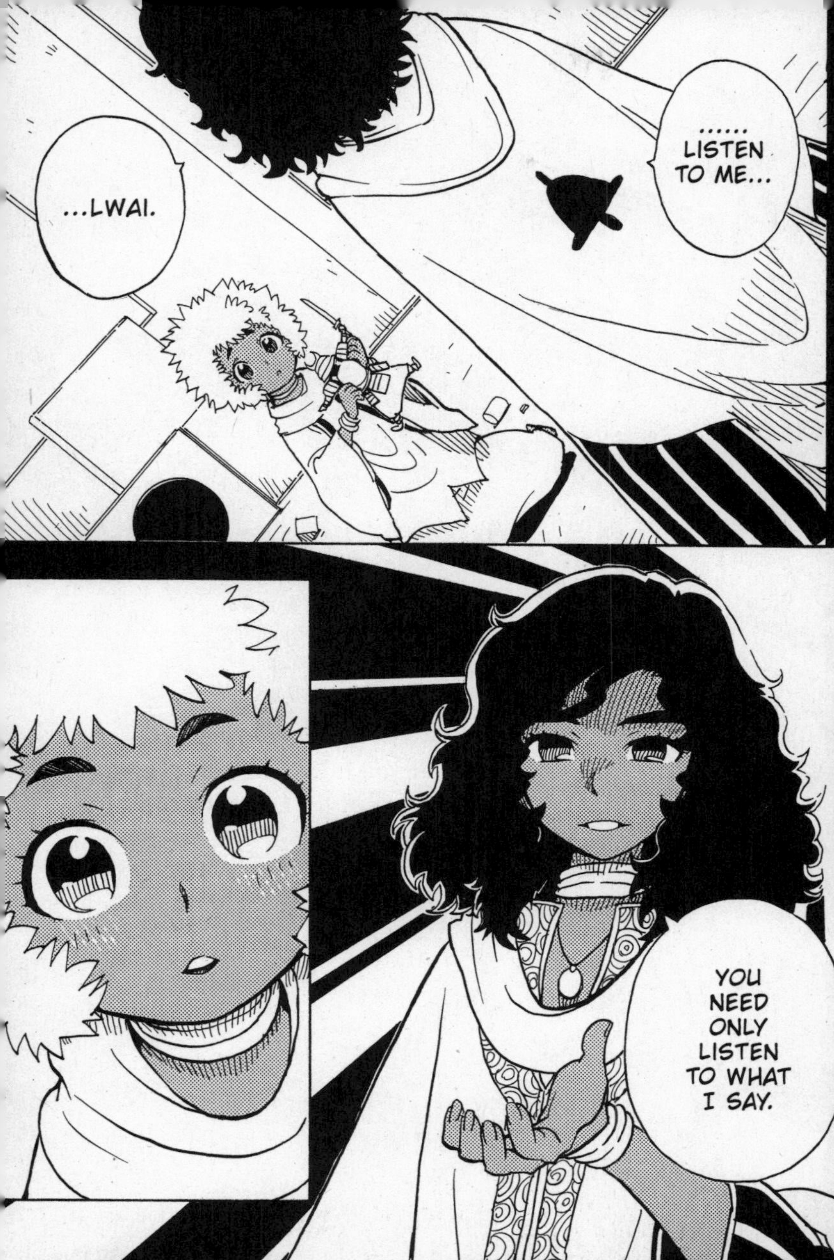
......LISTEN TO ME...
...LWAI.
YOU NEED ONLY LISTEN TO WHAT I SAY.

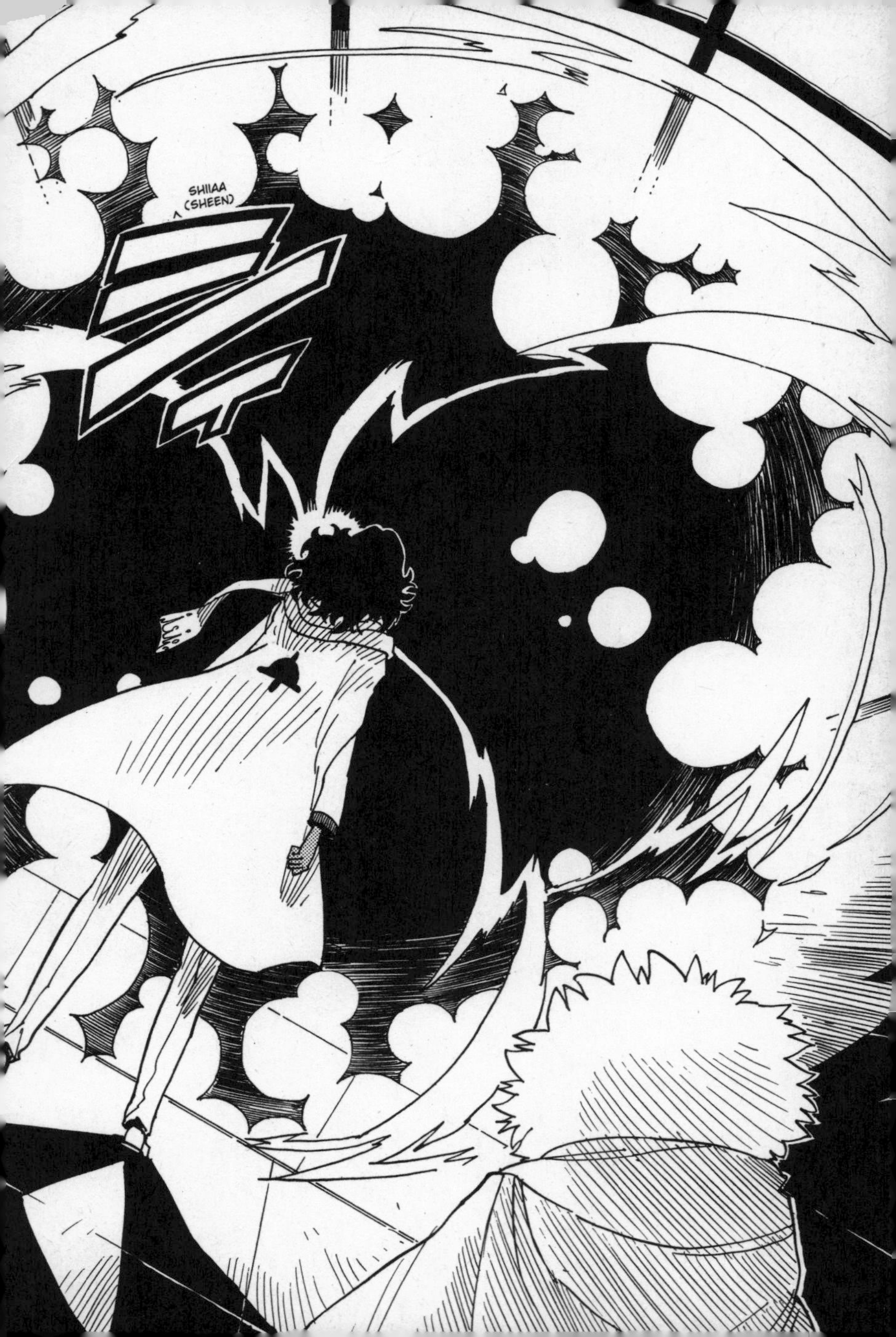
SHIIAA (SHEEN)

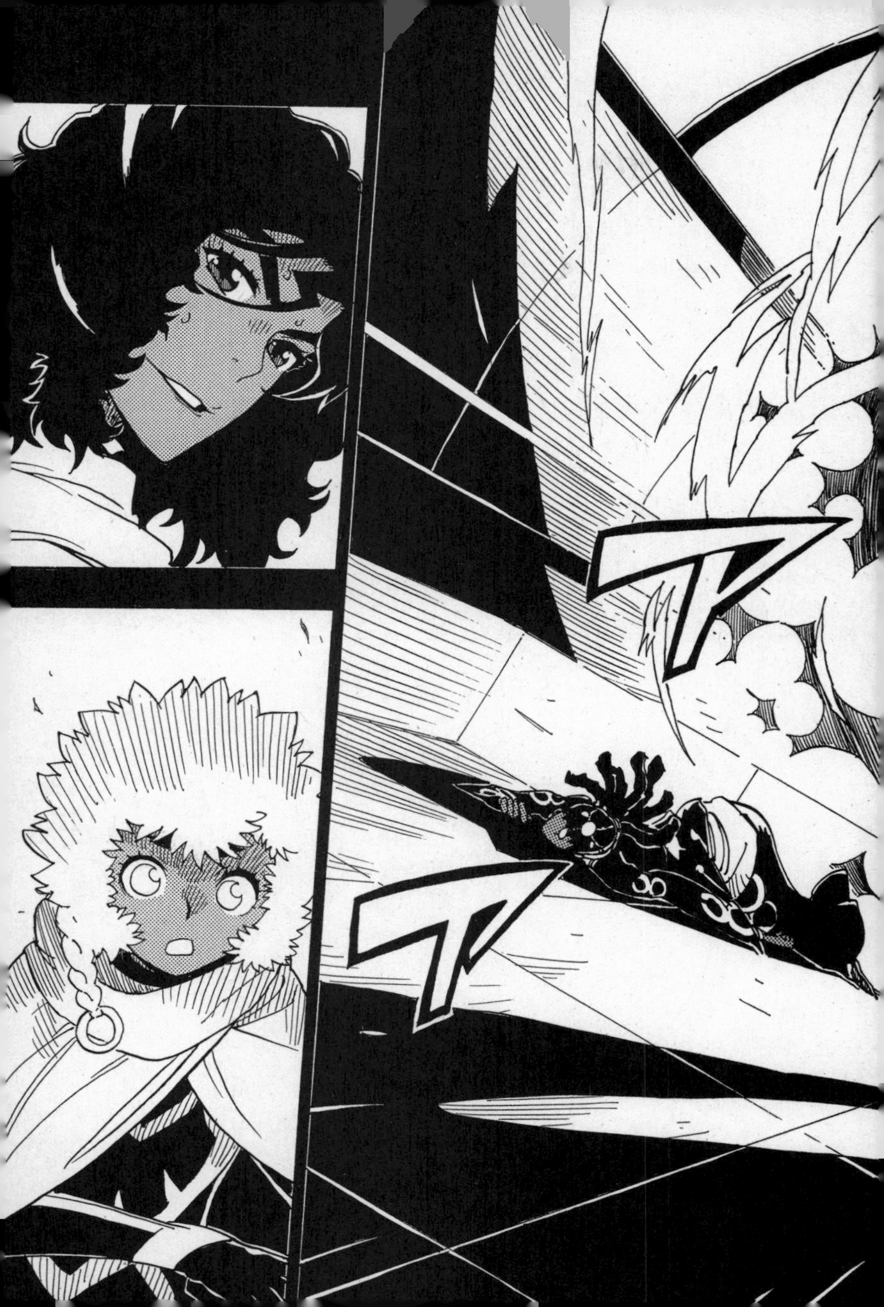

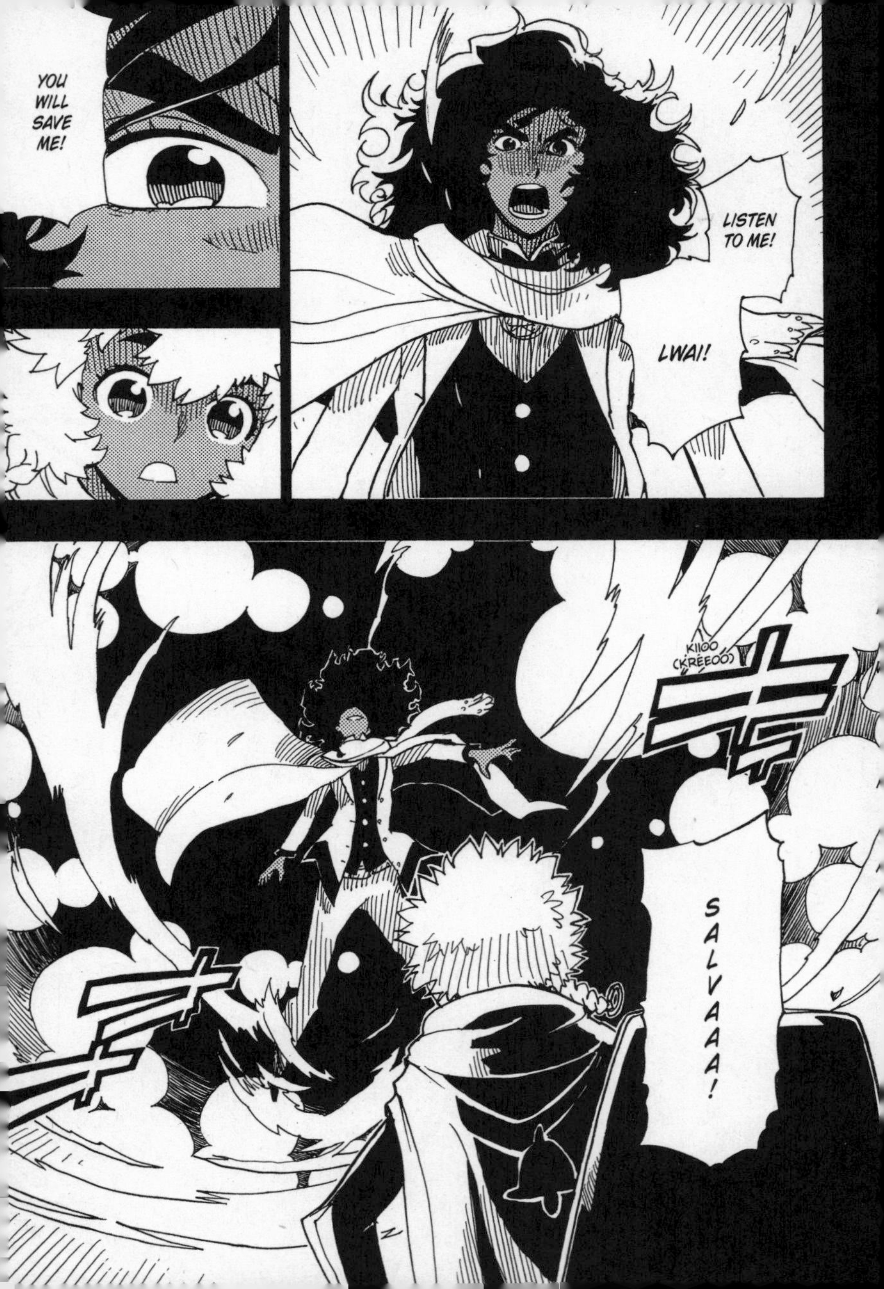
LISTEN TO ME!
LWAI!
YOU WILL SAVE ME!
KIIOO (KREEOO)
SALVAAA!

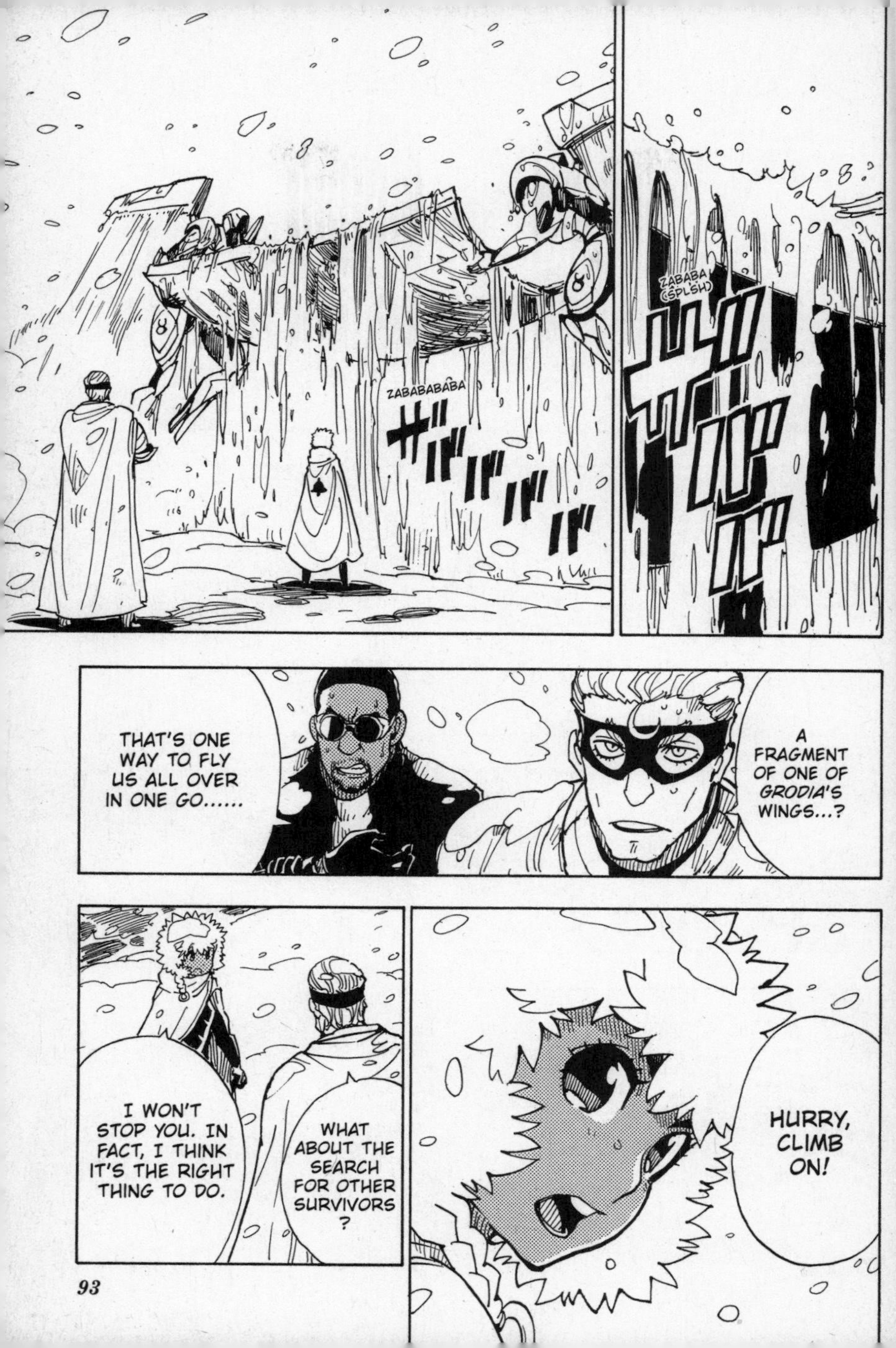
ZABABA (SPLSH)
ZABABABABA
A FRAGMENT OF ONE OF GRODIA'S WINGS...?
THAT'S ONE WAY TO FLY US ALL OVER IN ONE GO......
HURRY, CLIMB ON!
WHAT ABOUT THE SEARCH FOR OTHER SURVIVORS?
I WON'T STOP YOU. IN FACT, I THINK IT'S THE RIGHT THING TO DO.

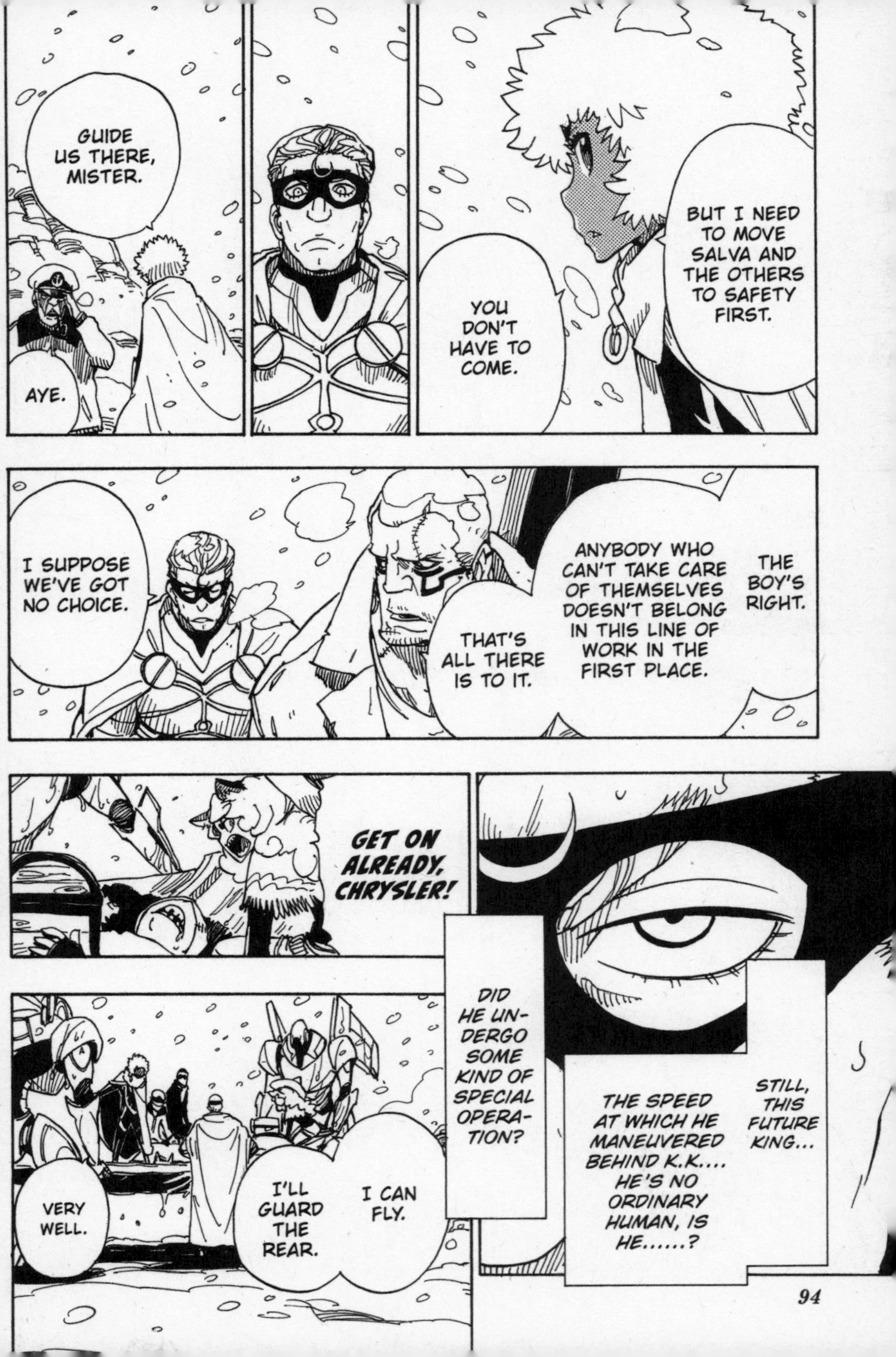
BUT I NEED TO MOVE SALVA AND THE OTHERS TO SAFETY FIRST.
YOU DON'T HAVE TO COME.
GUIDE US THERE, MISTER.
AYE.
THE BOY'S RIGHT.
ANYBODY WHO CAN'T TAKE CARE OF THEMSELVES DOESN'T BELONG IN THIS LINE OF WORK IN THE FIRST PLACE.
THAT'S ALL THERE IS TO IT.
I SUPPOSE WE'VE GOT NO CHOICE.
STILL, THIS FUTURE KING...
THE SPEED AT WHICH HE MANEUVERED BEHIND K.K.... HE'S NO ORDINARY HUMAN, IS HE......?
DID HE UNDERGO SOME KIND OF SPECIAL OPERATION?
GET ON ALREADY, CHRYSLER!
I CAN FLY.
I'LL GUARD THE REAR.
VERY WELL.

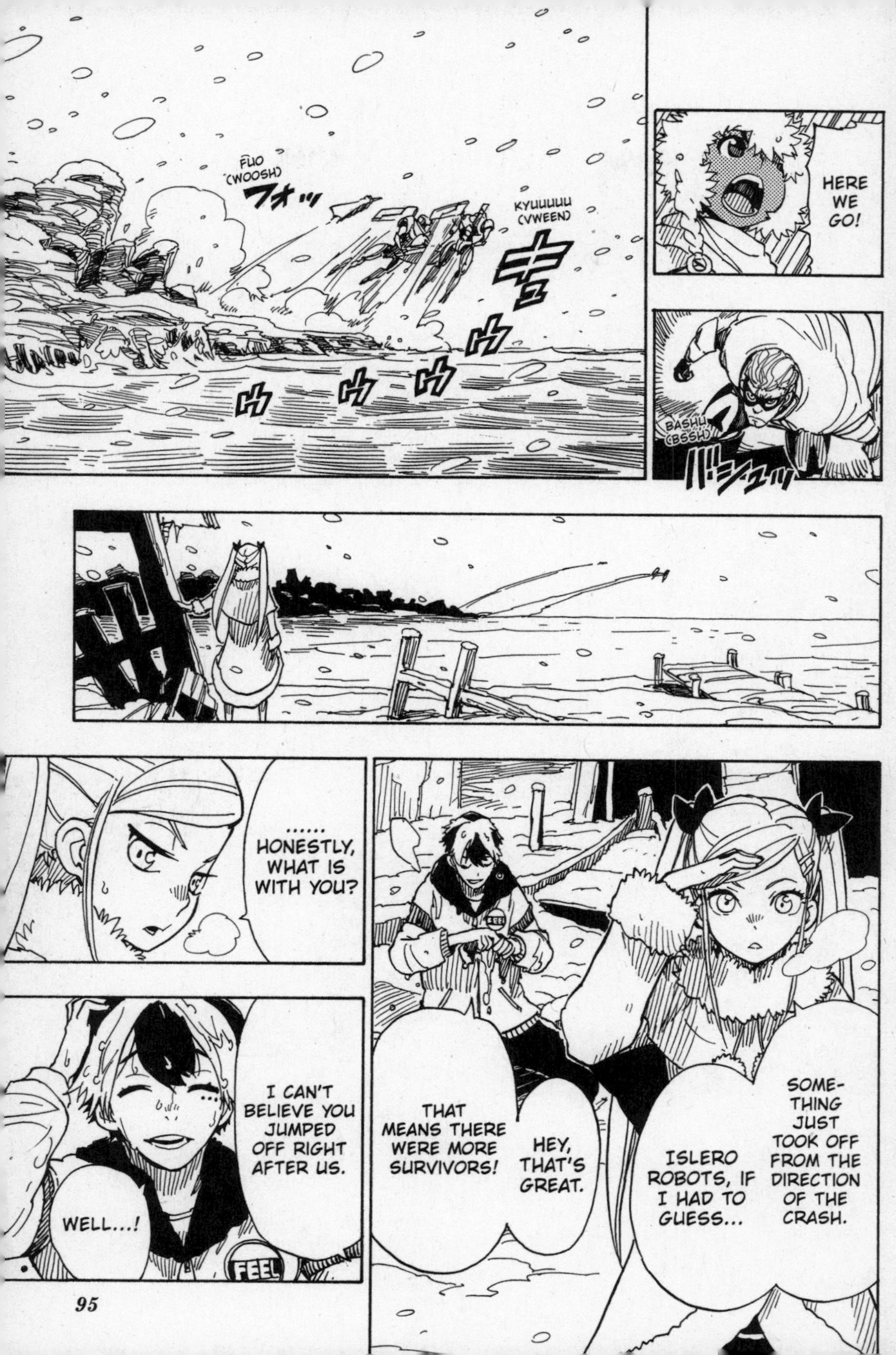
HERE WE GO!
BASHU (BSSH)
バシュッ
KYUUUUU (VWEEN)
FUO (WOOSH)
フォッ
SOMETHING JUST TOOK OFF FROM THE DIRECTION OF THE CRASH.
ISLERO ROBOTS, IF I HAD TO GUESS...
HEY, THAT'S GREAT.
THAT MEANS THERE WERE MORE SURVIVORS!
...... HONESTLY, WHAT IS WITH YOU?
I CAN'T BELIEVE YOU JUMPED OFF RIGHT AFTER US.
WELL...!

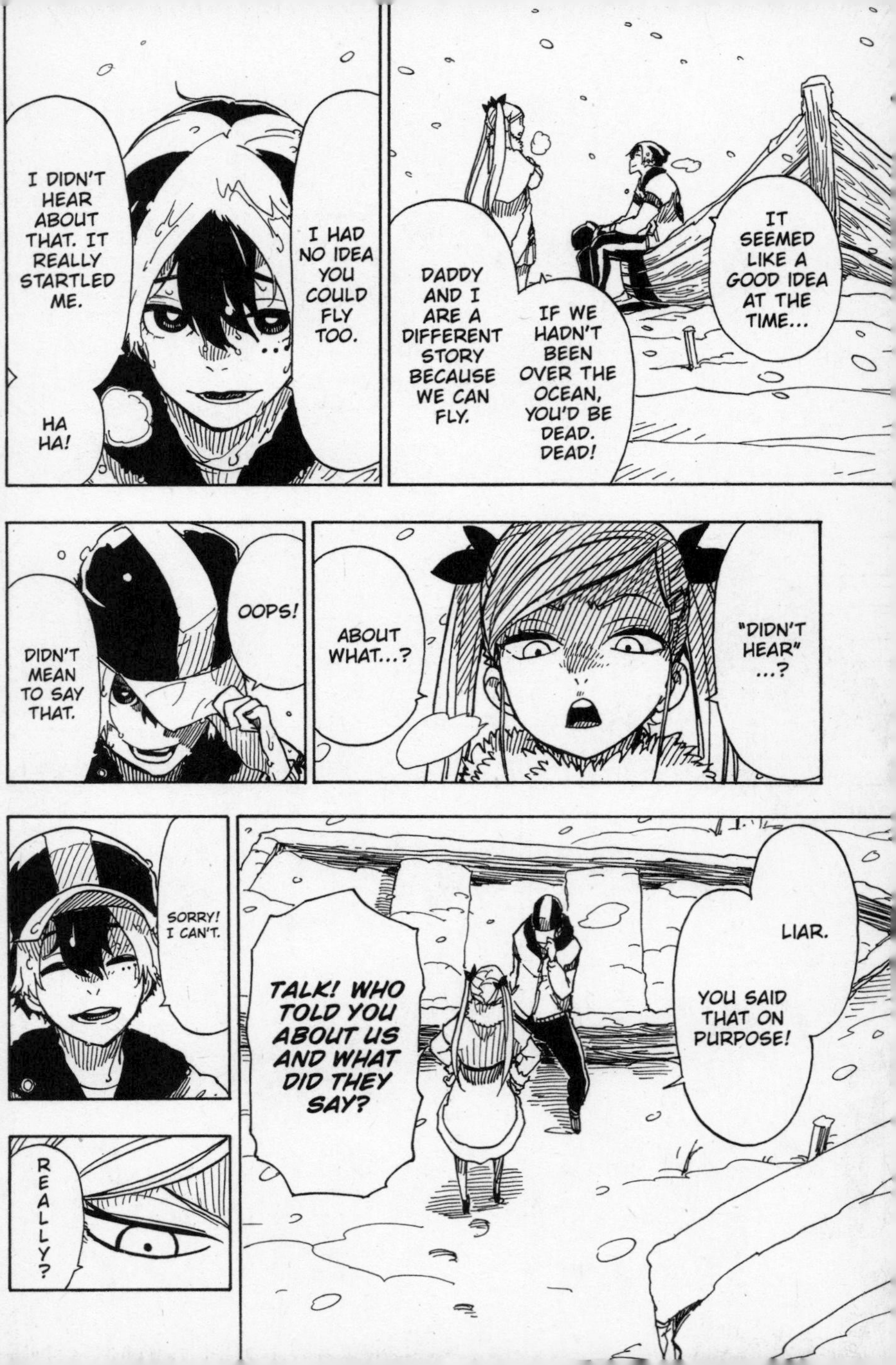
IT SEEMED LIKE A GOOD IDEA AT THE TIME...
IF WE HADN'T BEEN OVER THE OCEAN, YOU'D BE DEAD. DEAD!
DADDY AND I ARE A DIFFERENT STORY BECAUSE WE CAN FLY.
I HAD NO IDEA YOU COULD FLY TOO.
I DIDN'T HEAR ABOUT THAT. IT REALLY STARTLED ME.
HA HA!
"DIDN'T HEAR" ...?
ABOUT WHAT...?
OOPS!
DIDN'T MEAN TO SAY THAT.
LIAR.
YOU SAID THAT ON PURPOSE!
TALK! WHO TOLD YOU ABOUT US AND WHAT DID THEY SAY?
SORRY! I CAN'T.
REALLY?

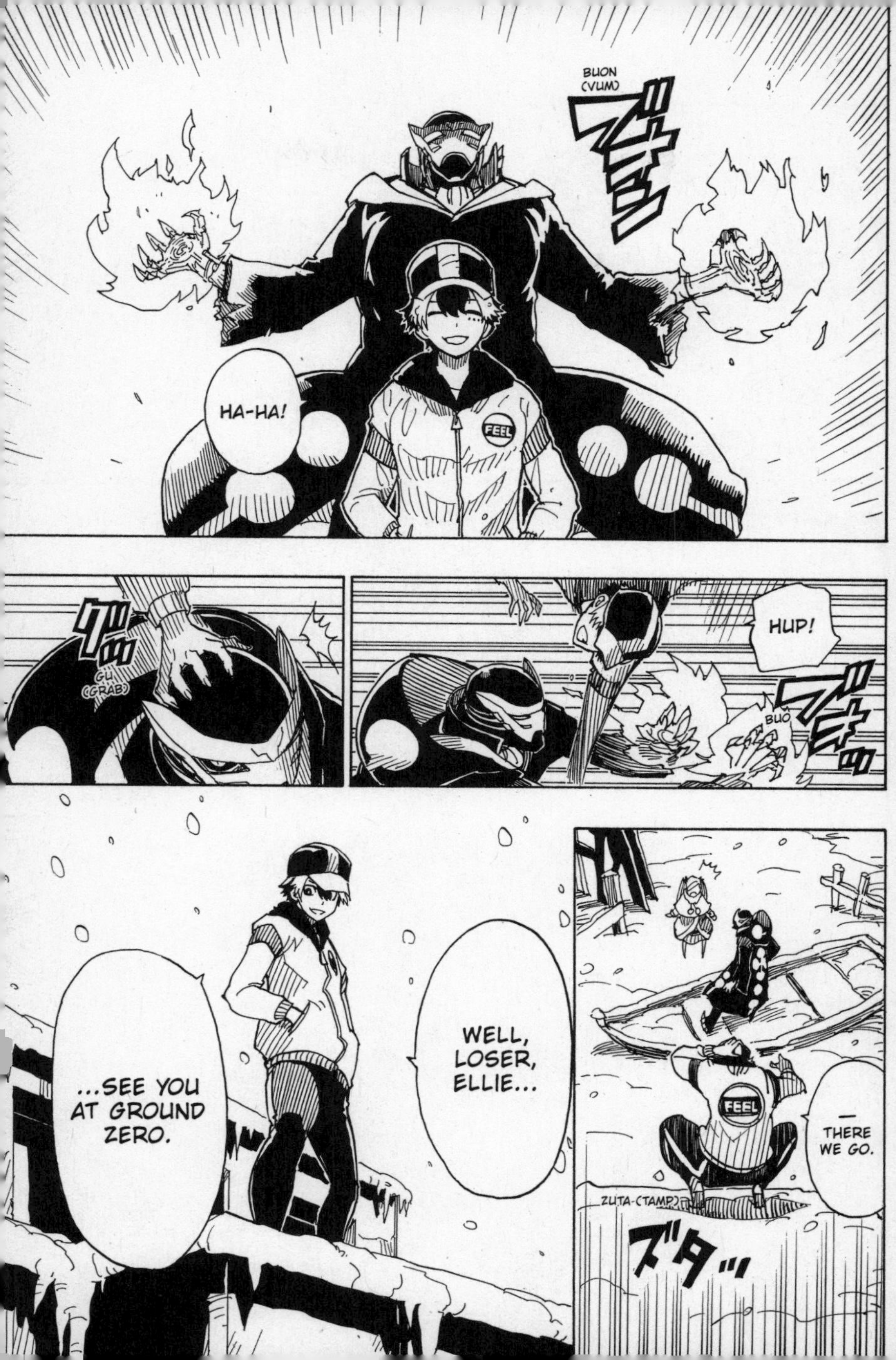
BUON (VUM)
HA-HA!
HUP!
BUO
GU (GRAB)
—THERE WE GO.
ZUTA-(TAMP)
WELL, LOSER, ELLIE...
...SEE YOU AT GROUND ZERO.

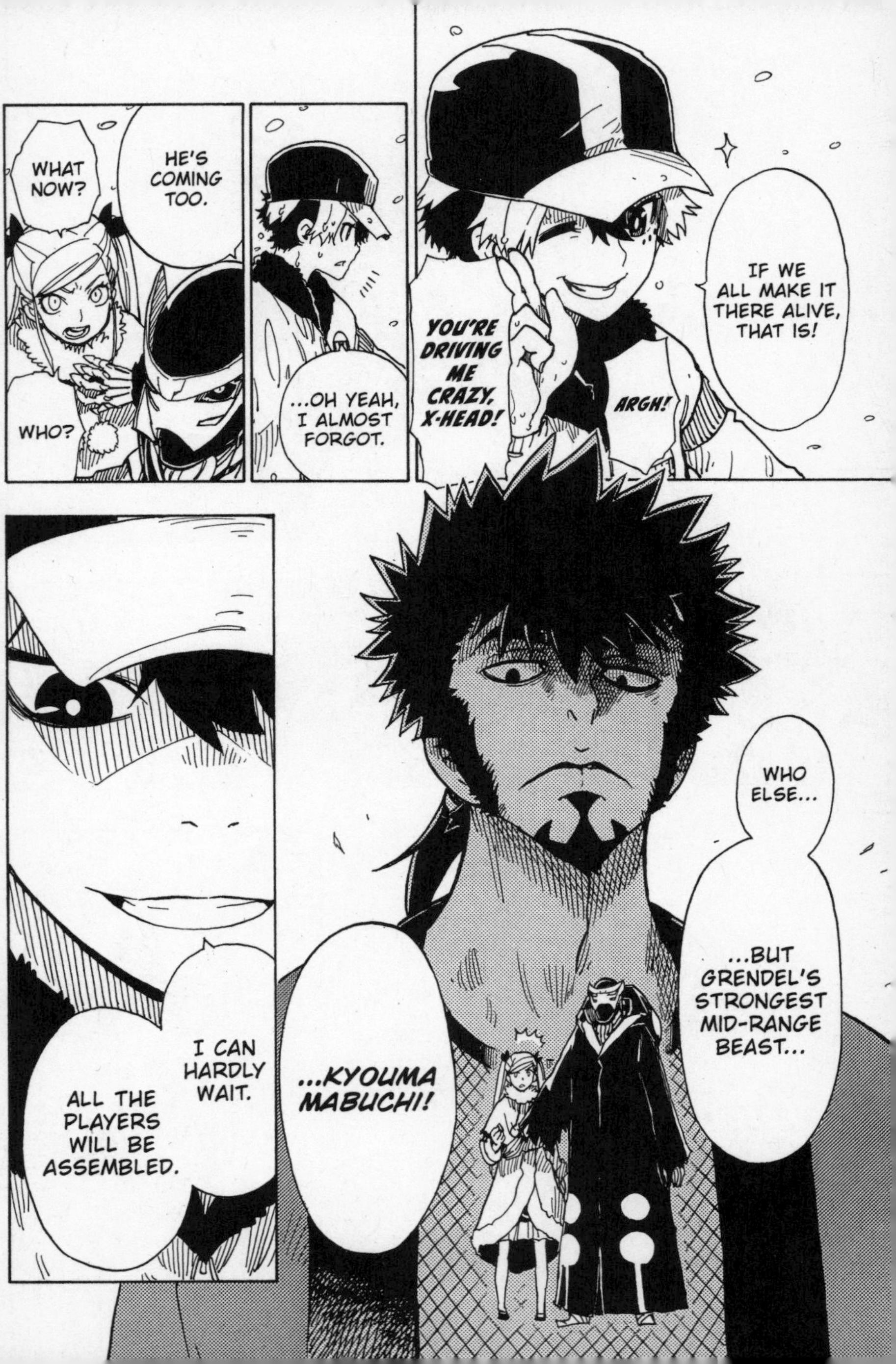
IF WE ALL MAKE IT THERE ALIVE, THAT IS!
ARGH!
YOU'RE DRIVING ME CRAZY, X-HEAD!
...OH YEAH, I ALMOST FORGOT.
HE'S COMING TOO.
WHAT NOW?
WHO?
WHO ELSE...
...BUT GRENDEL'S STRONGEST MID-RANGE BEAST...
...KYOUMA MABUCHI!
I CAN HARDLY WAIT.
ALL THE PLAYERS WILL BE ASSEMBLED.

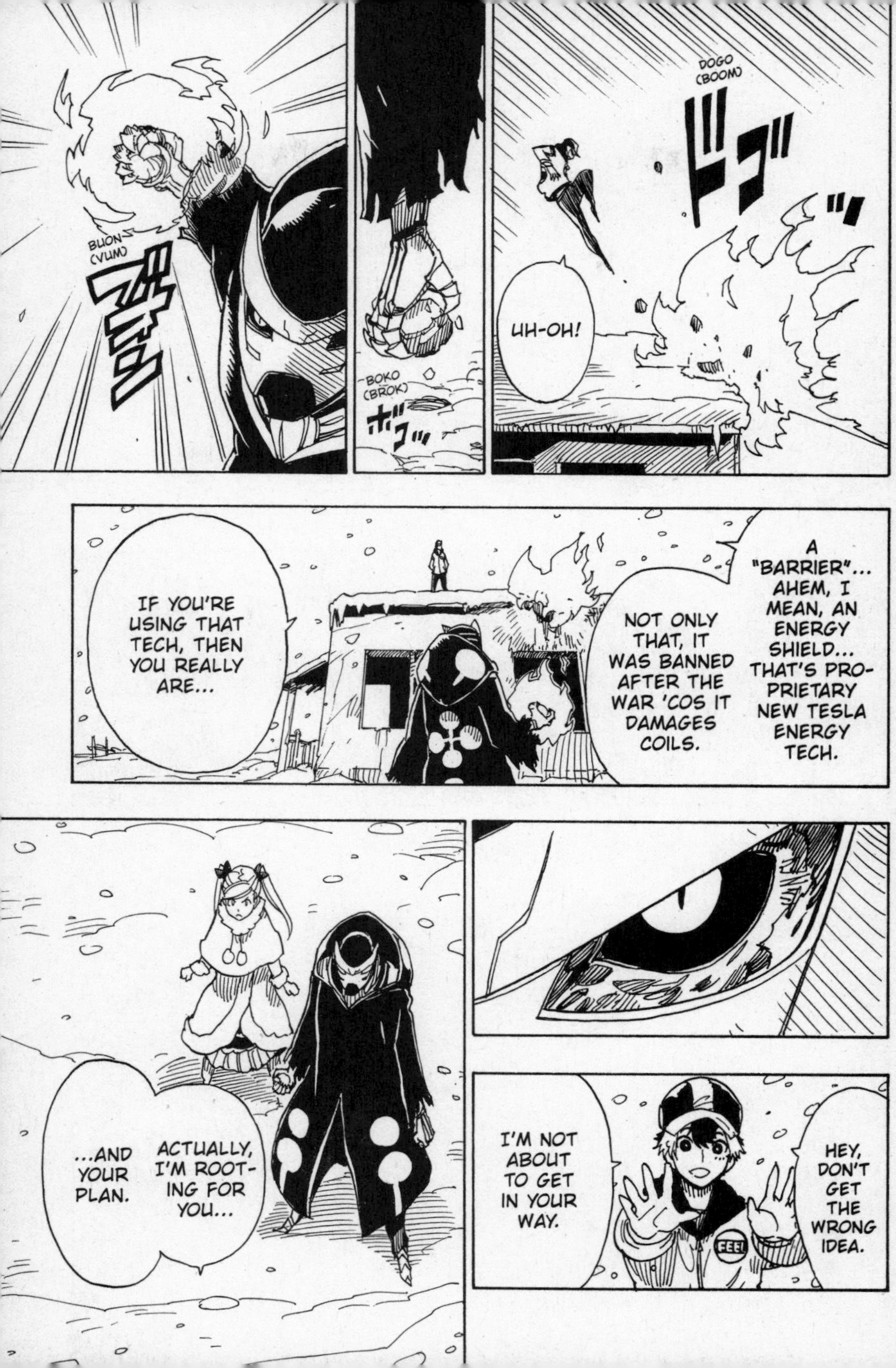
DOGO (BOOM)
UH-OH!
BOKO (BROK)
BUON (VUM)
A "BARRIER"... AHEM, I MEAN, AN ENERGY SHIELD... THAT'S PROPRIETARY NEW TESLA ENERGY TECH.
NOT ONLY THAT, IT WAS BANNED AFTER THE WAR 'COS IT DAMAGES COILS.
IF YOU'RE USING THAT TECH, THEN YOU REALLY ARE...
HEY, DON'T GET THE WRONG IDEA.
I'M NOT ABOUT TO GET IN YOUR WAY.
FEEL
ACTUALLY, I'M ROOTING FOR YOU...
...AND YOUR PLAN.

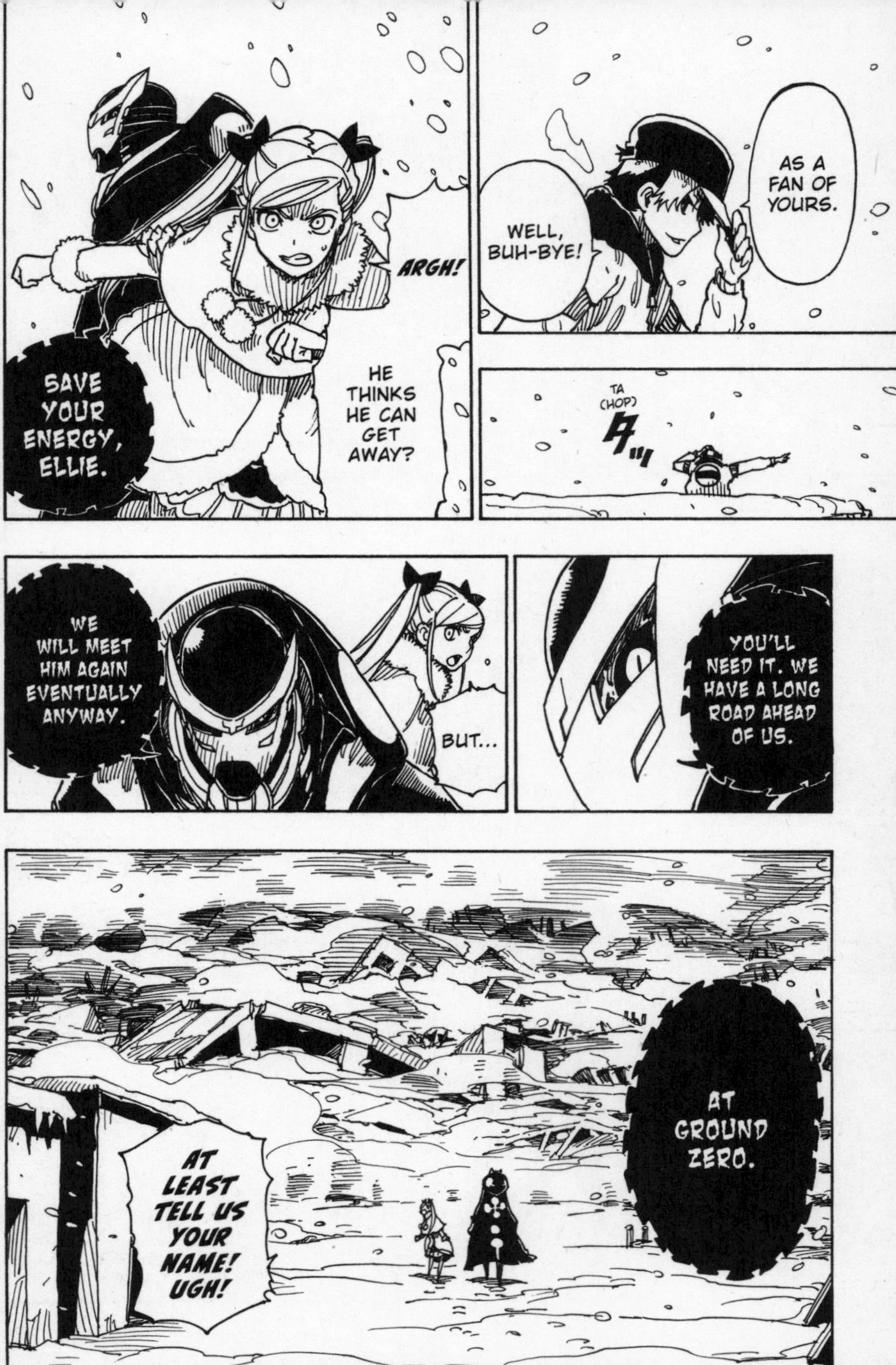
AS A FAN OF YOURS.
WELL, BUH-BYE!
TA (HOP)
ARGH!
HE THINKS HE CAN GET AWAY?
SAVE YOUR ENERGY, ELLIE.
YOU'LL NEED IT. WE HAVE A LONG ROAD AHEAD OF US.
BUT...
WE WILL MEET HIM AGAIN EVENTUALLY ANYWAY.
AT GROUND ZERO.
AT LEAST TELL US YOUR NAME! UGH!

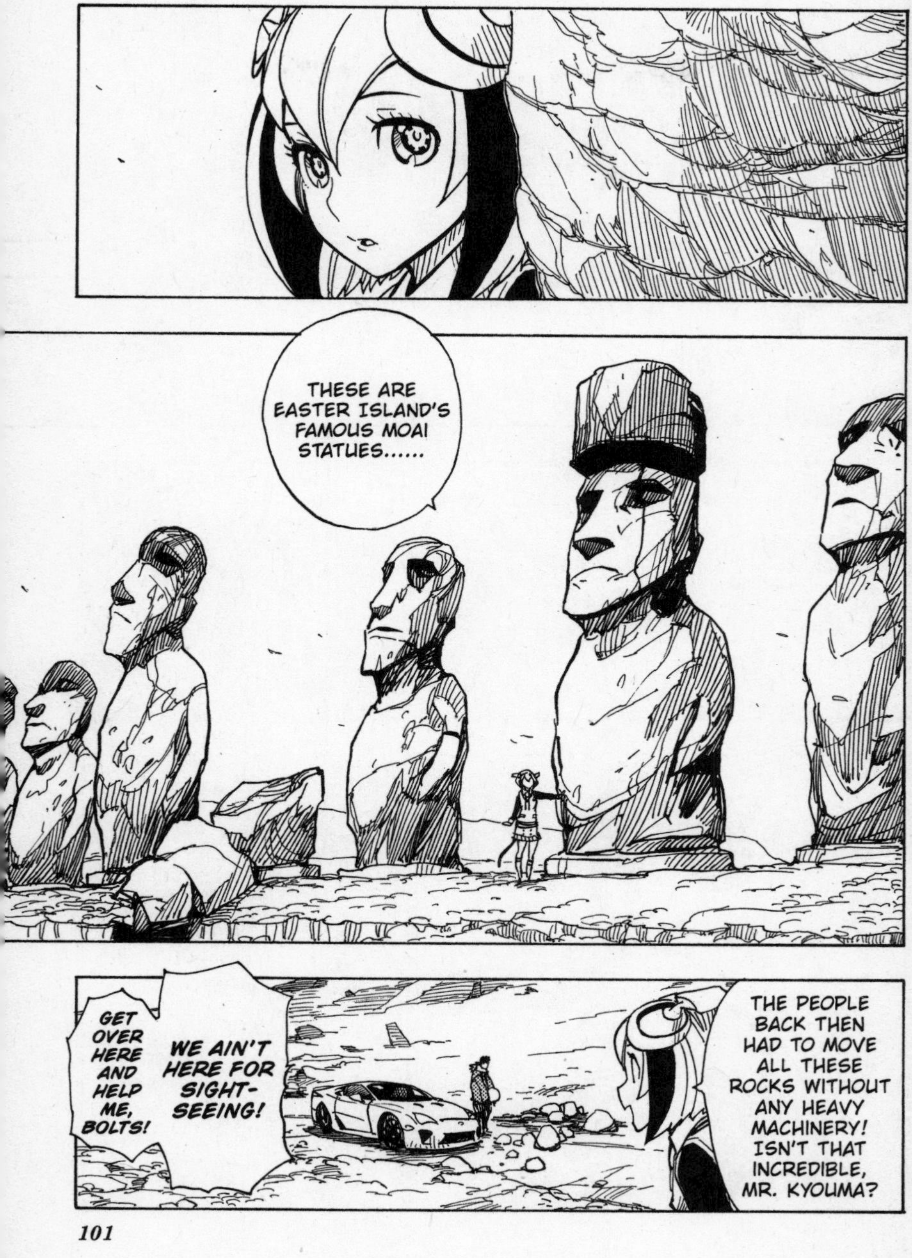
THESE ARE EASTER ISLAND'S FAMOUS MOAI STATUES......
THE PEOPLE BACK THEN HAD TO MOVE ALL THESE ROCKS WITHOUT ANY HEAVY MACHINERY! ISN'T THAT INCREDIBLE, MR. KYOUMA?
WE AIN'T HERE FOR SIGHT-SEEING!
GET OVER HERE AND HELP ME, BOLTS!

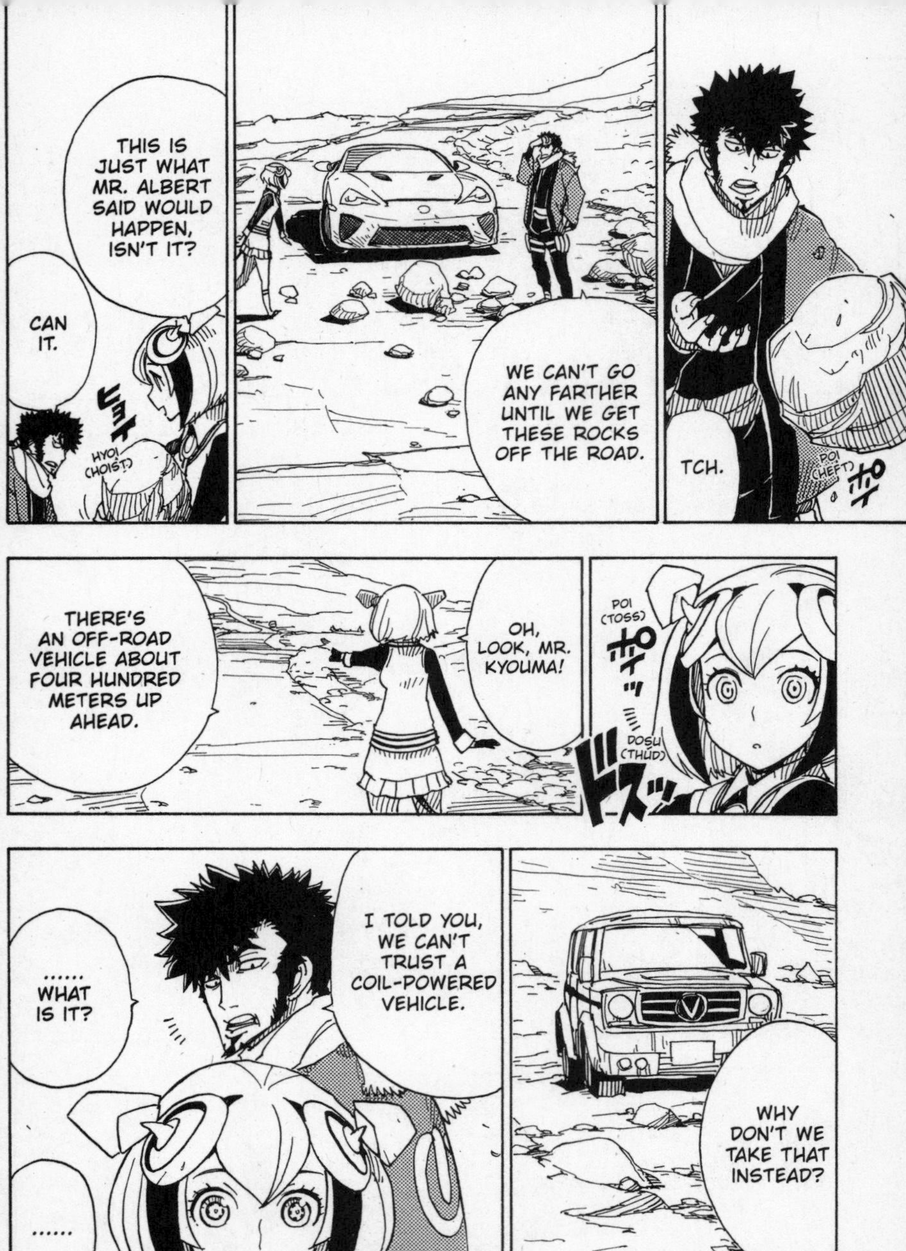
POI (HEFT)
ポイ
TCH.
WE CAN'T GO ANY FARTHER UNTIL WE GET THESE ROCKS OFF THE ROAD.
THIS IS JUST WHAT MR. ALBERT SAID WOULD HAPPEN, ISN'T IT?
CAN IT.
ヒョイ
HYO! (HOIST!)
POI (TOSS)
ポイッ
DOSU (THUD)
ドスッ
OH, LOOK, MR. KYOUMA!
THERE'S AN OFF-ROAD VEHICLE ABOUT FOUR HUNDRED METERS UP AHEAD.
WHY DON'T WE TAKE THAT INSTEAD?
I TOLD YOU, WE CAN'T TRUST A COIL-POWERED VEHICLE.
...... WHAT IS IT?
......

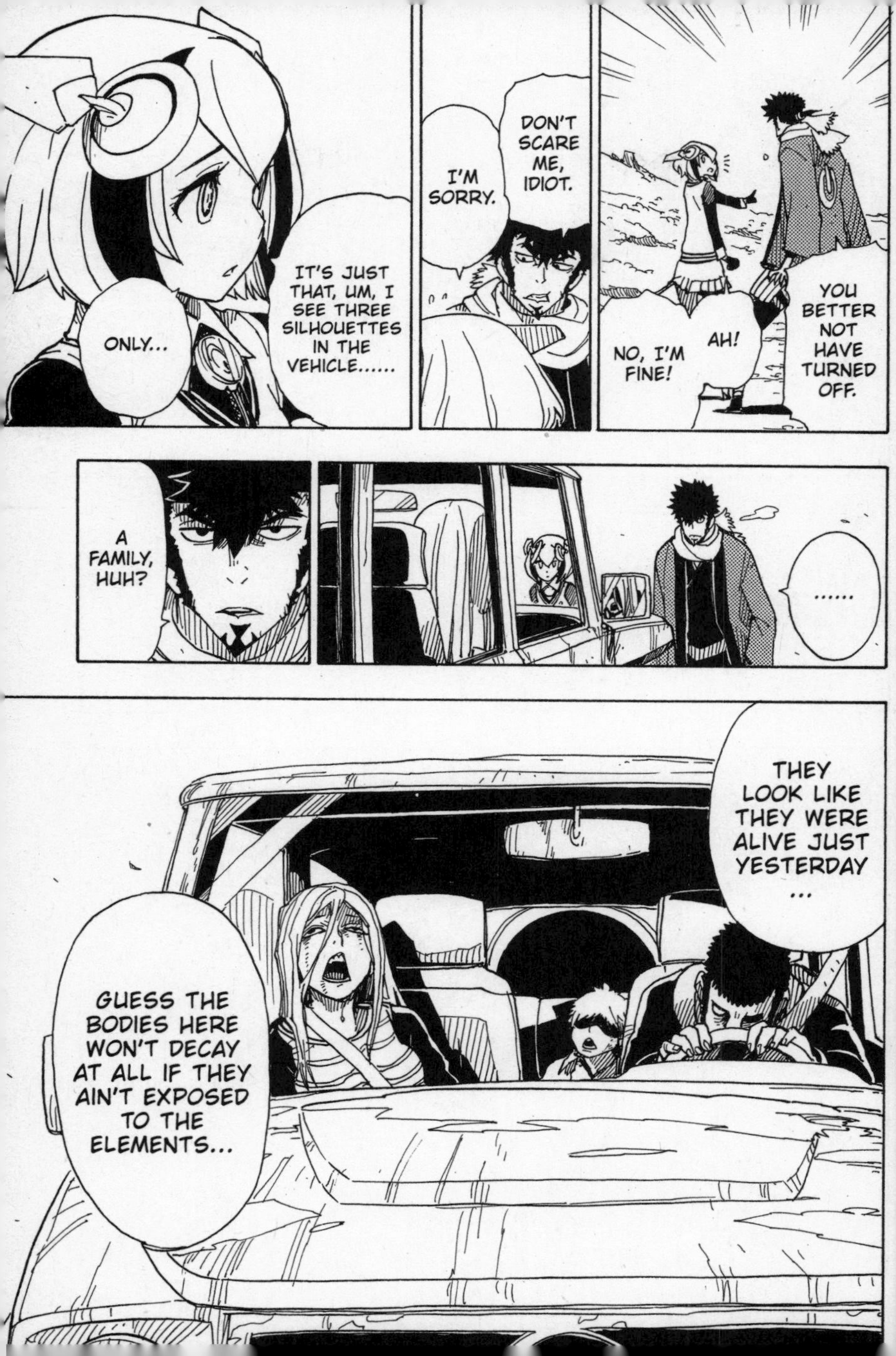
YOU BETTER NOT HAVE TURNED OFF.
AH!
NO, I'M FINE!
DON'T SCARE ME, IDIOT.
I'M SORRY.
IT'S JUST THAT, UM, I SEE THREE SILHOUETTES IN THE VEHICLE......
ONLY...
......
A FAMILY, HUH?
THEY LOOK LIKE THEY WERE ALIVE JUST YESTERDAY ...
GUESS THE BODIES HERE WON'T DECAY AT ALL IF THEY AIN'T EXPOSED TO THE ELEMENTS...

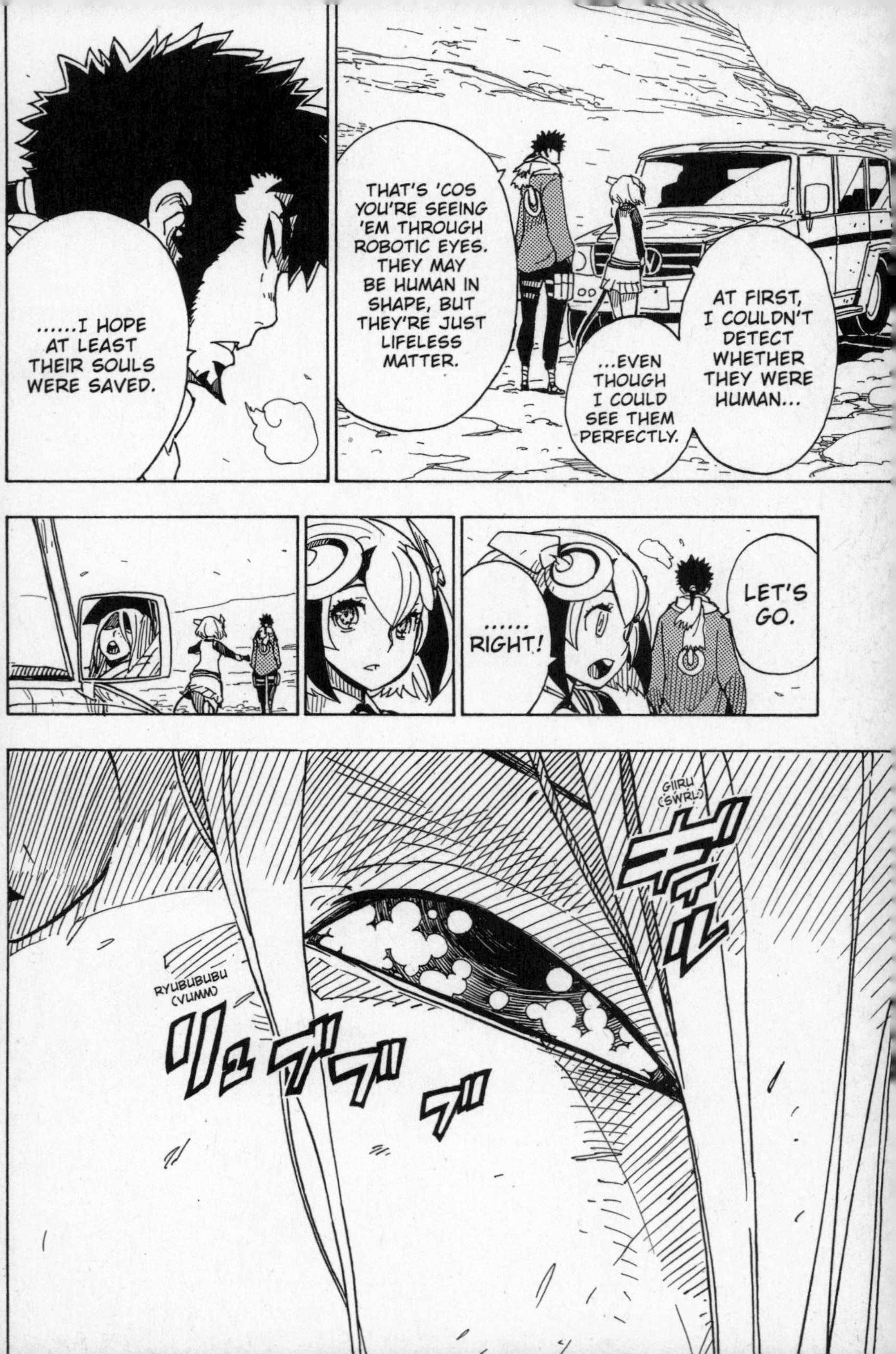
AT FIRST, I COULDN'T DETECT WHETHER THEY WERE HUMAN...
...EVEN THOUGH I COULD SEE THEM PERFECTLY.
THAT'S 'COS YOU'RE SEEING 'EM THROUGH ROBOTIC EYES. THEY MAY BE HUMAN IN SHAPE, BUT THEY'RE JUST LIFELESS MATTER.
......I HOPE AT LEAST THEIR SOULS WERE SAVED.
LET'S GO.
...... RIGHT!
GIIRU (SWRL)
RYUBUBUBU (VUMM)

Dimension W

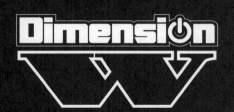

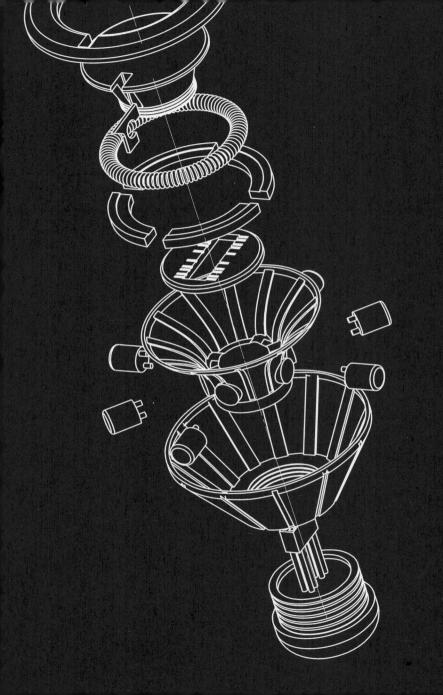

# FILE.44
# LOST TIME

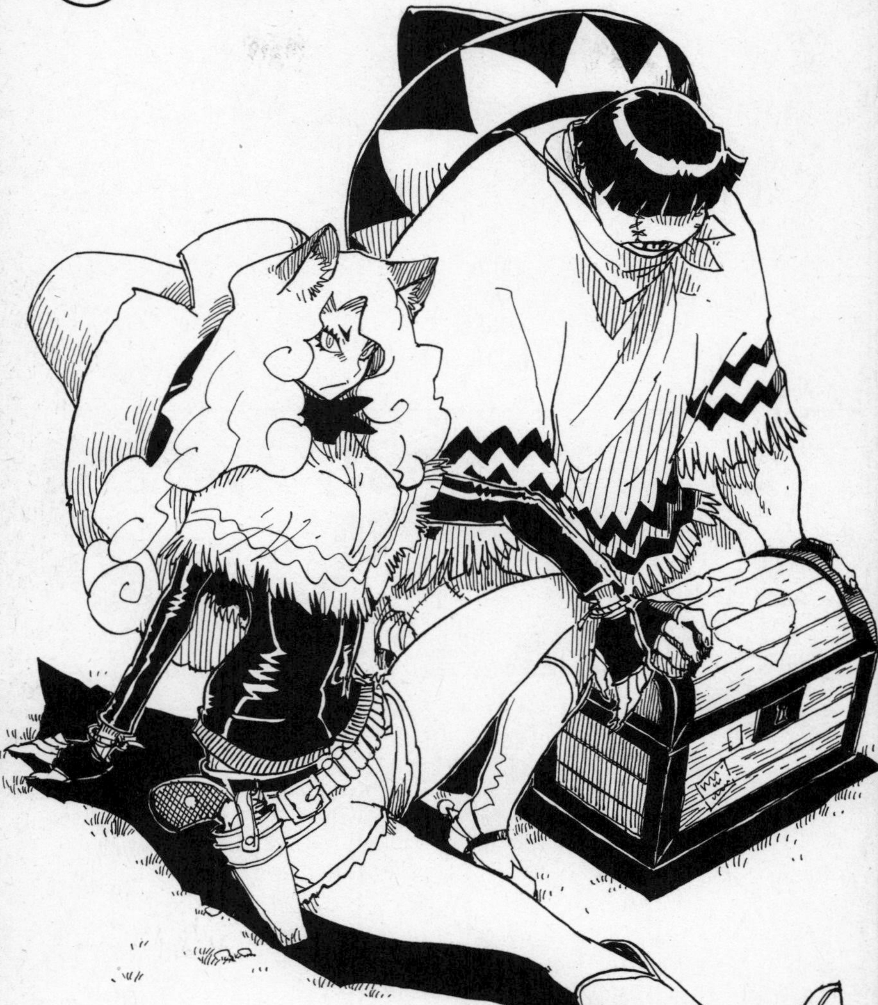

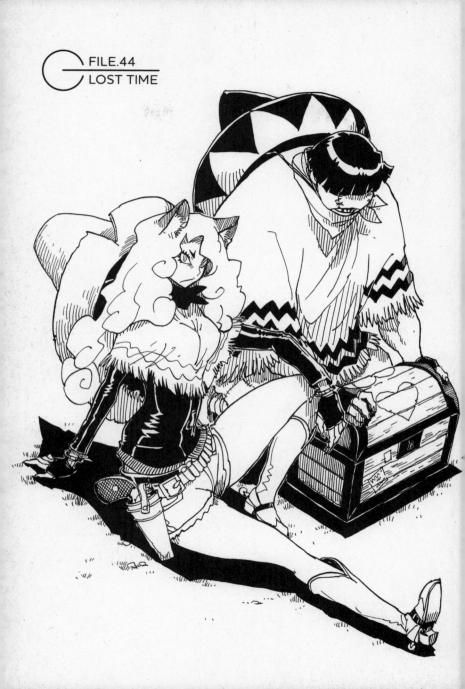

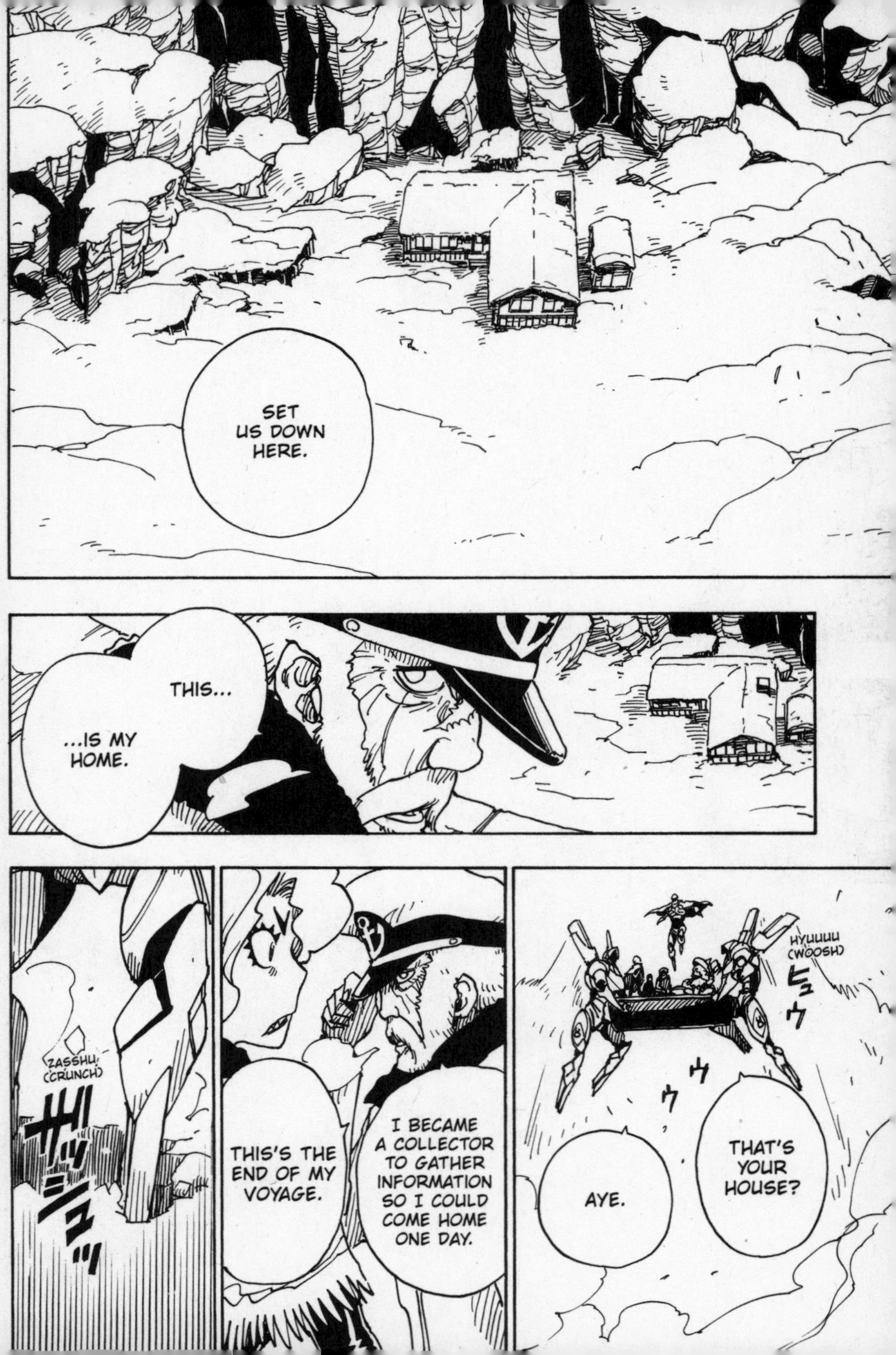
SET US DOWN HERE.
THIS...
...IS MY HOME.
HYUUUU (WOOSH)
ヒュウウウ
THAT'S YOUR HOUSE?
AYE.
I BECAME A COLLECTOR TO GATHER INFORMATION SO I COULD COME HOME ONE DAY.
THIS'S THE END OF MY VOYAGE.
ZASSHU (CRUNCH)
ザッシュッ

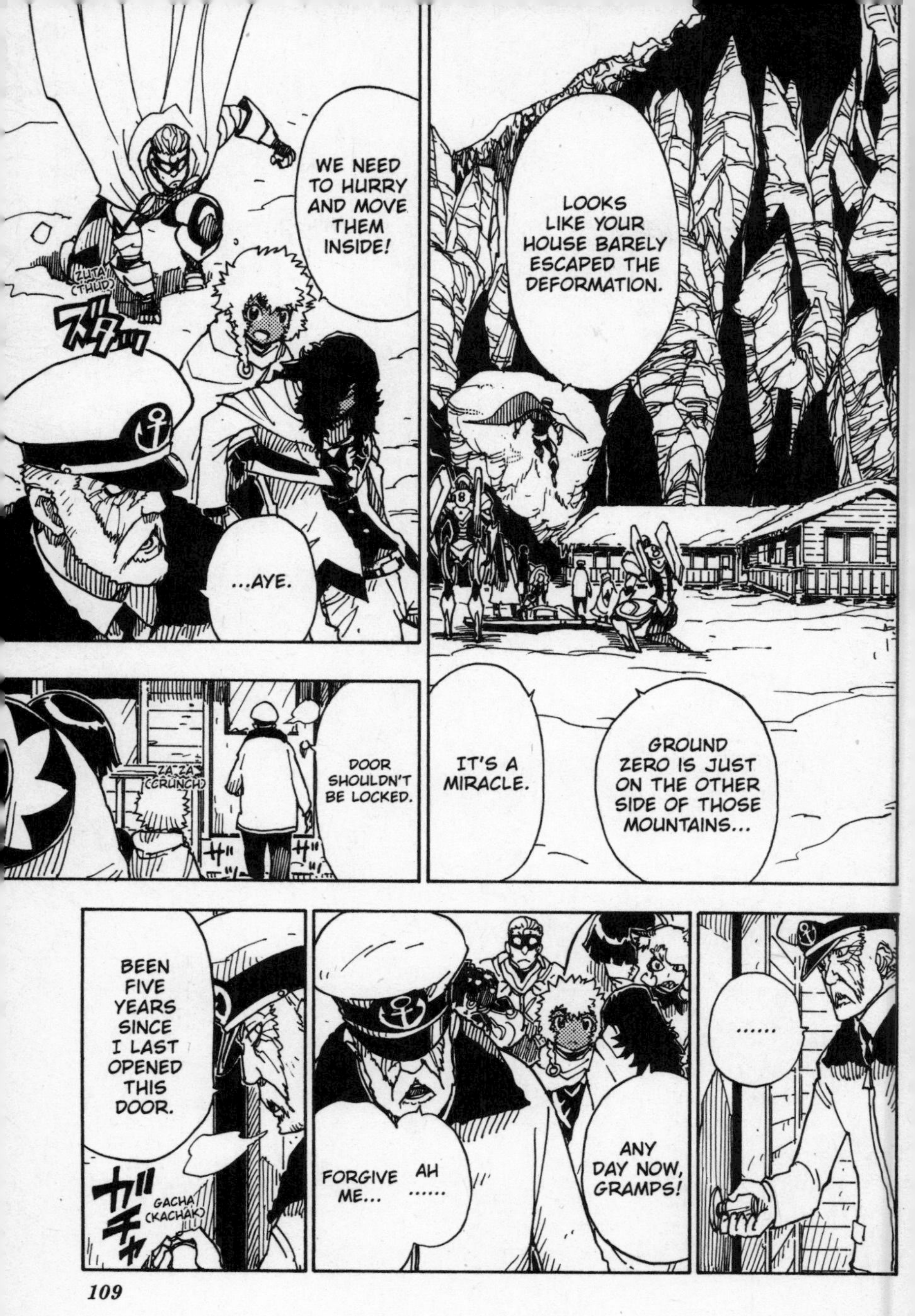
LOOKS LIKE YOUR HOUSE BARELY ESCAPED THE DEFORMATION.
GROUND ZERO IS JUST ON THE OTHER SIDE OF THOSE MOUNTAINS...
IT'S A MIRACLE.
WE NEED TO HURRY AND MOVE THEM INSIDE!
ZUTA (THUD)
...AYE.
DOOR SHOULDN'T BE LOCKED.
ZA ZA (CRUNCH)
......
ANY DAY NOW, GRAMPS!
AH ......
FORGIVE ME...
BEEN FIVE YEARS SINCE I LAST OPENED THIS DOOR.
GACHA (KACHAK)

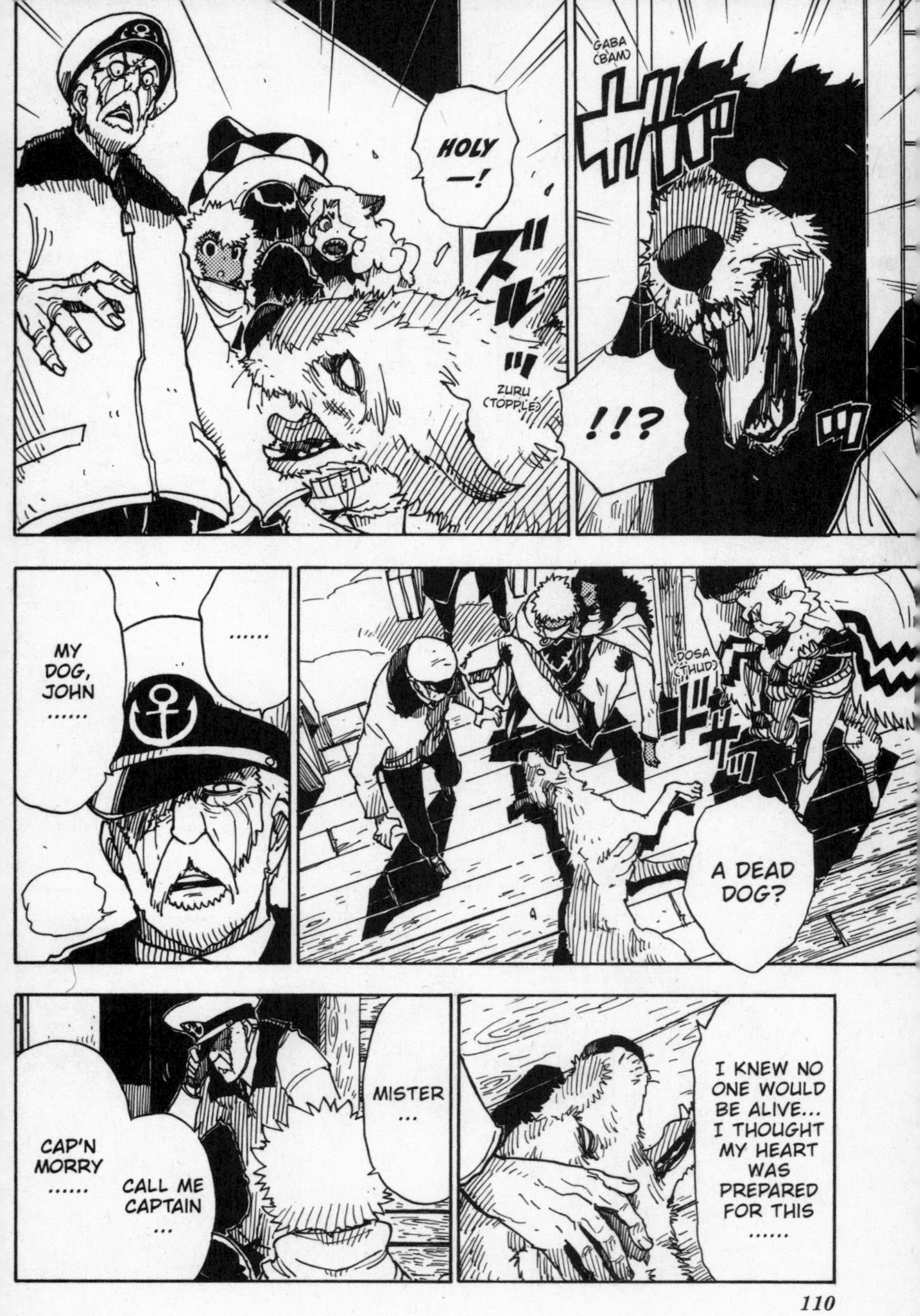
GABA (BAM)
!!?
HOLY —!
ZURU (TOPPLE)
DOSA (THUD)
A DEAD DOG?
......
MY DOG, JOHN ......
I KNEW NO ONE WOULD BE ALIVE... I THOUGHT MY HEART WAS PREPARED FOR THIS ......
MISTER ...
CALL ME CAPTAIN ...
CAP'N MORRY ......

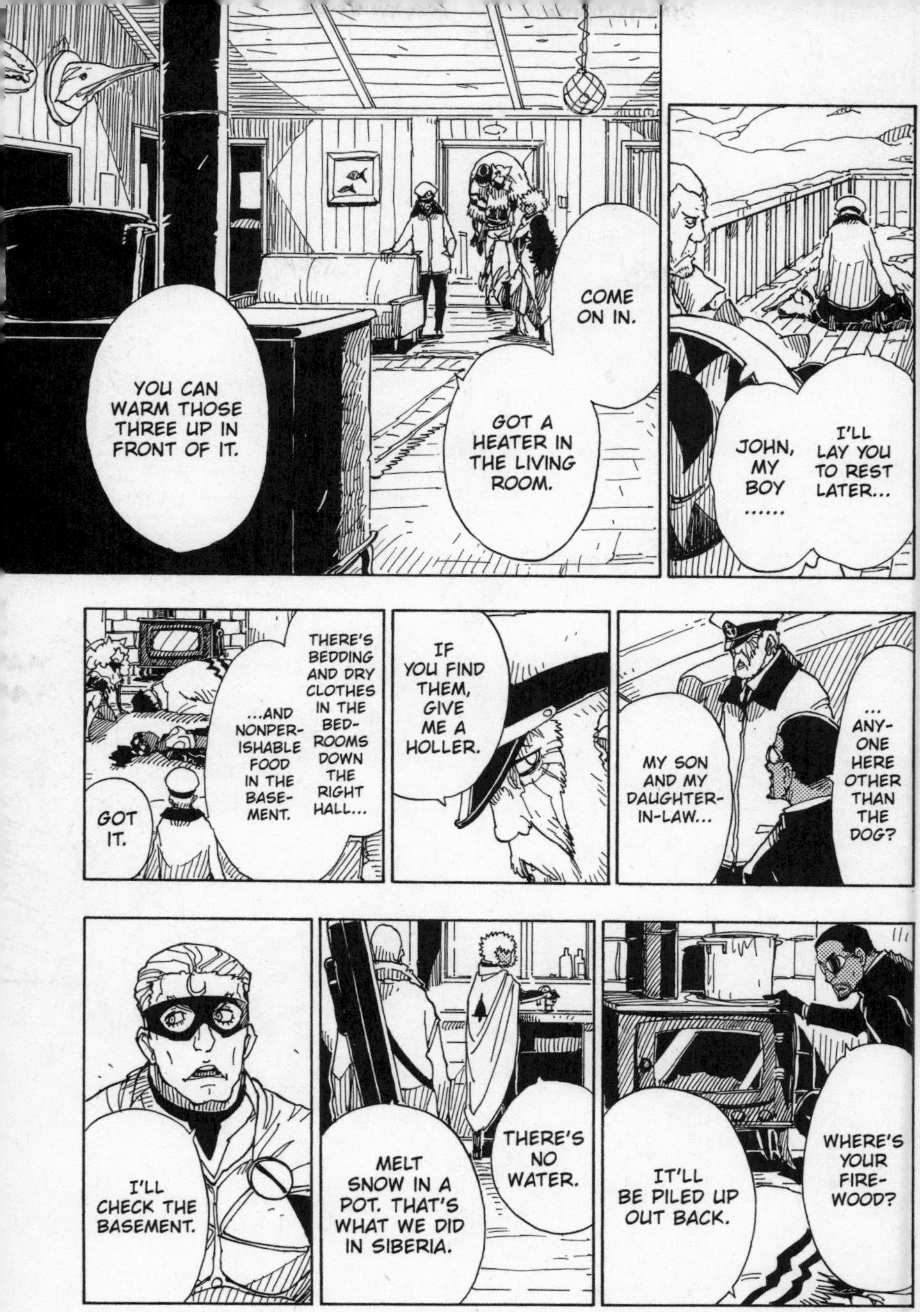
I'LL LAY YOU TO REST LATER...
JOHN, MY BOY ......
COME ON IN.
GOT A HEATER IN THE LIVING ROOM.
YOU CAN WARM THOSE THREE UP IN FRONT OF IT.
...ANYONE HERE OTHER THAN THE DOG?
MY SON AND MY DAUGHTER-IN-LAW...
IF YOU FIND THEM, GIVE ME A HOLLER.
THERE'S BEDDING AND DRY CLOTHES IN THE BEDROOMS DOWN THE RIGHT HALL...
...AND NONPERISHABLE FOOD IN THE BASEMENT.
GOT IT.
WHERE'S YOUR FIREWOOD?
IT'LL BE PILED UP OUT BACK.
THERE'S NO WATER.
MELT SNOW IN A POT. THAT'S WHAT WE DID IN SIBERIA.
I'LL CHECK THE BASEMENT.

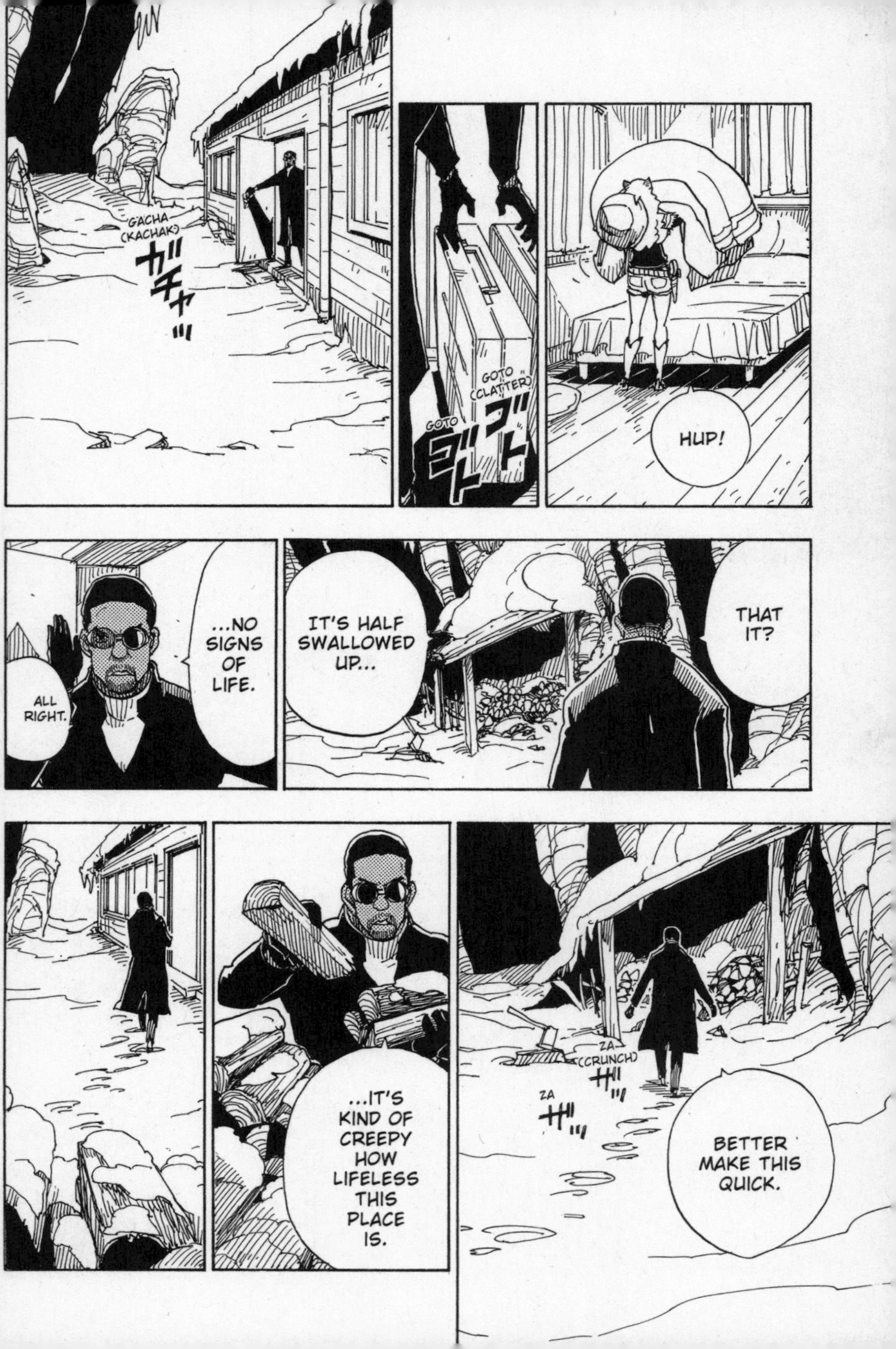
HUP!
GOTO (CLATTER)
ゴト
GOTO
ゴト
GACHA (KACHAK)
ガチャッ
THAT IT?
IT'S HALF SWALLOWED UP...
...NO SIGNS OF LIFE.
ALL RIGHT.
BETTER MAKE THIS QUICK.
ZA (CRUNCH)
ザッ
ZA
ザッ
...IT'S KIND OF CREEPY HOW LIFELESS THIS PLACE IS.

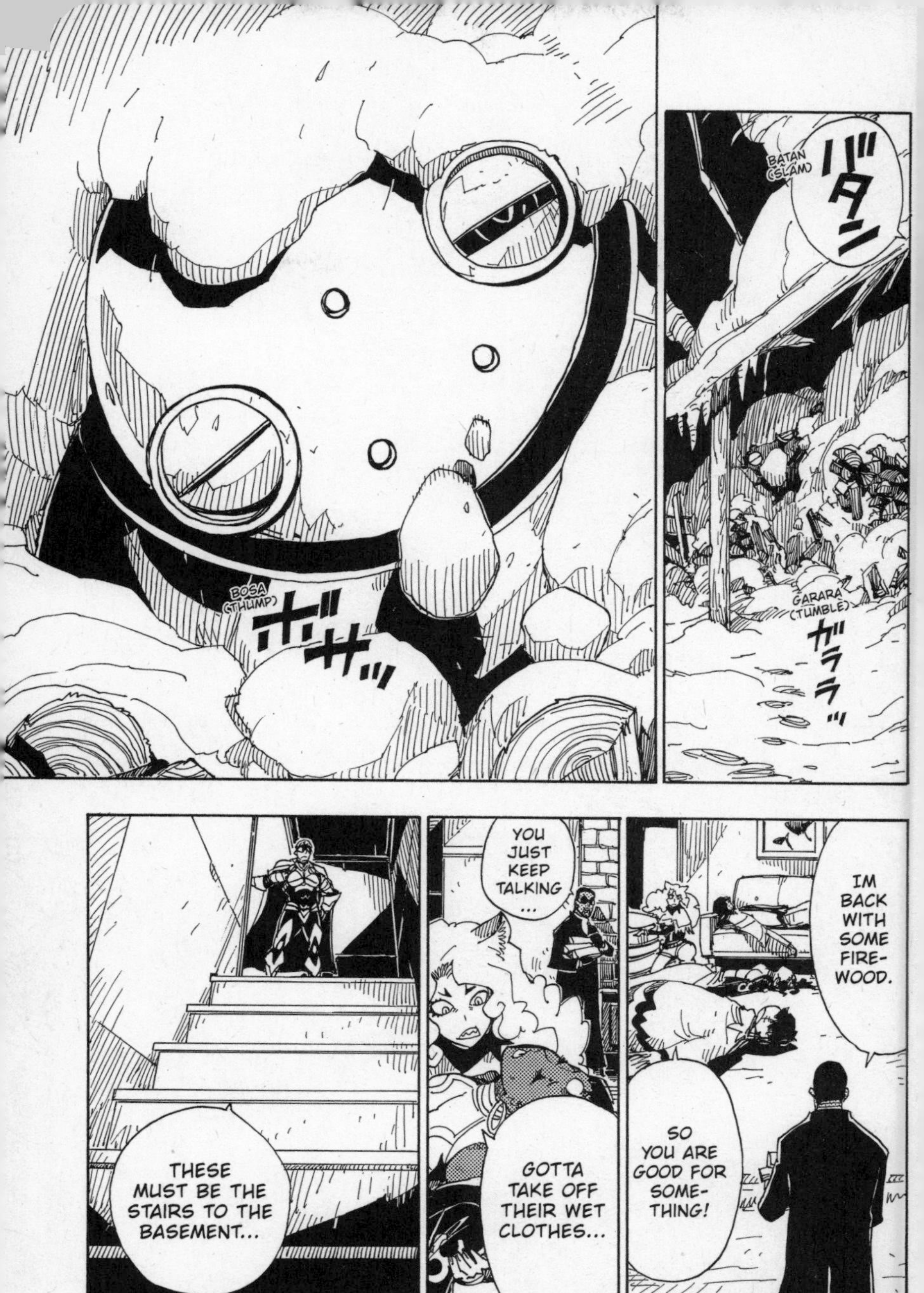
BATAN (SLAM)
バタン
GARARA (TUMBLE)
ガララッ
BOSA (THUMP)
ボサッ
IM BACK WITH SOME FIRE-WOOD.
SO YOU ARE GOOD FOR SOME-THING!
YOU JUST KEEP TALKING...
GOTTA TAKE OFF THEIR WET CLOTHES...
THESE MUST BE THE STAIRS TO THE BASEMENT...

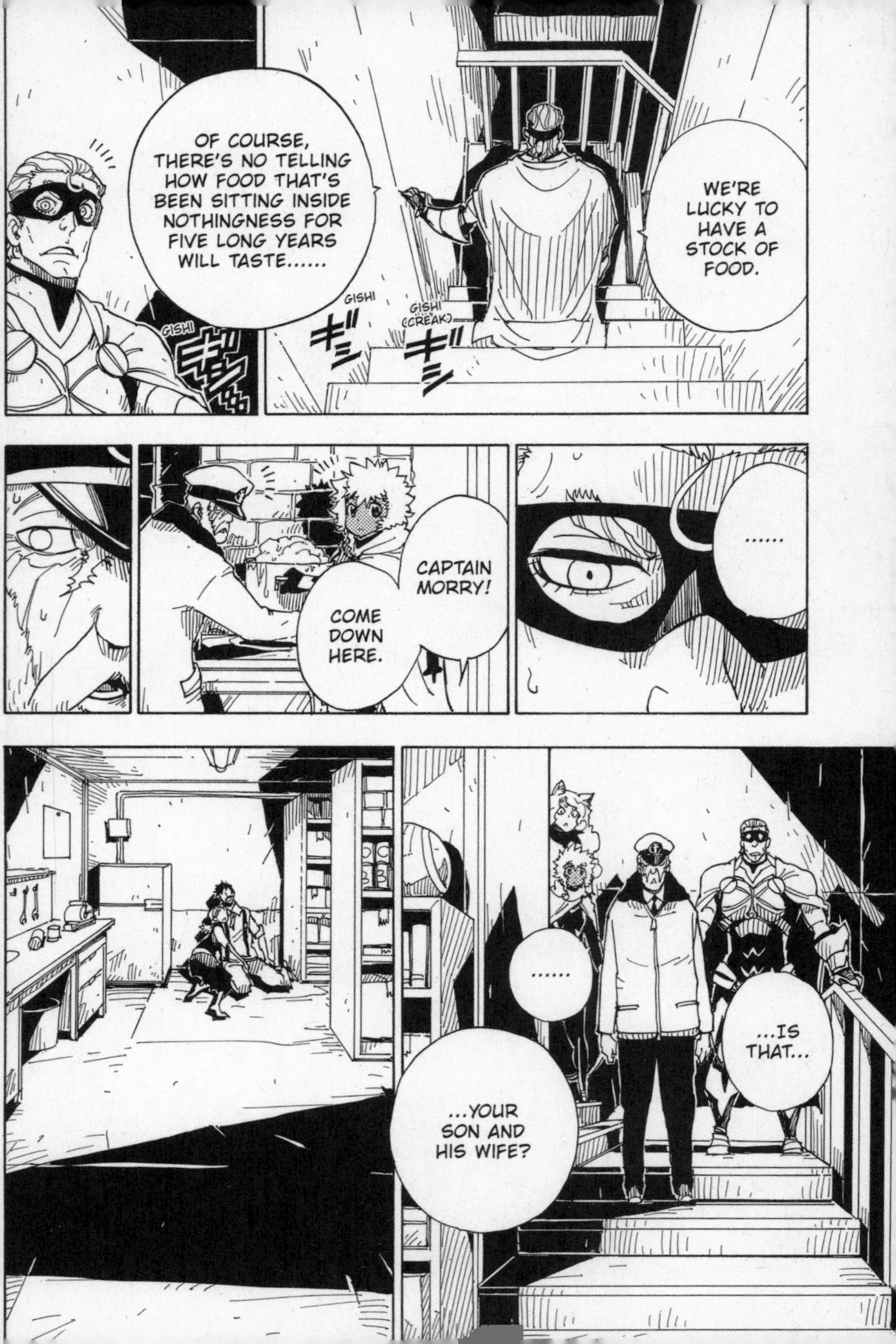

WE'RE LUCKY TO HAVE A STOCK OF FOOD.
GISHI (CREAK)
GISHI
OF COURSE, THERE'S NO TELLING HOW FOOD THAT'S BEEN SITTING INSIDE NOTHINGNESS FOR FIVE LONG YEARS WILL TASTE......
GISHI
......
CAPTAIN MORRY!
COME DOWN HERE.
...IS THAT...
......
...YOUR SON AND HIS WIFE?

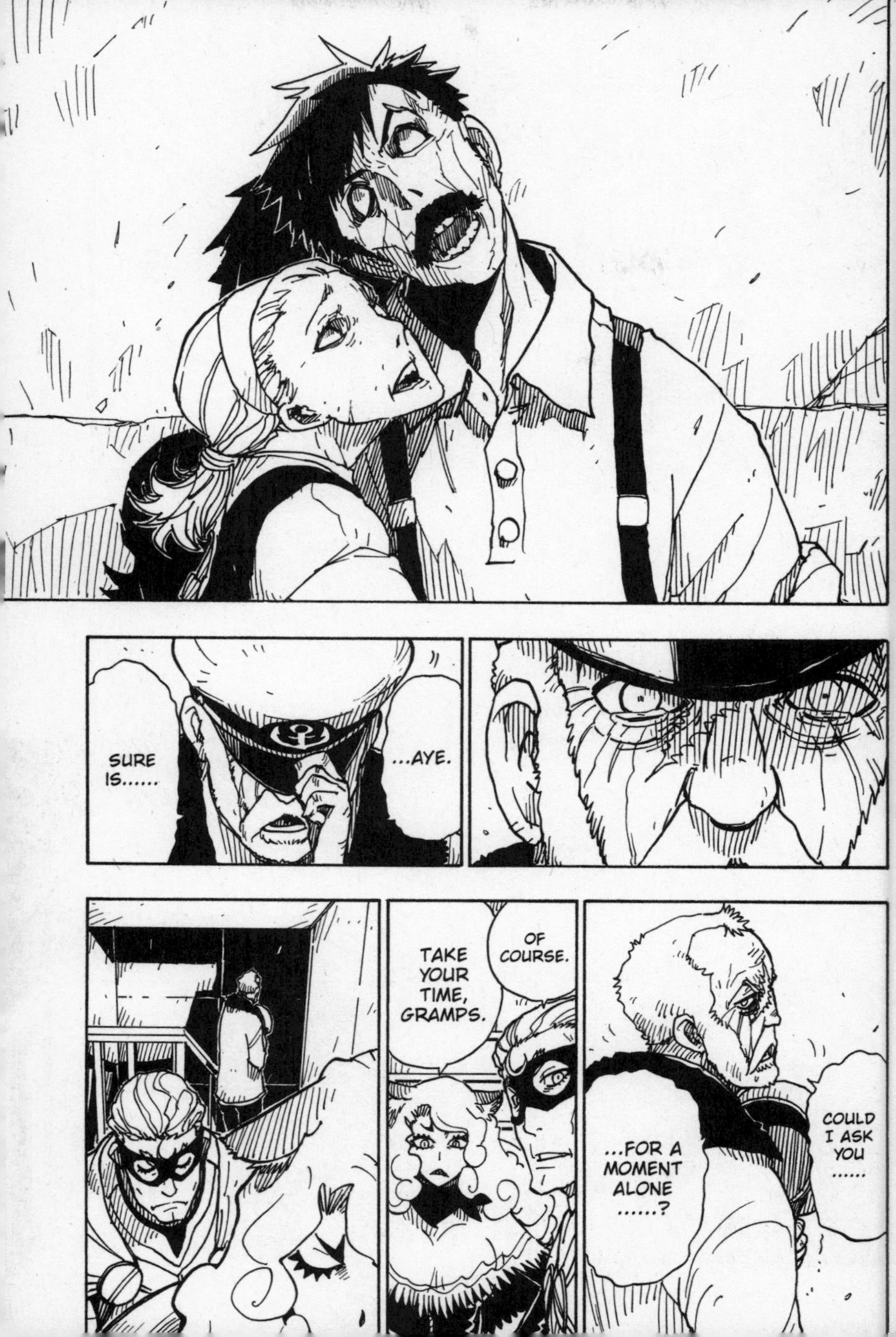
...AYE.
SURE IS......
COULD I ASK YOU ......
...FOR A MOMENT ALONE ......?
OF COURSE.
TAKE YOUR TIME, GRAMPS.

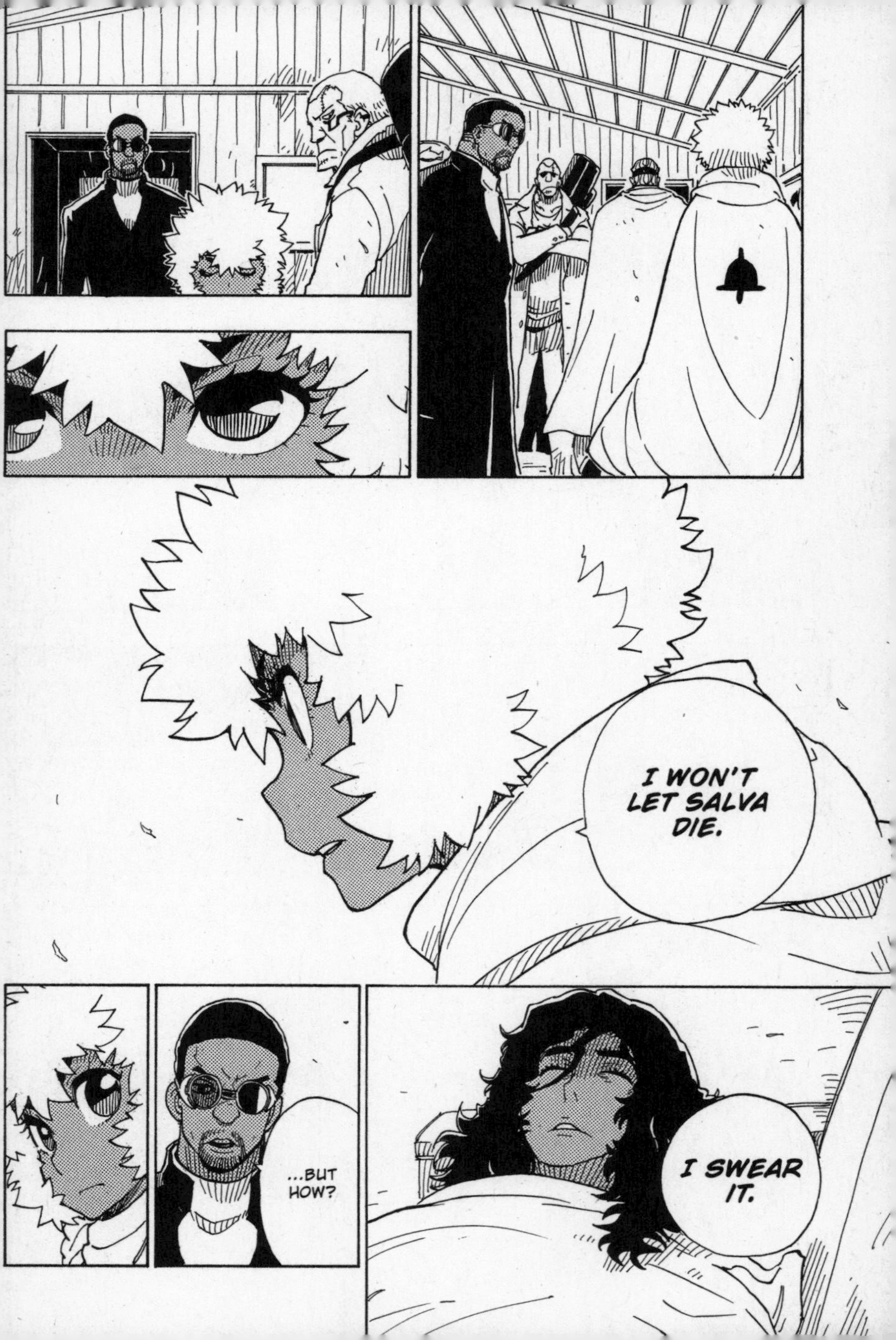
I WON'T LET SALVA DIE.
I SWEAR IT.
...BUT HOW?

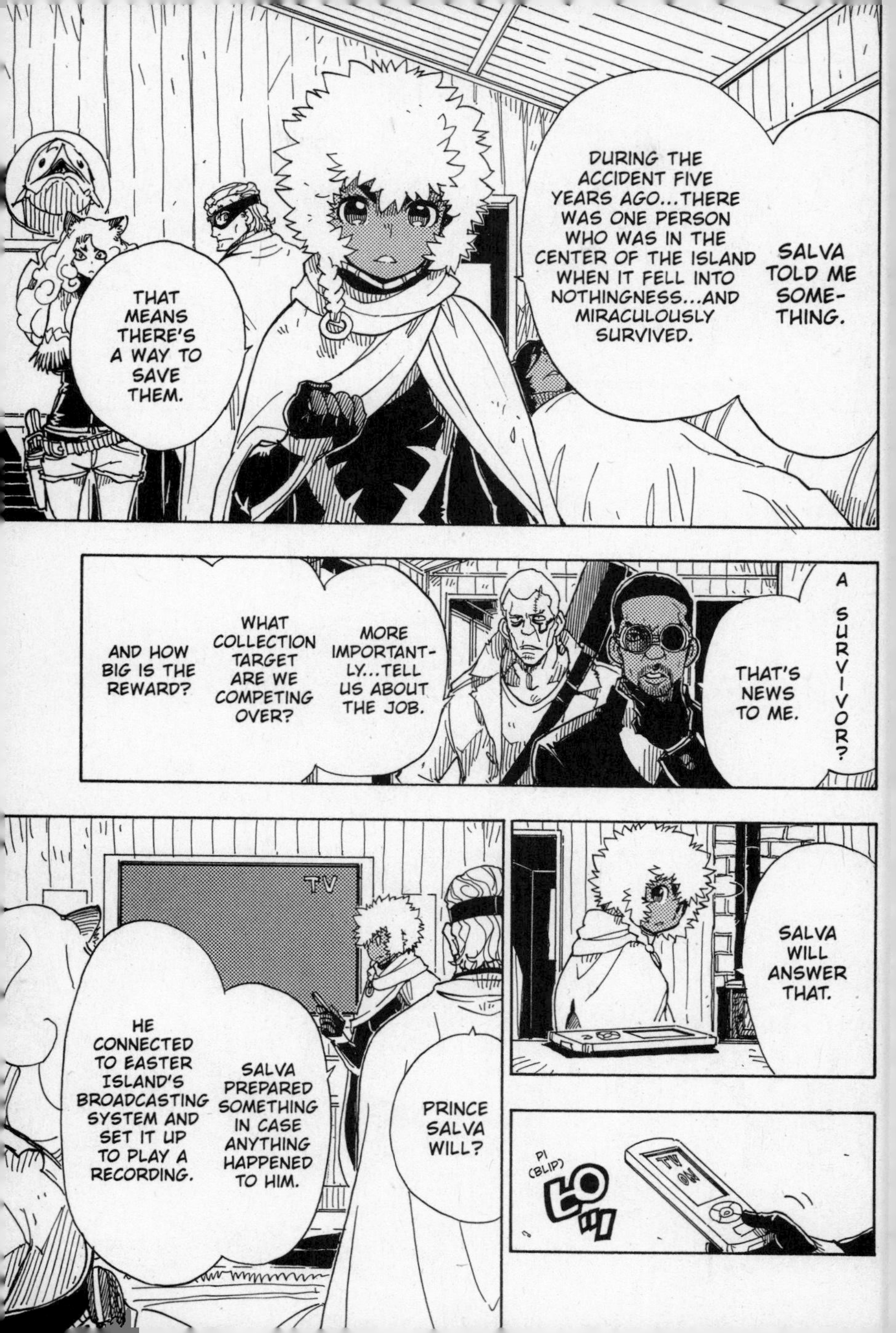
SALVA TOLD ME SOMETHING.
DURING THE ACCIDENT FIVE YEARS AGO...THERE WAS ONE PERSON WHO WAS IN THE CENTER OF THE ISLAND WHEN IT FELL INTO NOTHINGNESS...AND MIRACULOUSLY SURVIVED.
THAT MEANS THERE'S A WAY TO SAVE THEM.
A SURVIVOR?
THAT'S NEWS TO ME.
MORE IMPORTANTLY...TELL US ABOUT THE JOB.
WHAT COLLECTION TARGET ARE WE COMPETING OVER?
AND HOW BIG IS THE REWARD?
SALVA WILL ANSWER THAT.
PI (BLIP)
TV ON
PRINCE SALVA WILL?
SALVA PREPARED SOMETHING IN CASE ANYTHING HAPPENED TO HIM.
HE CONNECTED TO EASTER ISLAND'S BROADCASTING SYSTEM AND SET IT UP TO PLAY A RECORDING.
TV

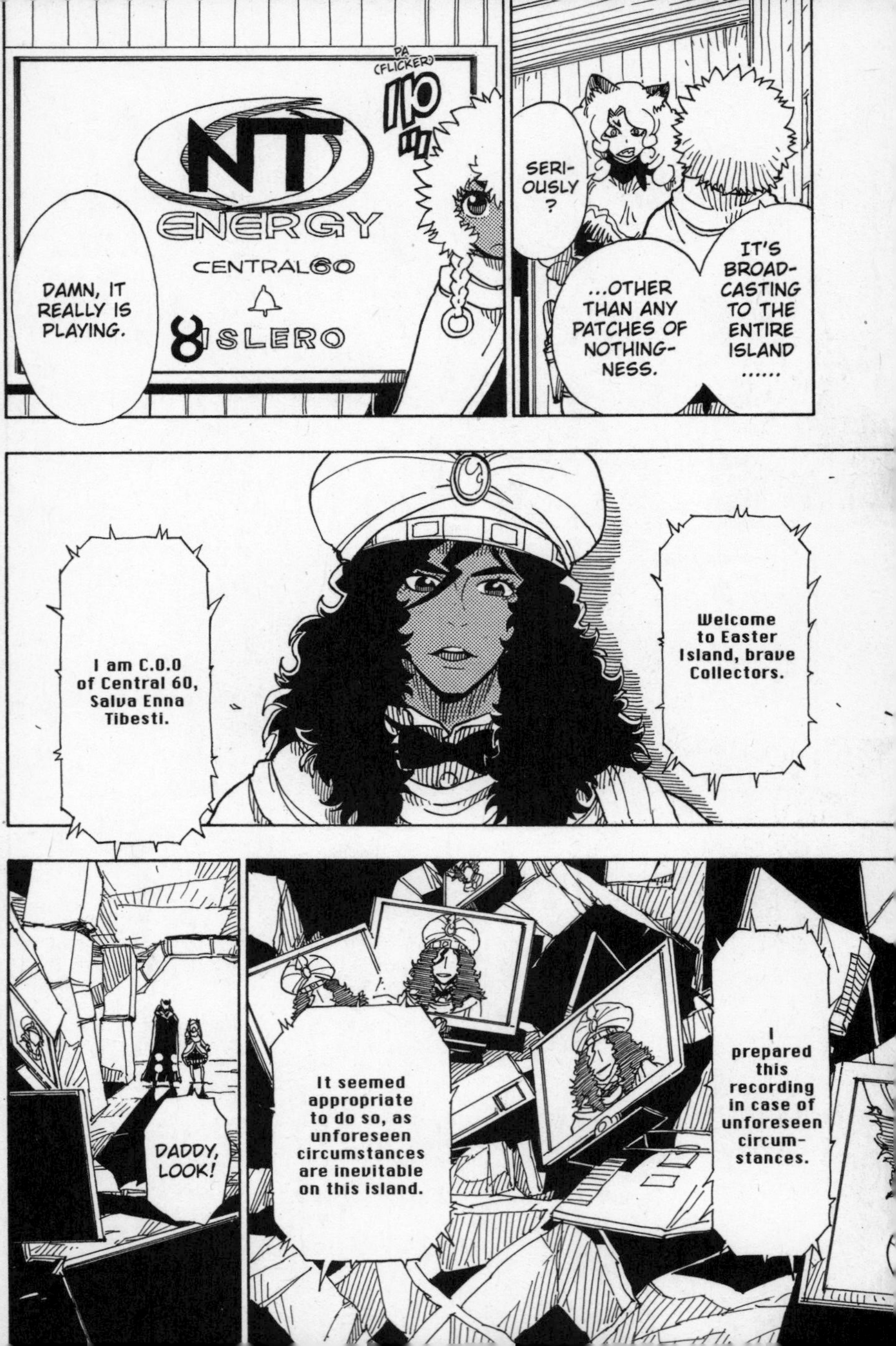
IT'S BROADCASTING TO THE ENTIRE ISLAND ......
...OTHER THAN ANY PATCHES OF NOTHINGNESS.
SERIOUSLY?
PA (FLICKER)
NT ENERGY
CENTRAL60
DAMN, IT REALLY IS PLAYING.
Welcome to Easter Island, brave Collectors.
I am C.O.O of Central 60, Salva Enna Tibesti.
I prepared this recording in case of unforeseen circumstances.
It seemed appropriate to do so, as unforeseen circumstances are inevitable on this island.
DADDY, LOOK!

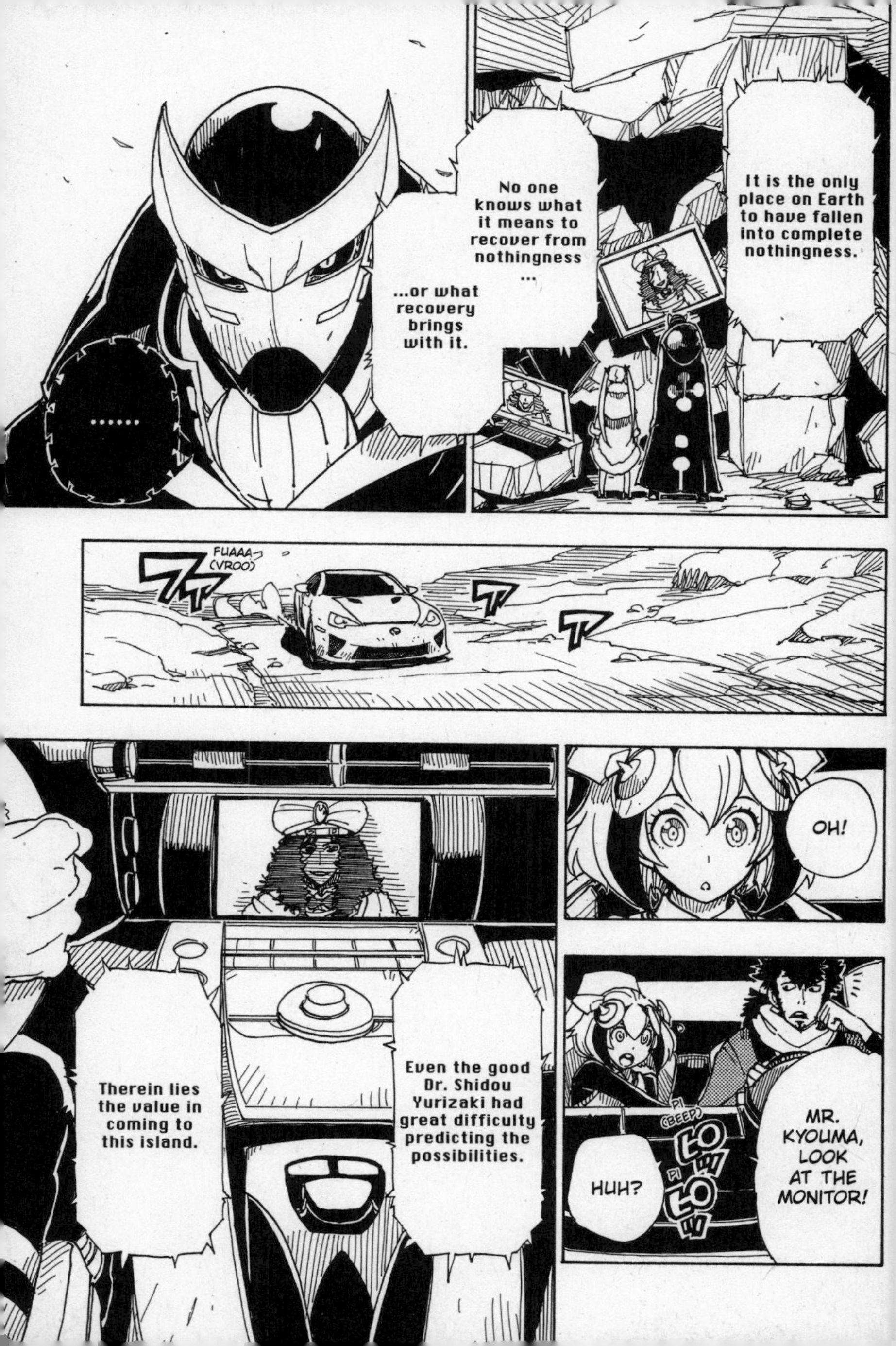
It is the only place on Earth to have fallen into complete nothingness.
No one knows what it means to recover from nothingness ...
...or what recovery brings with it.
......
FUAAA (VROO)
OH!
MR. KYOUMA, LOOK AT THE MONITOR!
PI (BEEP) PI
HUH?
Even the good Dr. Shidou Yurizaki had great difficulty predicting the possibilities.
Therein lies the value in coming to this island.

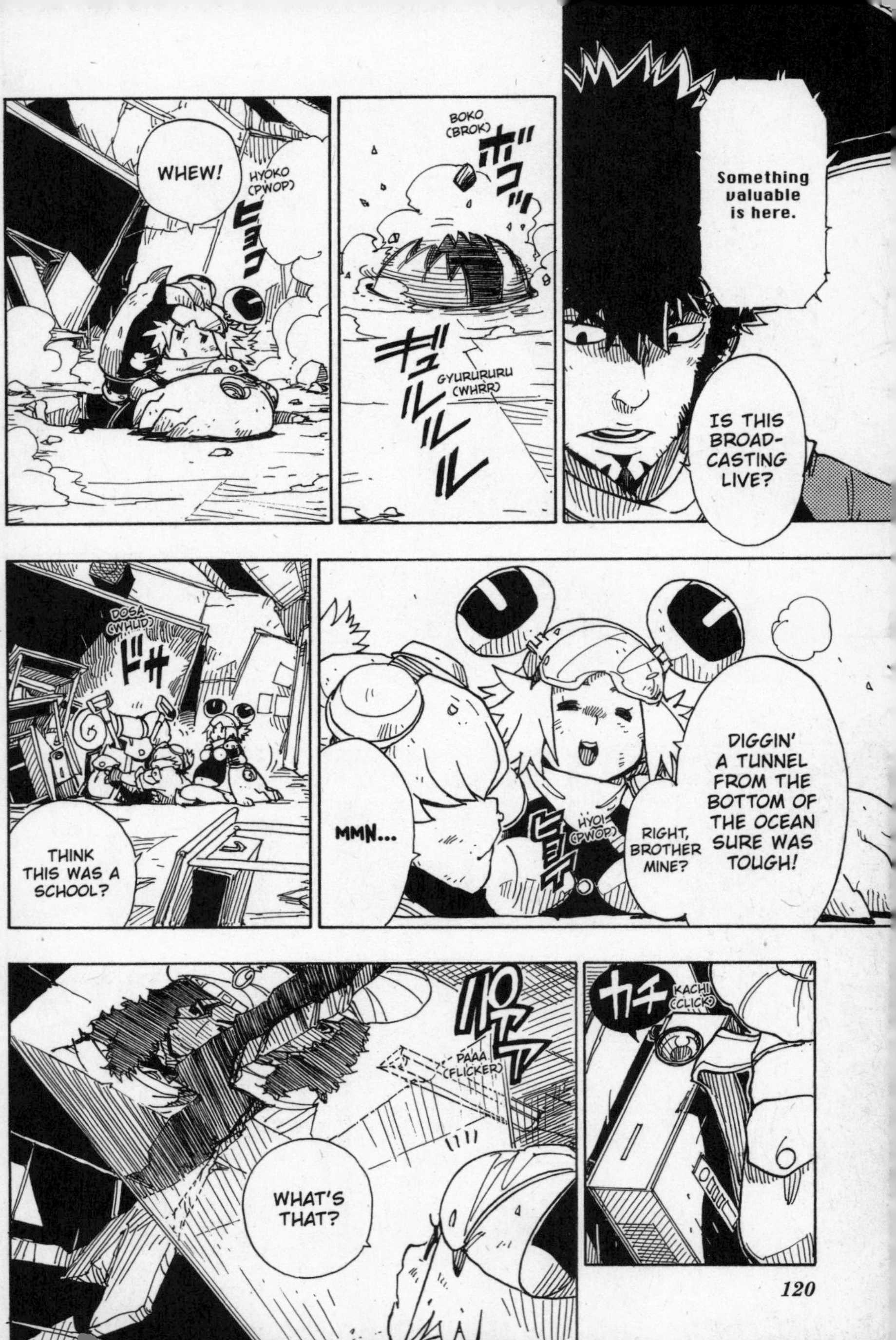

Something valuable is here.
IS THIS BROAD-CASTING LIVE?
BOKO (BROK)
GYURURURU (WHRR)
ギュルルル
WHEW!
HYOKO (PWOP)
ヒョコ
DIGGIN' A TUNNEL FROM THE BOTTOM OF THE OCEAN SURE WAS TOUGH!
RIGHT, BROTHER MINE?
HYOI (PWOP)
ヒョイ
MMN...
DOSA (WHUD)
ドサ
THINK THIS WAS A SCHOOL?
カチ
KACHI (CLICK)
PAAA (FLICKER)
WHAT'S THAT?

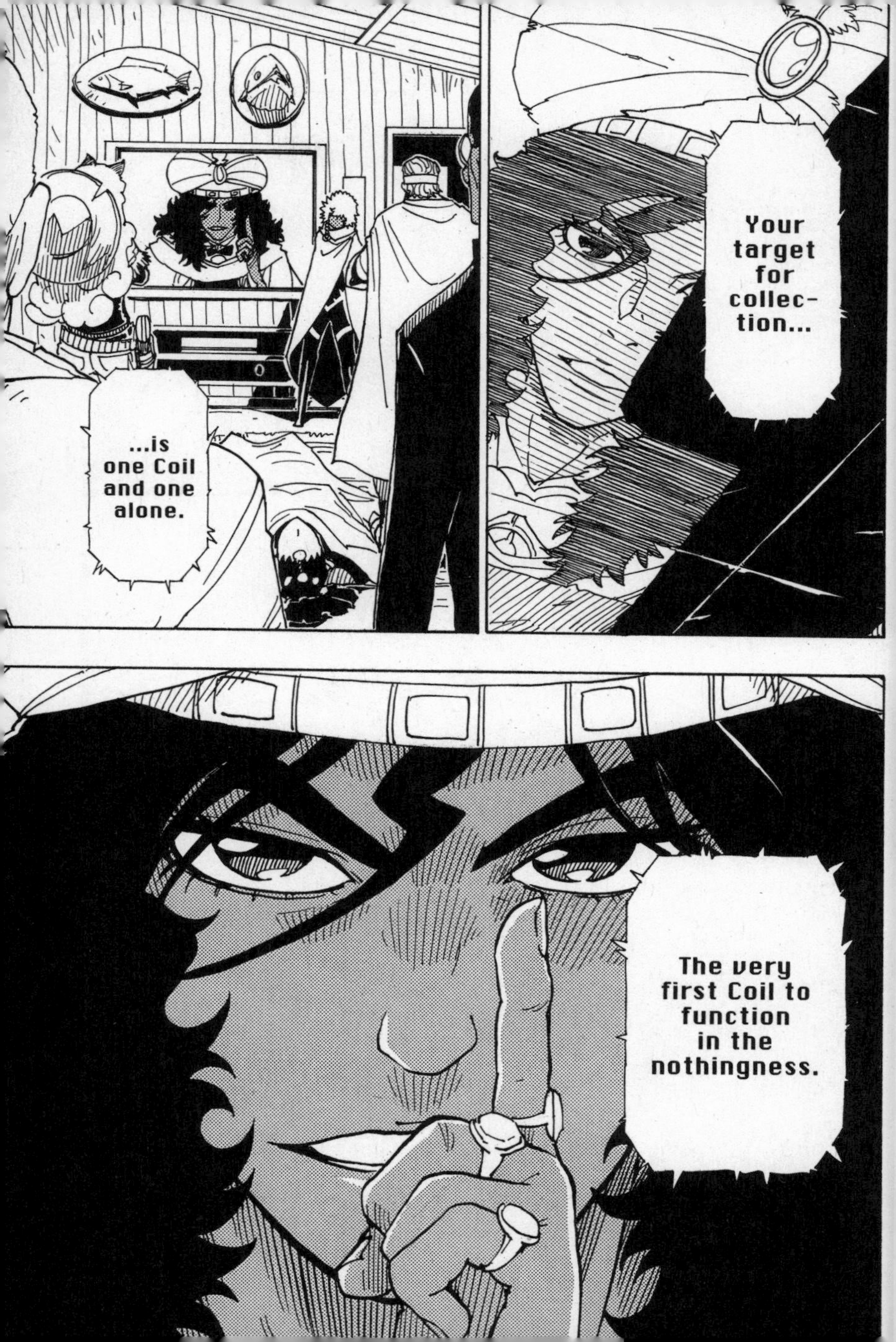
Your target for collection...
...is one Coil and one alone.
The very first Coil to function in the nothingness.

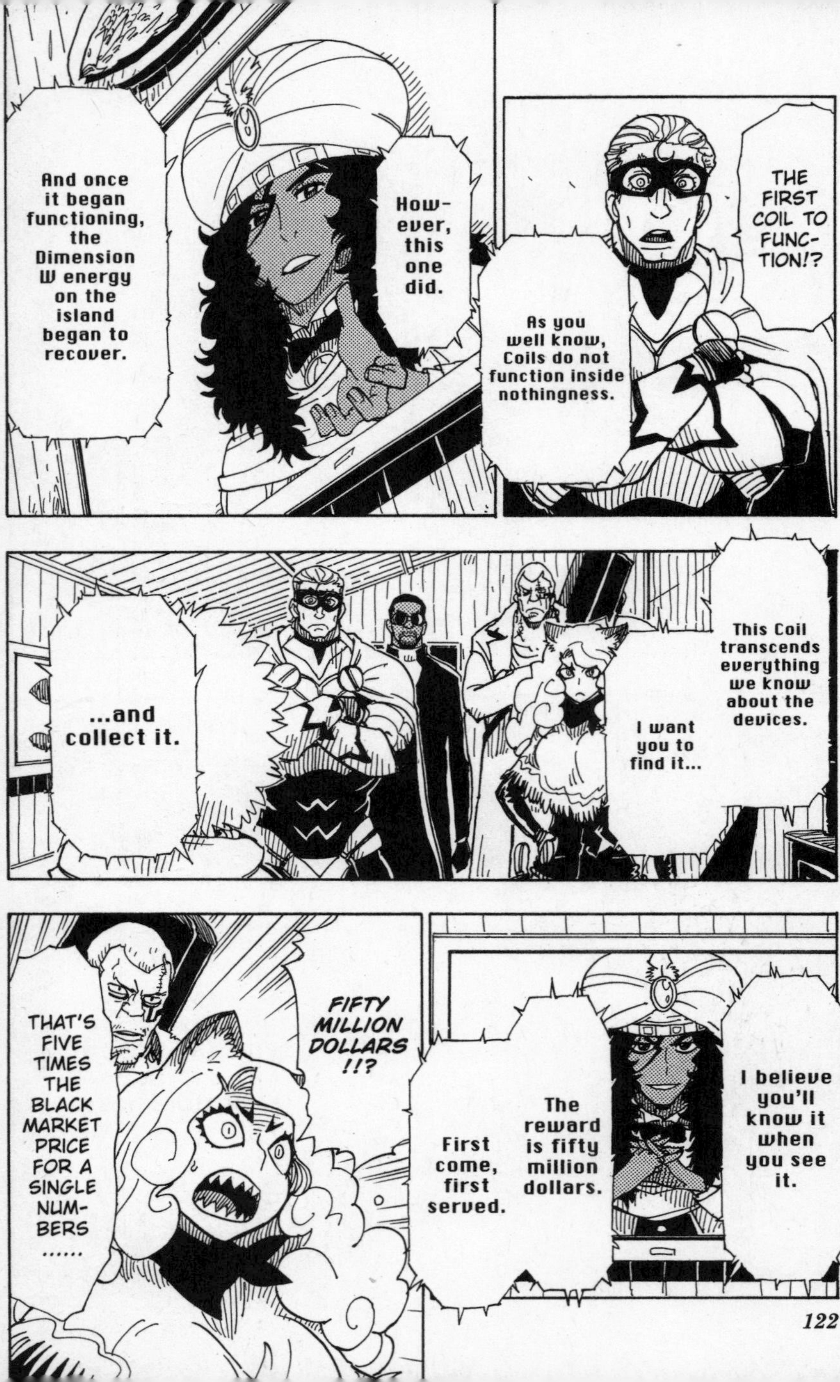
THE FIRST COIL TO FUNCTION!?
As you well know, Coils do not function inside nothingness.
However, this one did.
And once it began functioning, the Dimension W energy on the island began to recover.
This Coil transcends everything we know about the devices.
I want you to find it...
...and collect it.
I believe you'll know it when you see it.
The reward is fifty million dollars.
First come, first served.
FIFTY MILLION DOLLARS!!?
THAT'S FIVE TIMES THE BLACK MARKET PRICE FOR A SINGLE NUMBERS......

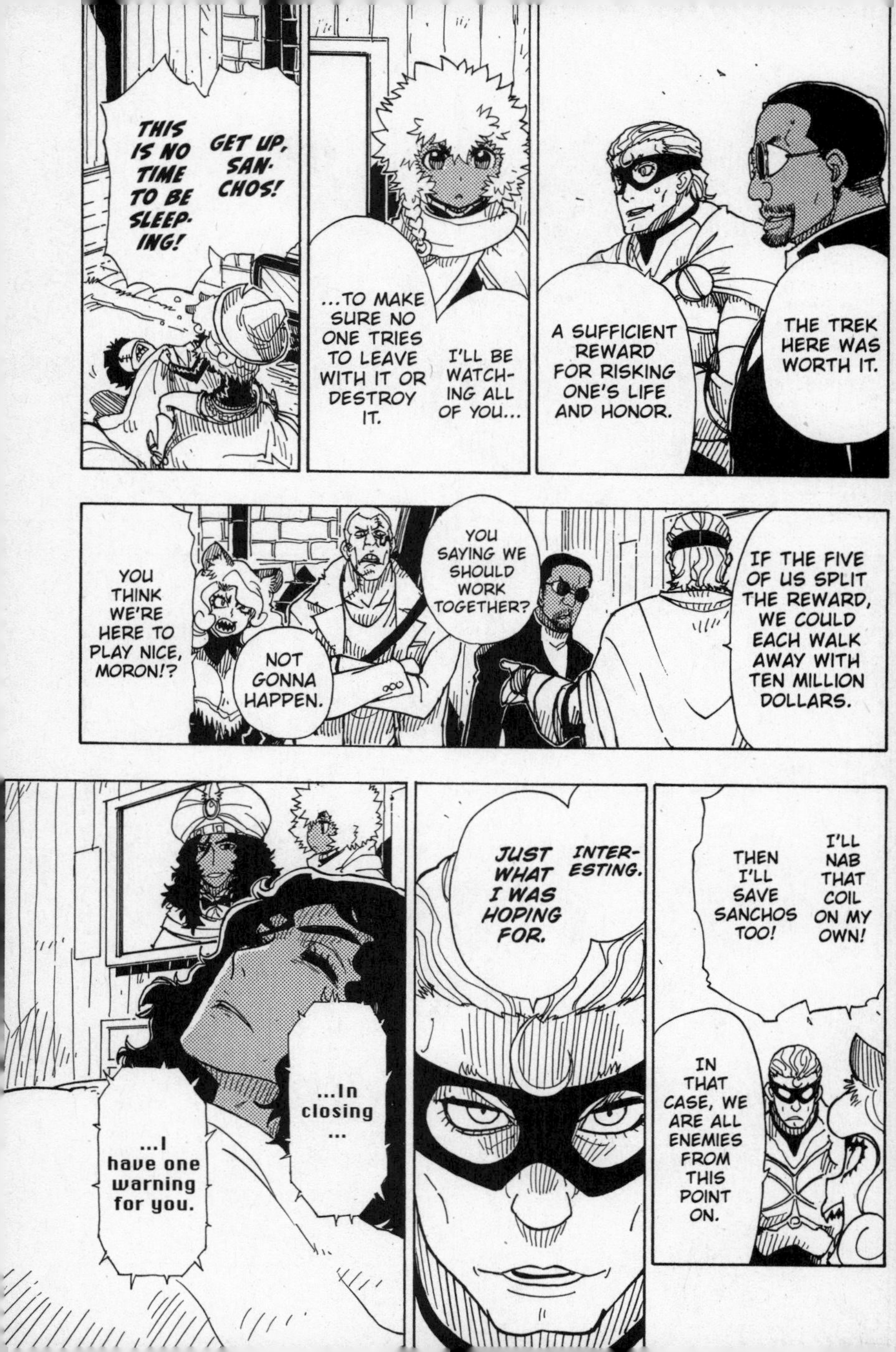
THE TREK HERE WAS WORTH IT.
A SUFFICIENT REWARD FOR RISKING ONE'S LIFE AND HONOR.
I'LL BE WATCHING ALL OF YOU...
...TO MAKE SURE NO ONE TRIES TO LEAVE WITH IT OR DESTROY IT.
GET UP, SANCHOS!
THIS IS NO TIME TO BE SLEEPING!
IF THE FIVE OF US SPLIT THE REWARD, WE COULD EACH WALK AWAY WITH TEN MILLION DOLLARS.
YOU SAYING WE SHOULD WORK TOGETHER?
NOT GONNA HAPPEN.
YOU THINK WE'RE HERE TO PLAY NICE, MORON!?
I'LL NAB THAT COIL ON MY OWN!
THEN I'LL SAVE SANCHOS TOO!
IN THAT CASE, WE ARE ALL ENEMIES FROM THIS POINT ON.
INTERESTING.
JUST WHAT I WAS HOPING FOR.
...In closing...
...I have one warning for you.

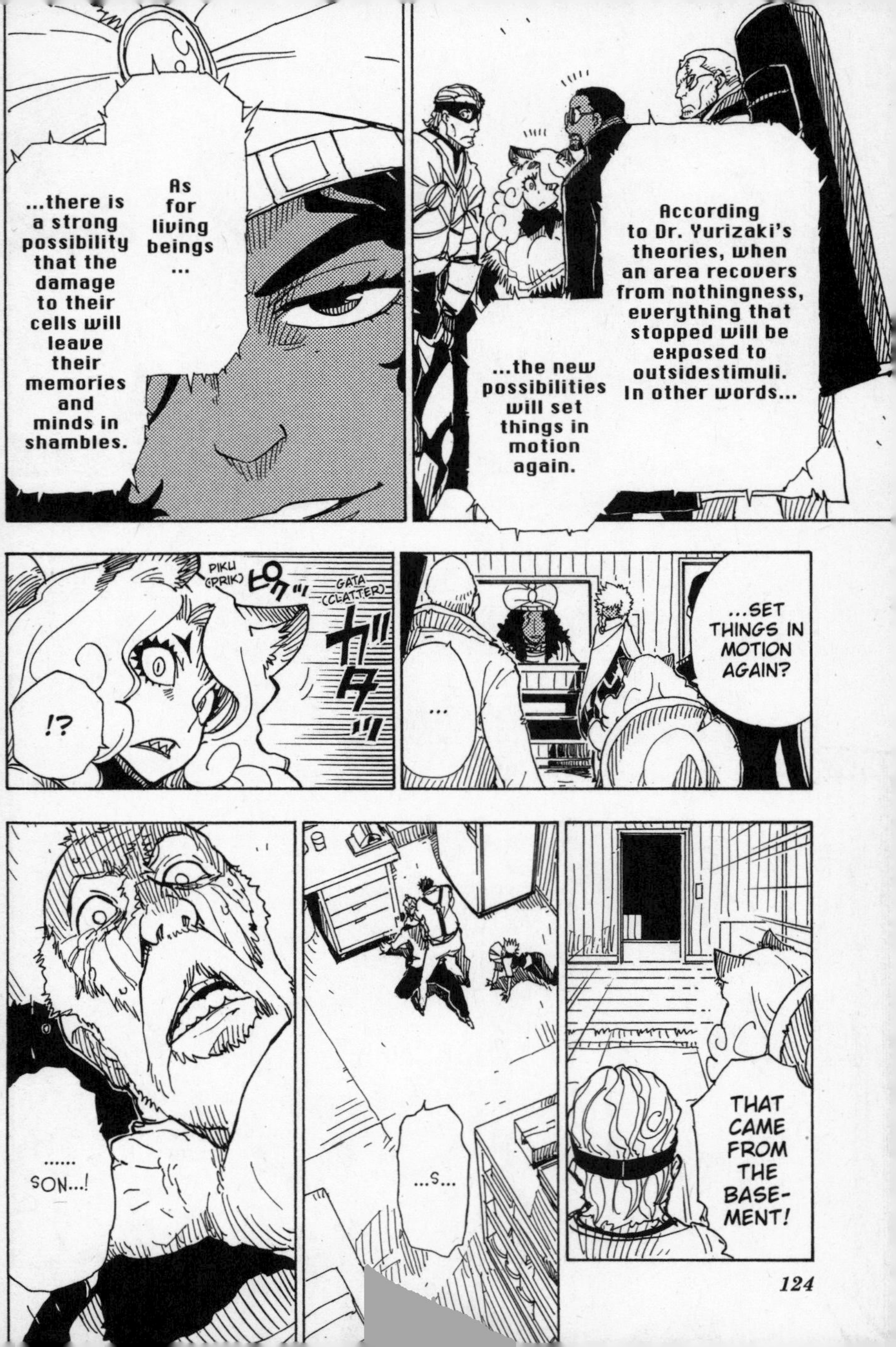
According to Dr. Yurizaki's theories, when an area recovers from nothingness, everything that stopped will be exposed to outsidestimuli. In other words...
...the new possibilities will set things in motion again.
As for living beings...
...there is a strong possibility that the damage to their cells will leave their memories and minds in shambles.
...SET THINGS IN MOTION AGAIN?
...
PIKU (PRIK)
GATA (CLATTER)
!?
THAT CAME FROM THE BASEMENT!
...S...
...... SON...!

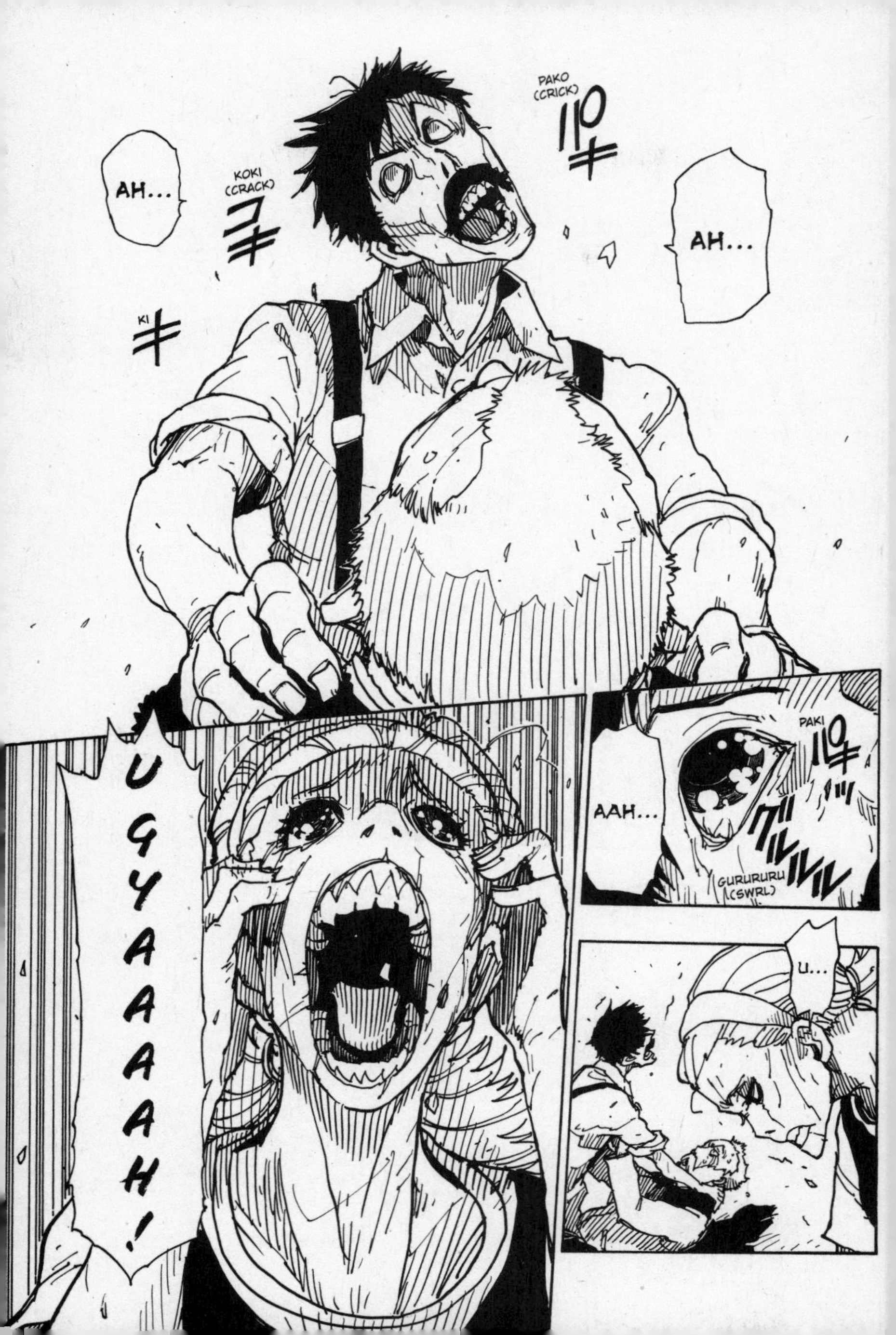
PAKO (CRICK)
AH...
KOKI (CRACK)
AH...
KI
PAKI
AAH...
GURURURU (SWRL)
U...
UGYAAAAAH!

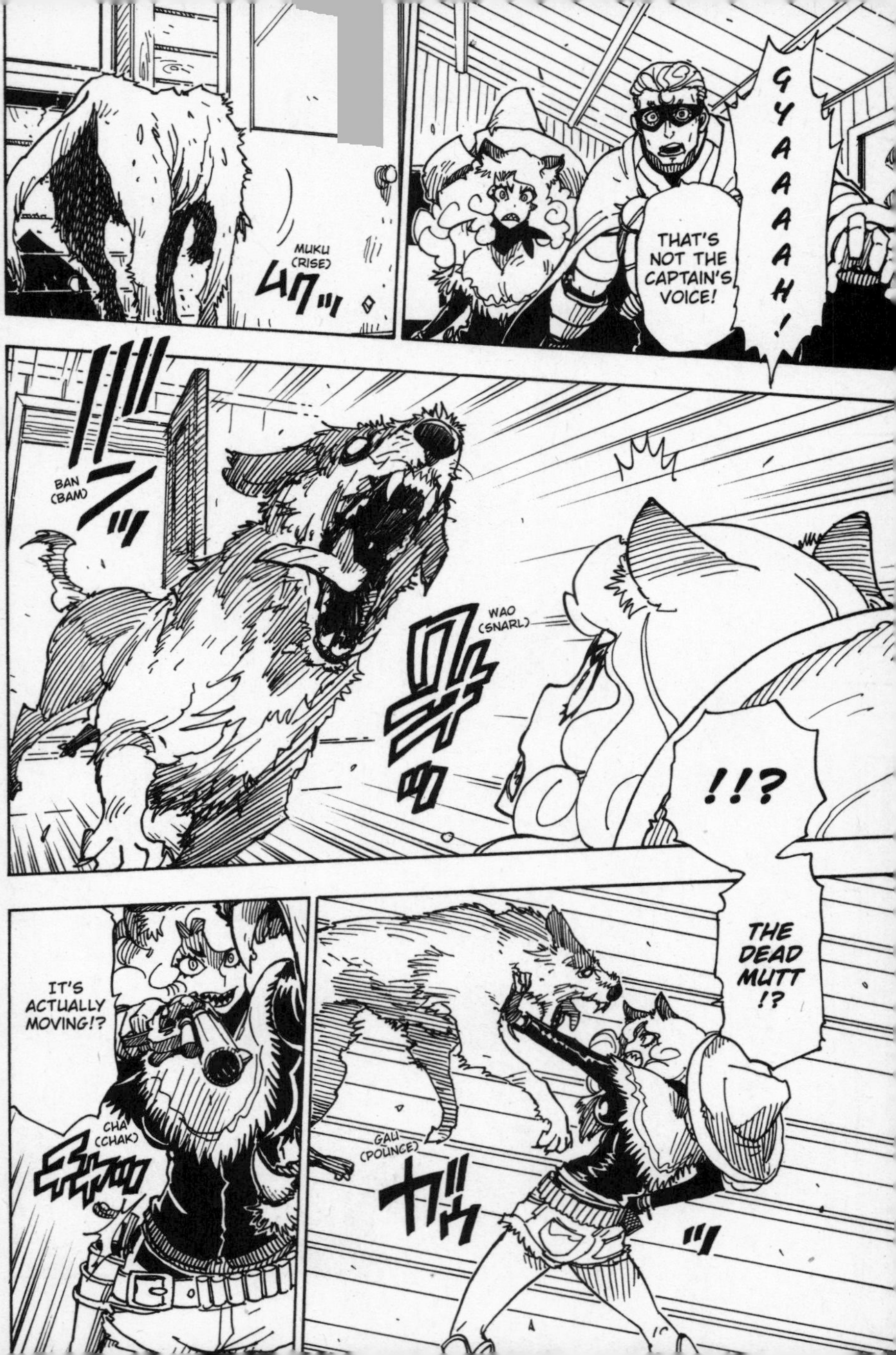
GYAAAAAH!
THAT'S NOT THE CAPTAIN'S VOICE!
MUKU (RISE)
ムクッ
!!?
WAO (SNARL)
ワオッ
BAN (BAM)
バンッ
THE DEAD MUTT!?
GAU (POUNCE)
ガウッ
IT'S ACTUALLY MOVING!?
CHA (CHAK)
チャッ

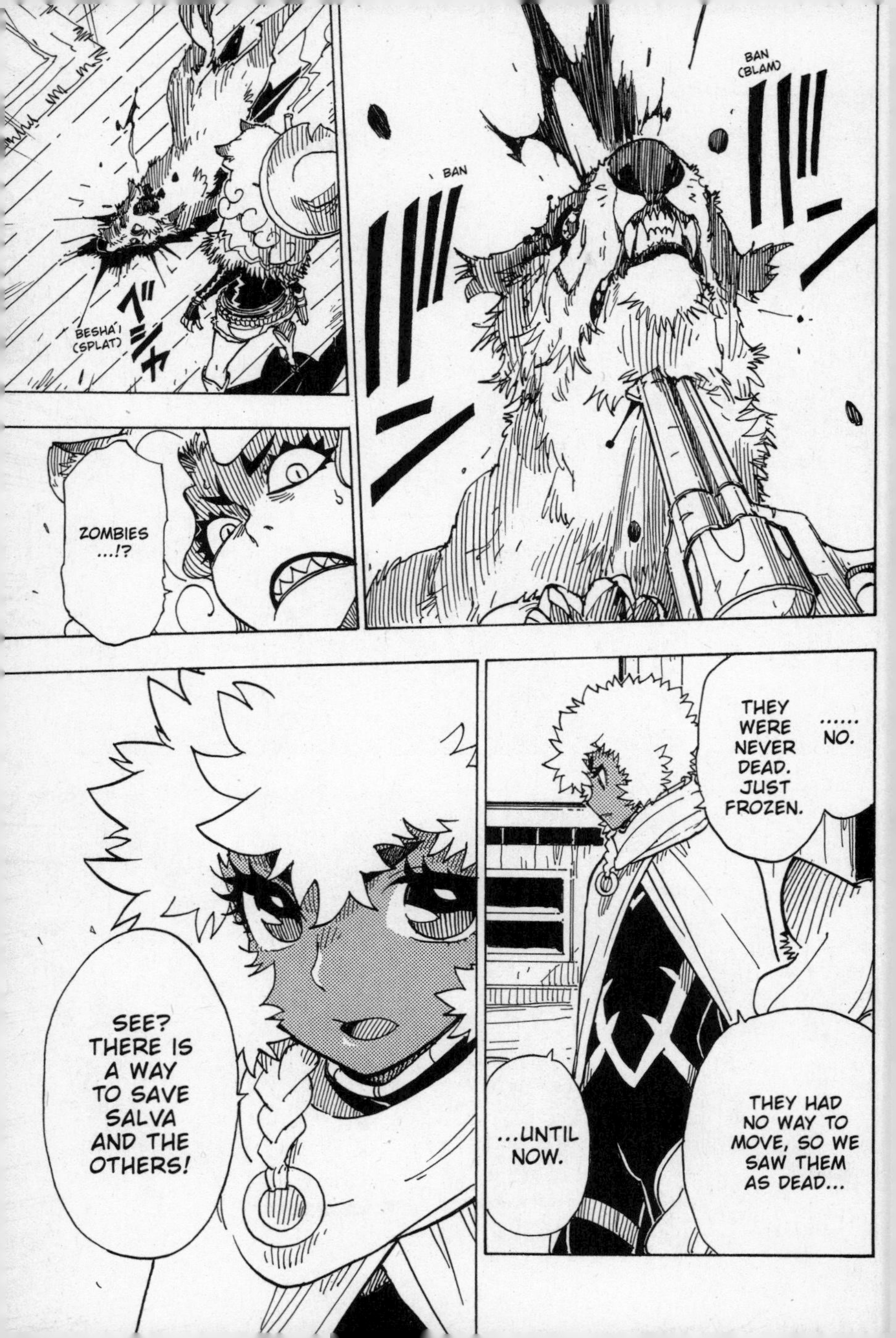
BAN (BLAM)
BAN
BESHA (SPLAT)
ZOMBIES ...!?
...... NO.
THEY WERE NEVER DEAD. JUST FROZEN.
THEY HAD NO WAY TO MOVE, SO WE SAW THEM AS DEAD...
...UNTIL NOW.
SEE? THERE IS A WAY TO SAVE SALVA AND THE OTHERS!

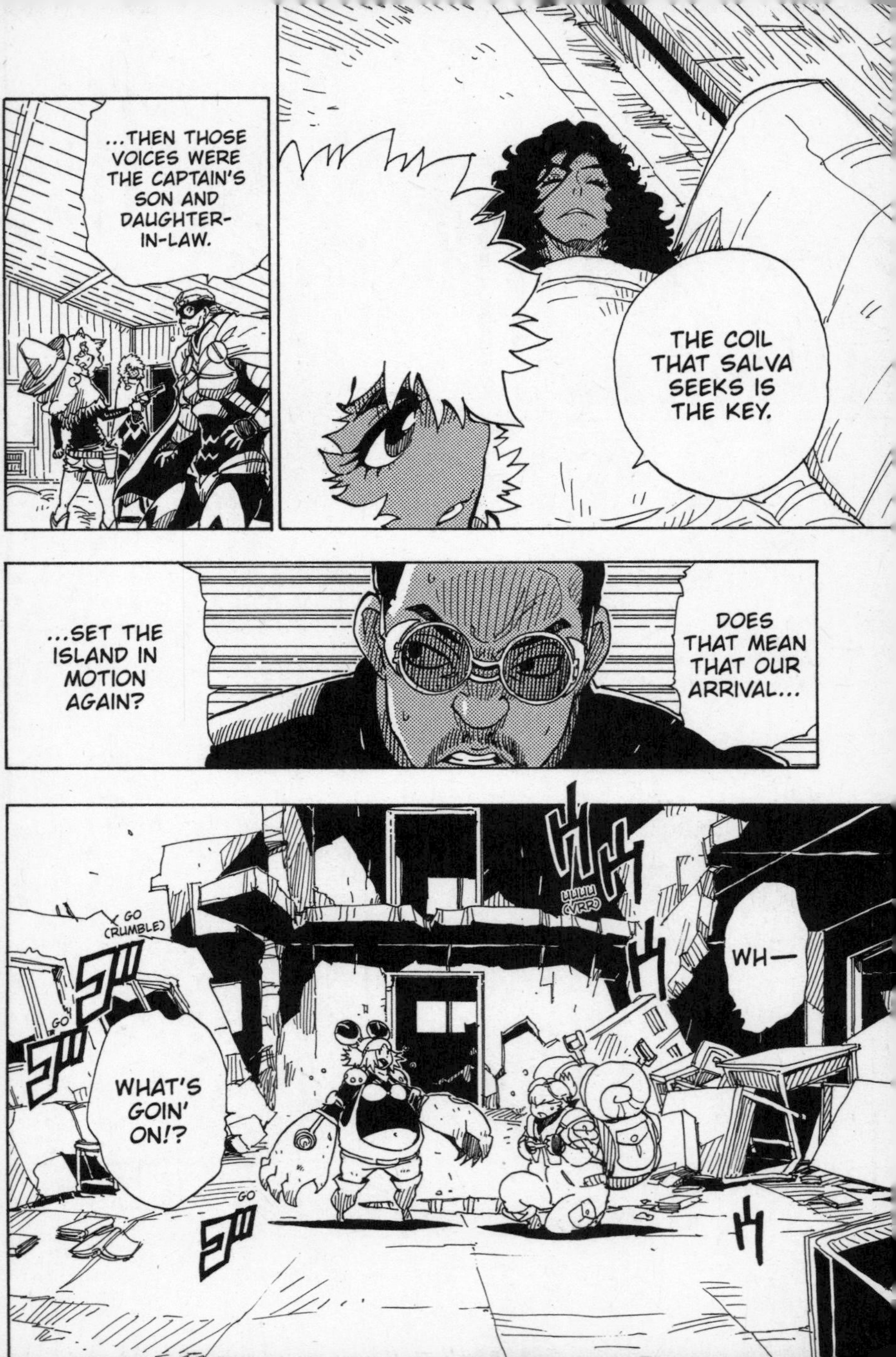
THE COIL THAT SALVA SEEKS IS THE KEY.
...THEN THOSE VOICES WERE THE CAPTAIN'S SON AND DAUGHTER-IN-LAW.
DOES THAT MEAN THAT OUR ARRIVAL...
...SET THE ISLAND IN MOTION AGAIN?
WH—
(VRR)
GO (RUMBLE)
GO
WHAT'S GOIN' ON!?
GO

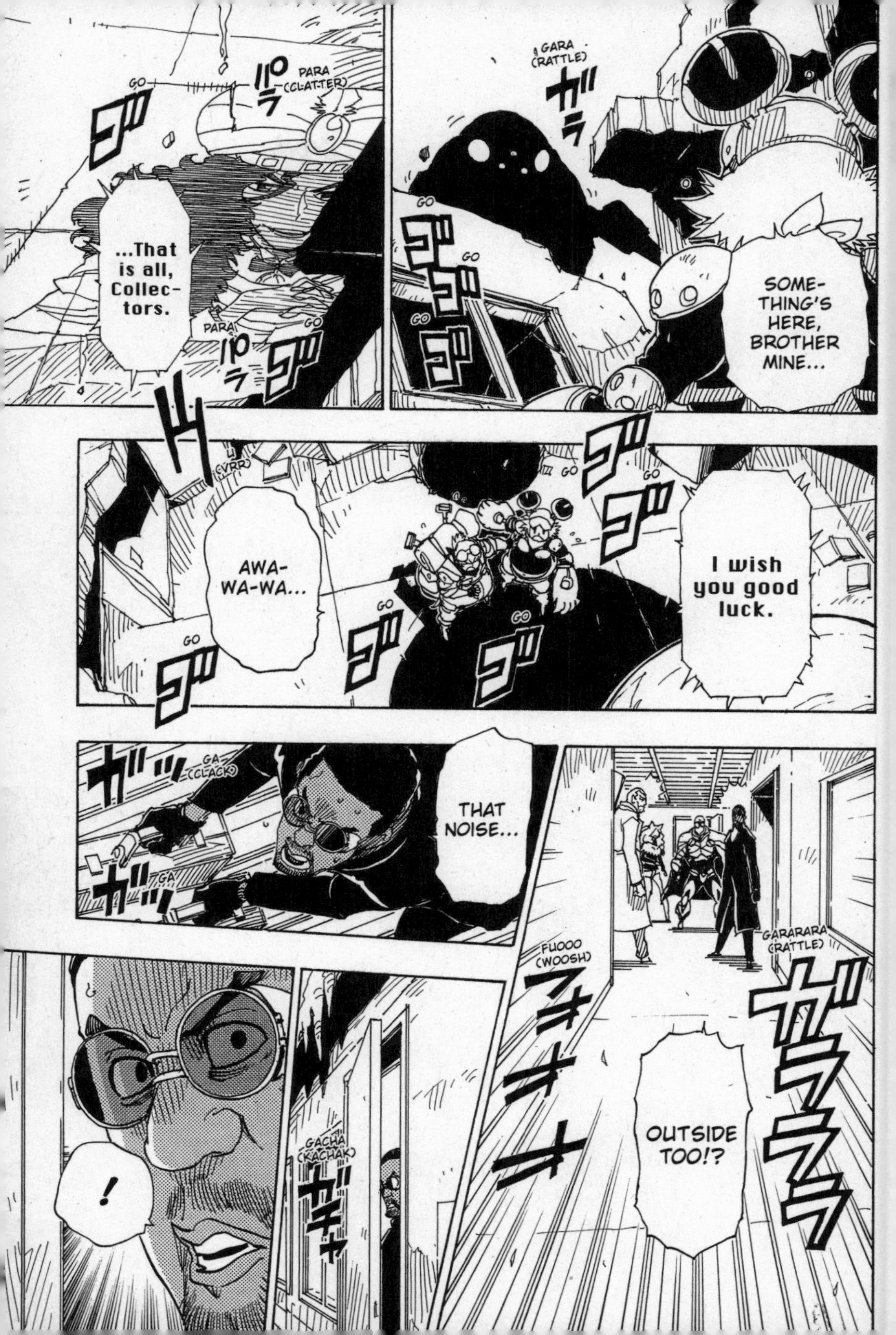
GARA (RATTLE)
GO
GO
GO
SOME-THING'S HERE, BROTHER MINE...
PARA (CLATTER)
GO
...That is all, Collectors.
PARA
GO
VRR
GO
GO
I wish you good luck.
GO
GO
AWA-WA-WA...
GO
GARARARA (RATTLE)
FUOOO (WOOSH)
OUTSIDE TOO!?
THAT NOISE...
GA (CLACK)
GA
GACHA (KACHAK)
!

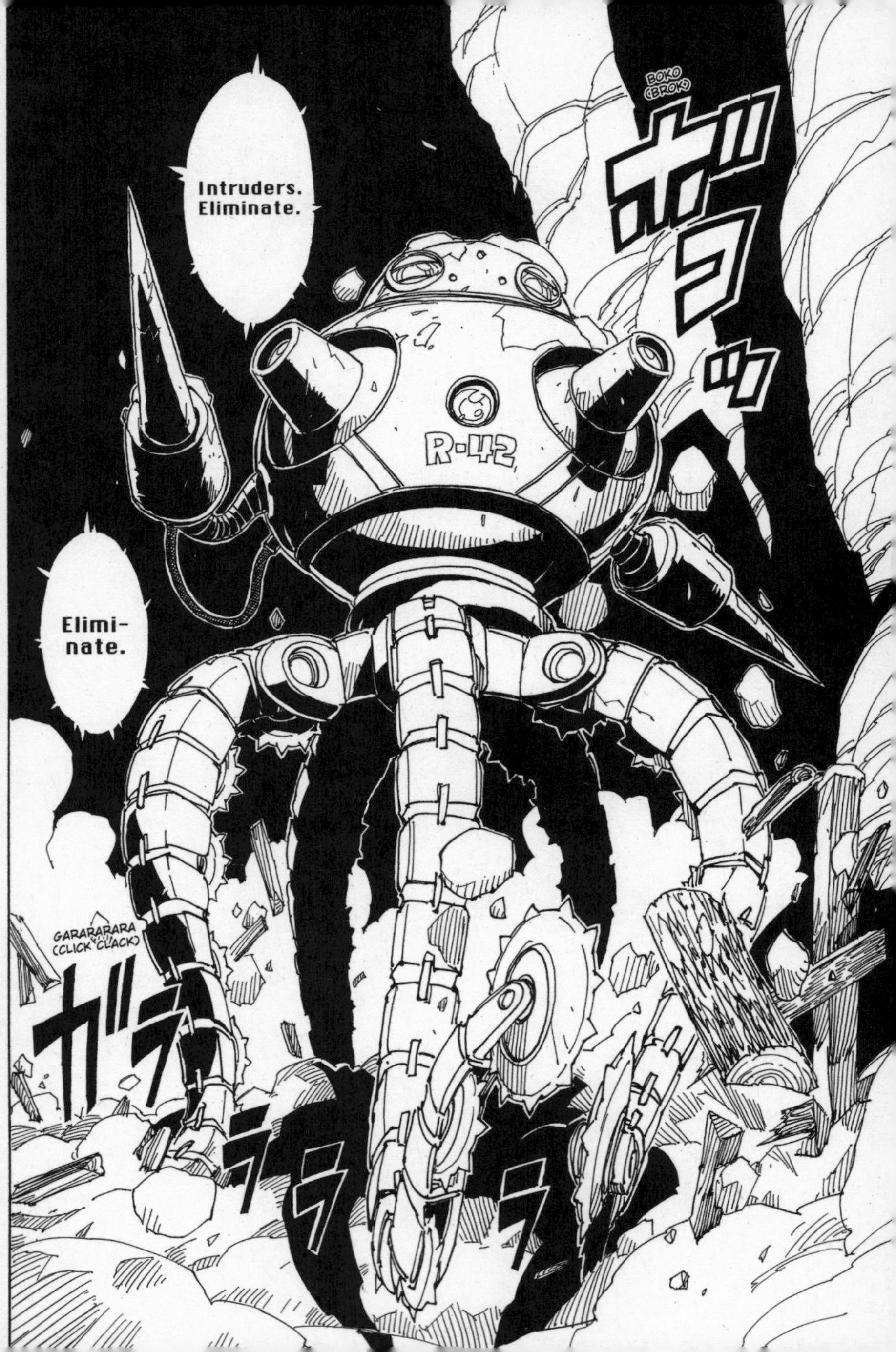
BOKO (BROK)
Intruders. Eliminate.
Elimi-nate.
GARARARARA (CLICK CLACK)

## FILE.45
## OLD ENEMIES

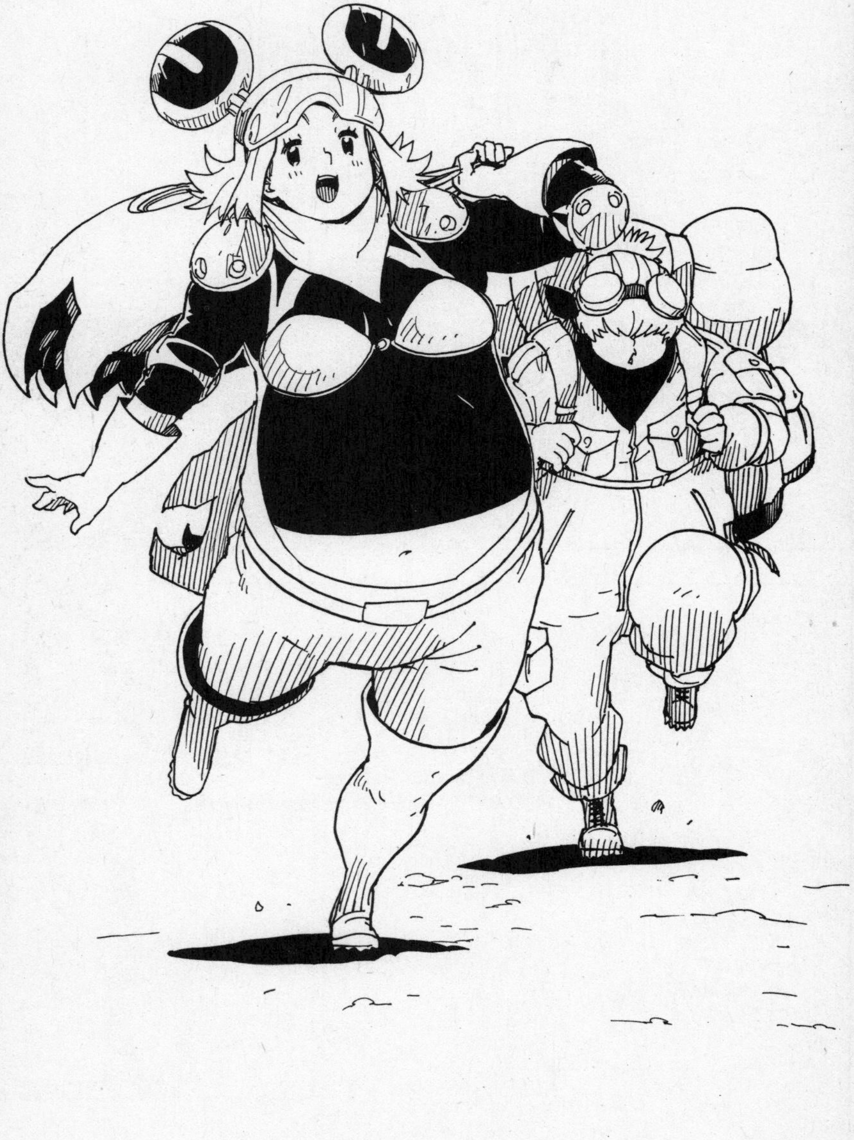

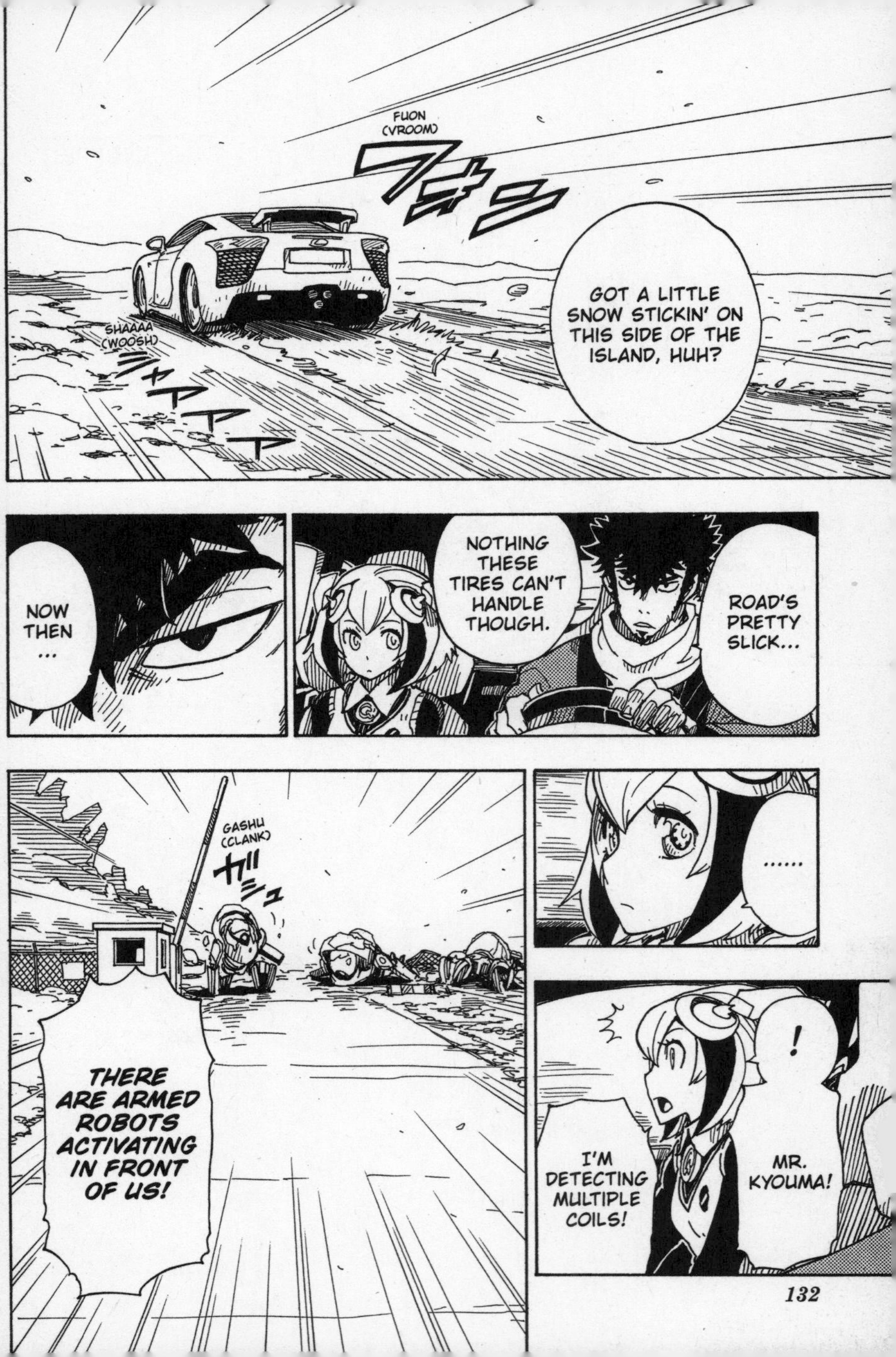
FUON (VROOM)
GOT A LITTLE SNOW STICKIN' ON THIS SIDE OF THE ISLAND, HUH?
SHAAAA (WOOSH)
ROAD'S PRETTY SLICK...
NOTHING THESE TIRES CAN'T HANDLE THOUGH.
NOW THEN ...
......
!
MR. KYOUMA!
I'M DETECTING MULTIPLE COILS!
GASHU (CLANK)
THERE ARE ARMED ROBOTS ACTIVATING IN FRONT OF US!

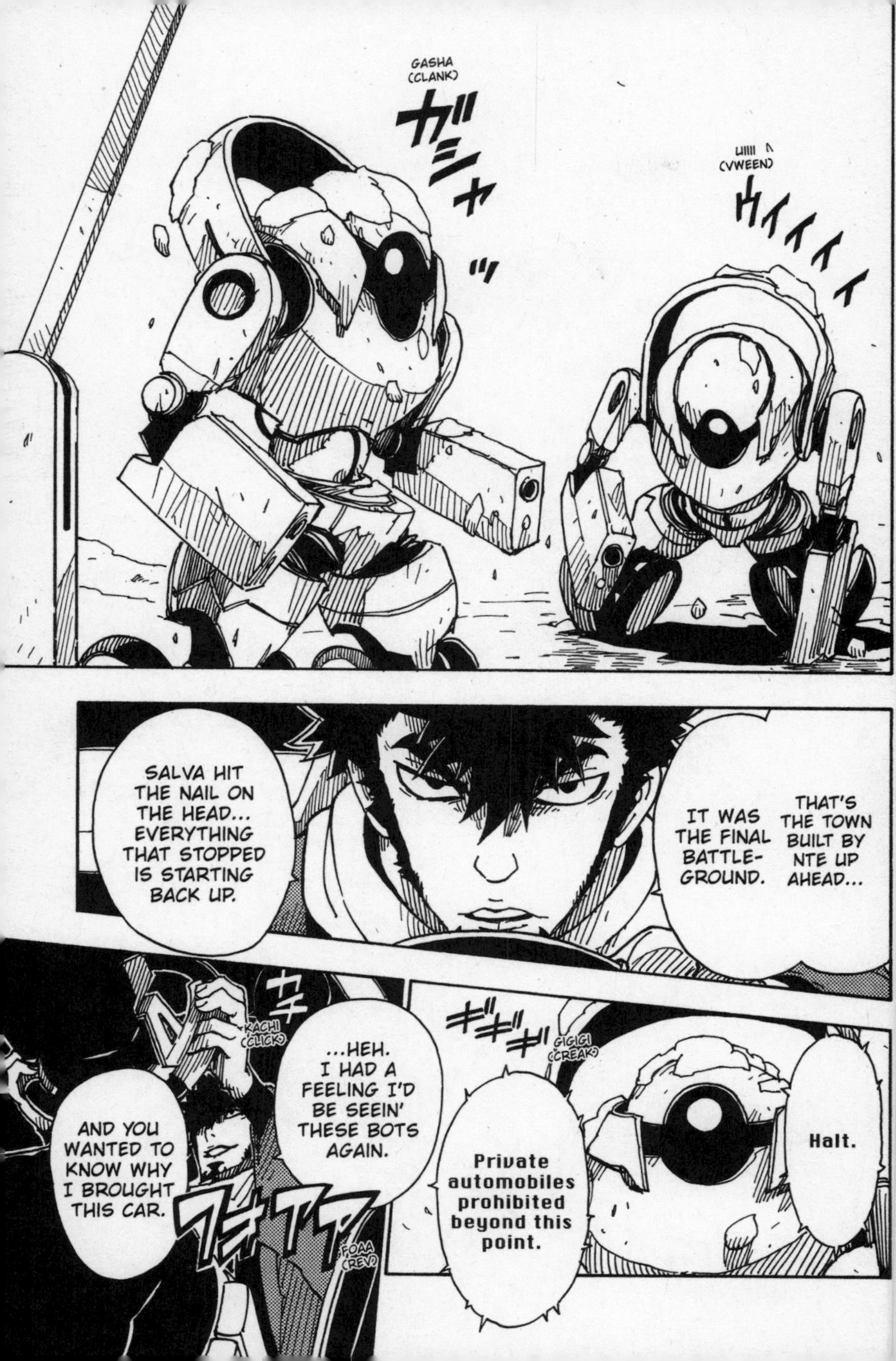
ウイイイイ
UIIII (VWEEN)
ガシャッ
GASHA (CLANK)
THAT'S THE TOWN BUILT BY NTE UP AHEAD...
IT WAS THE FINAL BATTLE-GROUND.
SALVA HIT THE NAIL ON THE HEAD... EVERYTHING THAT STOPPED IS STARTING BACK UP.
Halt.
Private automobiles prohibited beyond this point.
ギギギ
GIGIGI (CREAK)
...HEH. I HAD A FEELING I'D BE SEEIN' THESE BOTS AGAIN.
カチ
KACHI (CLICK)
AND YOU WANTED TO KNOW WHY I BROUGHT THIS CAR.
フォアア
FOAA (REV)

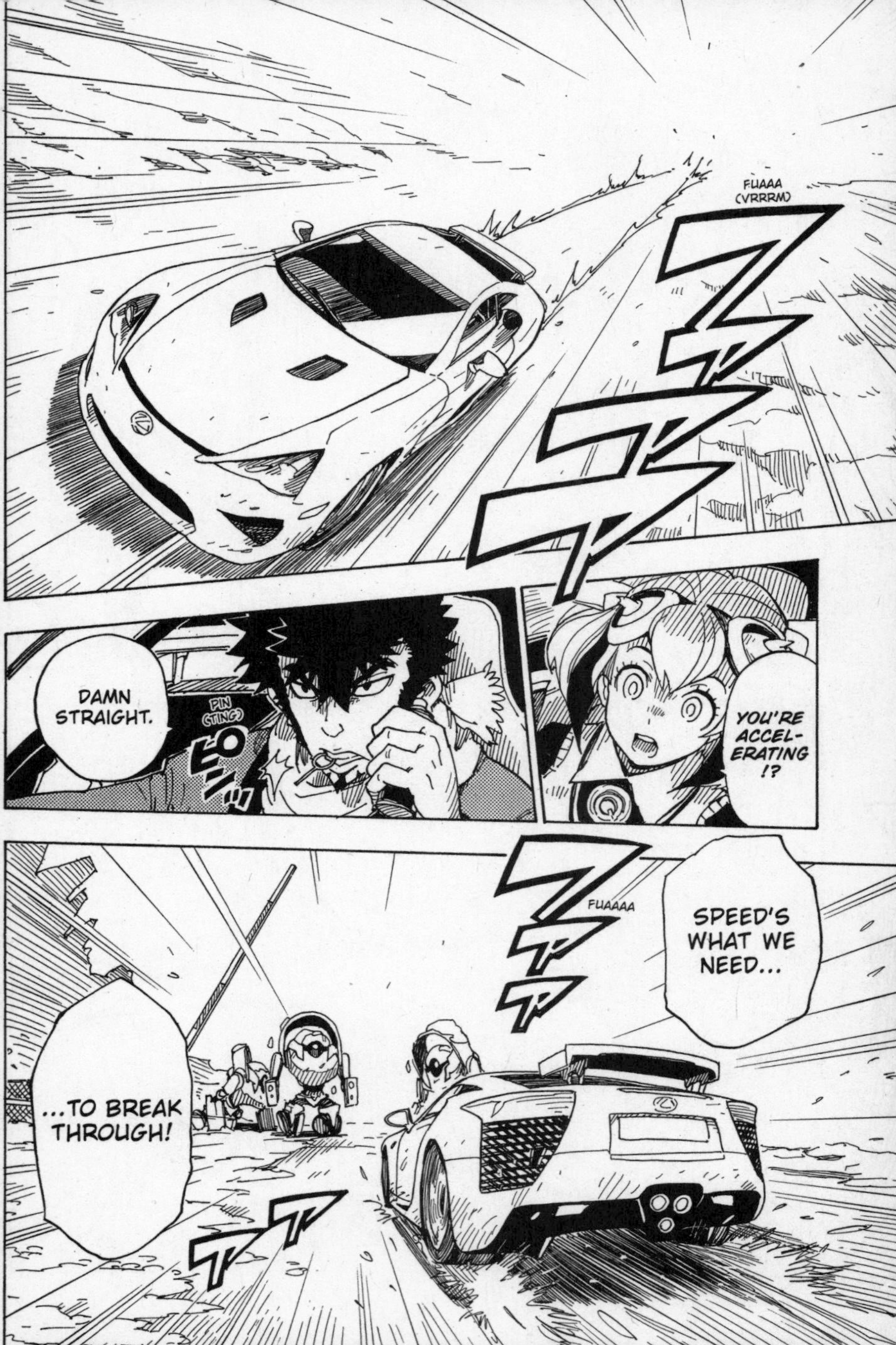
FUAAA
(VRRRM)
YOU'RE ACCEL-ERATING !?
DAMN STRAIGHT.
PIN
(TING)
SPEED'S WHAT WE NEED...
FUAAAA
...TO BREAK THROUGH!

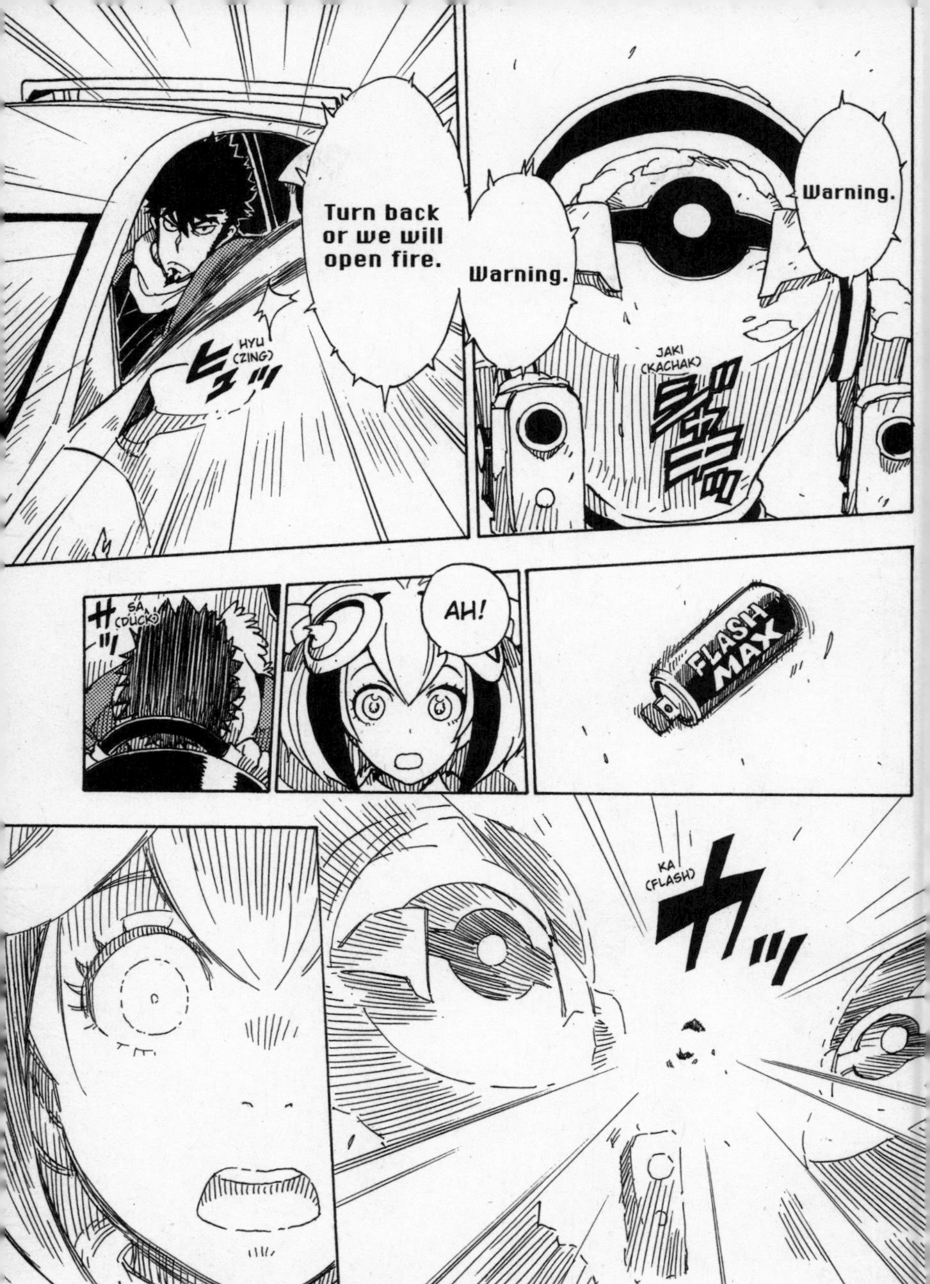
Warning.
Warning.
JAKI (KACHAK)
Turn back or we will open fire.
HYU (ZING)
FLASH MAX
AH!
SA (DUCK)
KA (FLASH)

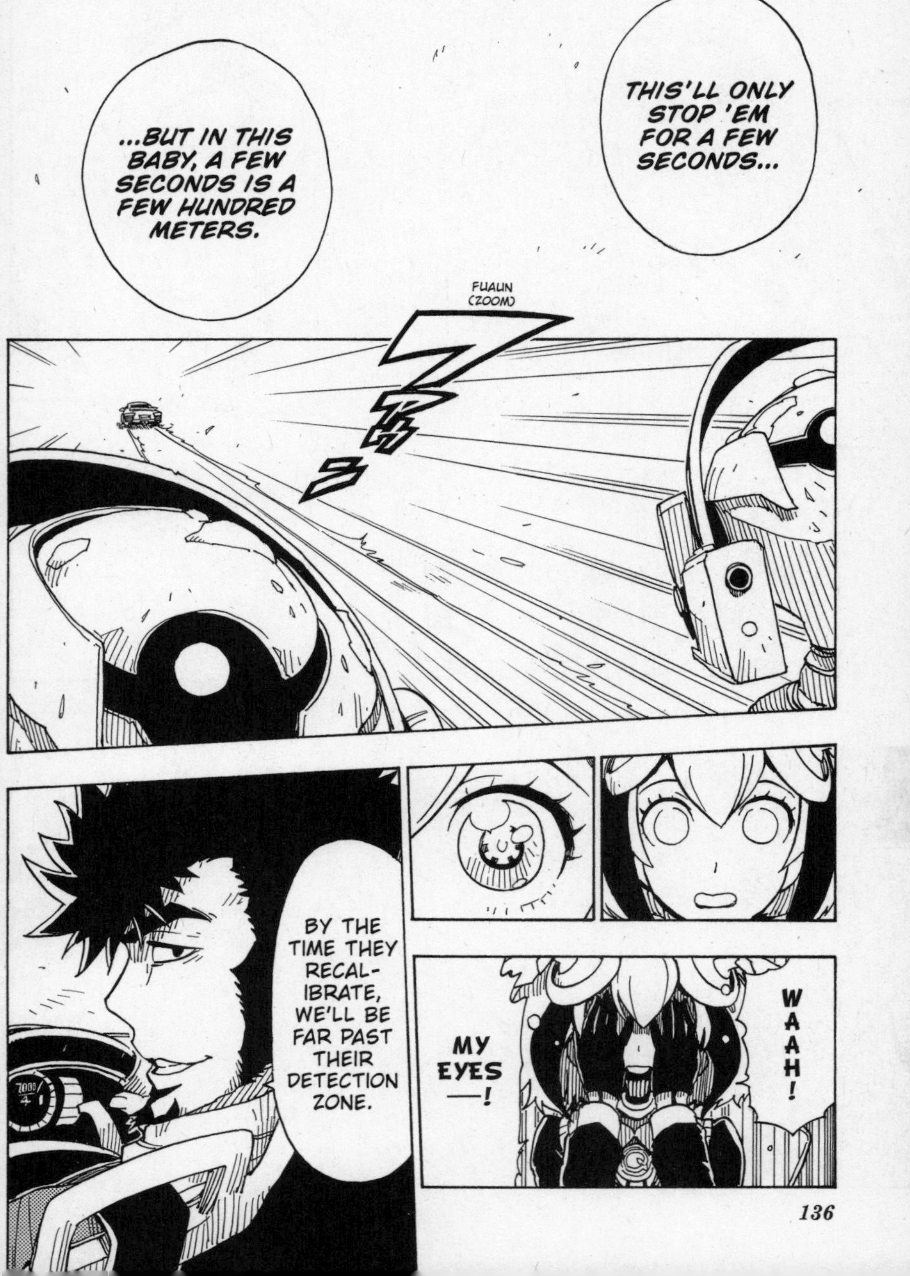
THIS'LL ONLY STOP 'EM FOR A FEW SECONDS...
...BUT IN THIS BABY, A FEW SECONDS IS A FEW HUNDRED METERS.
FUAUN (ZOOM)
WAAH!
MY EYES—!
BY THE TIME THEY RECAL-IBRATE, WE'LL BE FAR PAST THEIR DETECTION ZONE.

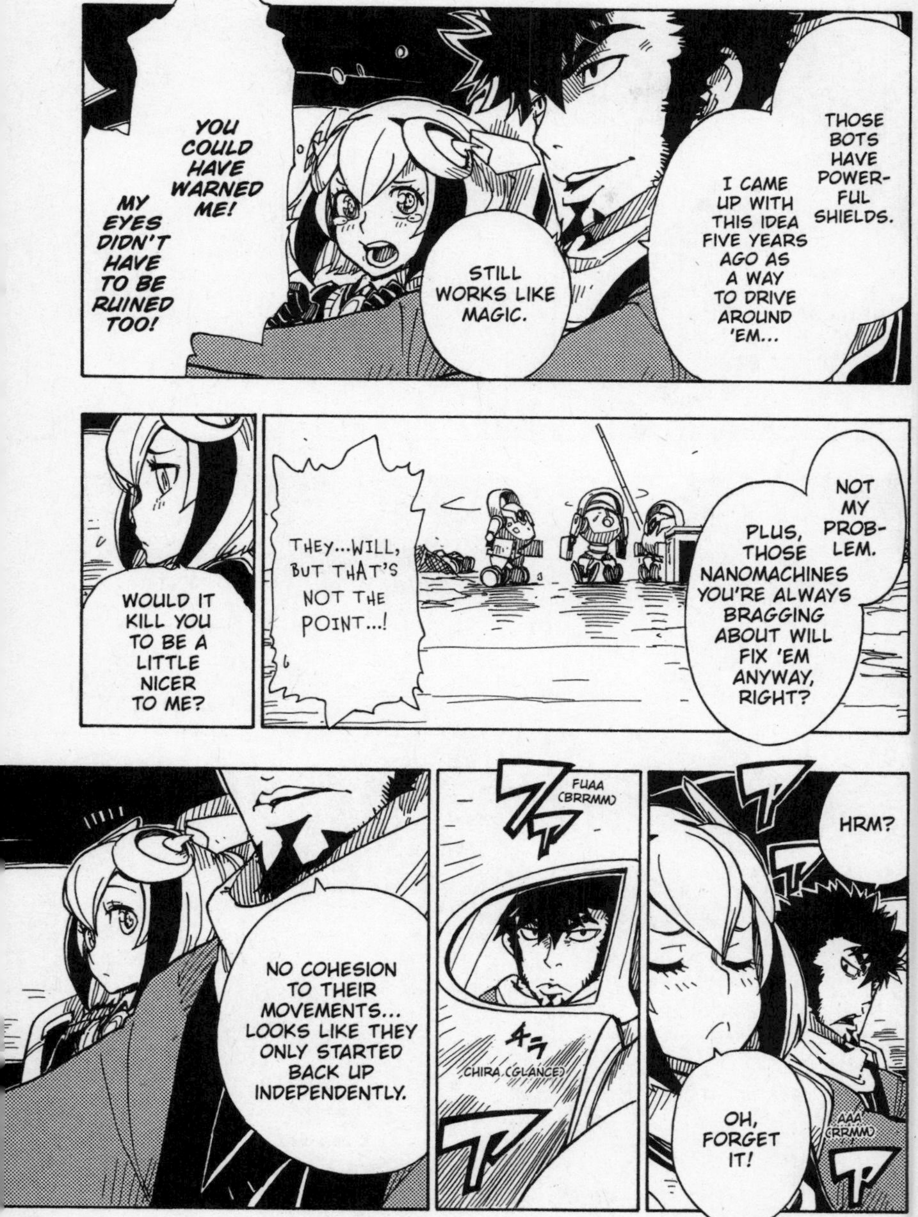
THOSE BOTS HAVE POWERFUL SHIELDS.
I CAME UP WITH THIS IDEA FIVE YEARS AGO AS A WAY TO DRIVE AROUND 'EM...
STILL WORKS LIKE MAGIC.
YOU COULD HAVE WARNED ME!
MY EYES DIDN'T HAVE TO BE RUINED TOO!
NOT MY PROBLEM.
PLUS, THOSE NANOMACHINES YOU'RE ALWAYS BRAGGING ABOUT WILL FIX 'EM ANYWAY, RIGHT?
THEY...WILL, BUT THAT'S NOT THE POINT...!
WOULD IT KILL YOU TO BE A LITTLE NICER TO ME?
HRM?
AAA (RRMM)
OH, FORGET IT!
FUAA (BRRMM)
CHIRA (GLANCE)
NO COHESION TO THEIR MOVEMENTS... LOOKS LIKE THEY ONLY STARTED BACK UP INDEPENDENTLY.

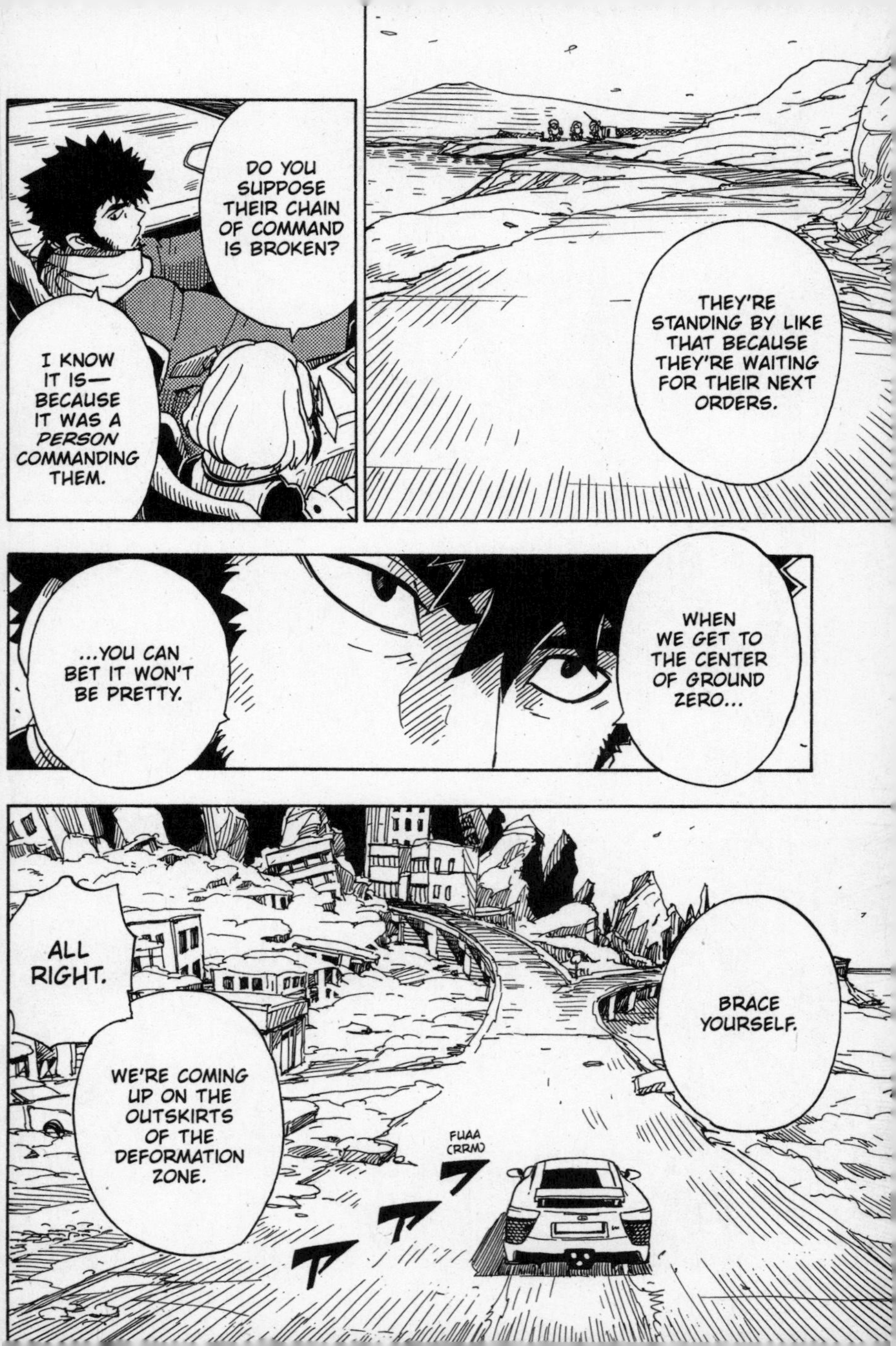
THEY'RE STANDING BY LIKE THAT BECAUSE THEY'RE WAITING FOR THEIR NEXT ORDERS.
DO YOU SUPPOSE THEIR CHAIN OF COMMAND IS BROKEN?
I KNOW IT IS— BECAUSE IT WAS A *PERSON* COMMANDING THEM.
WHEN WE GET TO THE CENTER OF GROUND ZERO...
...YOU CAN BET IT WON'T BE PRETTY.
WE'RE COMING UP ON THE OUTSKIRTS OF THE DEFORMATION ZONE.
BRACE YOURSELF.
ALL RIGHT.
FUAA (RRM)

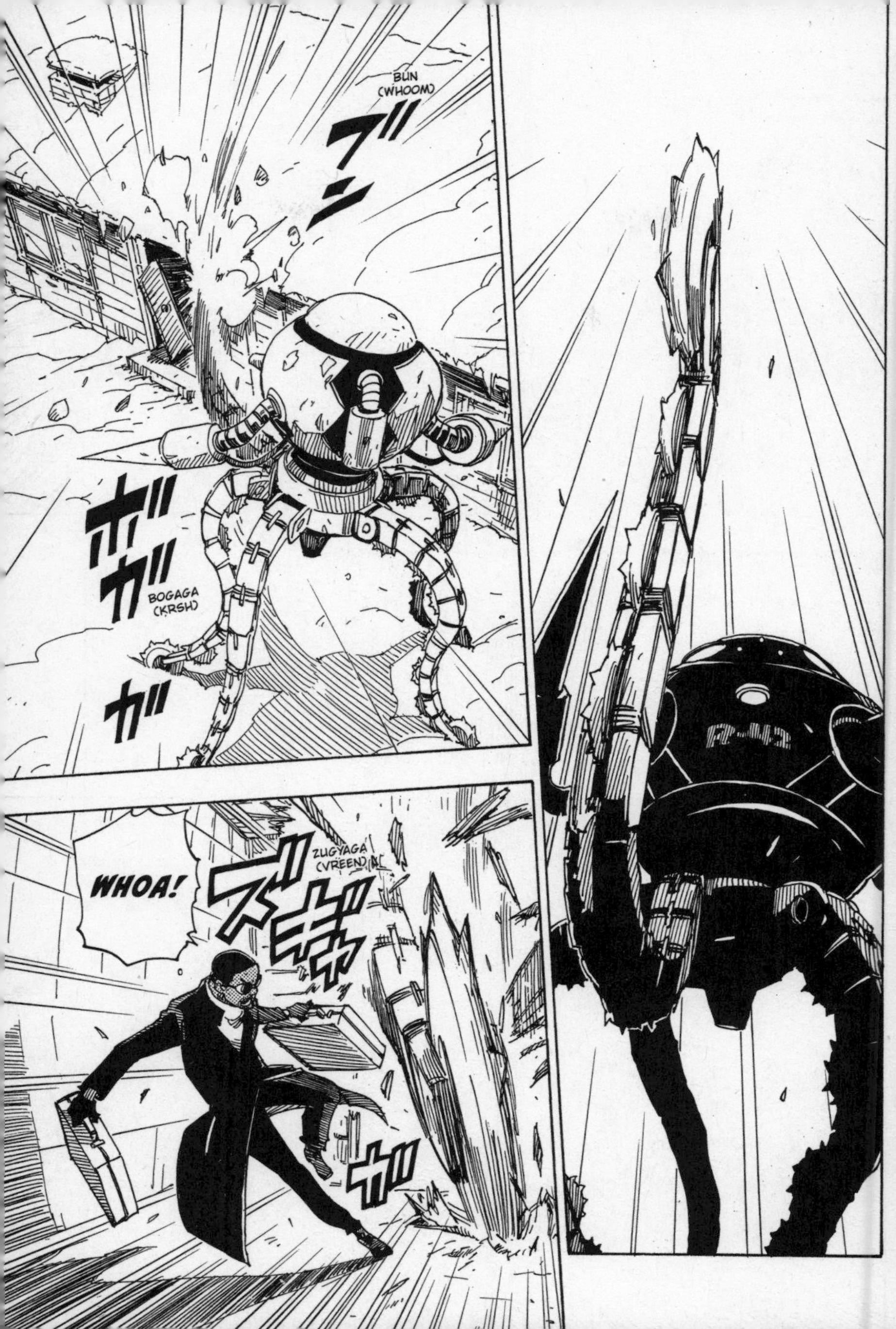
BUN (WHOOM)
ブン
ボガ
BOGAGA (KRSH)
ガ
WHOA!
ZUGYAGA (VREEN)
ズギャ
ガ

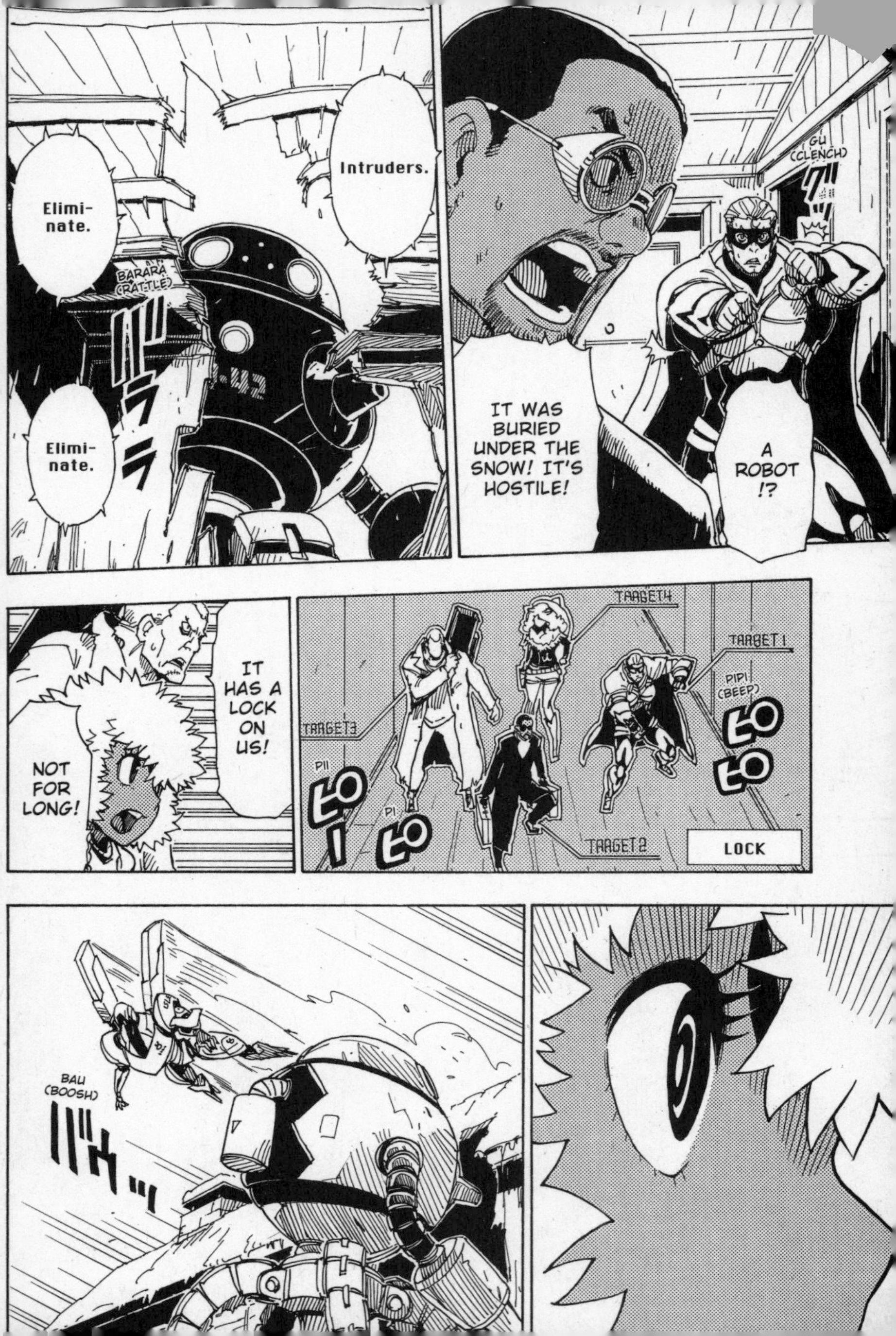
GU (CLENCH)
A ROBOT !?
IT WAS BURIED UNDER THE SNOW! IT'S HOSTILE!
Intruders.
Elimi-nate.
BARARA (RATTLE)
Elimi-nate.
TARGET4
TARGET 1
PIPI (BEEP)
TARGET3
PII
PI
TARGET2
LOCK
IT HAS A LOCK ON US!
NOT FOR LONG!
BAU (BOOSH)

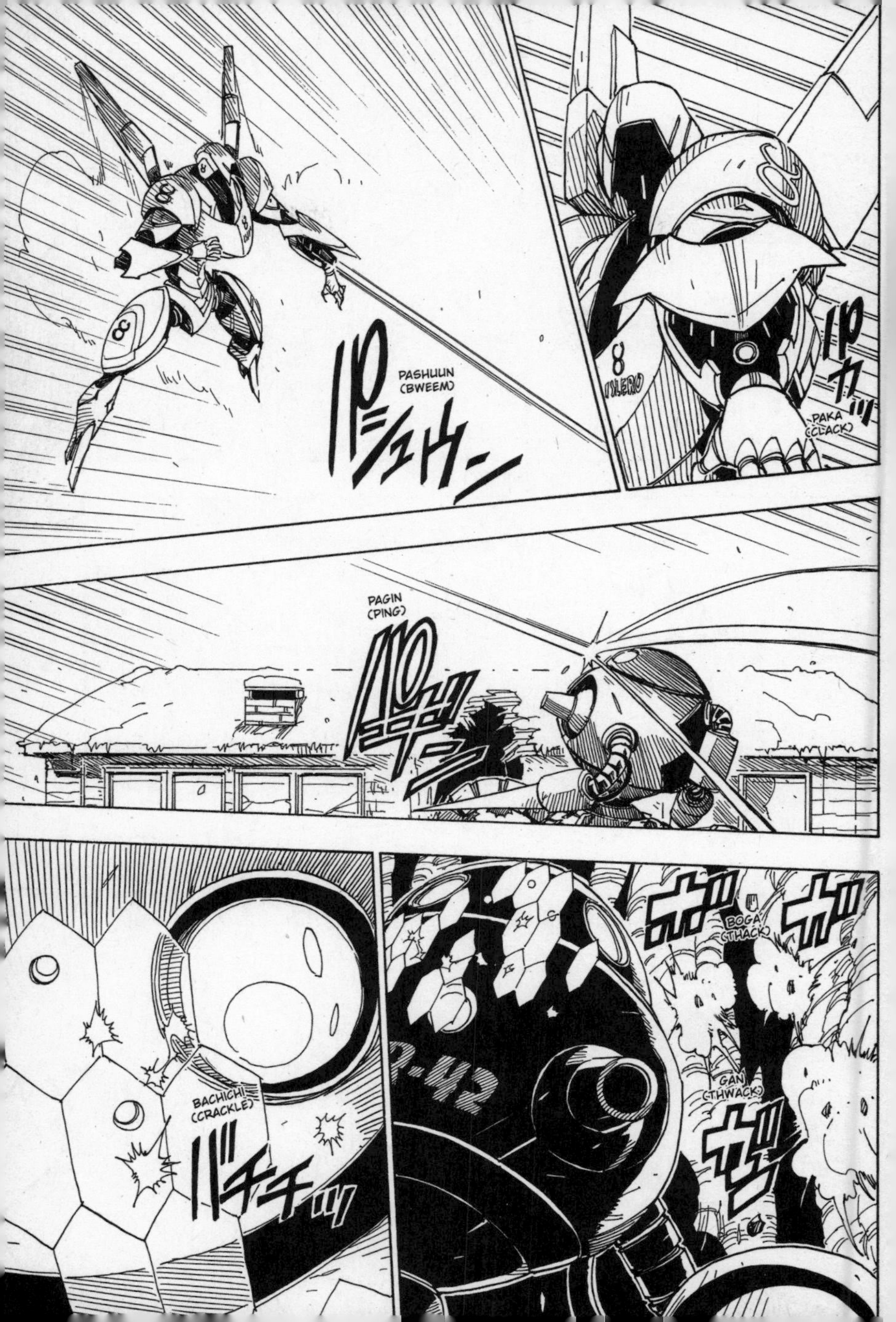
PAKA
(CLACK)
PASHUUN
(BWEEM)
PAGIN
(PING)
BOGA
(THACK)
GAN
(THWACK)
BACHICHI
(CRACKLE)

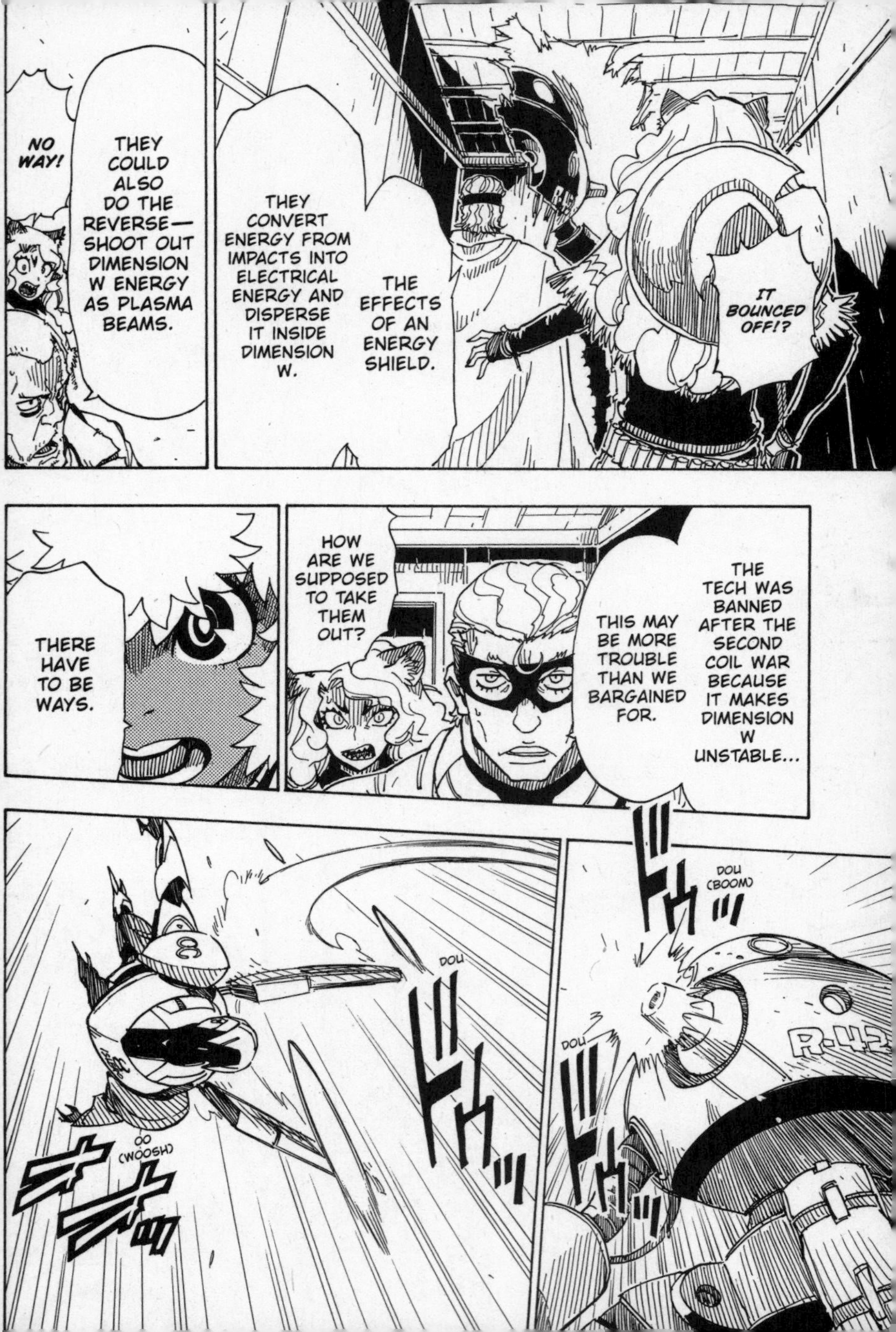
IT BOUNCED OFF!?
THE EFFECTS OF AN ENERGY SHIELD.
THEY CONVERT ENERGY FROM IMPACTS INTO ELECTRICAL ENERGY AND DISPERSE IT INSIDE DIMENSION W.
THEY COULD ALSO DO THE REVERSE—SHOOT OUT DIMENSION W ENERGY AS PLASMA BEAMS.
NO WAY!
THE TECH WAS BANNED AFTER THE SECOND COIL WAR BECAUSE IT MAKES DIMENSION W UNSTABLE...
THIS MAY BE MORE TROUBLE THAN WE BARGAINED FOR.
HOW ARE WE SUPPOSED TO TAKE THEM OUT?
THERE HAVE TO BE WAYS.
DOU (BOOM)
DOU
R-42
DOU
OO (WOOSH)

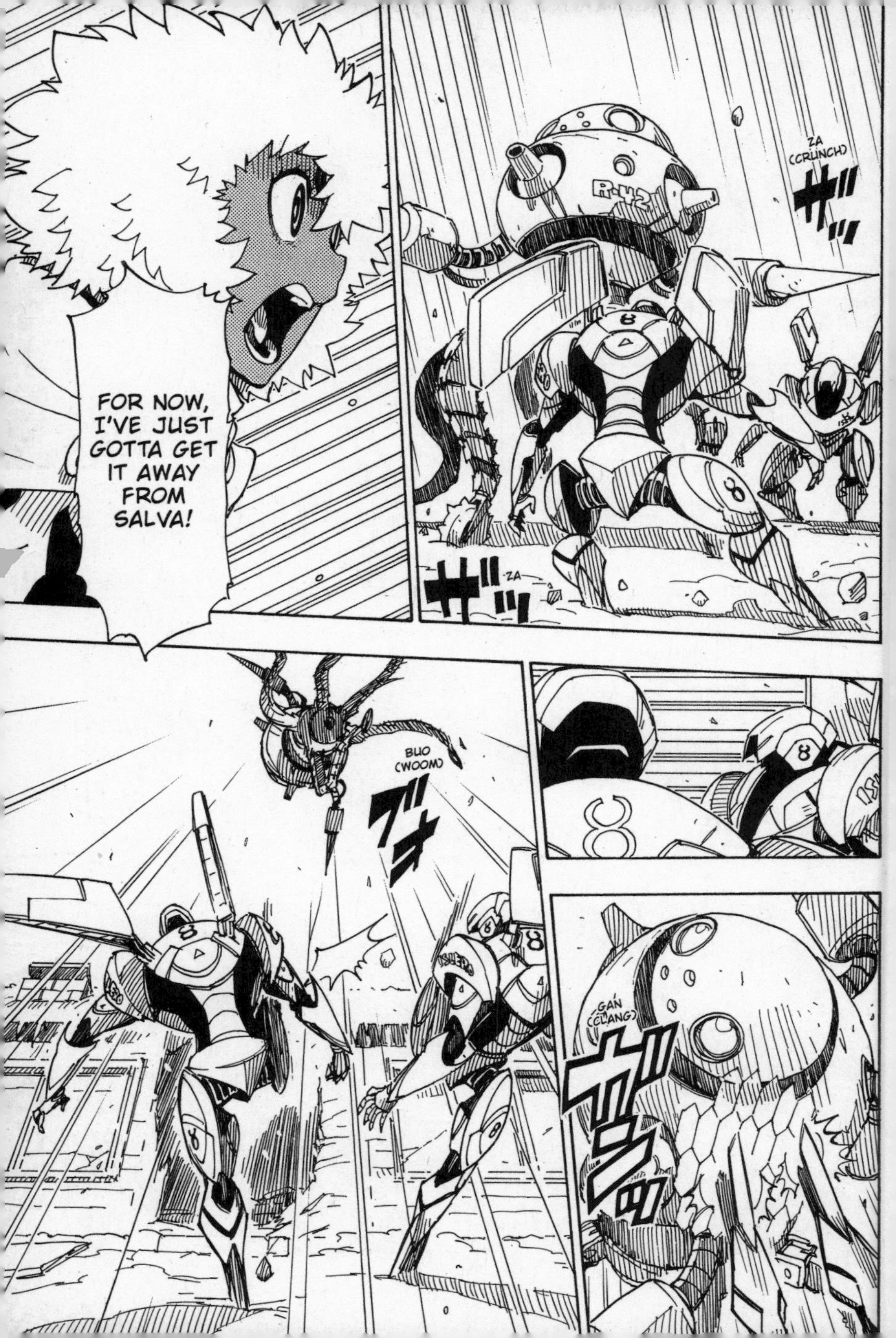
ZA (CRUNCH)
ZA
FOR NOW, I'VE JUST GOTTA GET IT AWAY FROM SALVA!
GAN (CLANG)
BUO (WOOM)

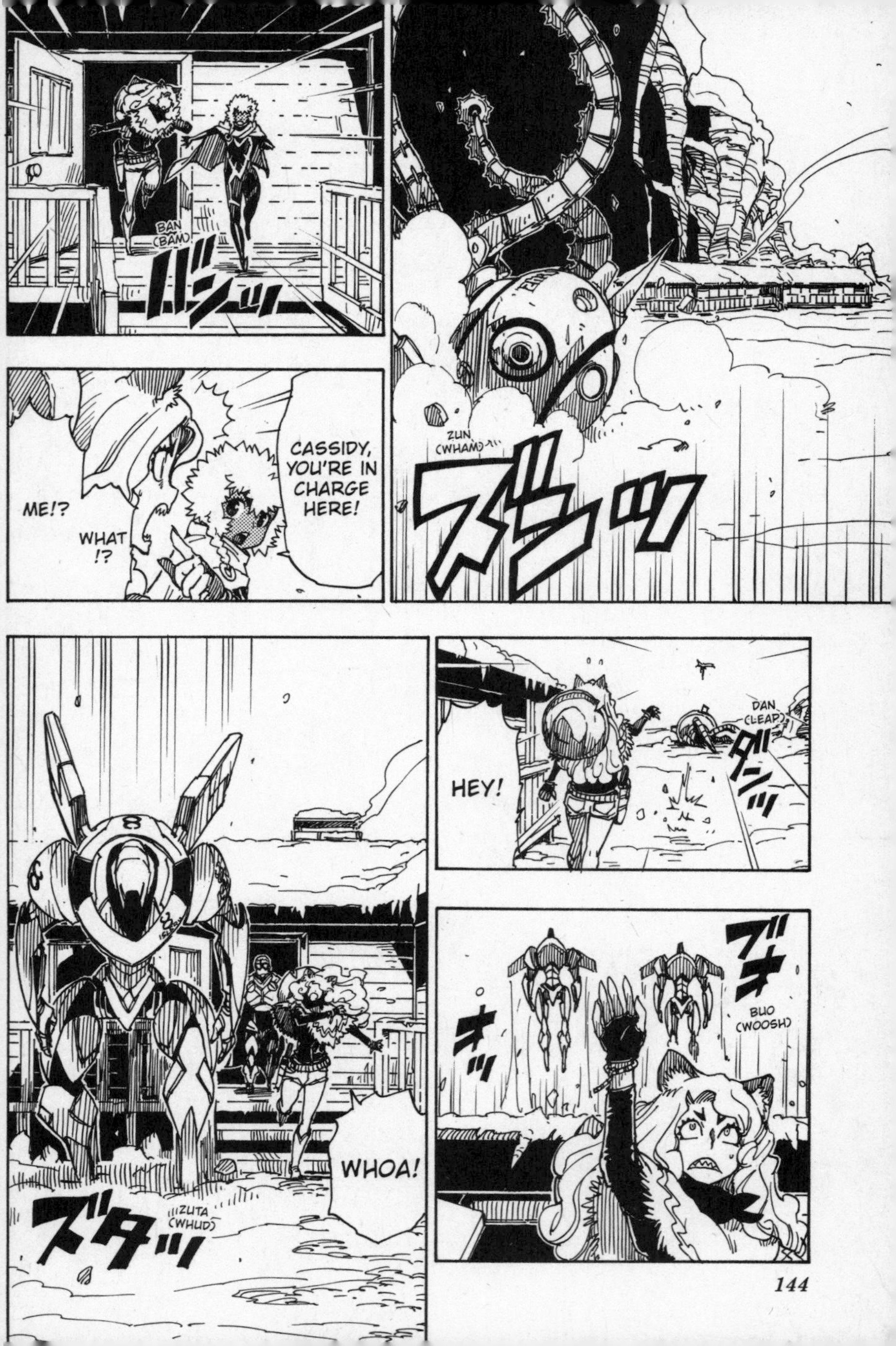
ZUN (WHAM)
ズシッ
BAN (BAM)
バシッ
CASSIDY, YOU'RE IN CHARGE HERE!
ME!?
WHAT !?
DAN (LEAP)
ダンッ
HEY!
ブオッ
BUO (WOOSH)
WHOA!
ZUTA (WHUD)
ズタッ

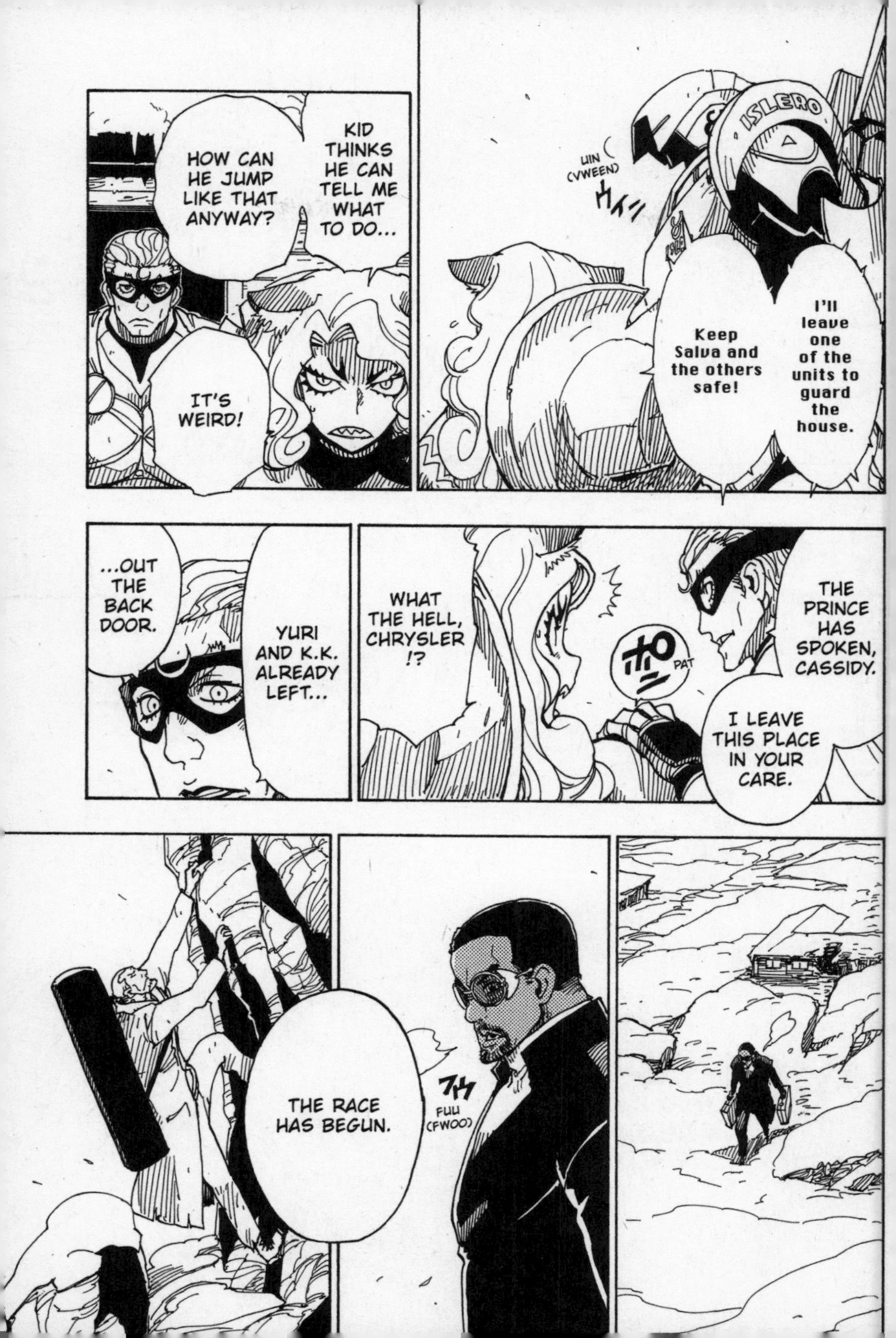
UIN (VWEEN)
I'll leave one of the units to guard the house.
Keep Salva and the others safe!
KID THINKS HE CAN TELL ME WHAT TO DO...
HOW CAN HE JUMP LIKE THAT ANYWAY?
IT'S WEIRD!
THE PRINCE HAS SPOKEN, CASSIDY.
I LEAVE THIS PLACE IN YOUR CARE.
PAT
WHAT THE HELL, CHRYSLER !?
YURI AND K.K. ALREADY LEFT...
...OUT THE BACK DOOR.
FUU (FWOO)
THE RACE HAS BEGUN.

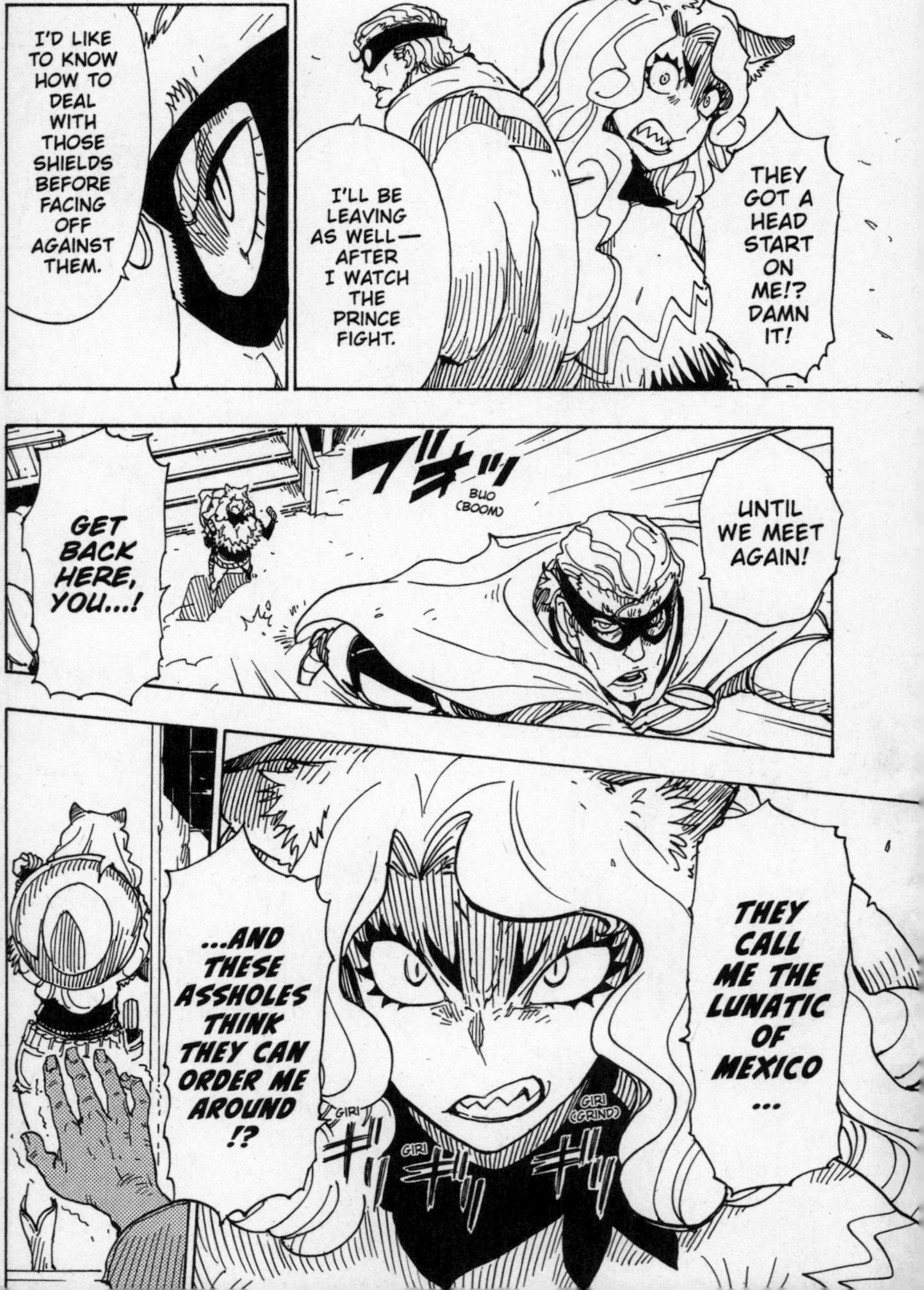
THEY GOT A HEAD START ON ME!? DAMN IT!
I'LL BE LEAVING AS WELL—AFTER I WATCH THE PRINCE FIGHT.
I'D LIKE TO KNOW HOW TO DEAL WITH THOSE SHIELDS BEFORE FACING OFF AGAINST THEM.
UNTIL WE MEET AGAIN!
BUO (BOOM)
GET BACK HERE, YOU...!
THEY CALL ME THE LUNATIC OF MEXICO ...
GIRI (GRIND)
GIRI
...AND THESE ASSHOLES THINK THEY CAN ORDER ME AROUND !?
GIRI

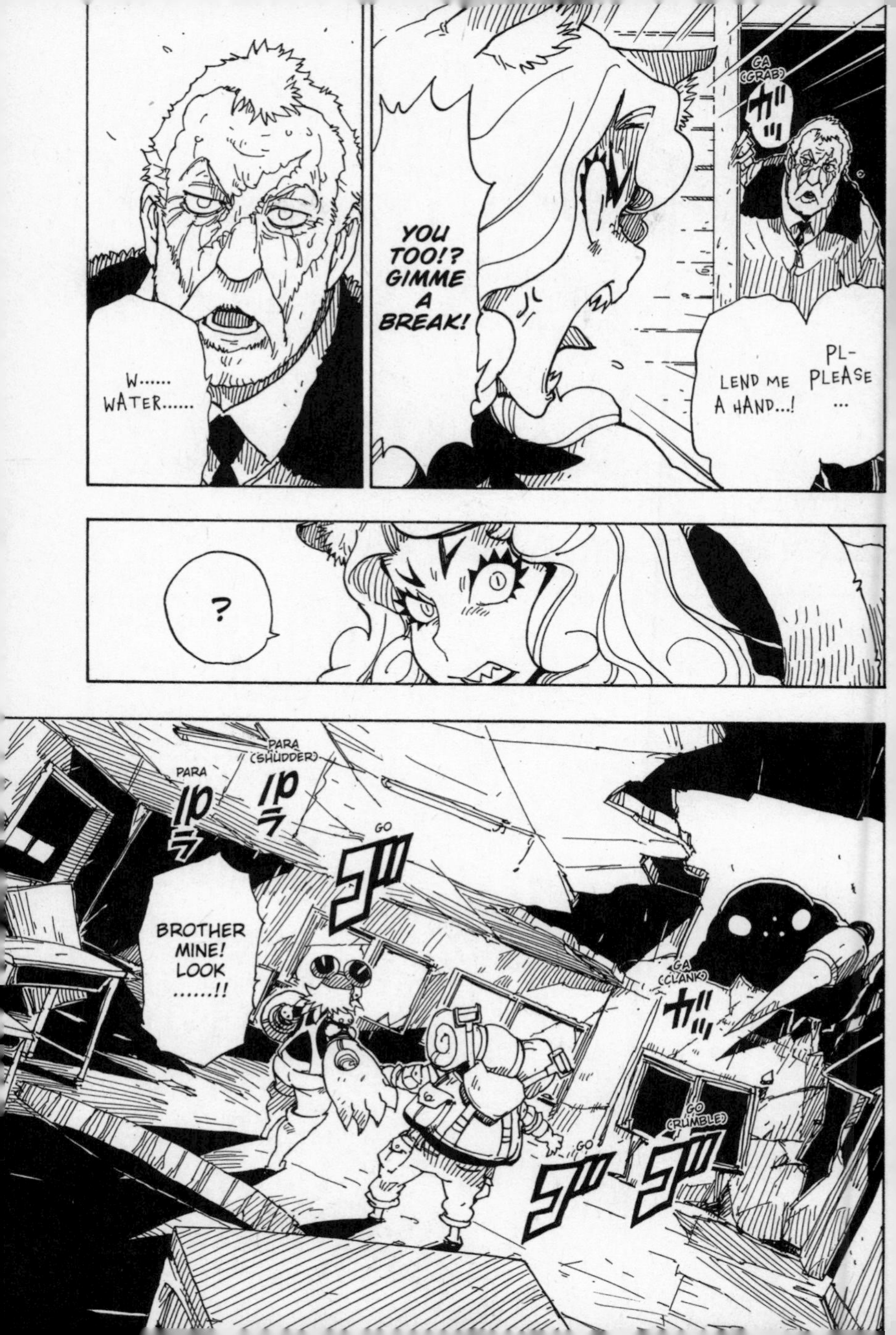
GA (GRAB)
PL-PLEASE ...
LEND ME A HAND...!
YOU TOO!? GIMME A BREAK!
W...... WATER......
?
PARA (SHUDDER)
PARA
GO
BROTHER MINE! LOOK ......!!
GA (CLANK)
GO (RUMBLE)
GO

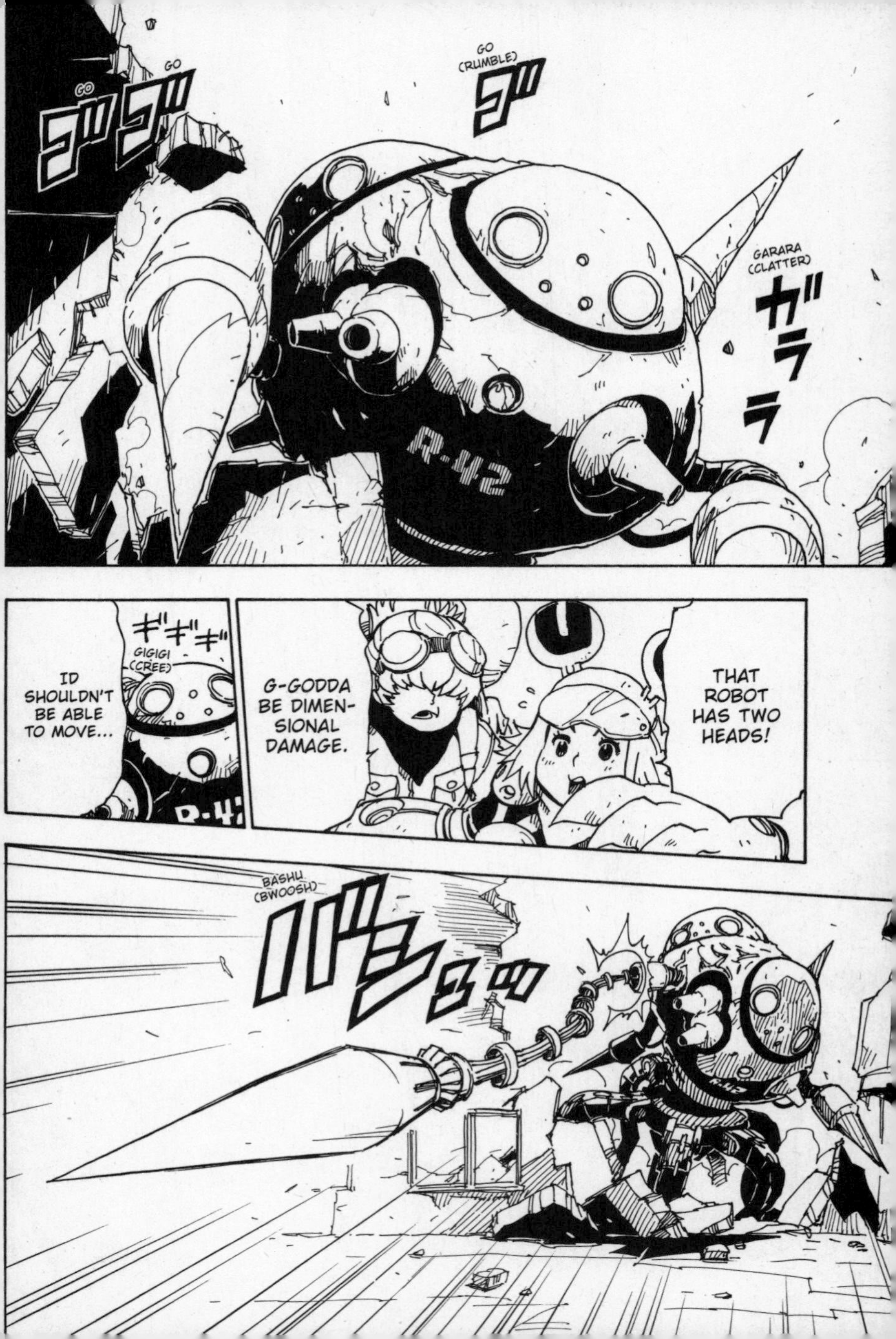
GARARA (CLATTER)
ガラ ラ
GO (RUMBLE)
GO
GO
THAT ROBOT HAS TWO HEADS!
G-GODDA BE DIMEN-SIONAL DAMAGE.
ギギギ
GIGIGI (CREE)
ID SHOULDN'T BE ABLE TO MOVE...
R-42
BASHU (BWOOSH)

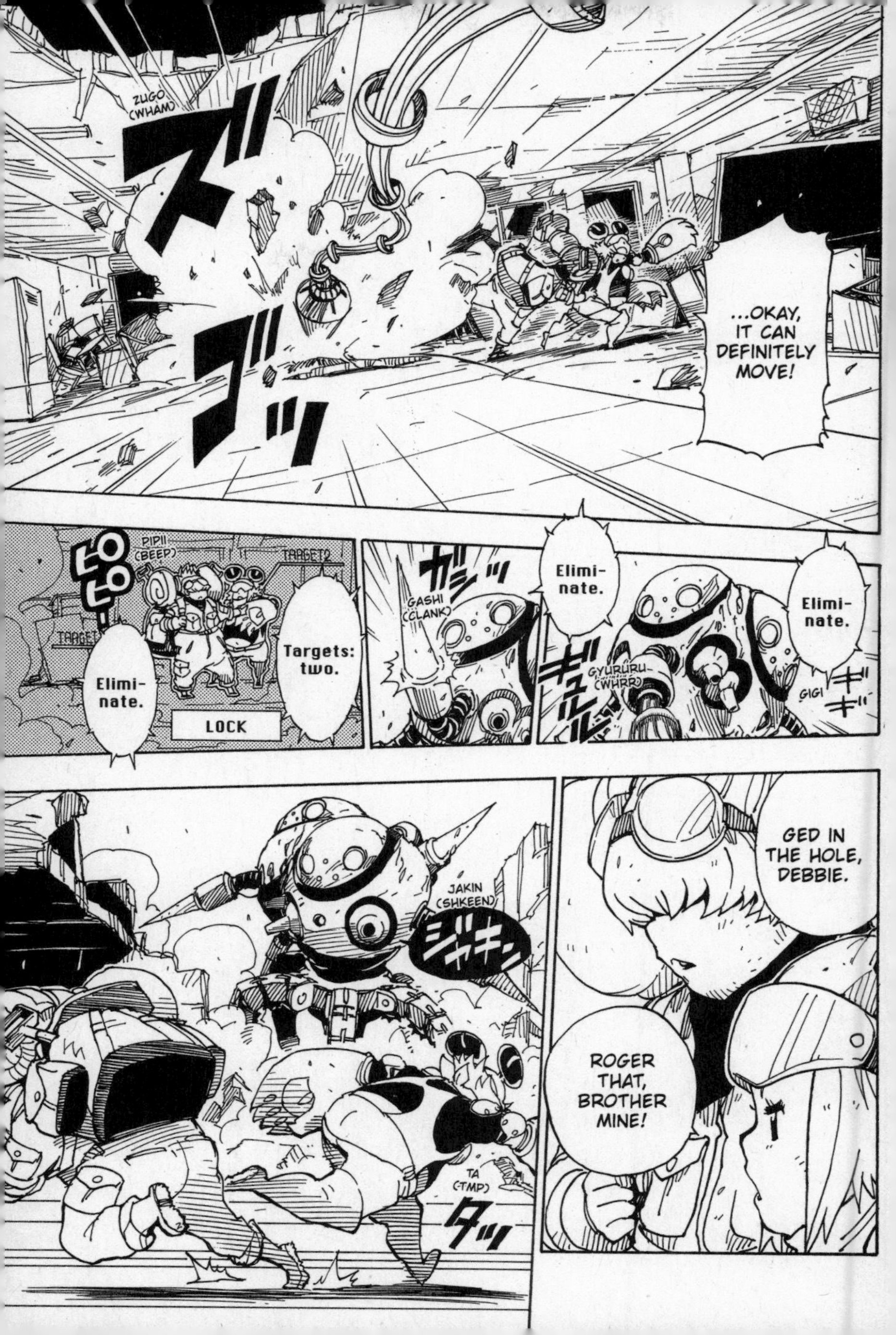
ZUGO (WHAM)
...OKAY, IT CAN DEFINITELY MOVE!
Elimi-nate.
GYURURU (WHRR)
GIGI
Elimi-nate.
GASHI (CLANK)
PIPII (BEEP)
TARGET2
Targets: two.
TARGET
LOCK
Elimi-nate.
GED IN THE HOLE, DEBBIE.
ROGER THAT, BROTHER MINE!
JAKIN (SHKEEN)
TA (TMP)

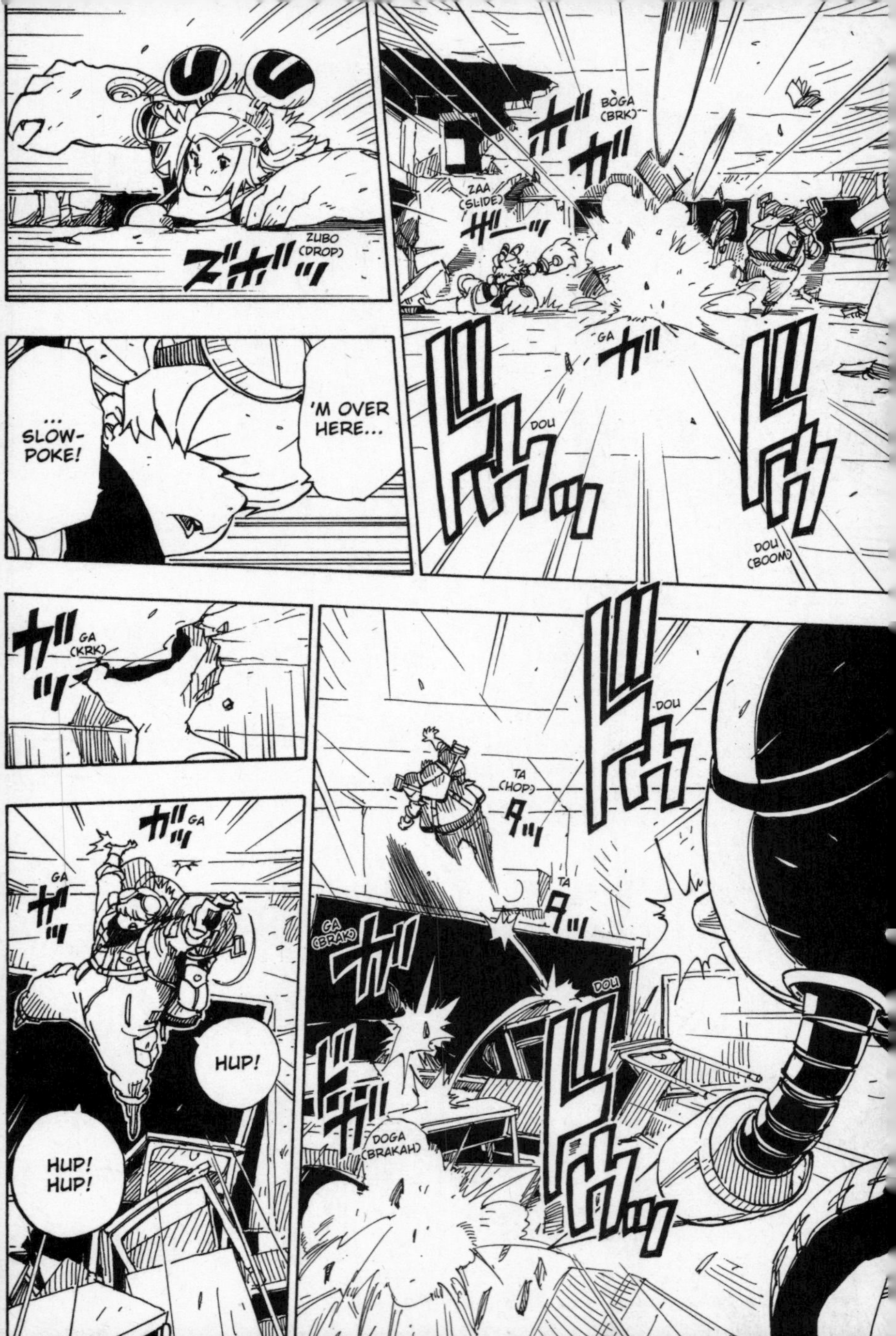
BOGA (BRK)
ZAA (SLIDE)
ZUBO (DROP)
GA
DOU
DOU (BOOM)
'M OVER HERE...
... SLOW-POKE!
DOU
TA (HOP)
TA
GA (BRAK)
DOU
DOGA (BRAKAH)
GA (KRK)
GA
GA
HUP!
HUP! HUP!

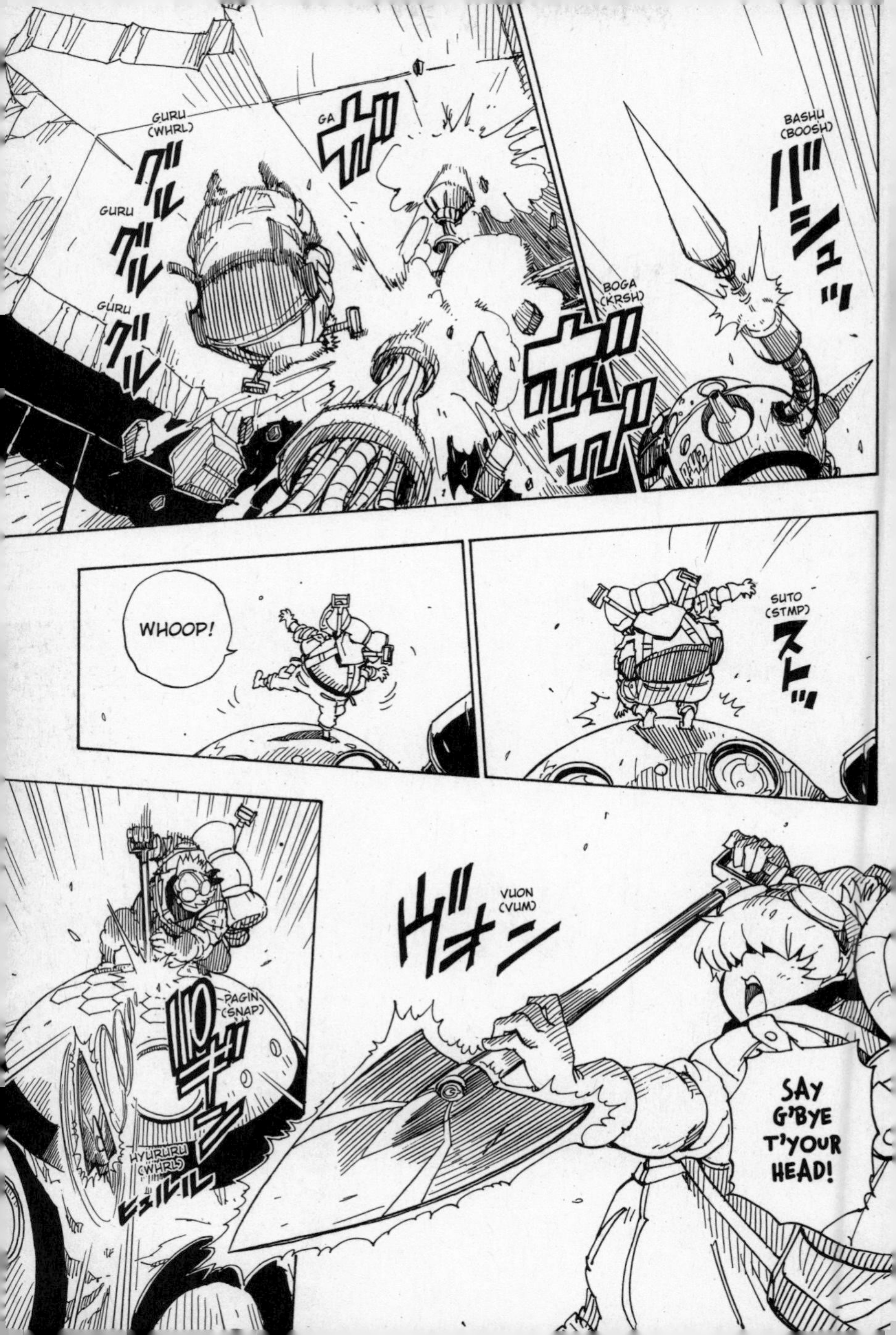
BASHU (BOOSH)
バシュッ
BOGA (KRSH)
ボガガ
GA
ガッ
GURU (WHRL)
GURU
GURU
グルグルグル
SUTO (STMP)
ストッ
WHOOP!
VUON (VUM)
ヴォン
SAY G'BYE T'YOUR HEAD!
PAGIN (SNAP)
パギン
HYURURU (WHRL)
ヒュルル

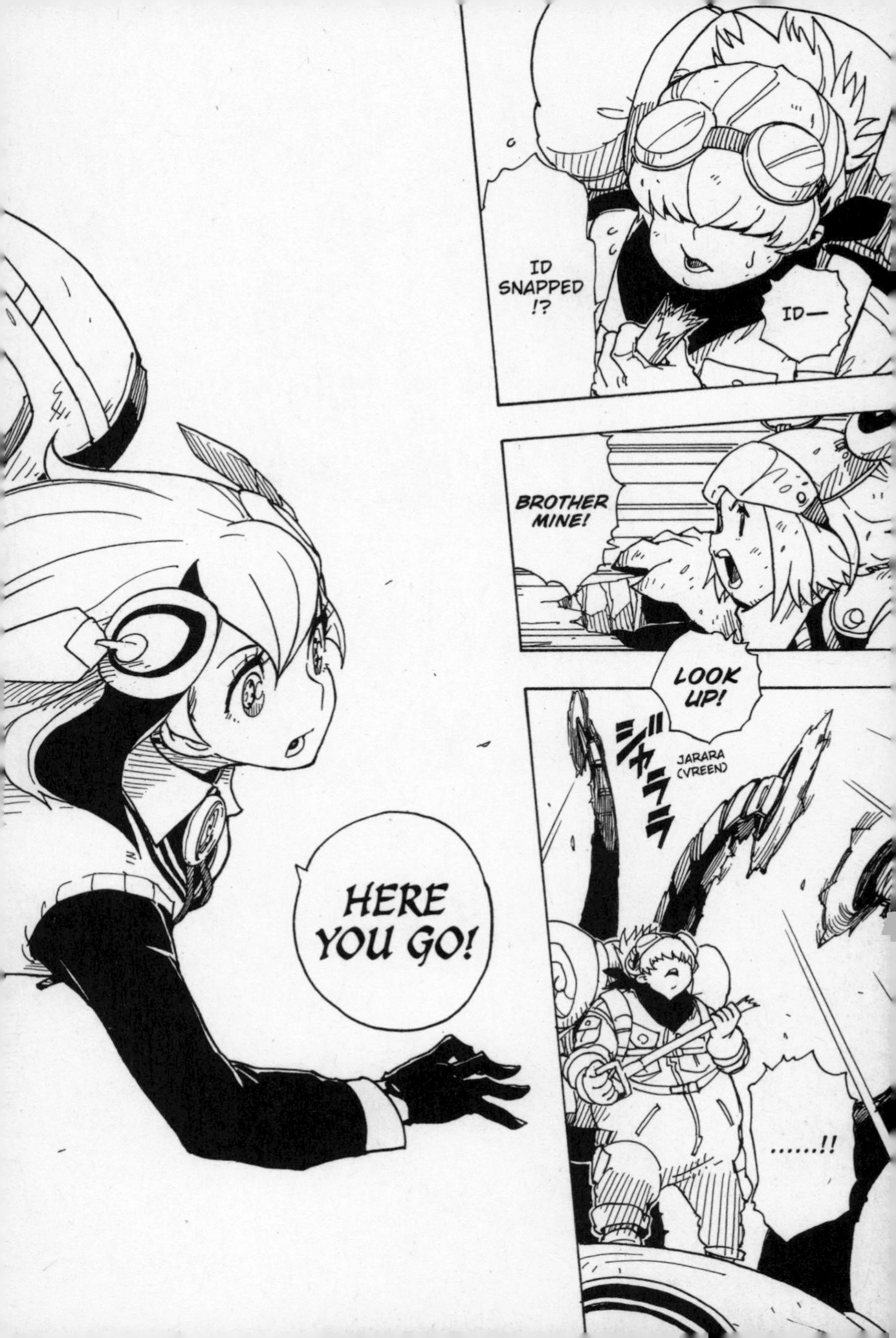
ID—
ID SNAPPED !?
BROTHER MINE!
LOOK UP!
ジャララ
JARARA (VREEN)
......!!
HERE YOU GO!

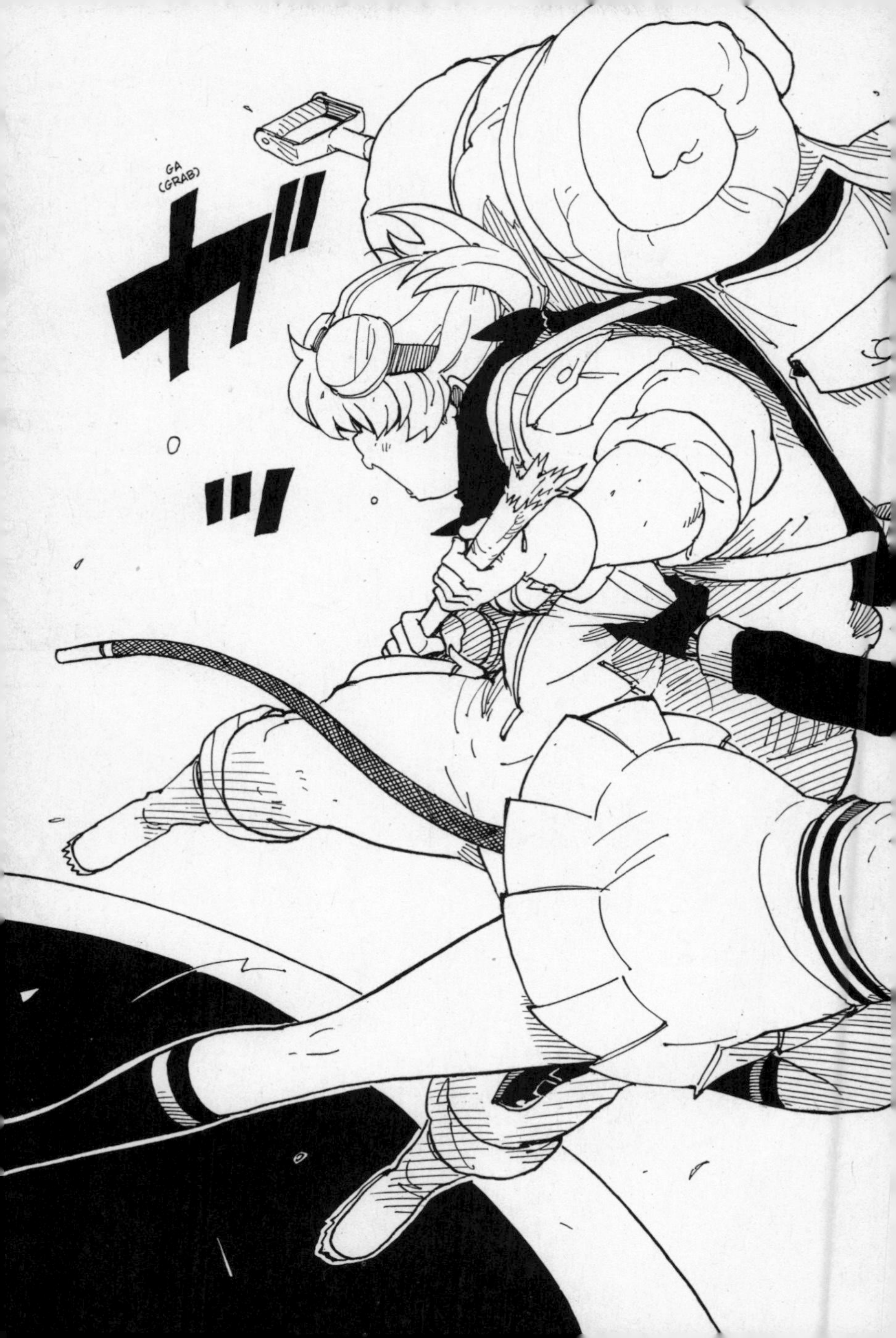
GA
(GRAB)
ガッ

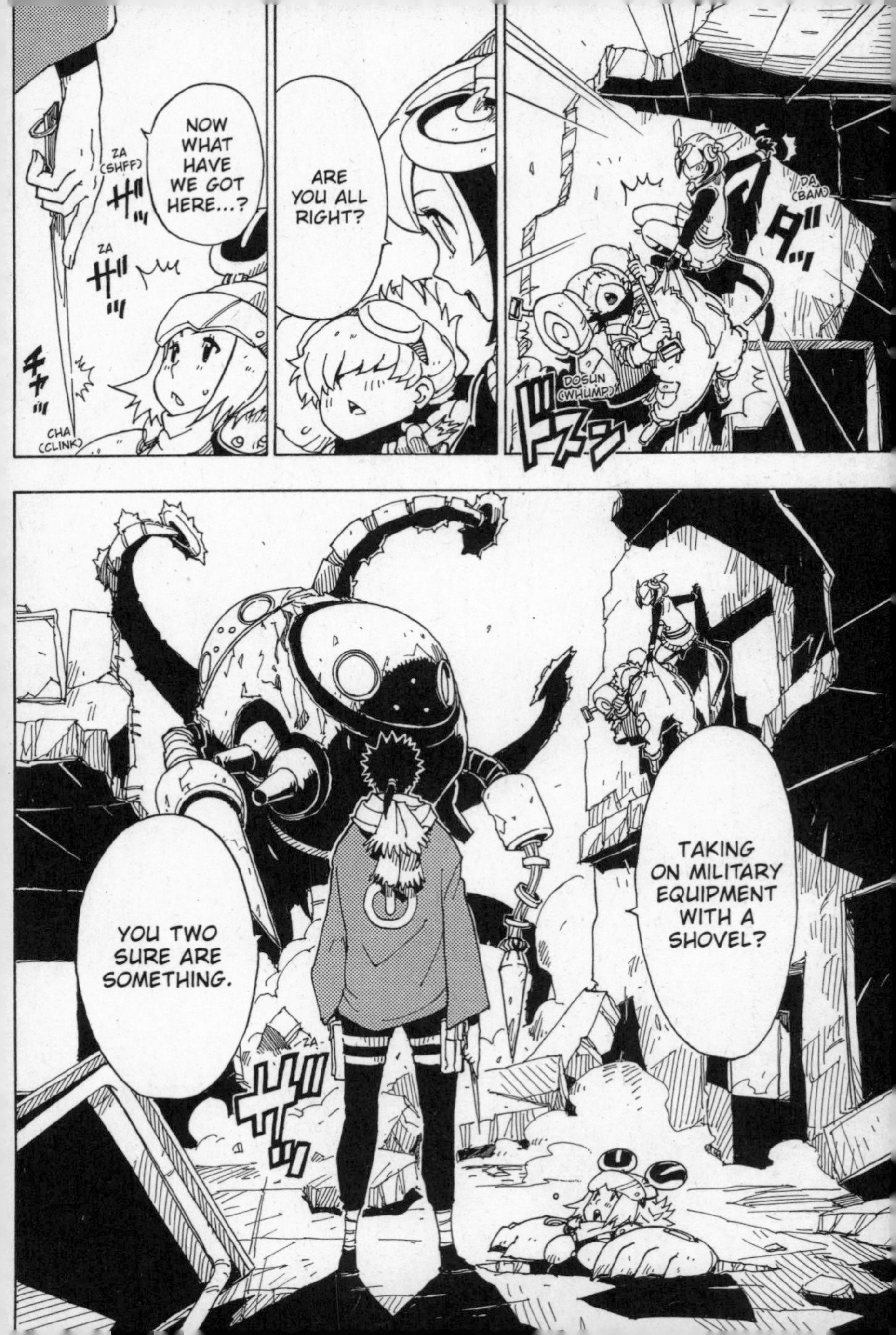
DA (BAM)
DOSUN (WHUMP)
ARE YOU ALL RIGHT?
ZA (SHFF)
NOW WHAT HAVE WE GOT HERE...?
ZA
CHA (CLINK)
TAKING ON MILITARY EQUIPMENT WITH A SHOVEL?
YOU TWO SURE ARE SOMETHING.
ZA

Dimension W

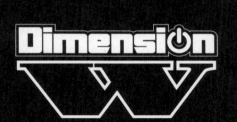

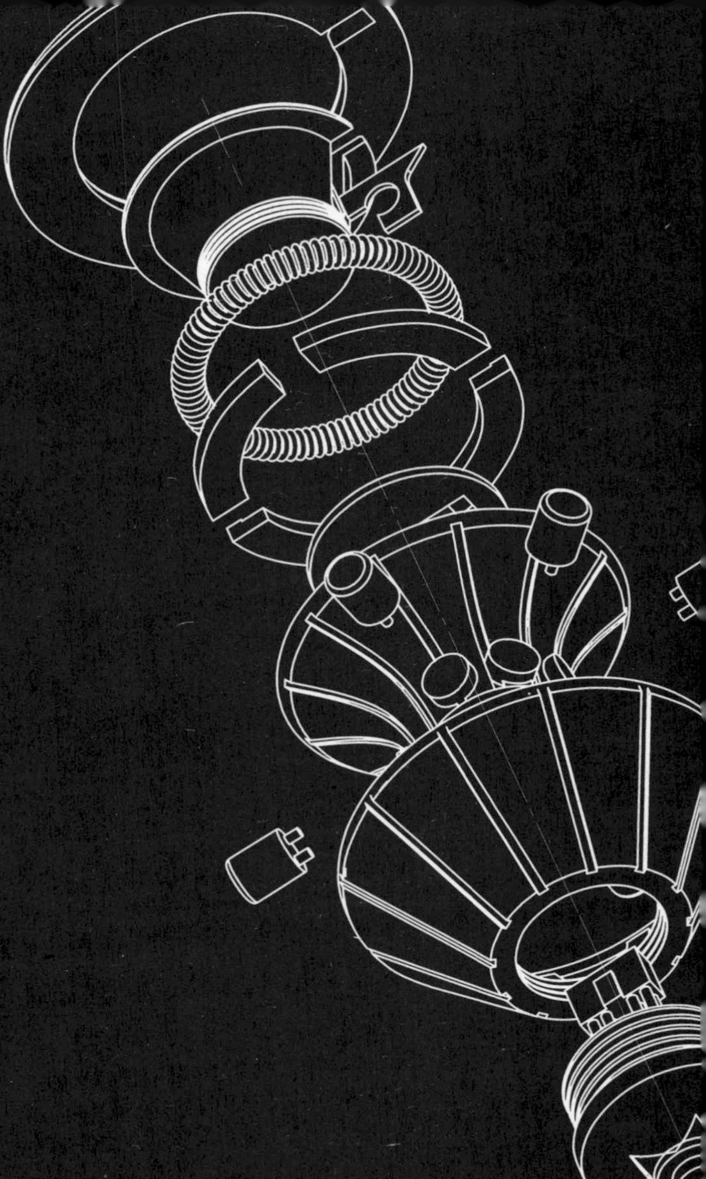

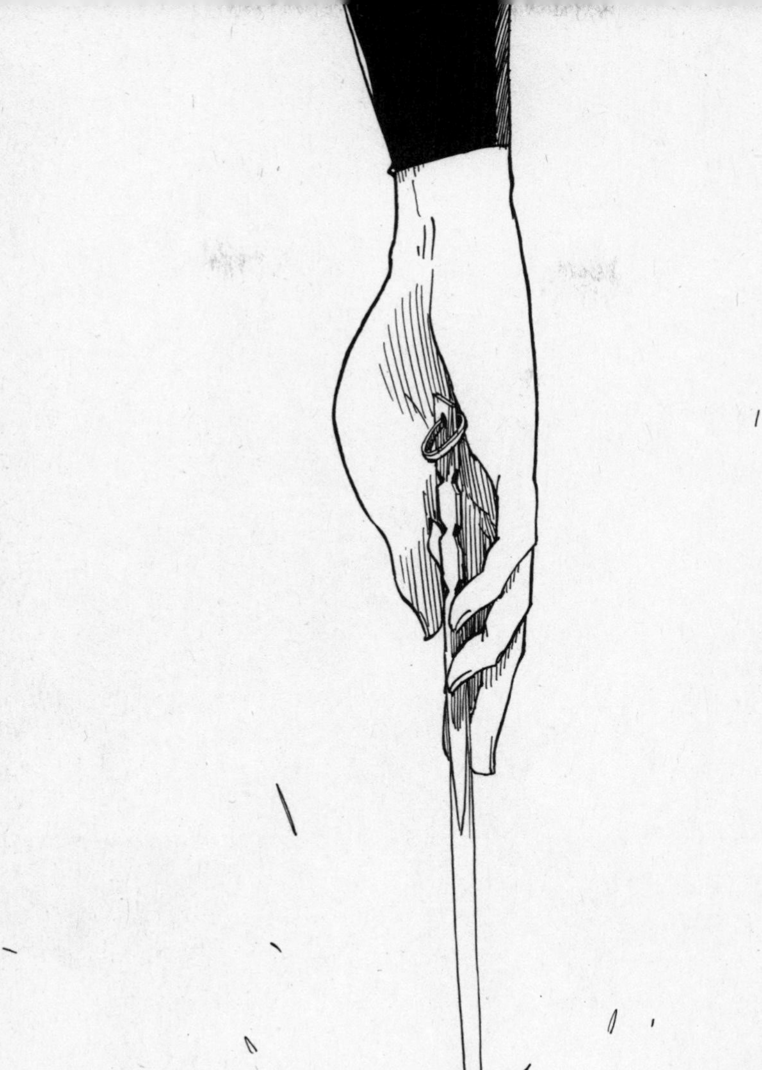

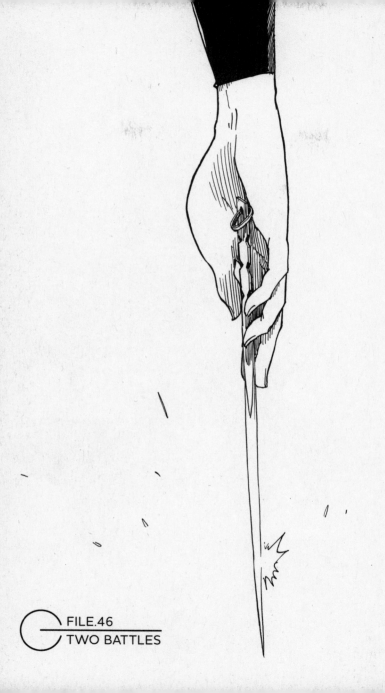

# FILE.46
# TWO BATTLES

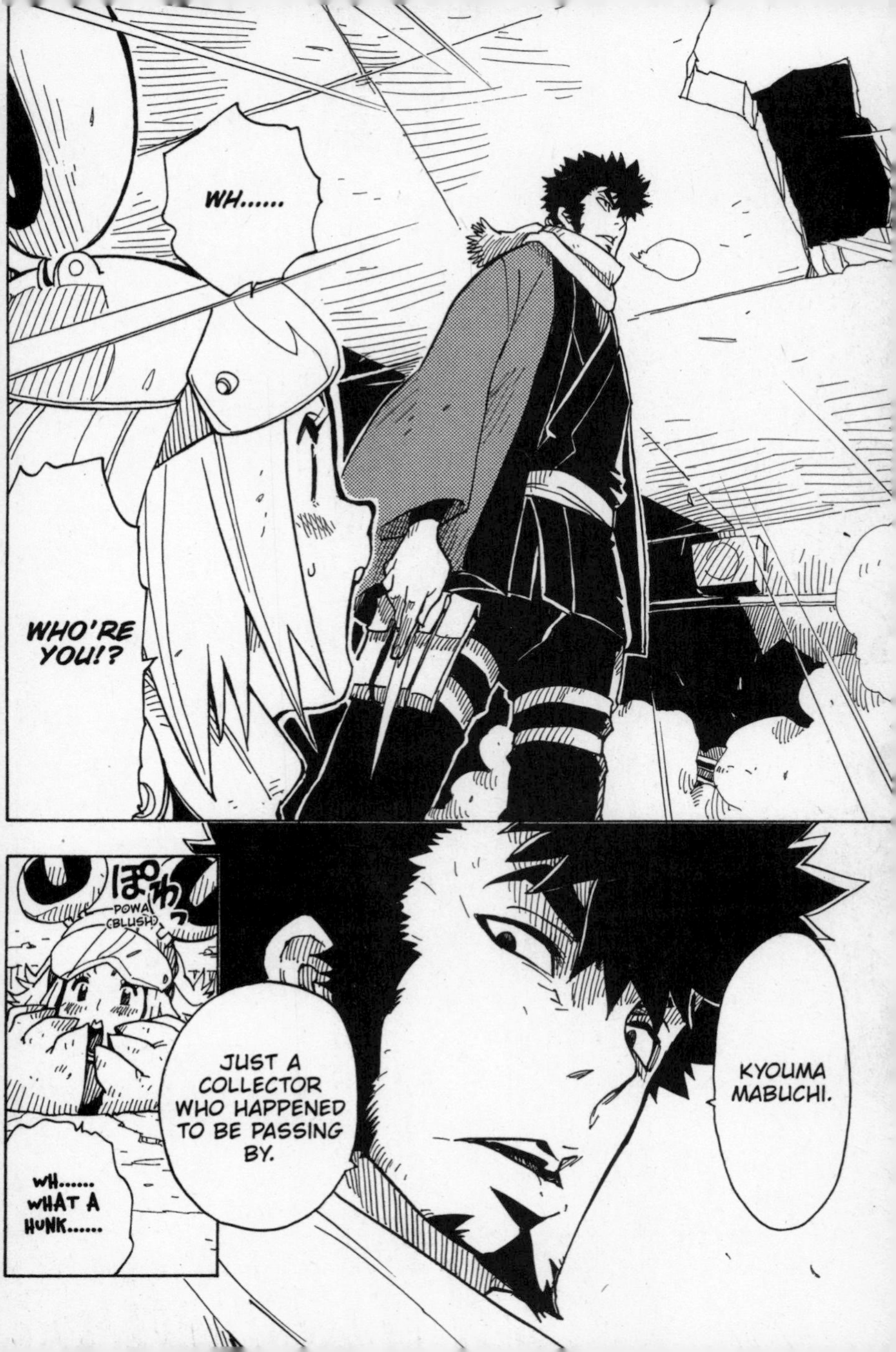
WH......
WHO'RE YOU!?
JUST A COLLECTOR WHO HAPPENED TO BE PASSING BY.
KYOUMA MABUCHI.
ぽわっ
POWA (BLUSH)
WH...... WHAT A HUNK......

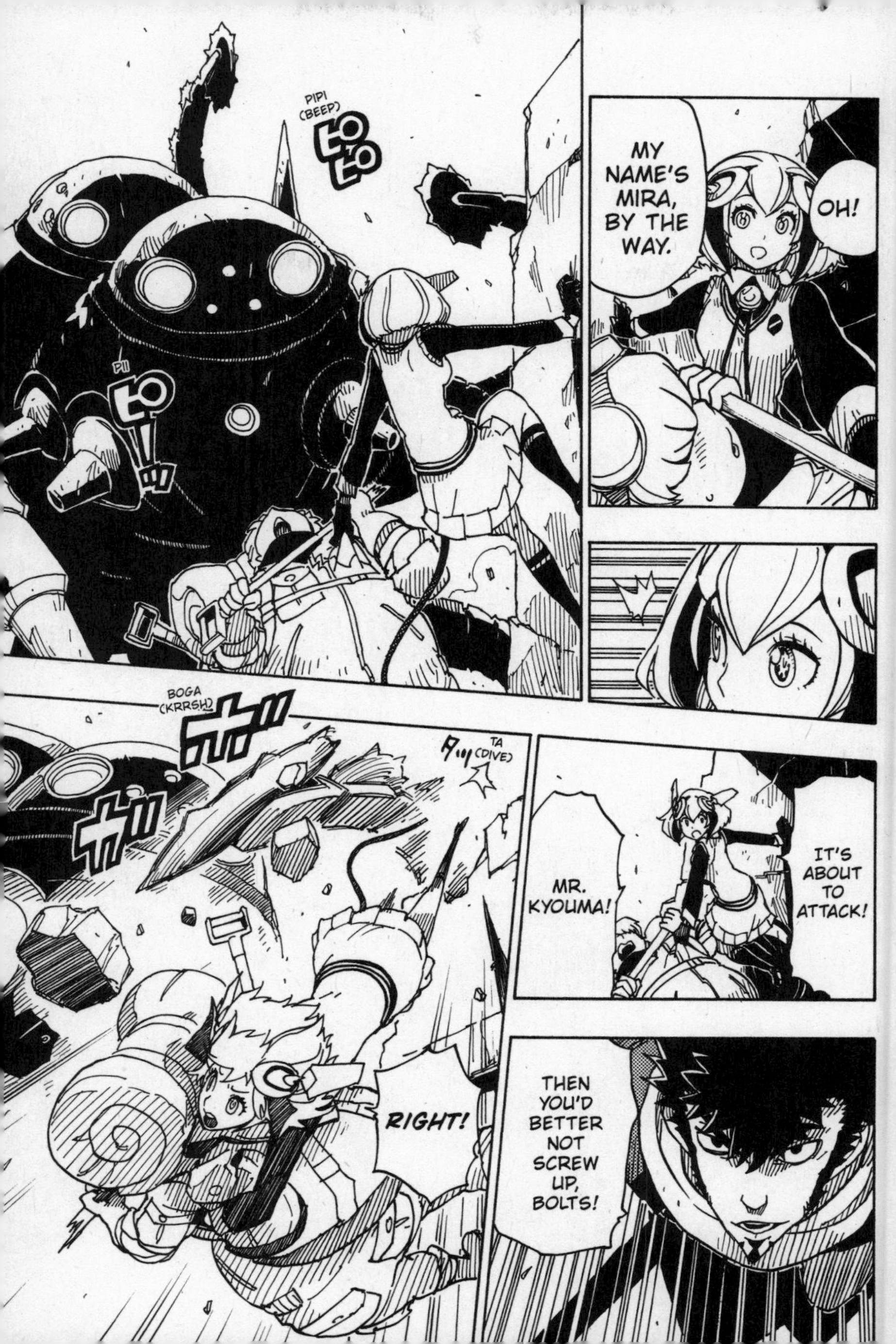
OH!
MY NAME'S MIRA, BY THE WAY.
PIPI (BEEP)
PII
MR. KYOUMA!
IT'S ABOUT TO ATTACK!
THEN YOU'D BETTER NOT SCREW UP, BOLTS!
TA (DIVE)
BOGA (KRRSH)
RIGHT!

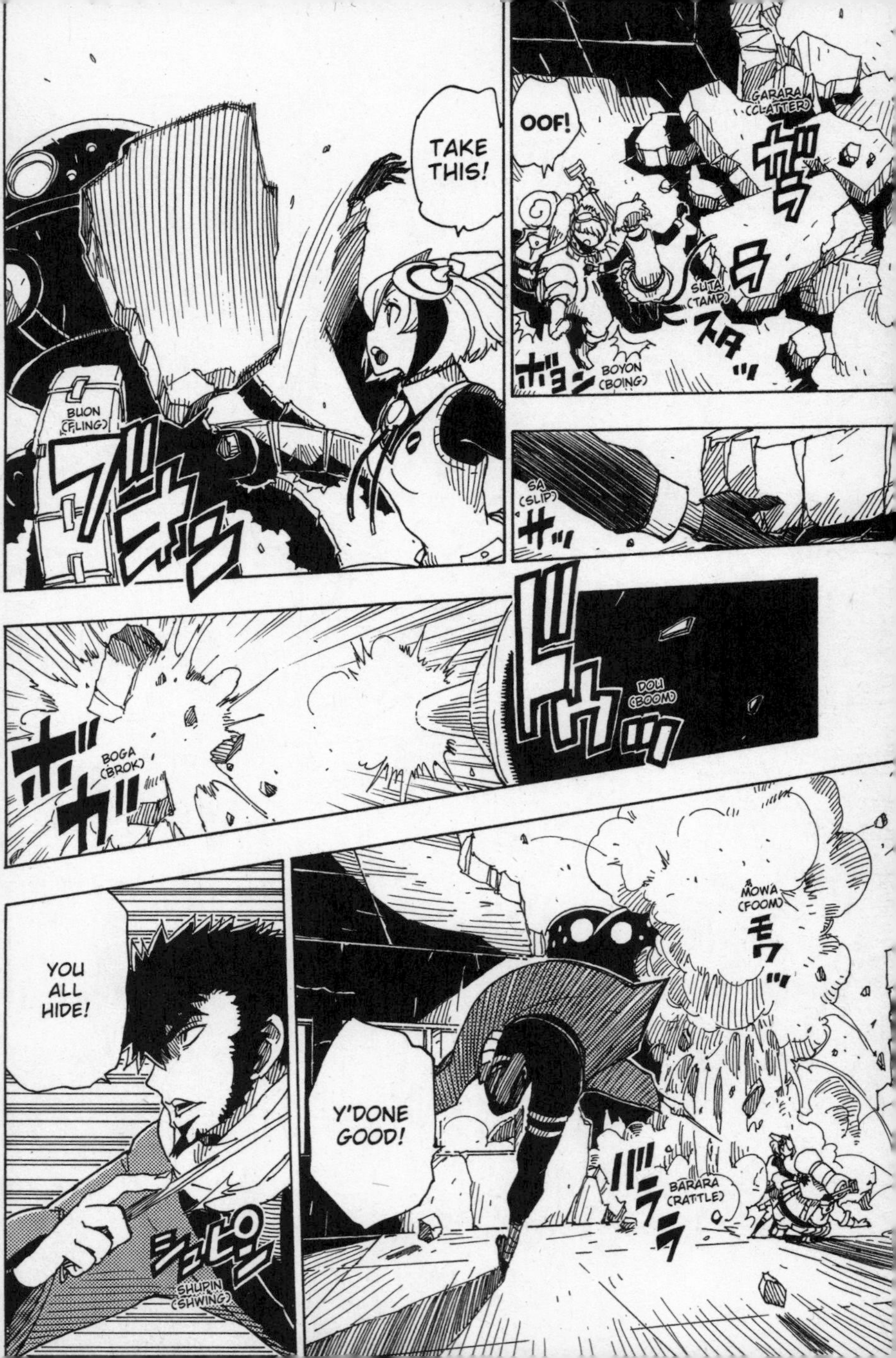
OOF!
GARARA (CLATTER)
SUTA (TAMP)
BOYON (BOING)
SA (SLIP)
TAKE THIS!
BUON (FLING)
DOU (BOOM)
BOGA (BROK)
MOWA (FOOM)
Y'DONE GOOD!
BARARA (RATTLE)
YOU ALL HIDE!
SHUPIN (SHWING)

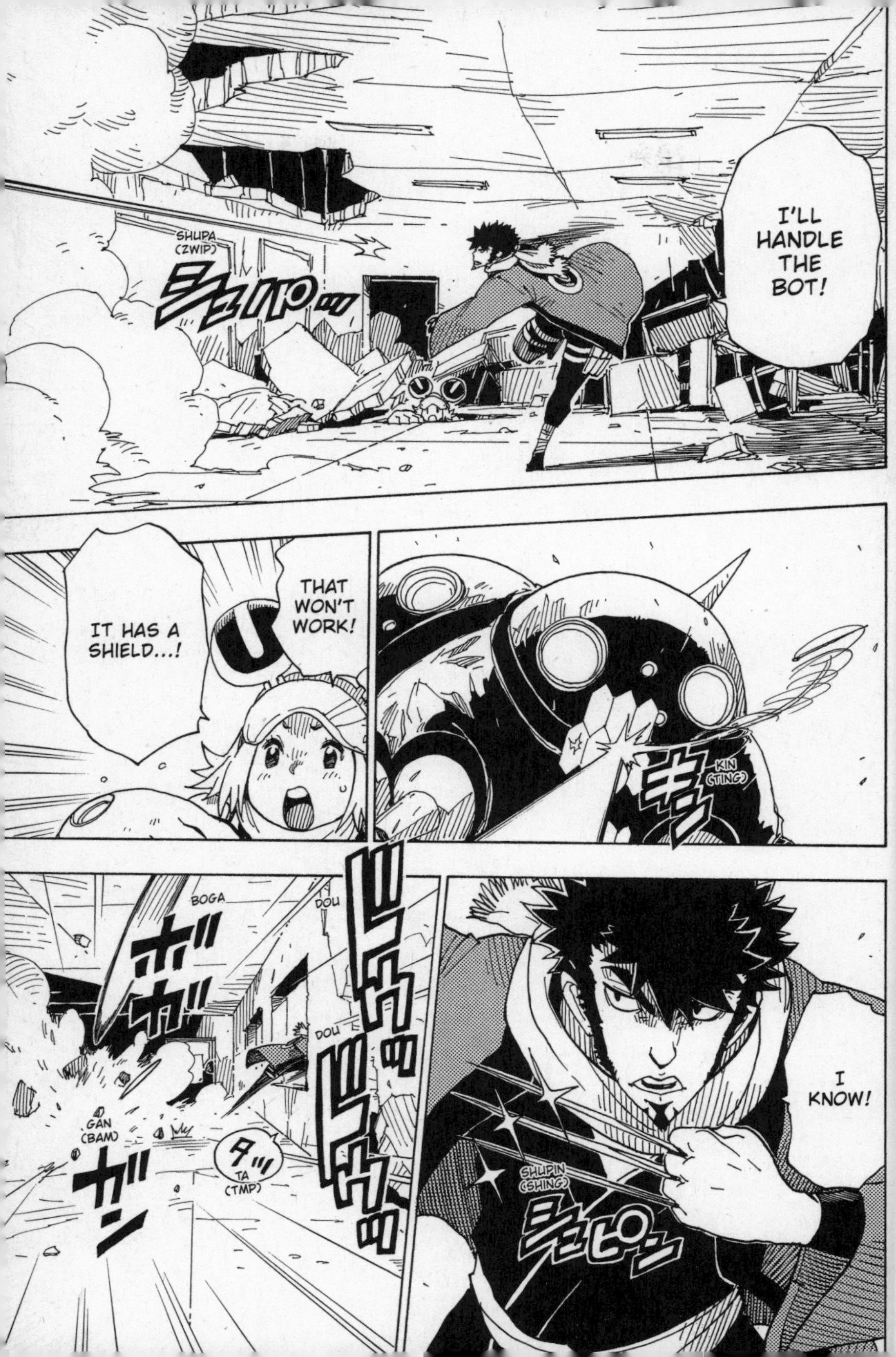
I'LL HANDLE THE BOT!
SHUPA (ZWIP)
KIN (TING)
THAT WON'T WORK!
IT HAS A SHIELD...!
I KNOW!
SHUPIN (SHING)
DOU
DOU
BOGA
GAN (BAM)
TA (TMP)

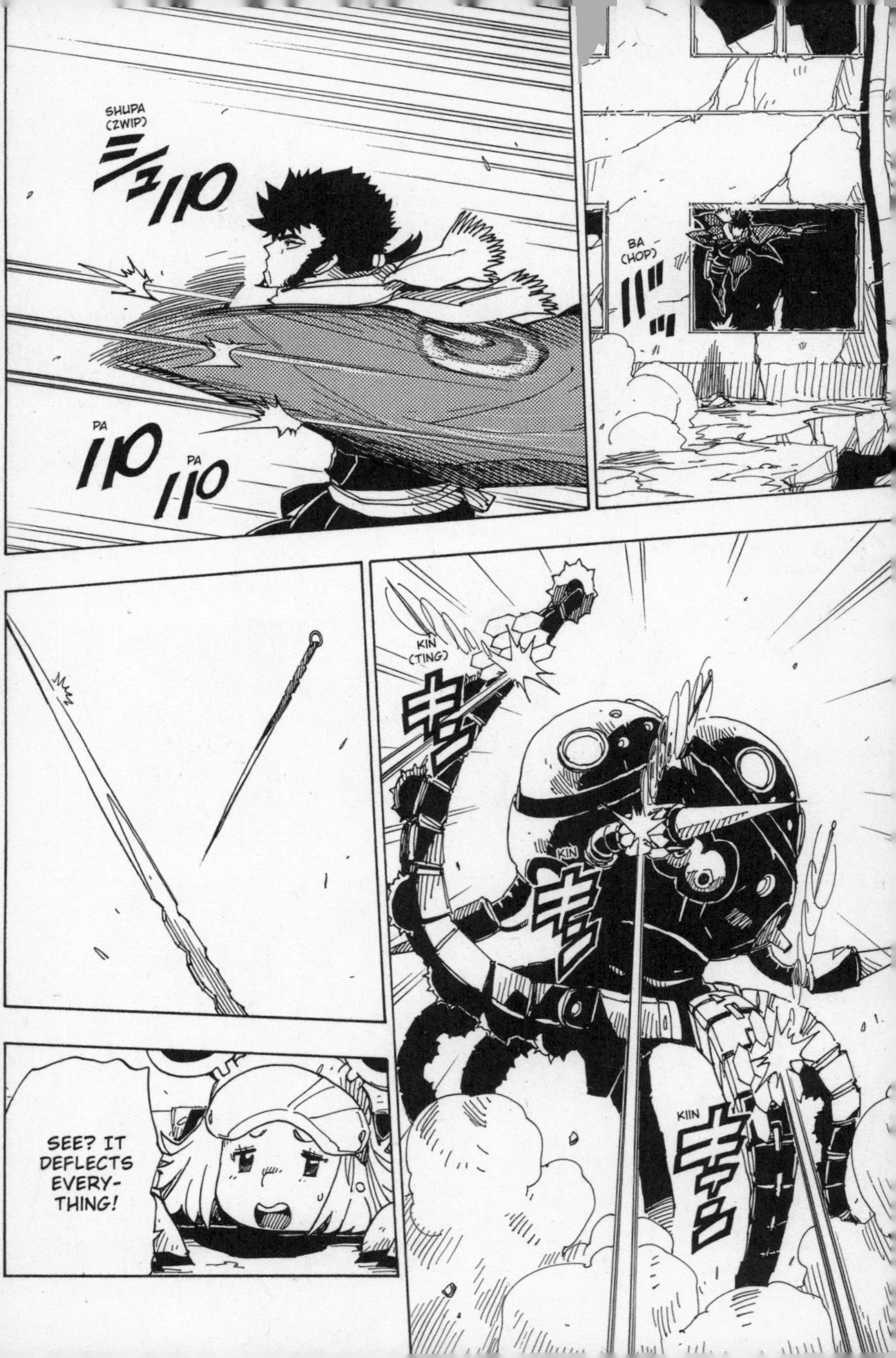
BA (HOP)
SHUPA (ZWIP)
PA
PA
KIN (TING)
KIN
KIIN
SEE? IT DEFLECTS EVERY-THING!

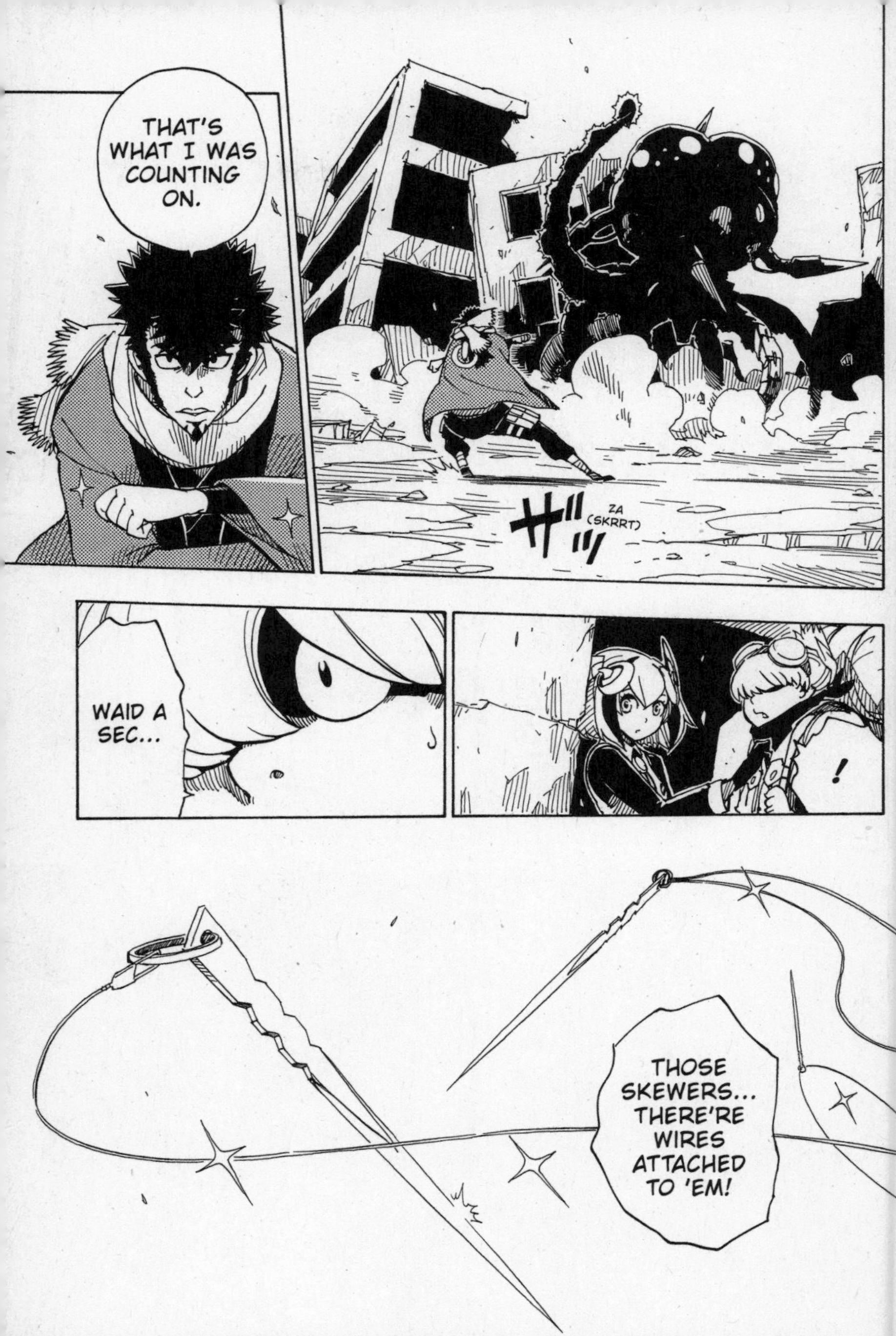
ザッ
ZA (SKRRT)
THAT'S WHAT I WAS COUNTING ON.
!
WAID A SEC...
THOSE SKEWERS... THERE'RE WIRES ATTACHED TO 'EM!

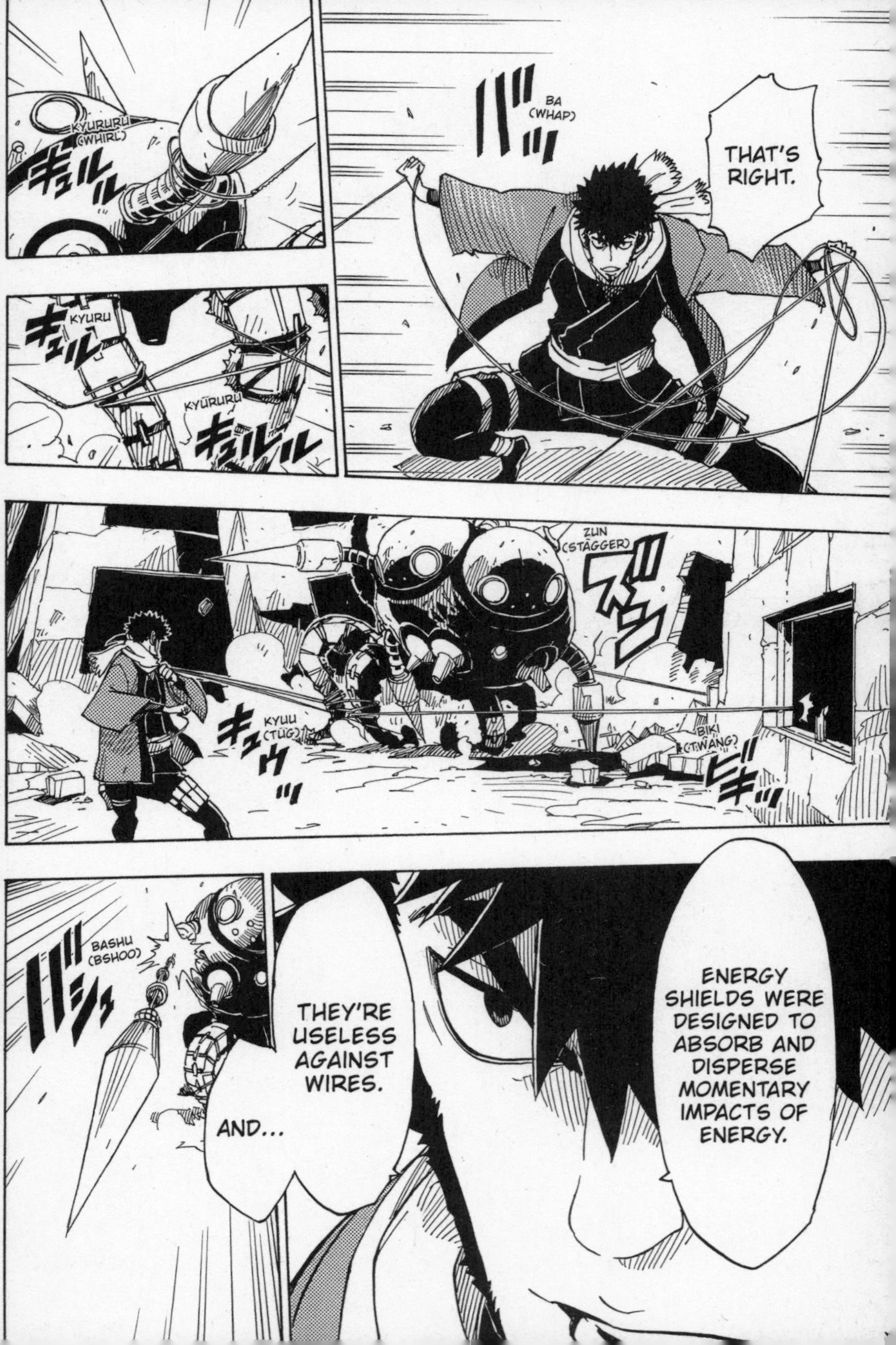
BA (WHAP)
THAT'S RIGHT.
KYURURU (WHIRL)
KYURU
KYURURU
ZUN (STAGGER)
BIKI (TWANG)
KYUU (TUG)
ENERGY SHIELDS WERE DESIGNED TO ABSORB AND DISPERSE MOMENTARY IMPACTS OF ENERGY.
THEY'RE USELESS AGAINST WIRES.
AND...
BASHU (BSHOO)

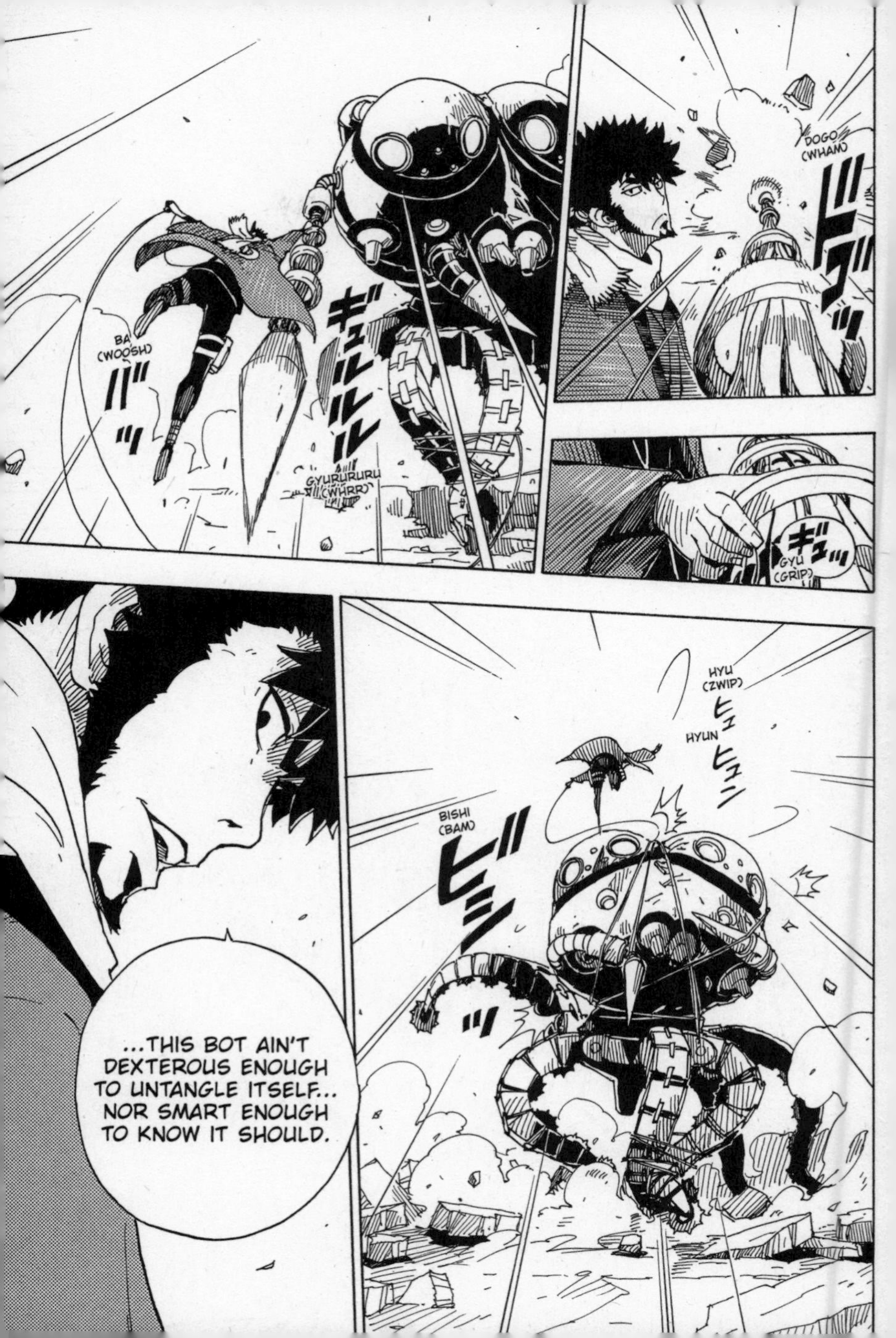
DOGO (WHAM)
ドゴッ
GYU (GRIP)
ギュッ
ギュルルル
GYURURURU (WHRR)
BA (WOOSH)
バッ
HYU (ZWIP)
ヒュ
HYUN
ヒュン
BISHI (BAM)
ビシッ
...THIS BOT AIN'T DEXTEROUS ENOUGH TO UNTANGLE ITSELF... NOR SMART ENOUGH TO KNOW IT SHOULD.

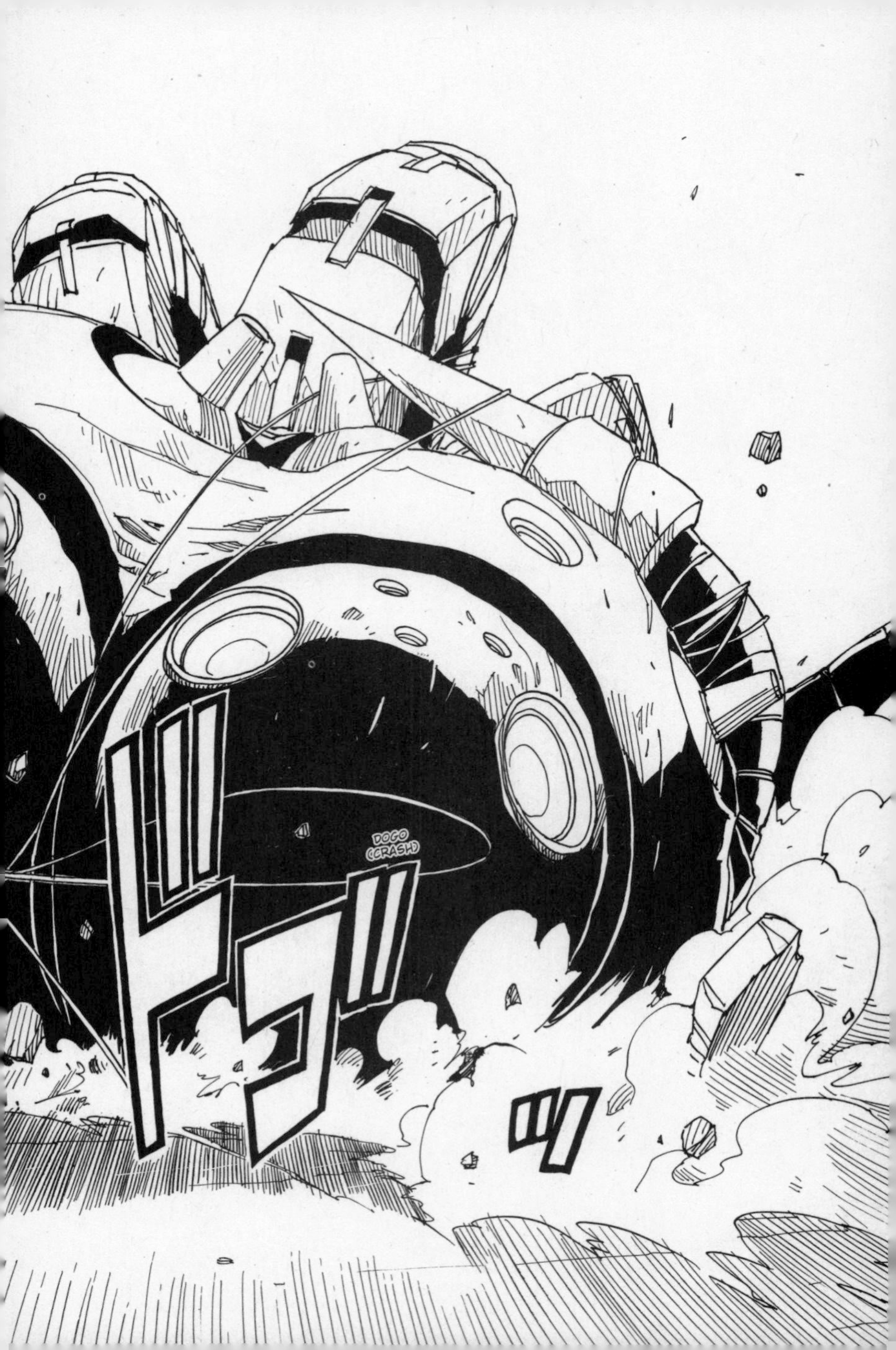
ドゴッ
DOGO
(CRASH)

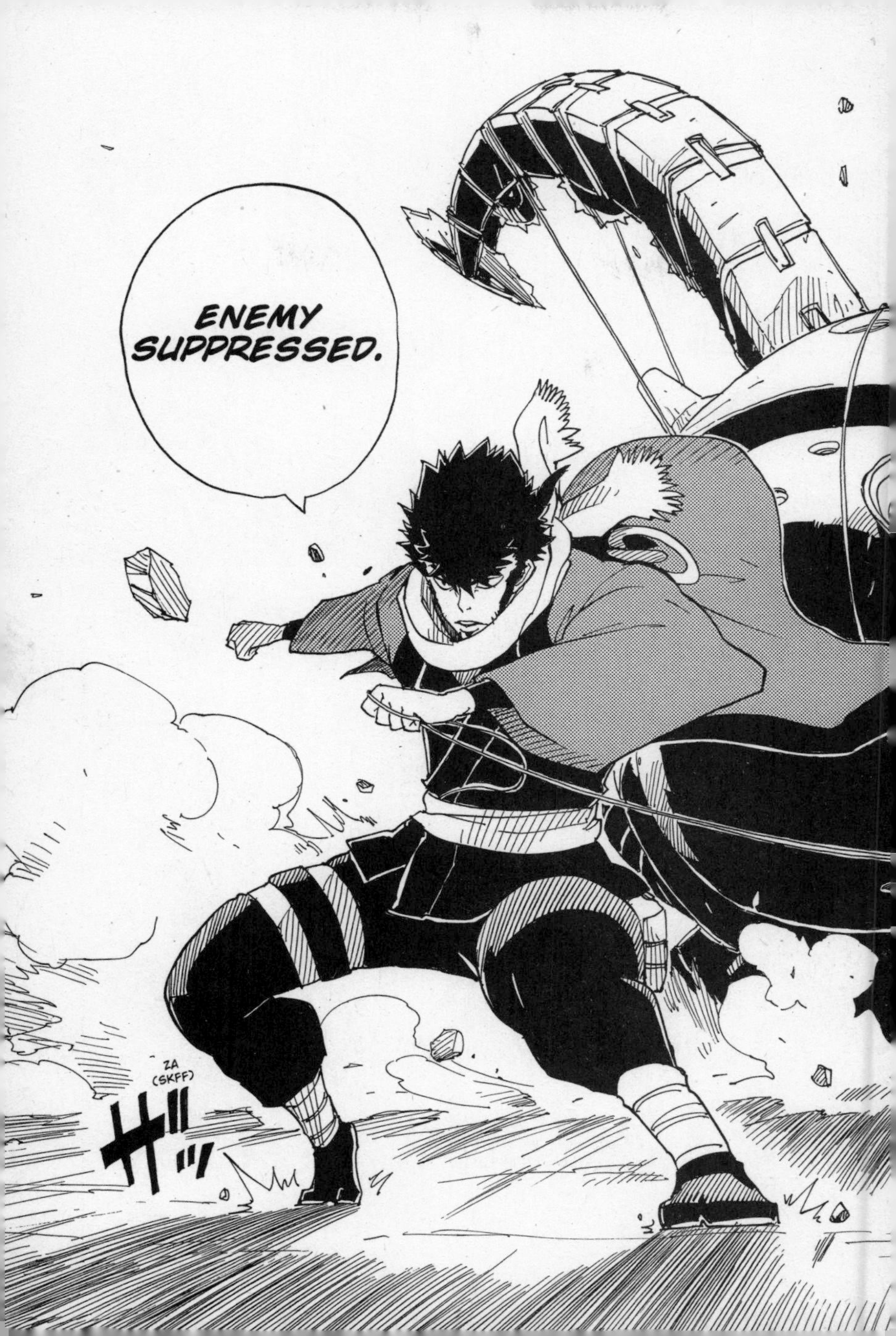
ENEMY SUPPRESSED.
ZA (SKFF)

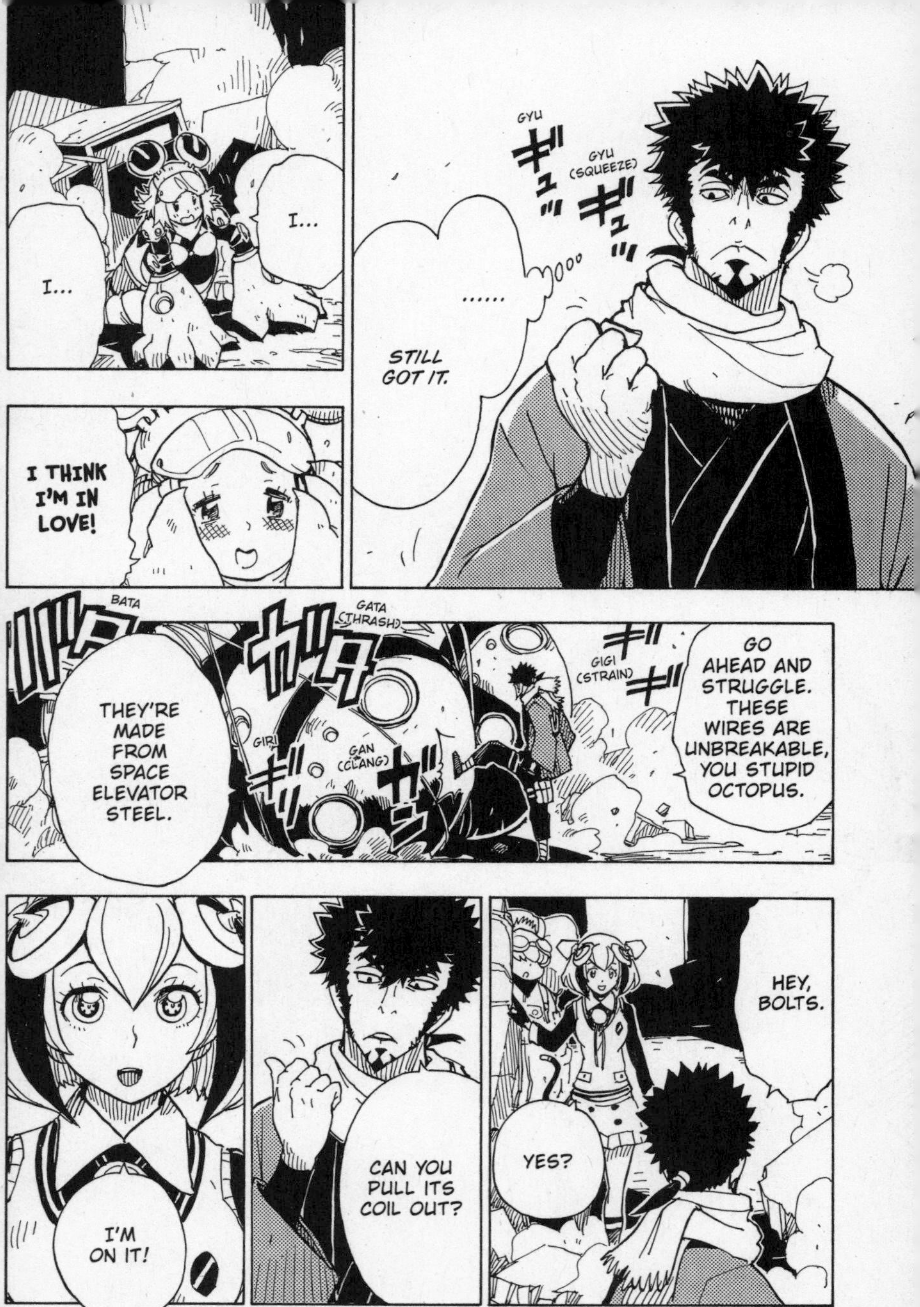
GYU
GYU (SQUEEZE)
......
STILL GOT IT.
I...
I...
I THINK I'M IN LOVE!
GIGI (STRAIN)
GO AHEAD AND STRUGGLE. THESE WIRES ARE UNBREAKABLE, YOU STUPID OCTOPUS.
GATA (THRASH)
GAN (CLANG)
GIRI
BATA
THEY'RE MADE FROM SPACE ELEVATOR STEEL.
HEY, BOLTS.
YES?
CAN YOU PULL ITS COIL OUT?
I'M ON IT!

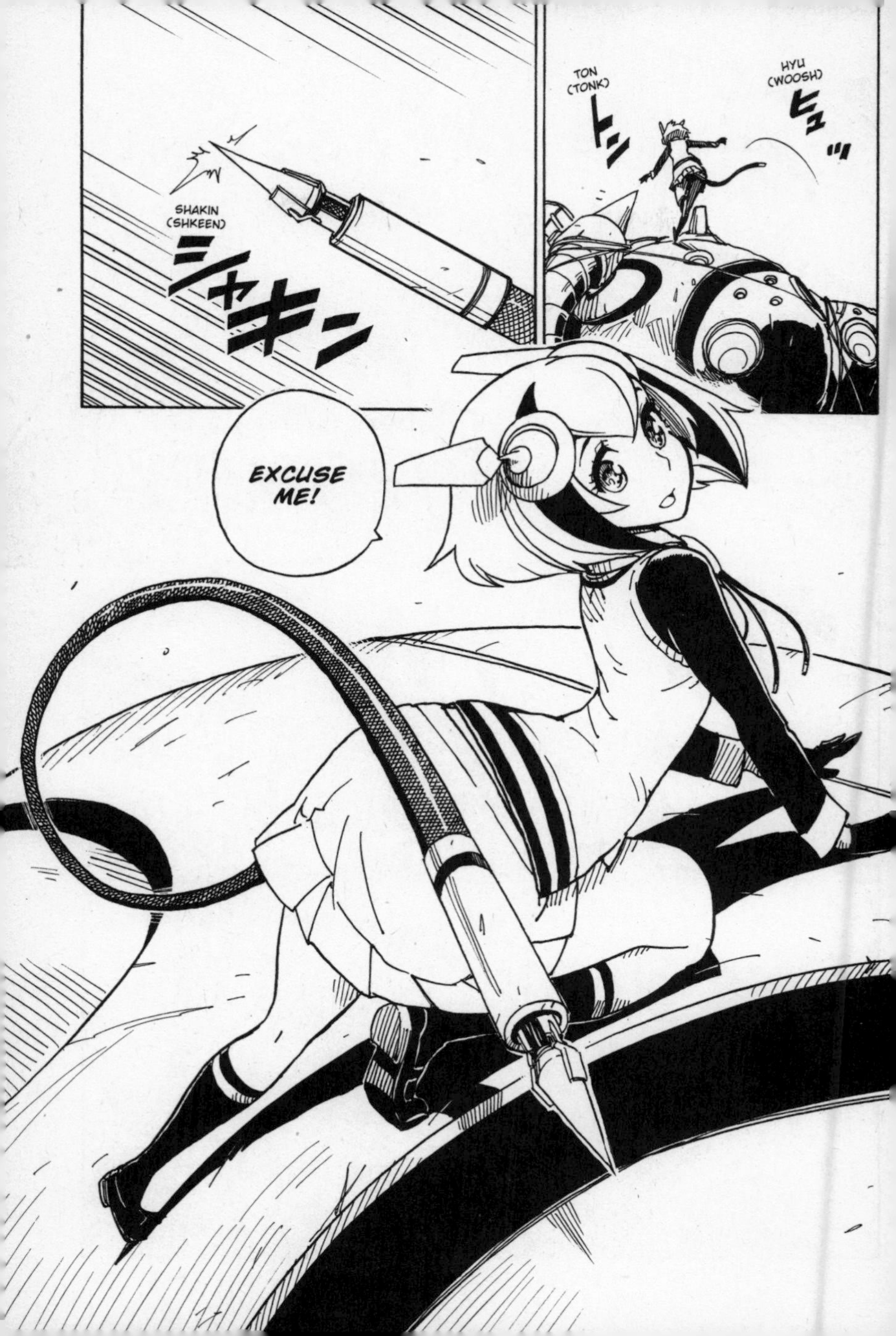
HYU (WOOSH)
ヒュッ
TON (TONK)
トン
SHAKIN (SHKEEN)
シャキン
EXCUSE ME!

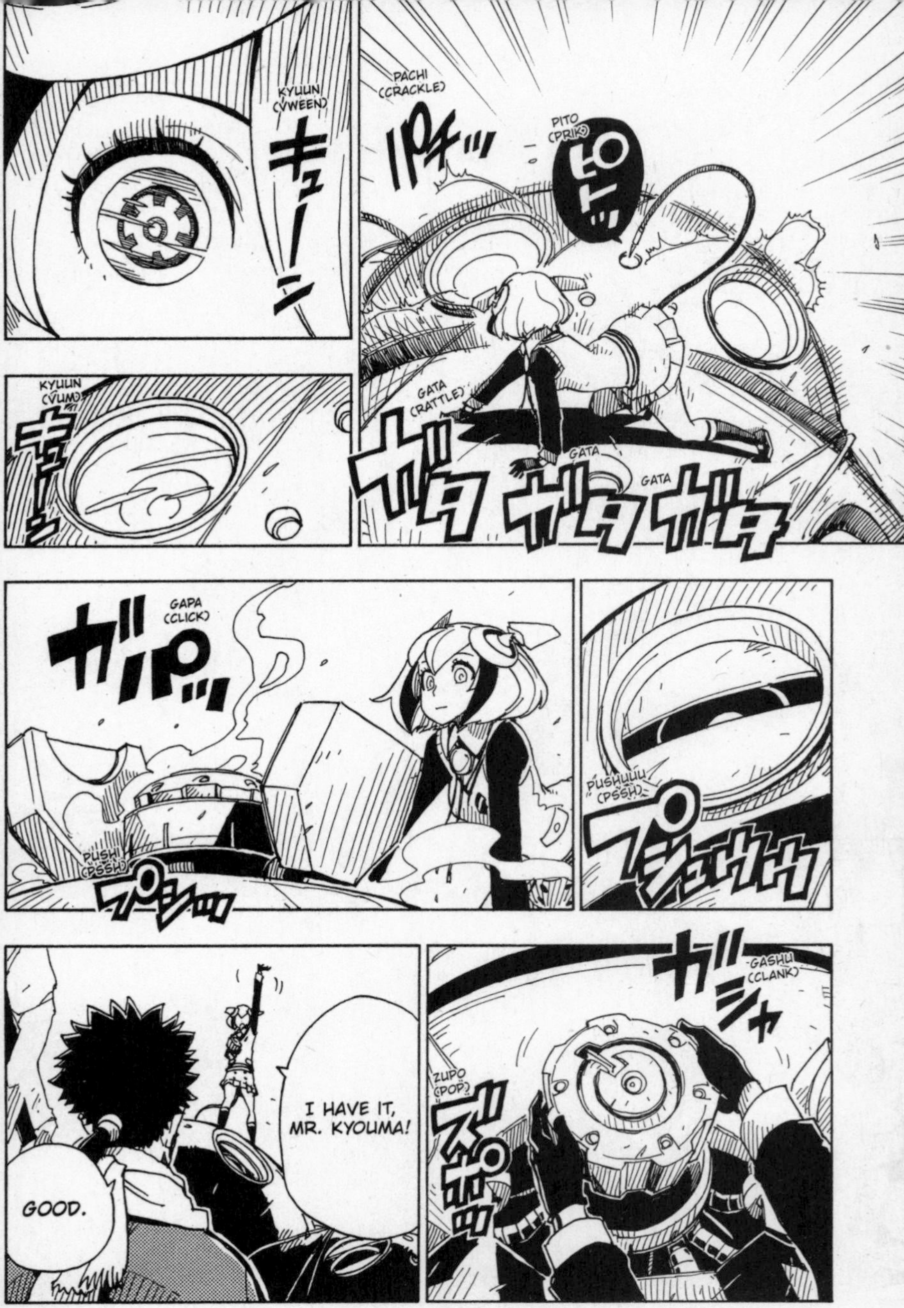
PACHI (CRACKLE)
PITO (PRIK)
GATA (RATTLE)
GATA
GATA
KYUUN (VWEEN)
KYUUN (VUM)
PUSHUUU (PSSH)
GAPA (CLICK)
PUSH (PSSH)
GASHU (CLANK)
ZUPO (POP)
I HAVE IT, MR. KYOUMA!
GOOD.

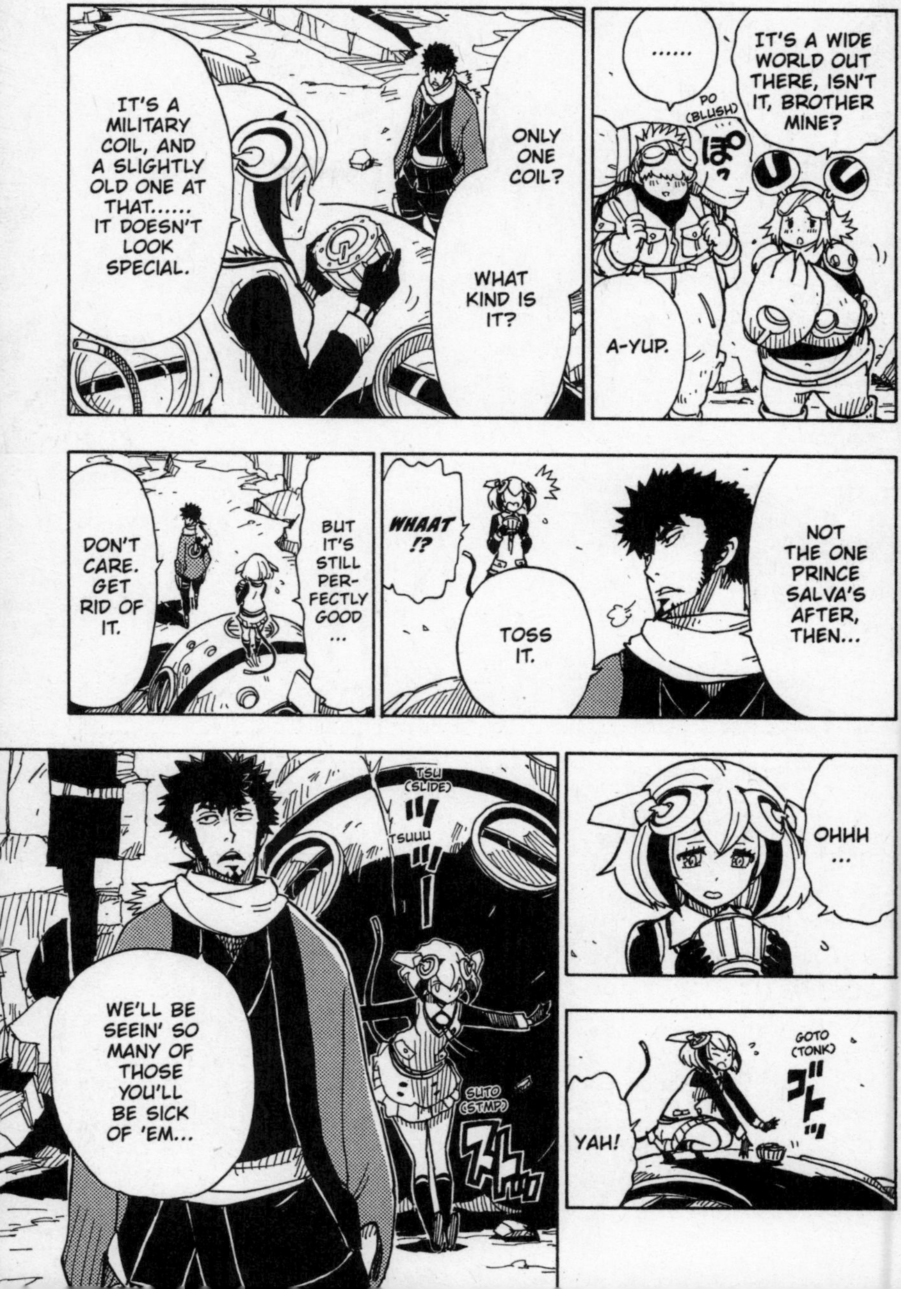
IT'S A WIDE WORLD OUT THERE, ISN'T IT, BROTHER MINE?
......
PO (BLUSH)
ぽっ
A-YUP.
ONLY ONE COIL?
WHAT KIND IS IT?
IT'S A MILITARY COIL, AND A SLIGHTLY OLD ONE AT THAT...... IT DOESN'T LOOK SPECIAL.
NOT THE ONE PRINCE SALVA'S AFTER, THEN...
TOSS IT.
WHAAT!?
BUT IT'S STILL PER-FECTLY GOOD...
DON'T CARE. GET RID OF IT.
OHHH...
GOTO (TONK)
ゴトッ
YAH!
TSU (SLIDE)
TSUUU
SUTO (STMP)
WE'LL BE SEEIN' SO MANY OF THOSE YOU'LL BE SICK OF 'EM...

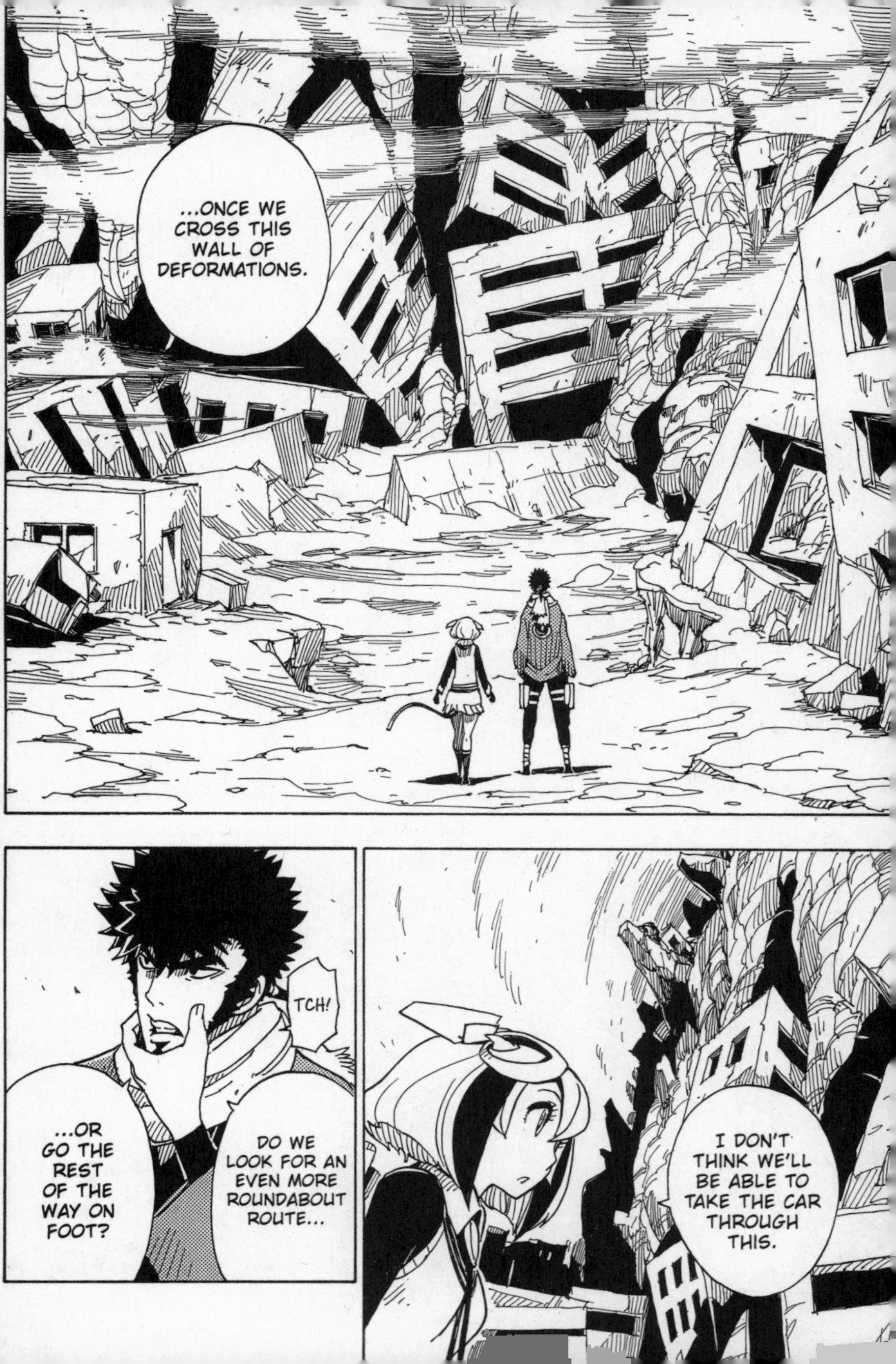
...ONCE WE CROSS THIS WALL OF DEFORMATIONS.
I DON'T THINK WE'LL BE ABLE TO TAKE THE CAR THROUGH THIS.
TCH!
DO WE LOOK FOR AN EVEN MORE ROUNDABOUT ROUTE...
...OR GO THE REST OF THE WAY ON FOOT?

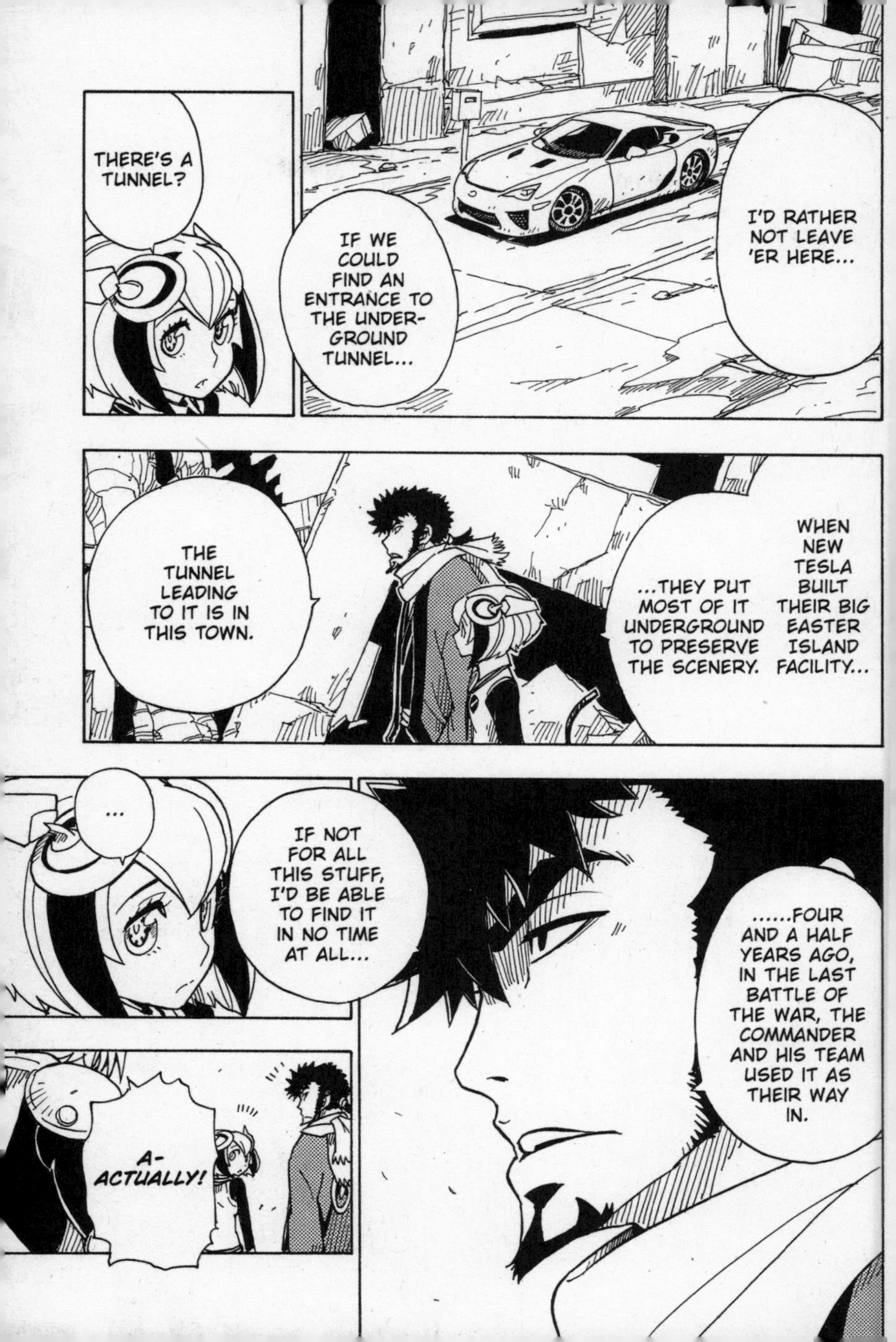
I'D RATHER NOT LEAVE 'ER HERE...
IF WE COULD FIND AN ENTRANCE TO THE UNDER-GROUND TUNNEL...
THERE'S A TUNNEL?
WHEN NEW TESLA BUILT THEIR BIG EASTER ISLAND FACILITY...
...THEY PUT MOST OF IT UNDERGROUND TO PRESERVE THE SCENERY.
THE TUNNEL LEADING TO IT IS IN THIS TOWN.
......FOUR AND A HALF YEARS AGO, IN THE LAST BATTLE OF THE WAR, THE COMMANDER AND HIS TEAM USED IT AS THEIR WAY IN.
IF NOT FOR ALL THIS STUFF, I'D BE ABLE TO FIND IT IN NO TIME AT ALL...
...
A- ACTUALLY!

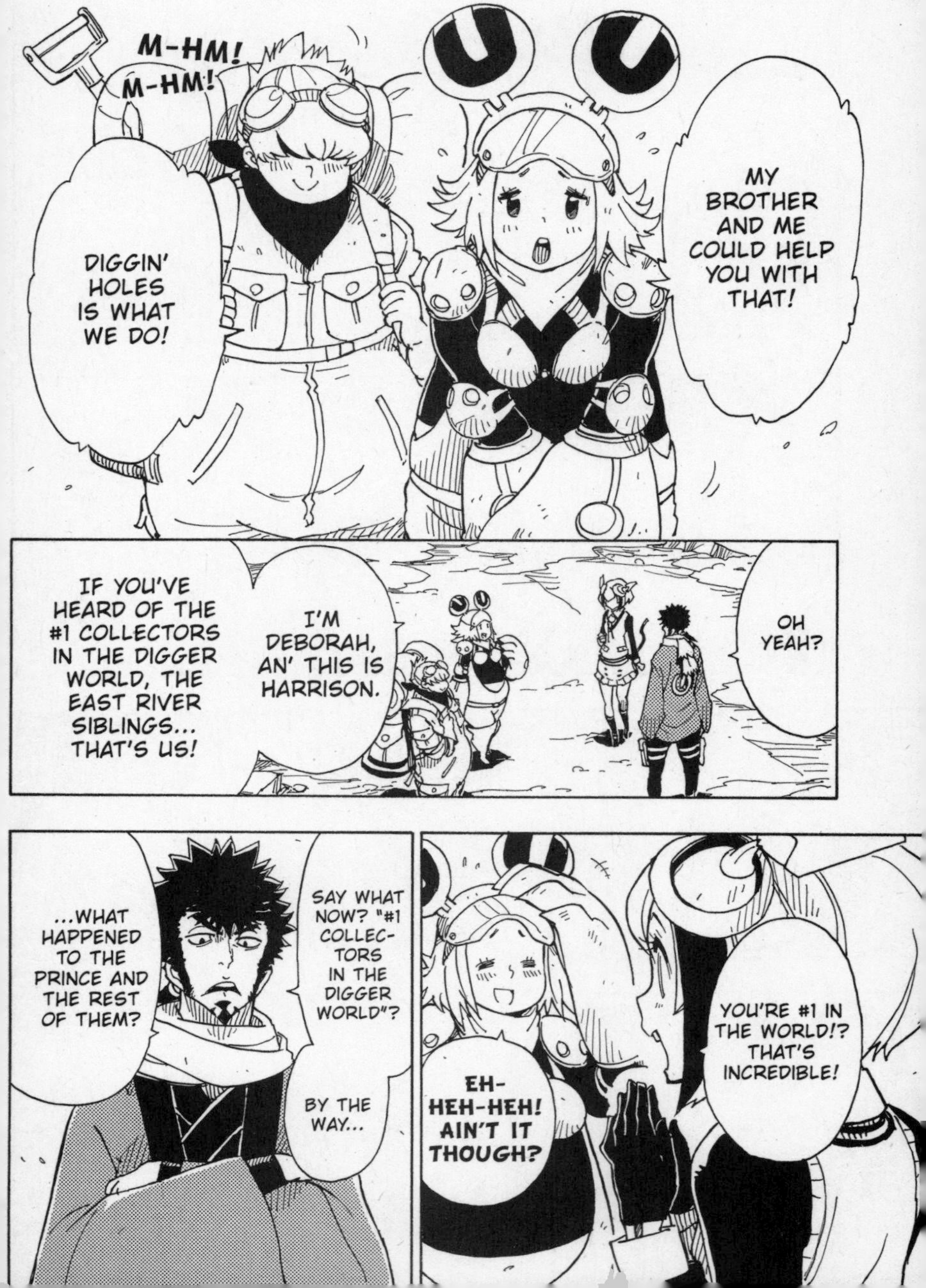
MY BROTHER AND ME COULD HELP YOU WITH THAT!
M-HM!
M-HM!
DIGGIN' HOLES IS WHAT WE DO!
OH YEAH?
I'M DEBORAH, AN' THIS IS HARRISON.
IF YOU'VE HEARD OF THE #1 COLLECTORS IN THE DIGGER WORLD, THE EAST RIVER SIBLINGS... THAT'S US!
YOU'RE #1 IN THE WORLD!? THAT'S INCREDIBLE!
EH-HEH-HEH! AIN'T IT THOUGH?
SAY WHAT NOW? "#1 COLLEC-TORS IN THE DIGGER WORLD"?
BY THE WAY...
...WHAT HAPPENED TO THE PRINCE AND THE REST OF THEM?

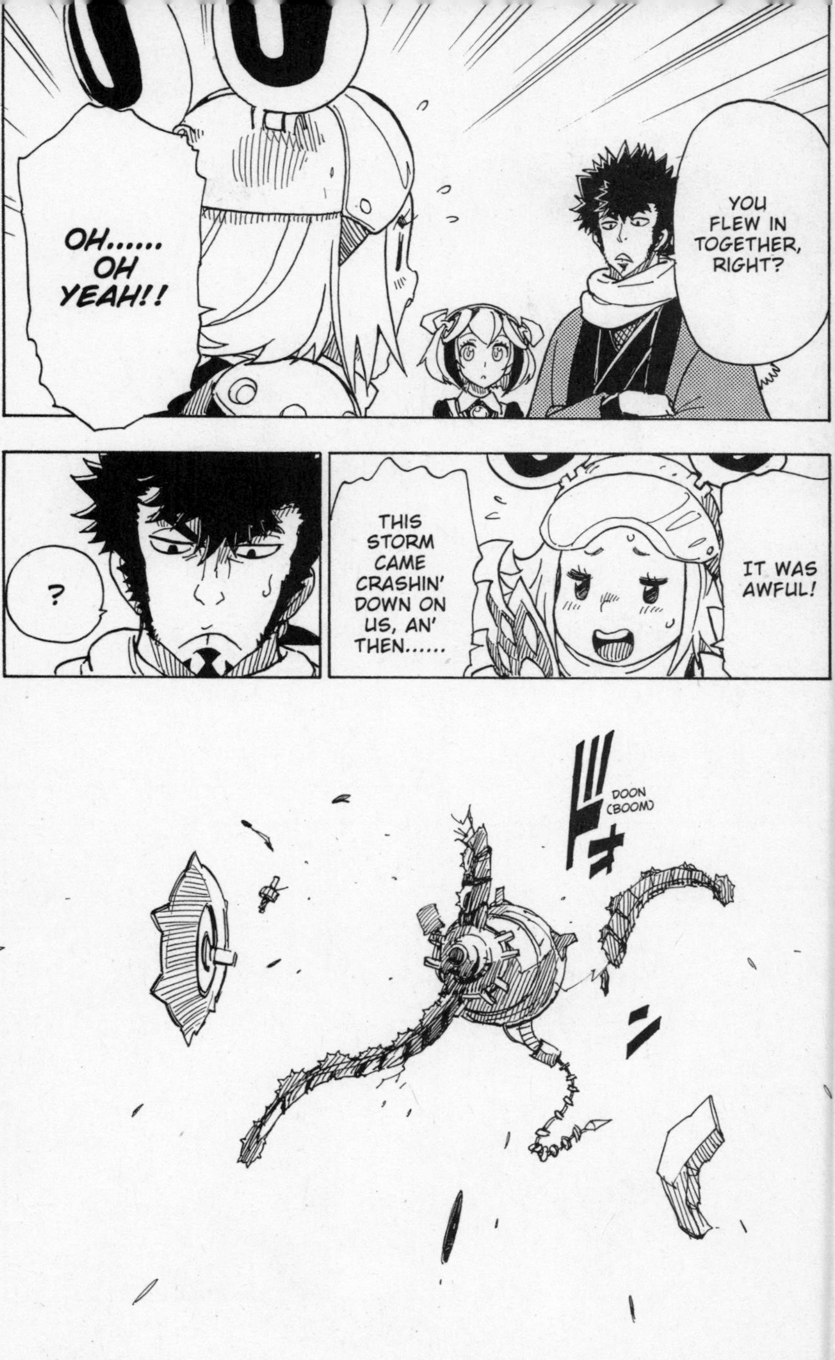
YOU FLEW IN TOGETHER, RIGHT?
OH...... OH YEAH!!
IT WAS AWFUL!
THIS STORM CAME CRASHIN' DOWN ON US, AN' THEN......
?
DOON (BOOM)

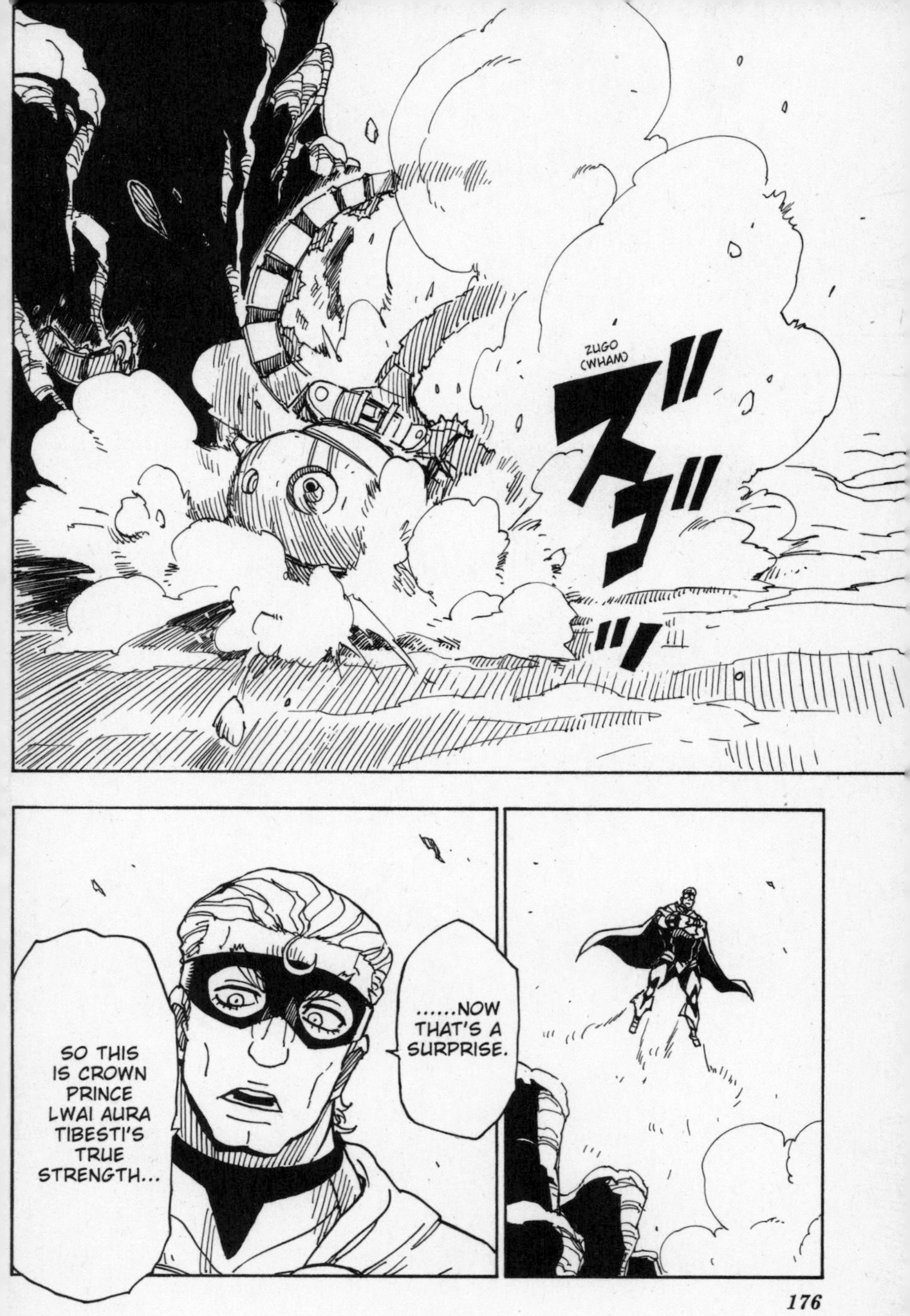
ZUGO (WHAM)
ズゴッ
......NOW THAT'S A SURPRISE.
SO THIS IS CROWN PRINCE LWAI AURA TIBESTI'S TRUE STRENGTH...

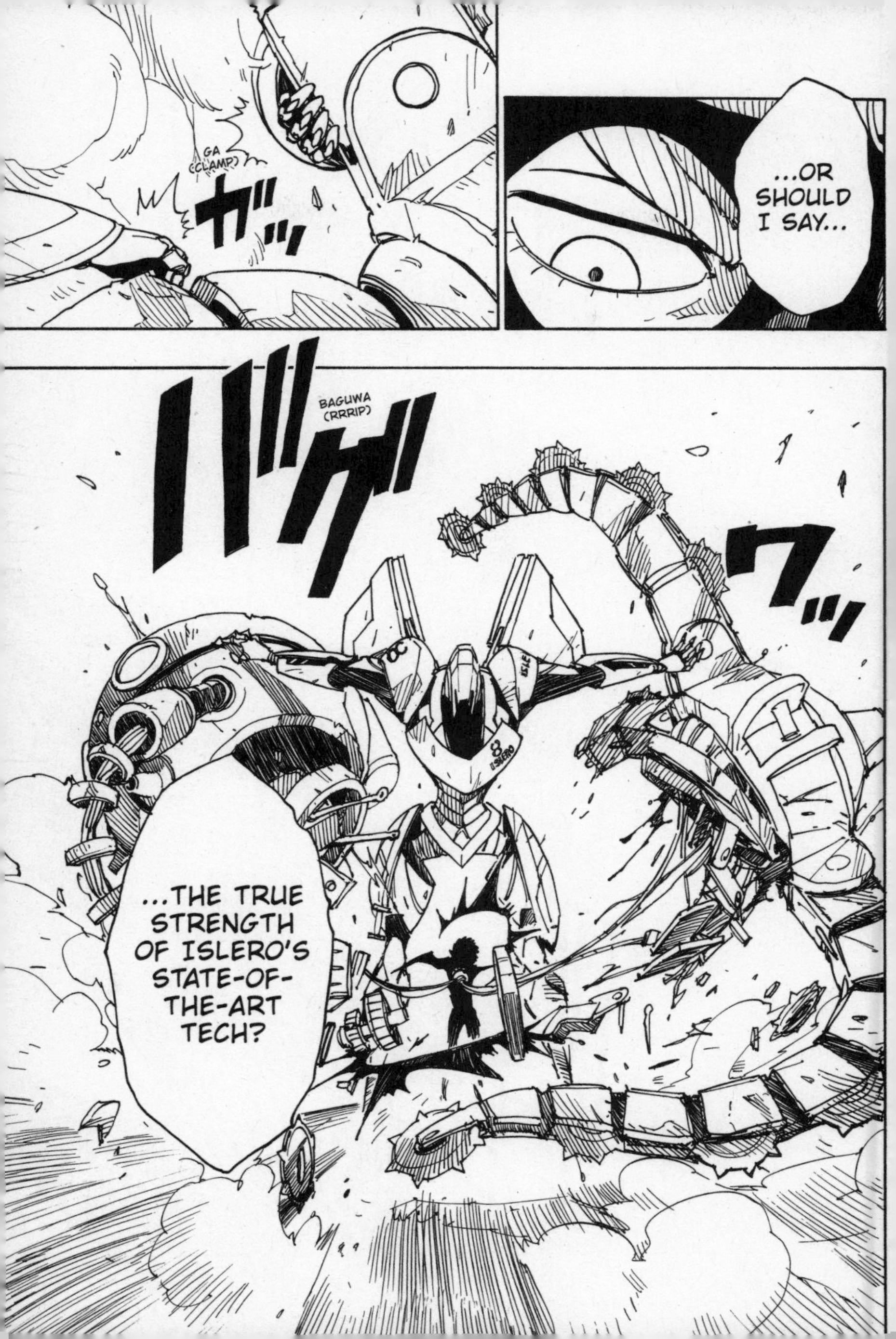
...OR SHOULD I SAY...
GA (CLAMP)
ガッ
BAGUWA (RRRIP)
バグワッ
...THE TRUE STRENGTH OF ISLERO'S STATE-OF-THE-ART TECH?

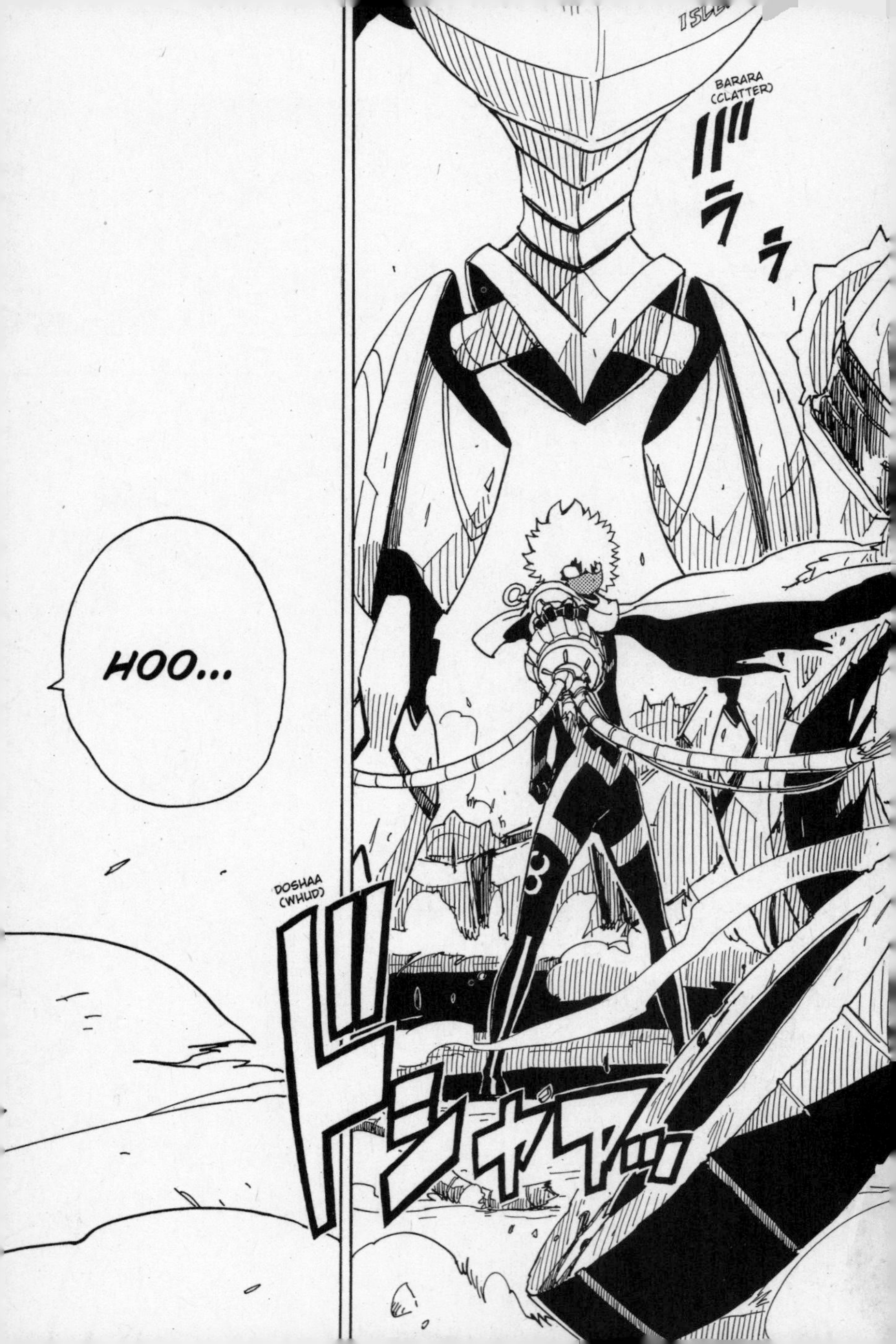
BARARA (CLATTER)
DOSHAA (WHUD)
HOO...

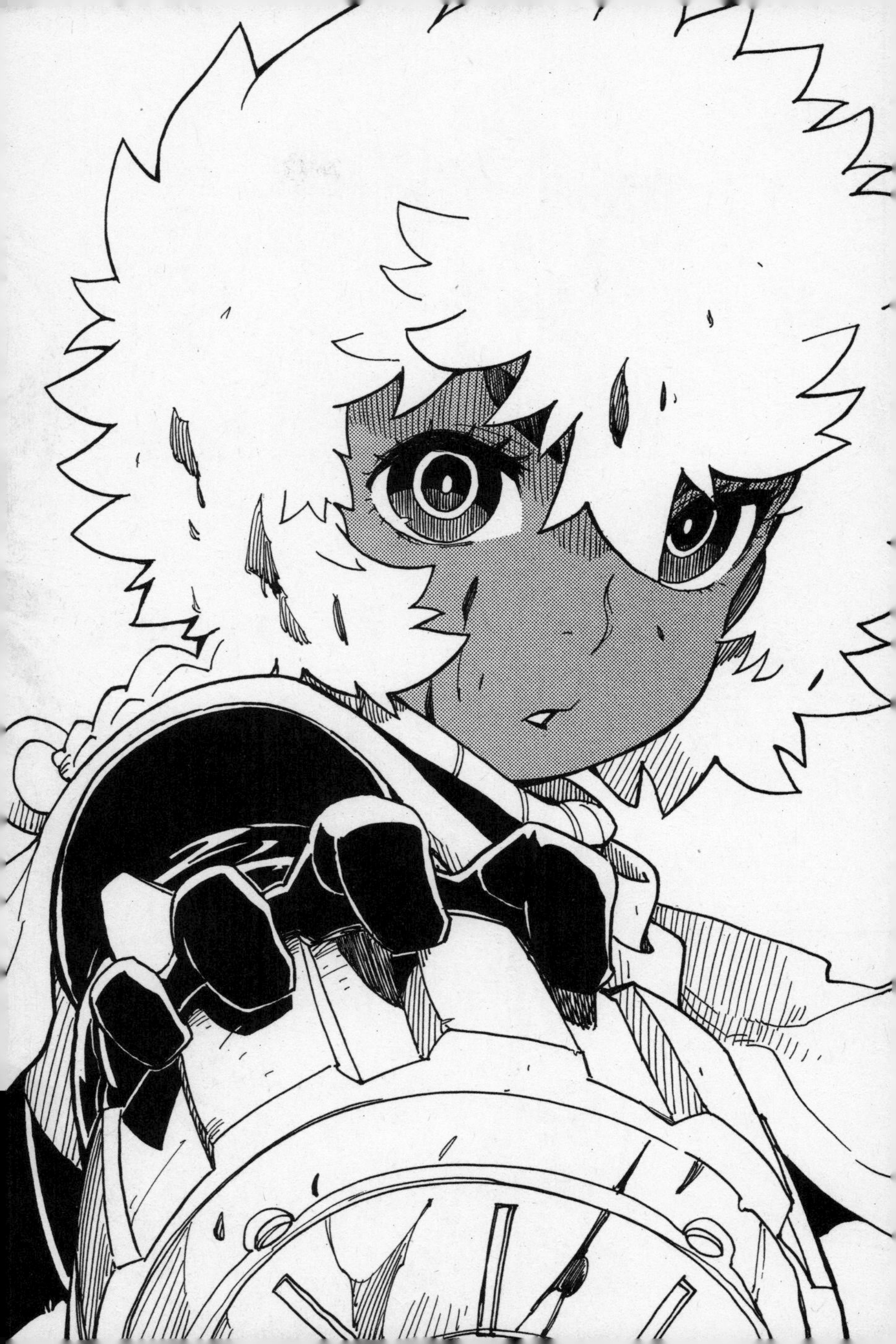

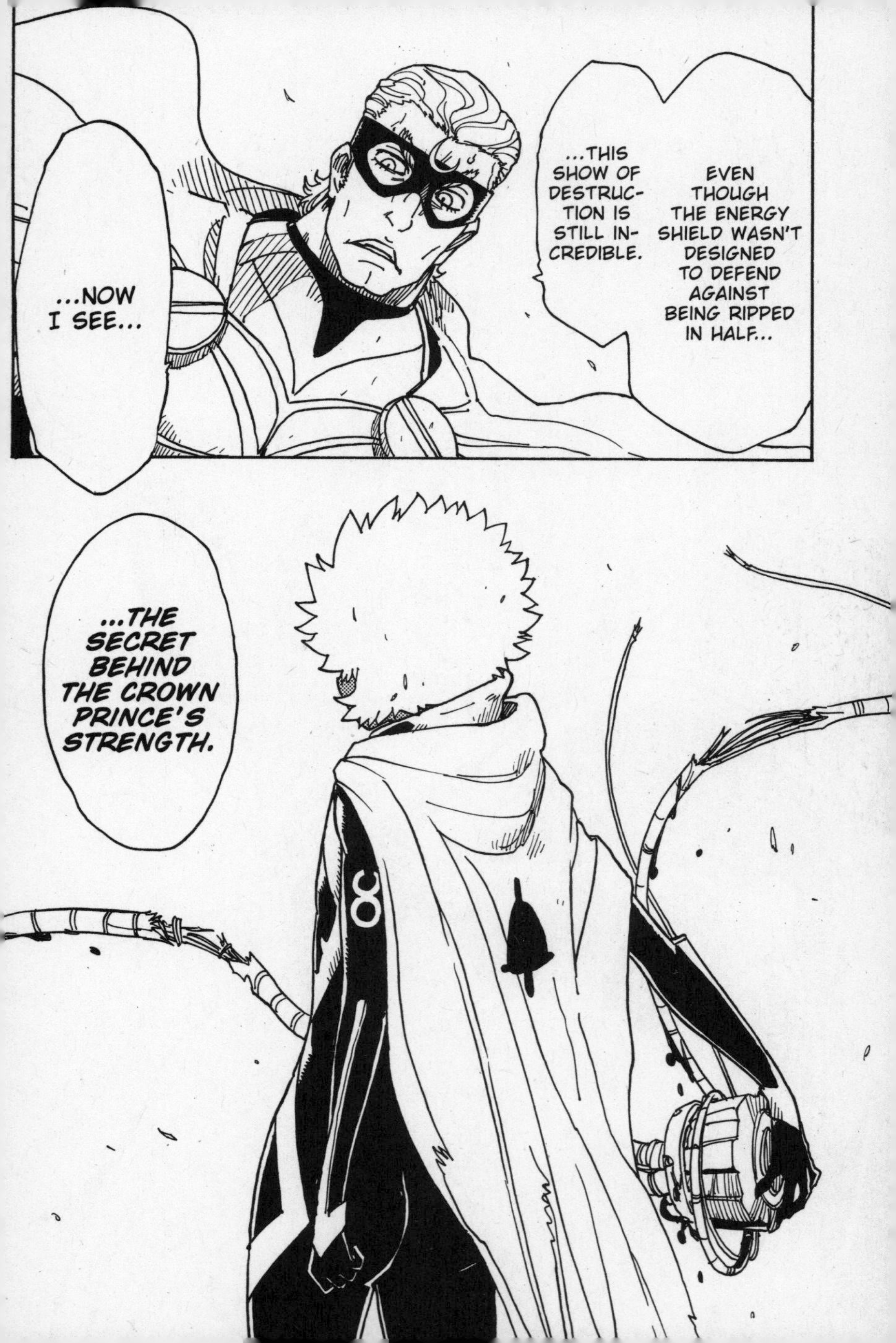
EVEN THOUGH THE ENERGY SHIELD WASN'T DESIGNED TO DEFEND AGAINST BEING RIPPED IN HALF...
...THIS SHOW OF DESTRUC- TION IS STILL IN- CREDIBLE.
...NOW I SEE...
...THE SECRET BEHIND THE CROWN PRINCE'S STRENGTH.

FILE.47

A DEATH LONG OVERDUE

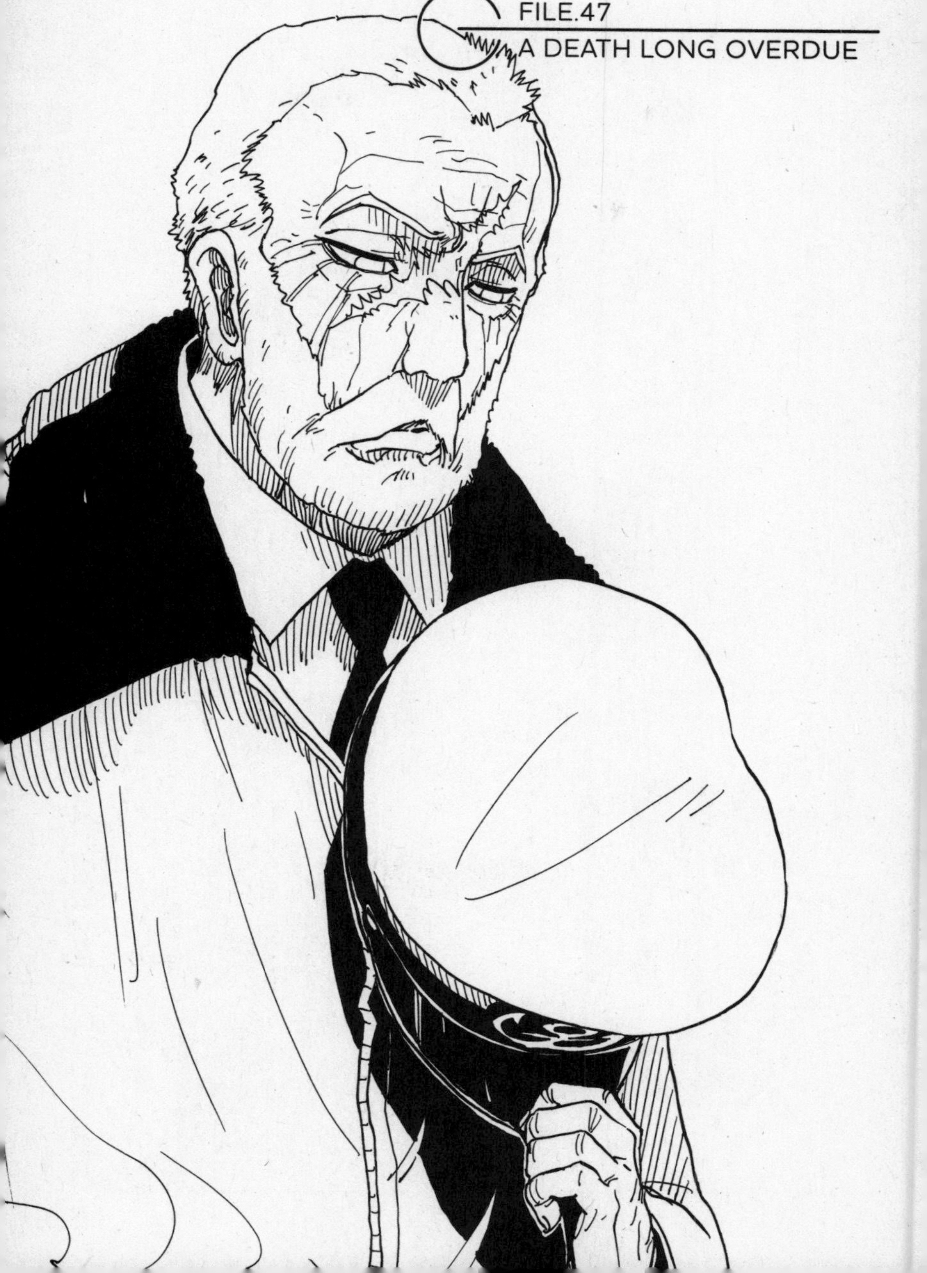

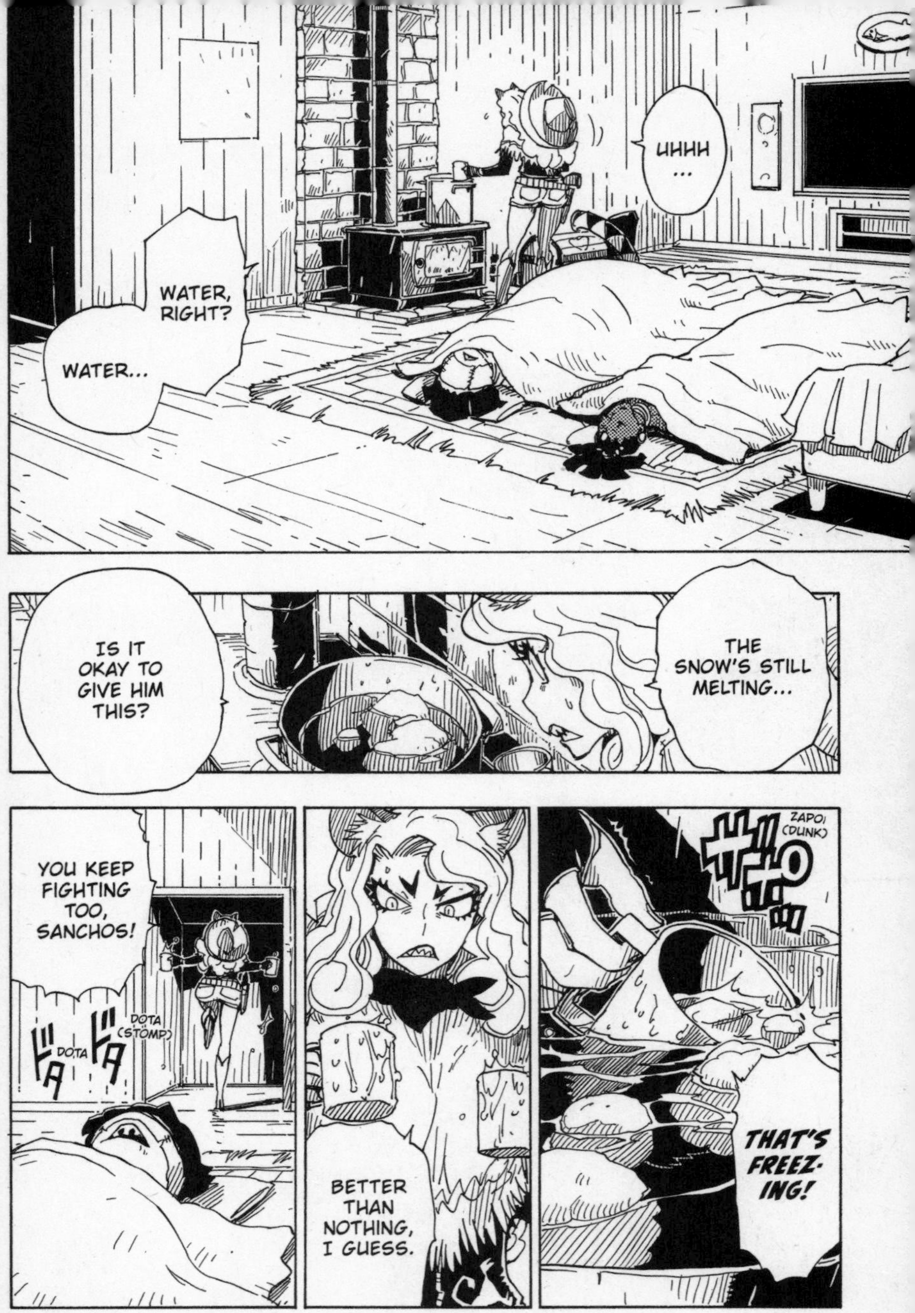
UHHH ...
WATER, RIGHT?
WATER...
THE SNOW'S STILL MELTING...
IS IT OKAY TO GIVE HIM THIS?
ZAPOI (DUNK)
THAT'S FREEZ-ING!
BETTER THAN NOTHING, I GUESS.
YOU KEEP FIGHTING TOO, SANCHOS!
DOTA (STOMP)
DOTA

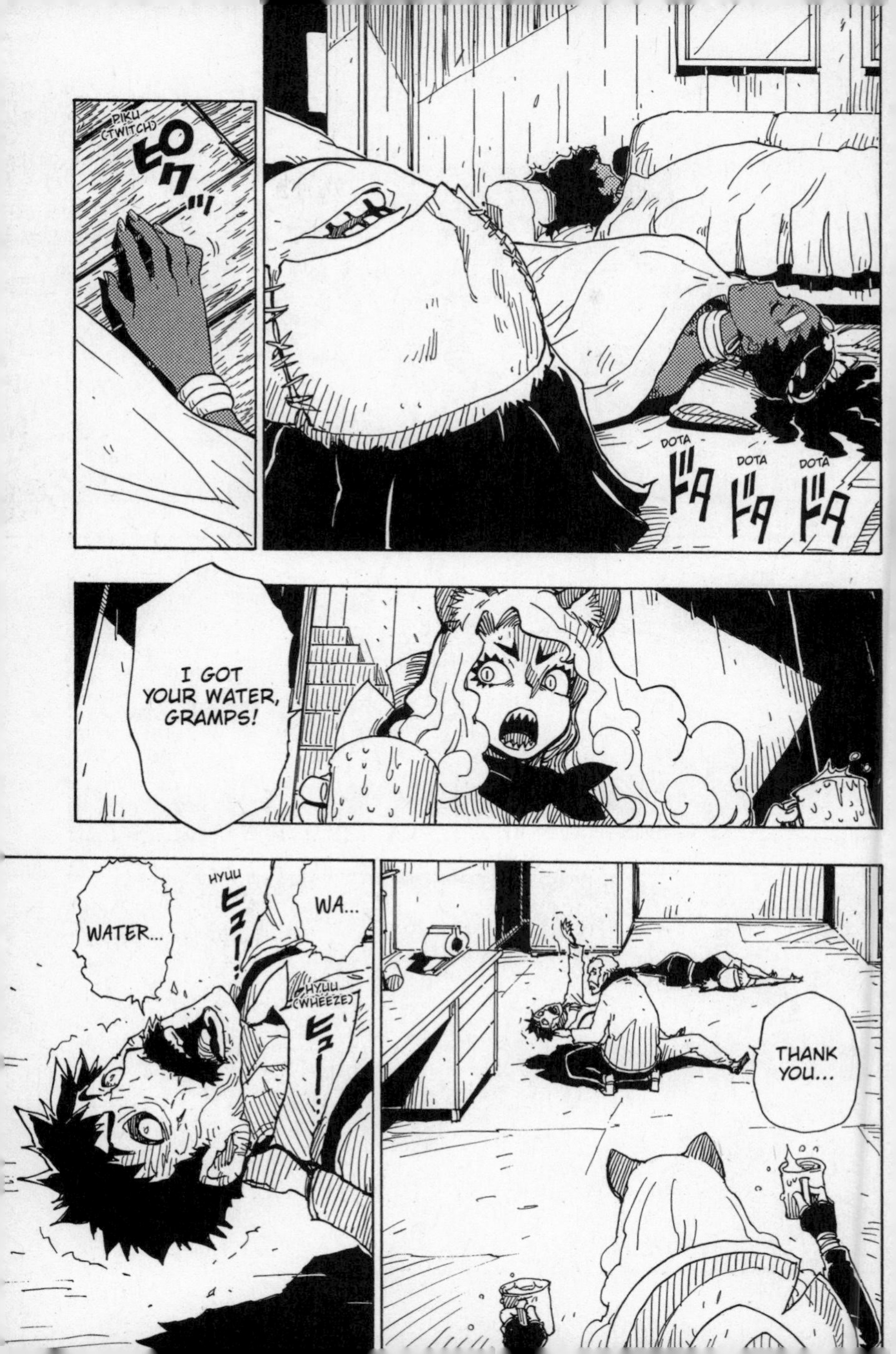
DOTA
DOTA
DOTA
PIKU (TWITCH)
I GOT YOUR WATER, GRAMPS!
THANK YOU...
WA...
HYUU
WATER...
HYUU (WHEEZE)

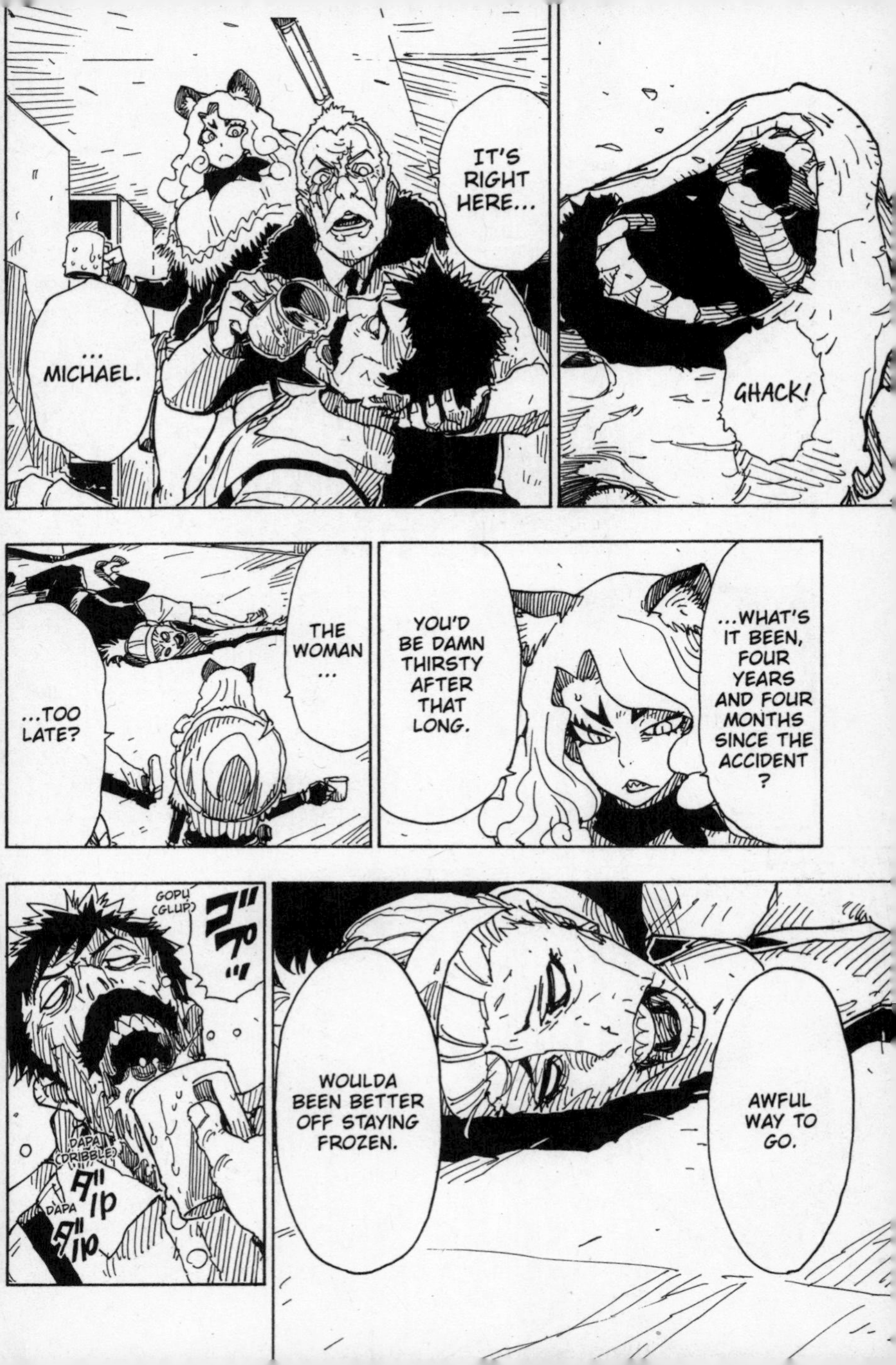
GHACK!
IT'S RIGHT HERE...
...MICHAEL.
...WHAT'S IT BEEN, FOUR YEARS AND FOUR MONTHS SINCE THE ACCIDENT?
YOU'D BE DAMN THIRSTY AFTER THAT LONG.
THE WOMAN...
...TOO LATE?
AWFUL WAY TO GO.
WOULDA BEEN BETTER OFF STAYING FROZEN.
GOPU (GLUP)
DAPA (DRIBBLE)
DAPA

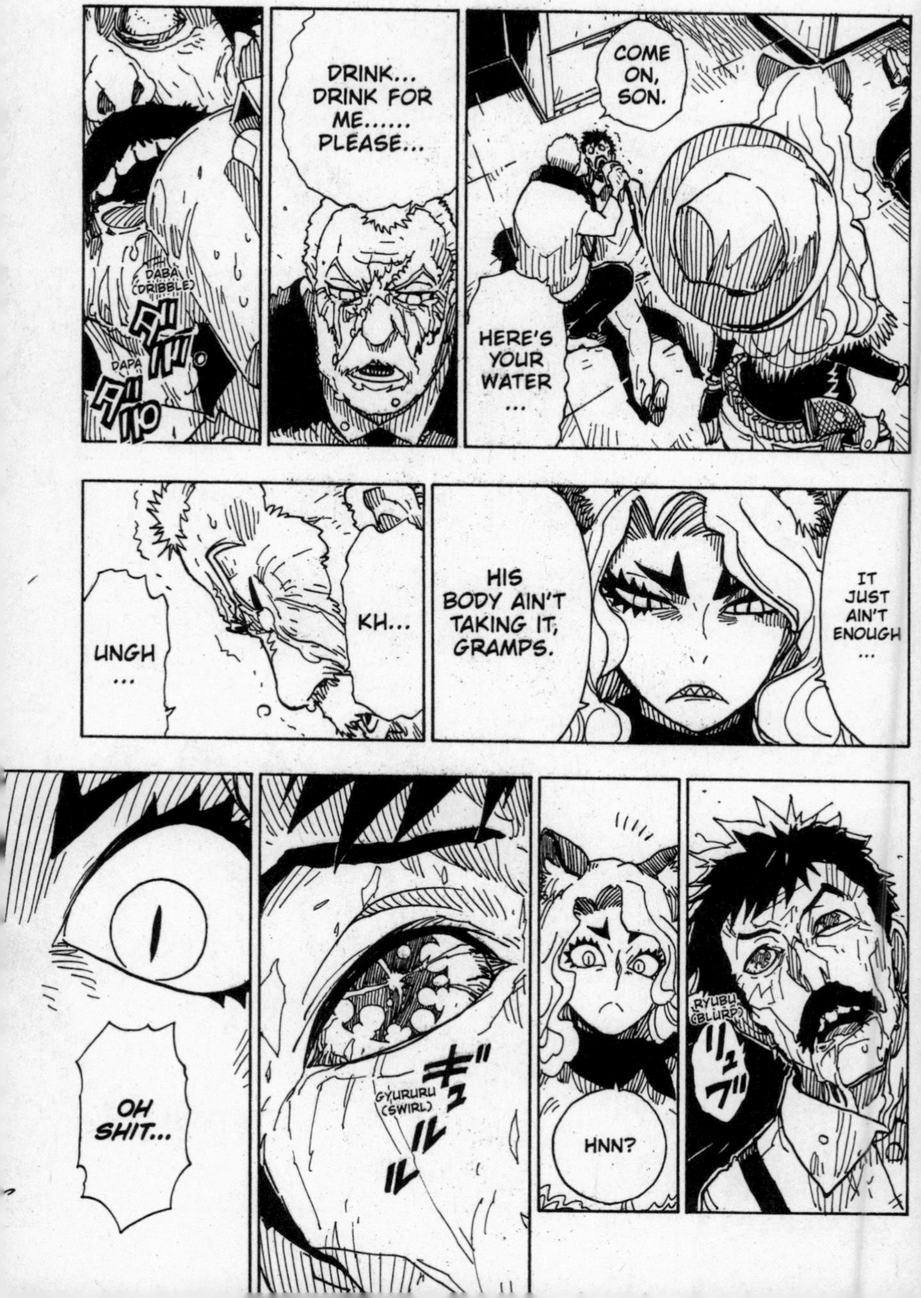
COME ON, SON.
HERE'S YOUR WATER ...
DRINK... DRINK FOR ME...... PLEASE...
DABA (DRIBBLE)
DAPA
IT JUST AIN'T ENOUGH ...
HIS BODY AIN'T TAKING IT, GRAMPS.
KH...
UNGH ...
RYUBU (BLURP)
HNN?
GYURURU (SWIRL)
OH SHIT...

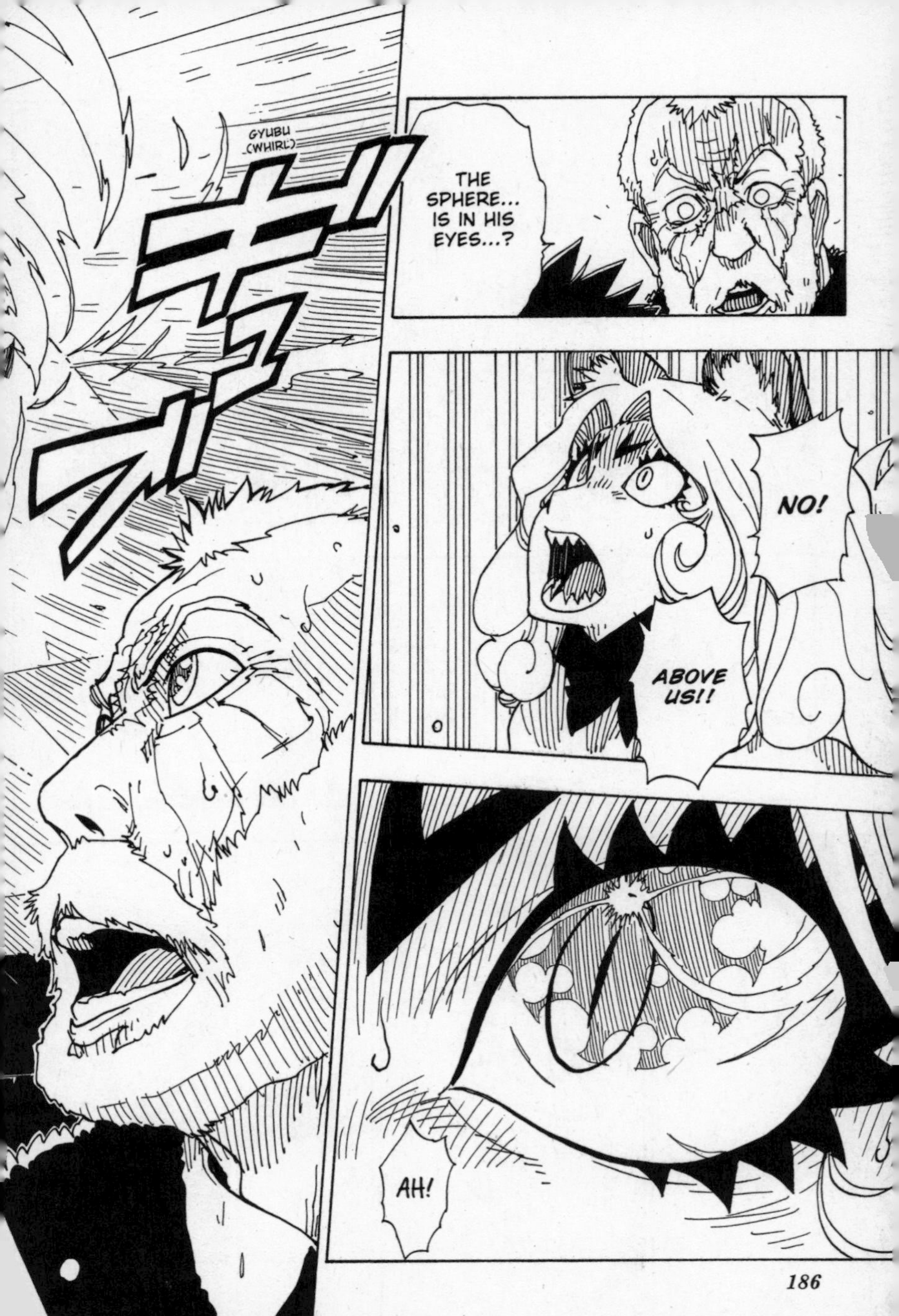
THE SPHERE... IS IN HIS EYES...?
NO!
ABOVE US!!
AH!
GYUBU (WHIRL)

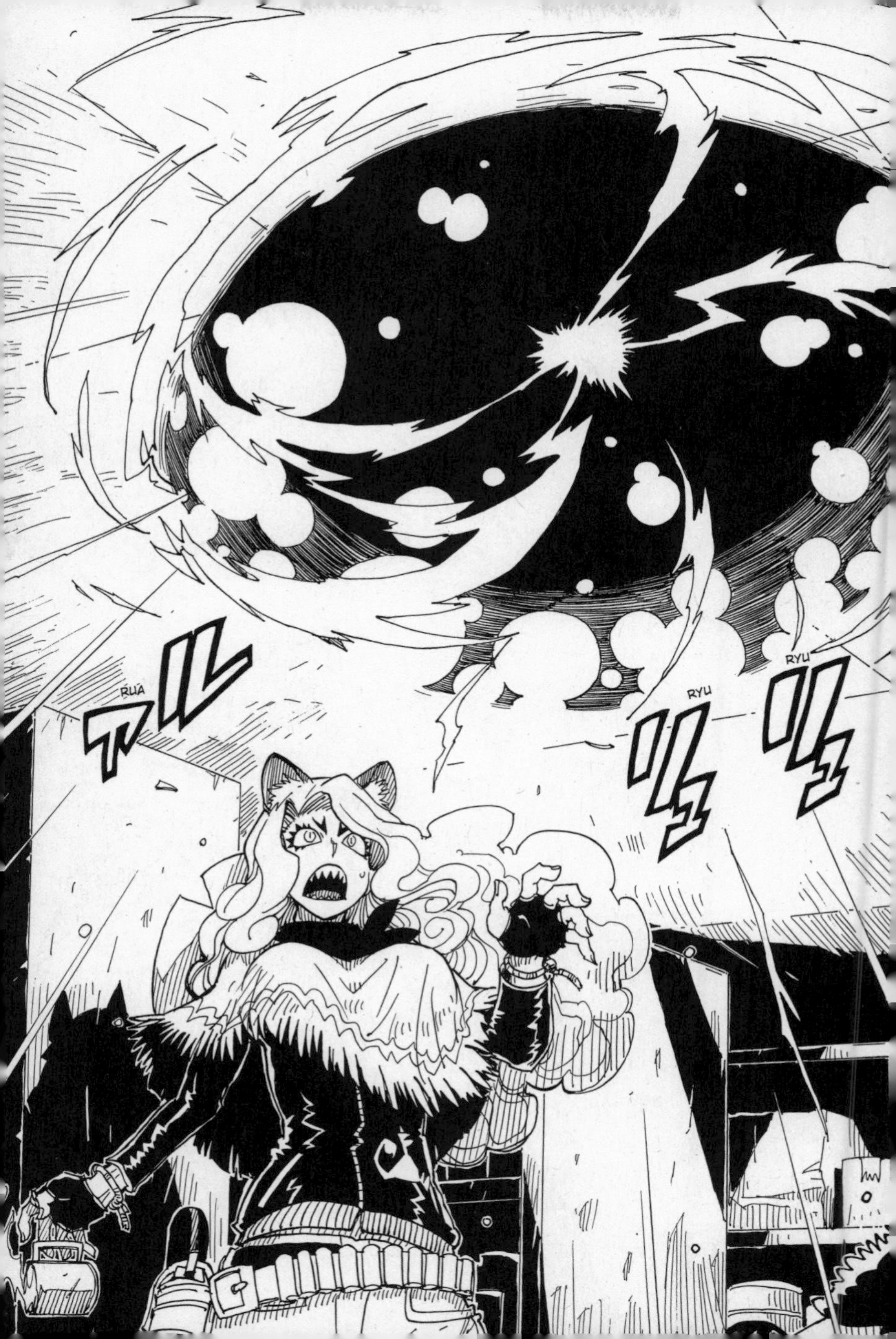
RYU
RYU
RUA

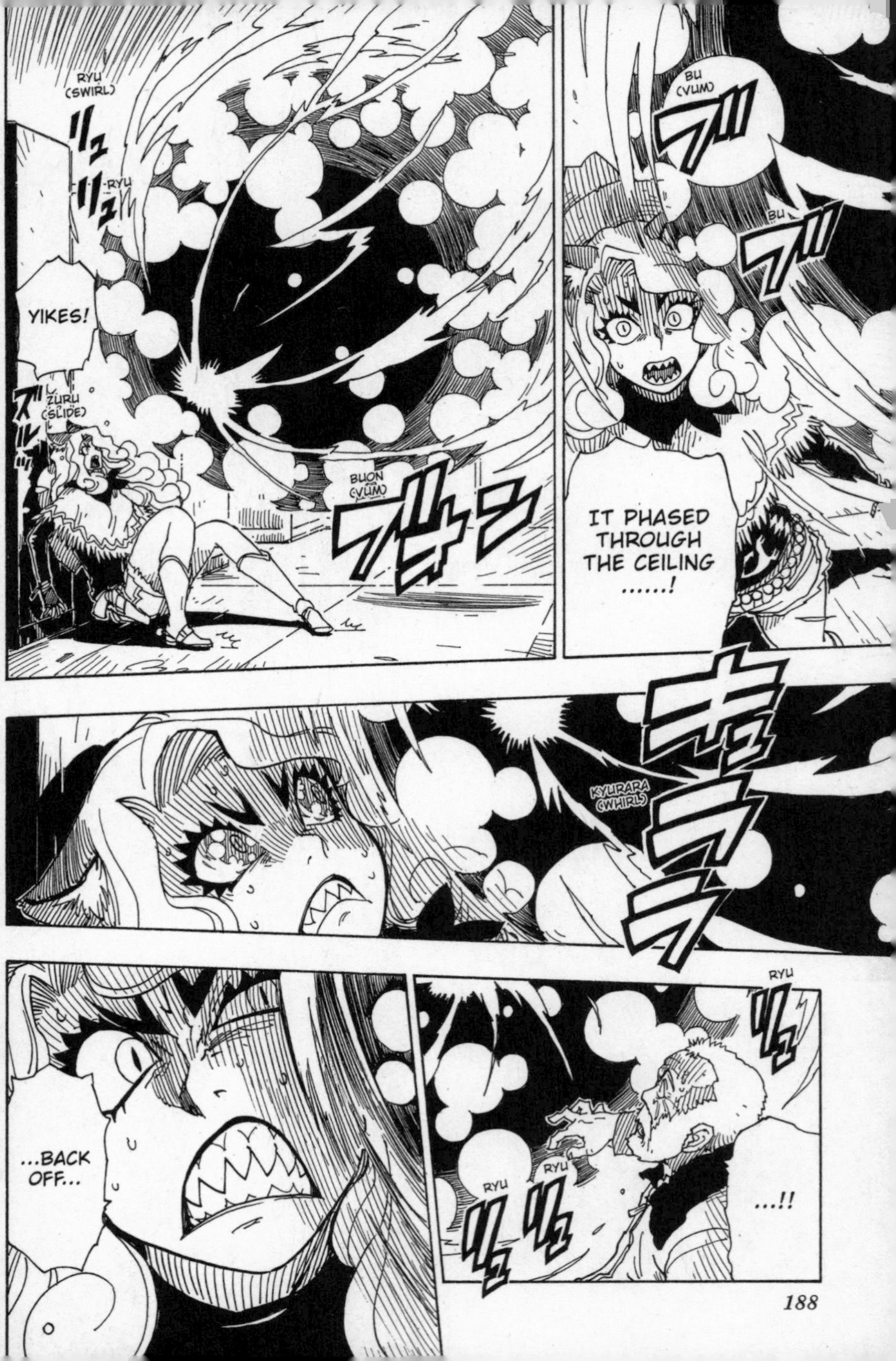
BU (VUM)
BU
IT PHASED THROUGH THE CEILING ......!
RYU (SWIRL)
RYU
YIKES!
ZURU (SLIDE)
BUON (VUM)
KYURARA (WHIRL)
RYU
RYU
RYU
...!!
...BACK OFF...

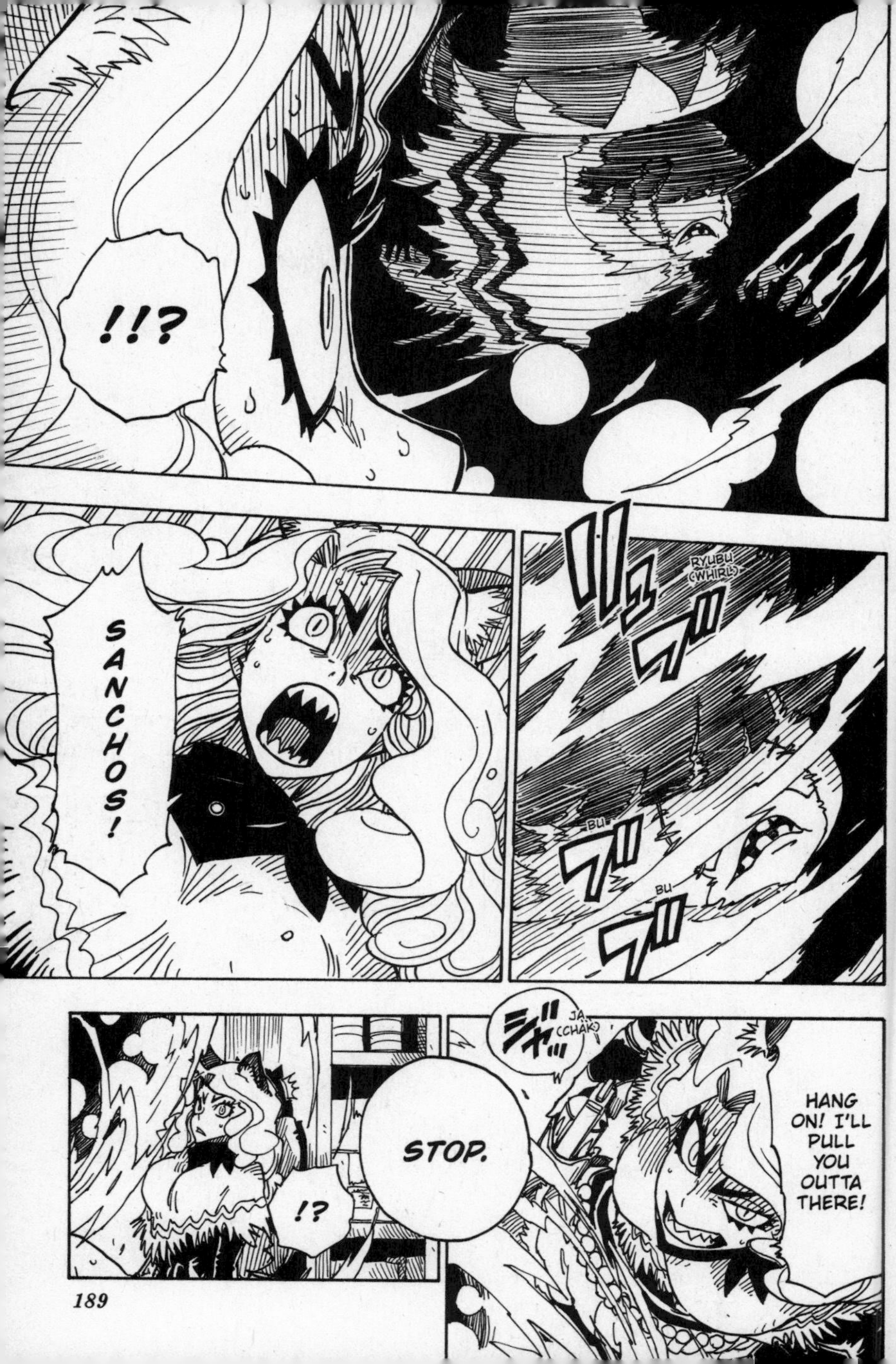
!!?
RYUBU (WHIRL)
BU
BU
SANCHOS!
JA (CHAK)
HANG ON! I'LL PULL YOU OUTTA THERE!
STOP.
!?

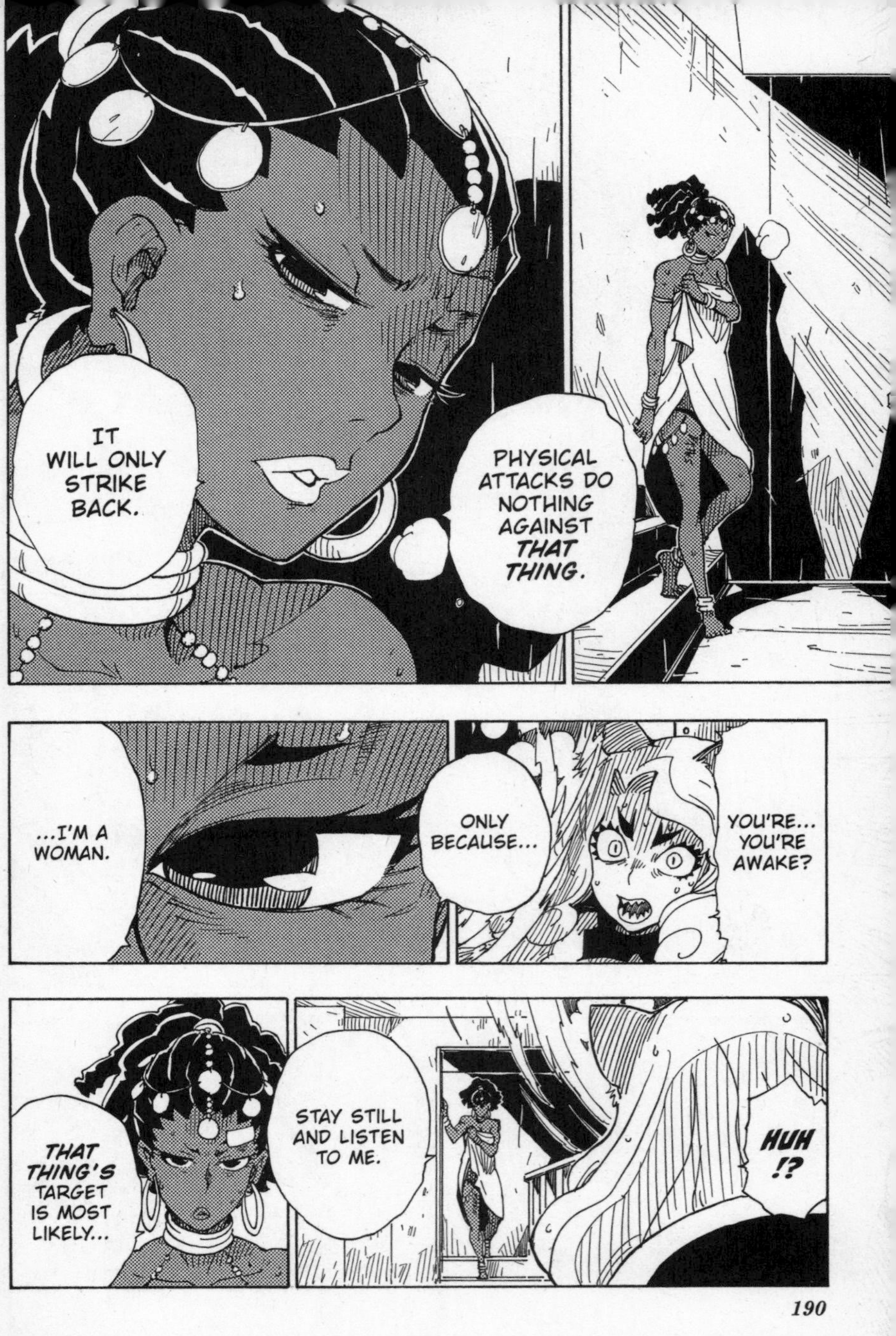
PHYSICAL ATTACKS DO NOTHING AGAINST *THAT THING*.
IT WILL ONLY STRIKE BACK.
YOU'RE... YOU'RE AWAKE?
ONLY BECAUSE...
...I'M A WOMAN.
*HUH!?*
STAY STILL AND LISTEN TO ME.
*THAT THING'S* TARGET IS MOST LIKELY...

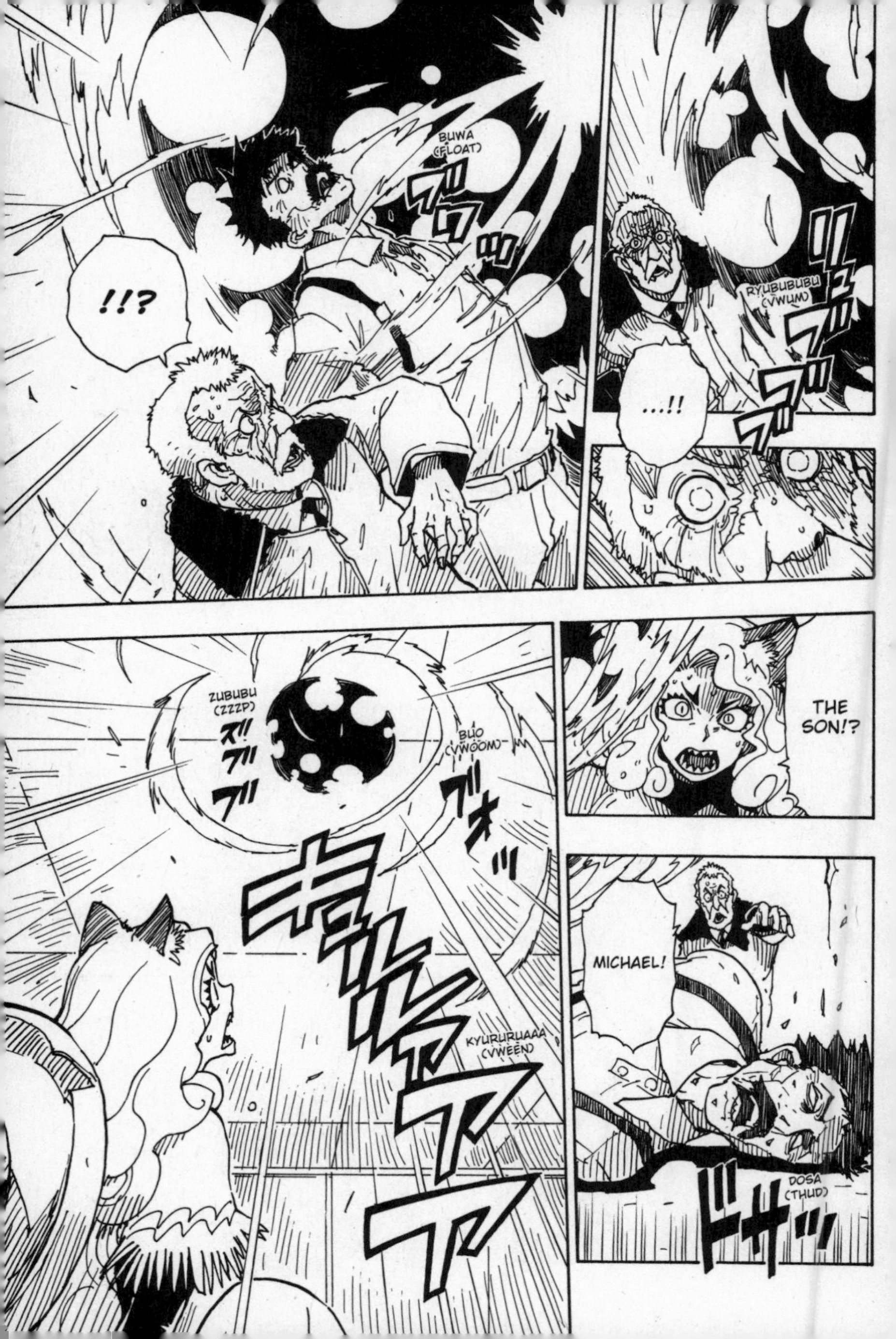
RYUBUBUBU (VWUM)
...!!
BUWA (FLOAT)
!!?
THE SON!?
MICHAEL!
DOSA (THUD)
ZUBUBU (ZZZP)
BUO (VWOOM)
KYURURUAAA (VWEEN)

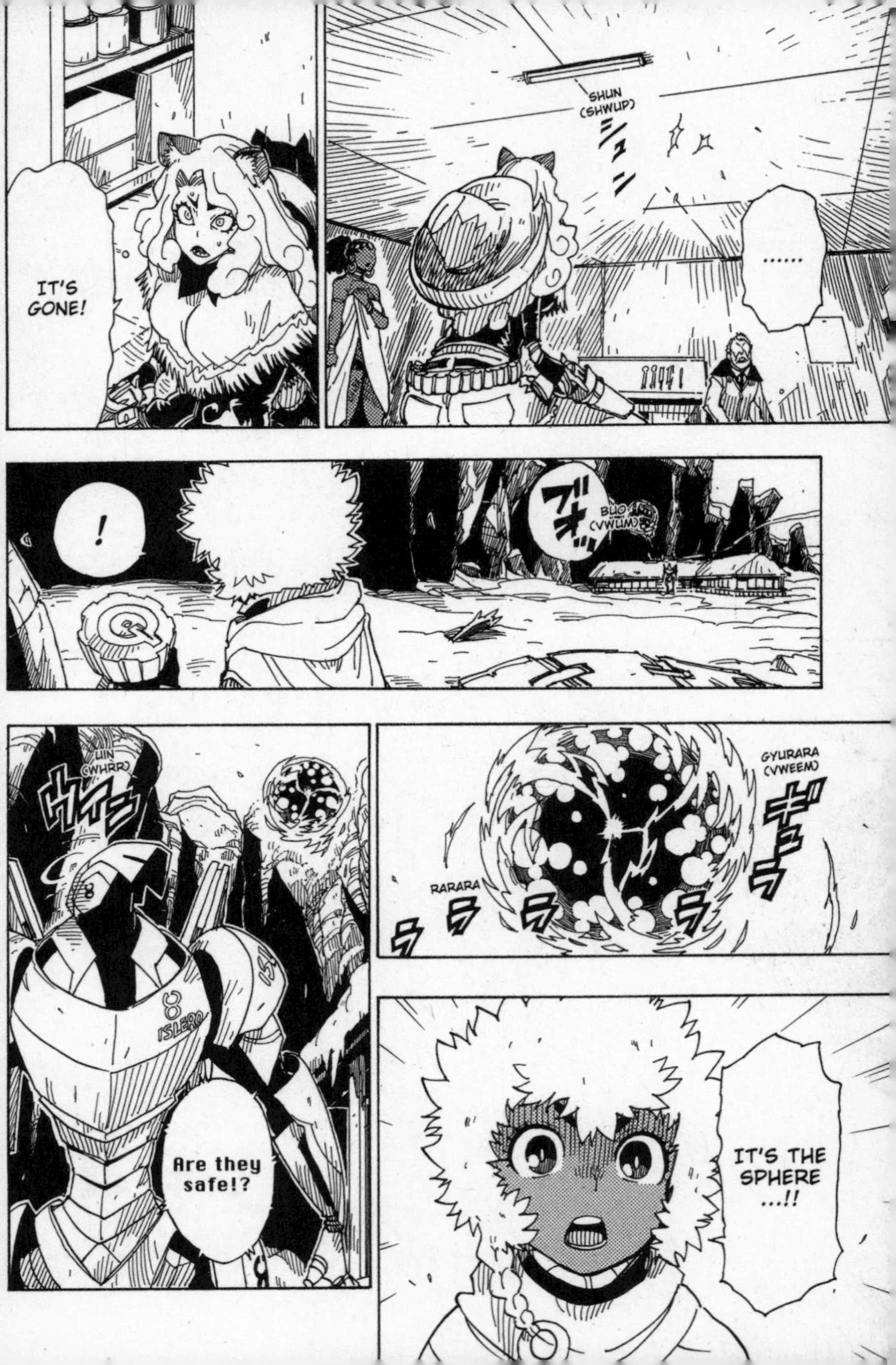
SHUN (SHWUP)
......
IT'S GONE!
BUO (VWUM)
!
GYURARA (VWEEM)
RARARA
IT'S THE SPHERE ...!!
UIN (WHRR)
ISLERO
Are they safe!?

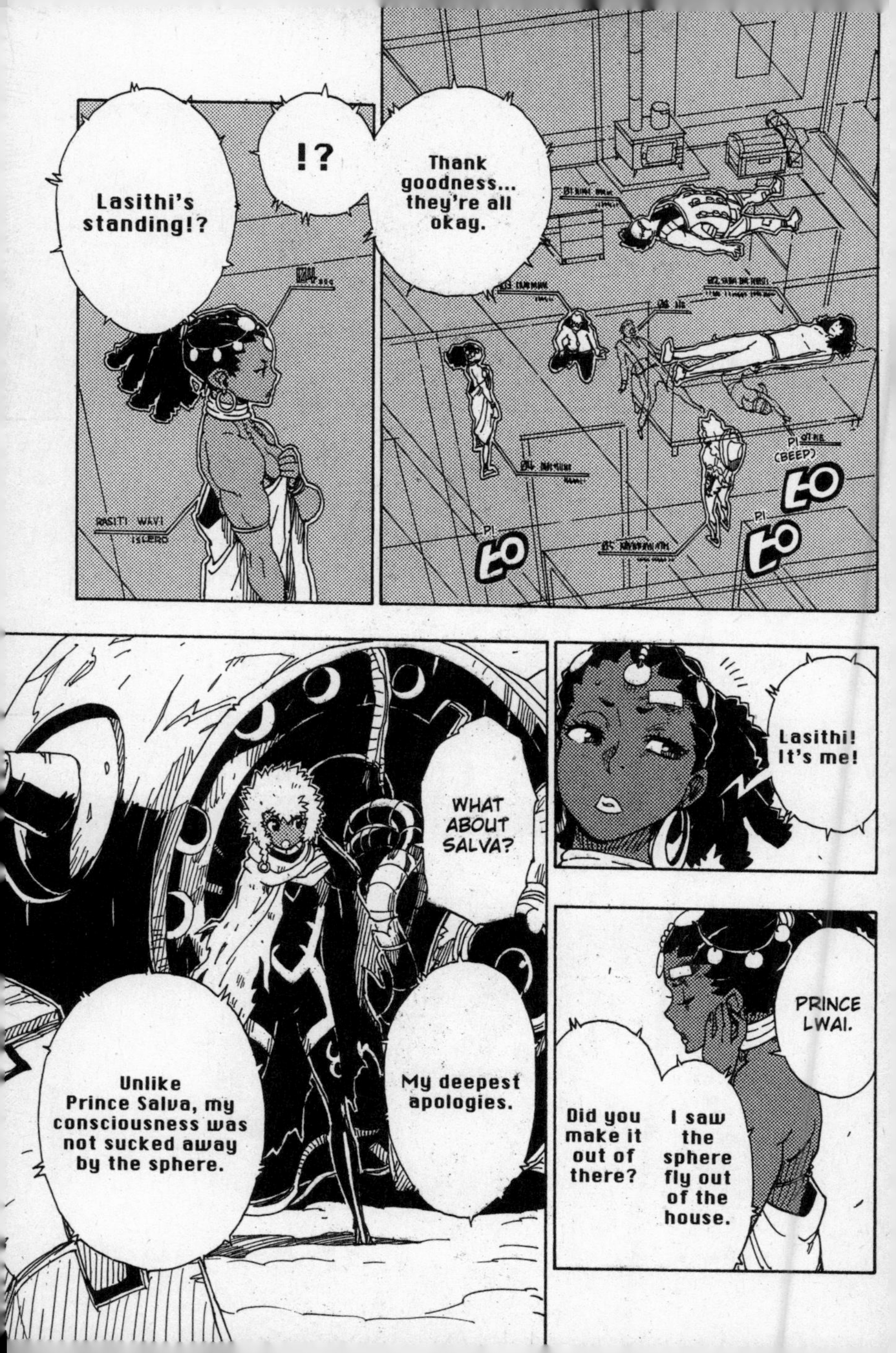
Thank goodness... they're all okay.
PI (BEEP)
PI
PI
!?
Lasithi's standing!?
RASITI WAVI ISLERO
Lasithi! It's me!
PRINCE LWAI.
I saw the sphere fly out of the house.
Did you make it out of there?
WHAT ABOUT SALVA?
My deepest apologies.
Unlike Prince Salva, my consciousness was not sucked away by the sphere.

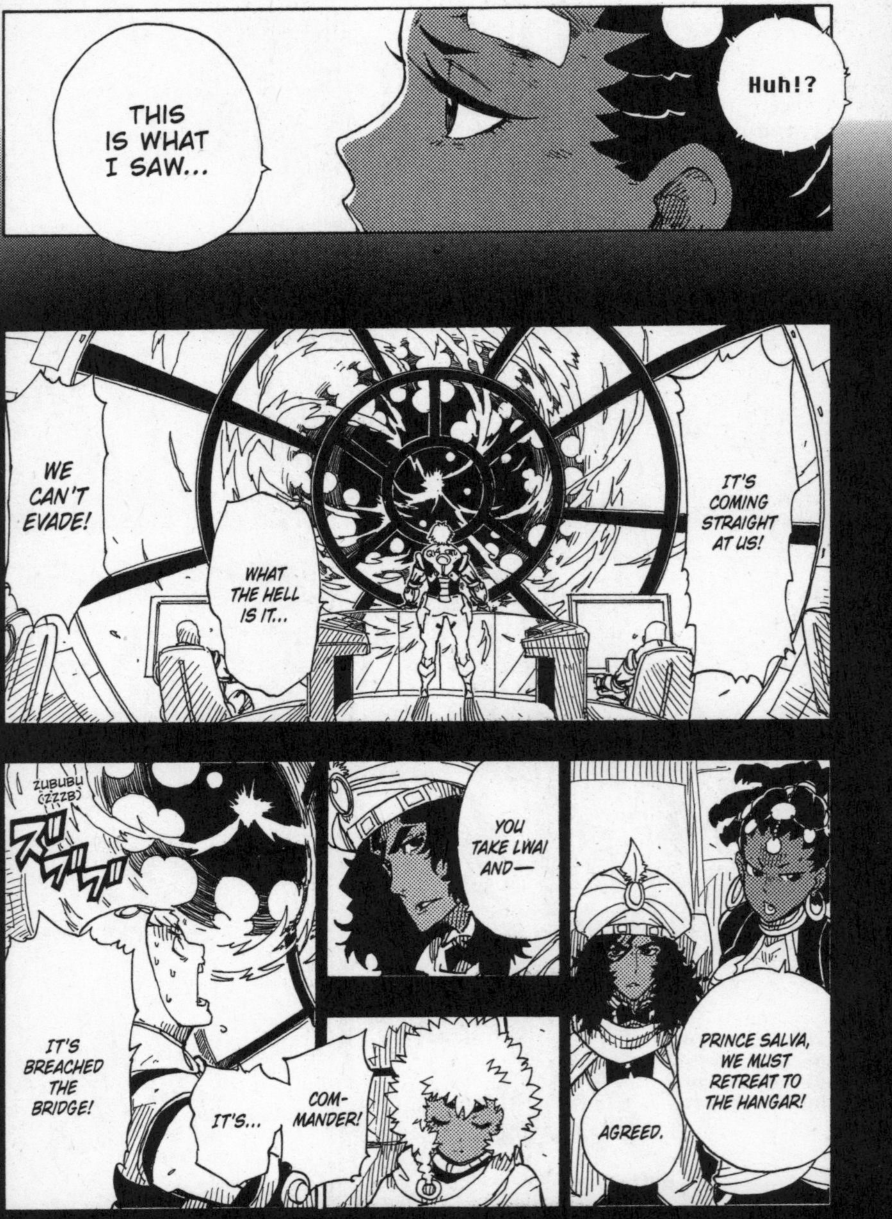
Huh!?
THIS IS WHAT I SAW...
IT'S COMING STRAIGHT AT US!
WHAT THE HELL IS IT...
WE CAN'T EVADE!
PRINCE SALVA, WE MUST RETREAT TO THE HANGAR!
AGREED.
YOU TAKE LWAI AND—
COM-MANDER!
IT'S...
ZUBUBU (ZZZB)
IT'S BREACHED THE BRIDGE!

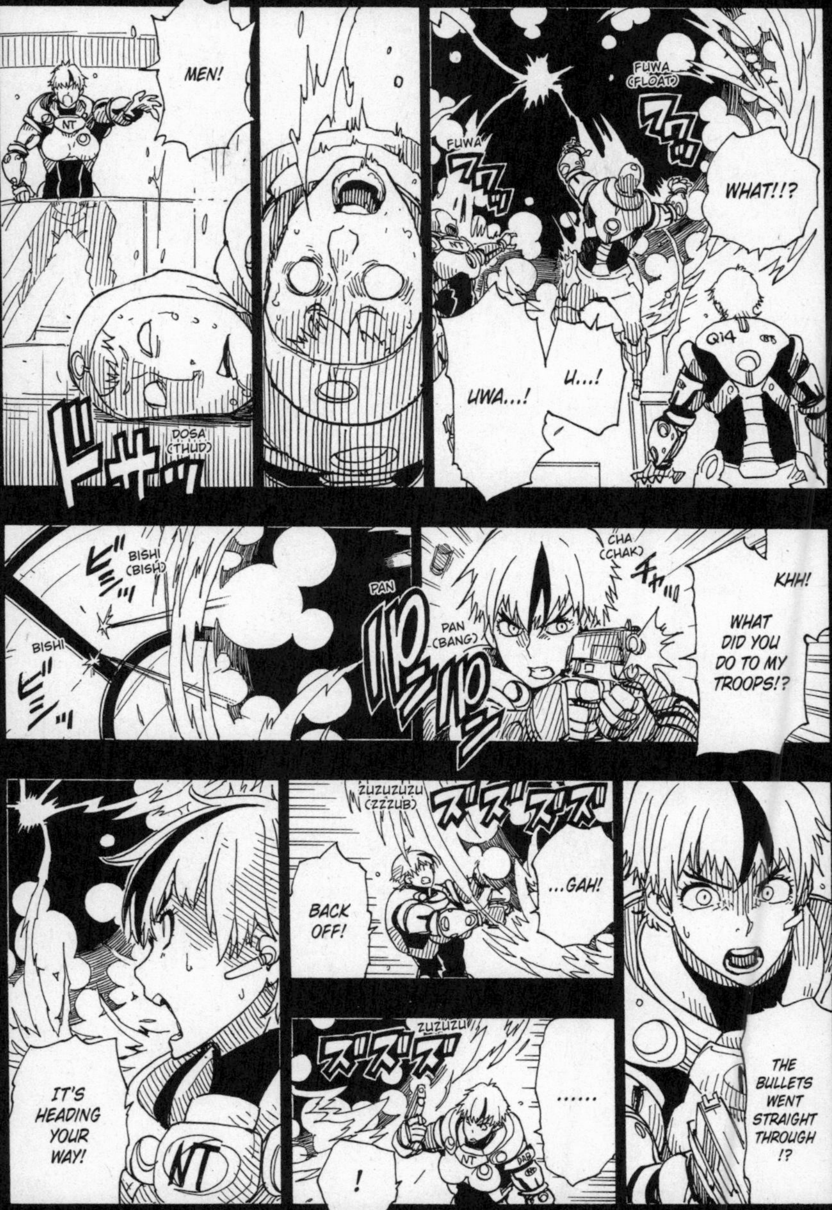
FUWA (FLOAT)
WHAT!!?
FUWA
U...!
UWA...!
MEN!
DOSA (THUD)
KHH!
WHAT DID YOU DO TO MY TROOPS!?
CHA (CHAK)
PAN
PAN (BANG)
BISHI (BISH)
BISHI
THE BULLETS WENT STRAIGHT THROUGH !?
ZUZUZUZU (ZZZUB)
...GAH!
BACK OFF!
ZUZUZU
......
!
IT'S HEADING YOUR WAY!

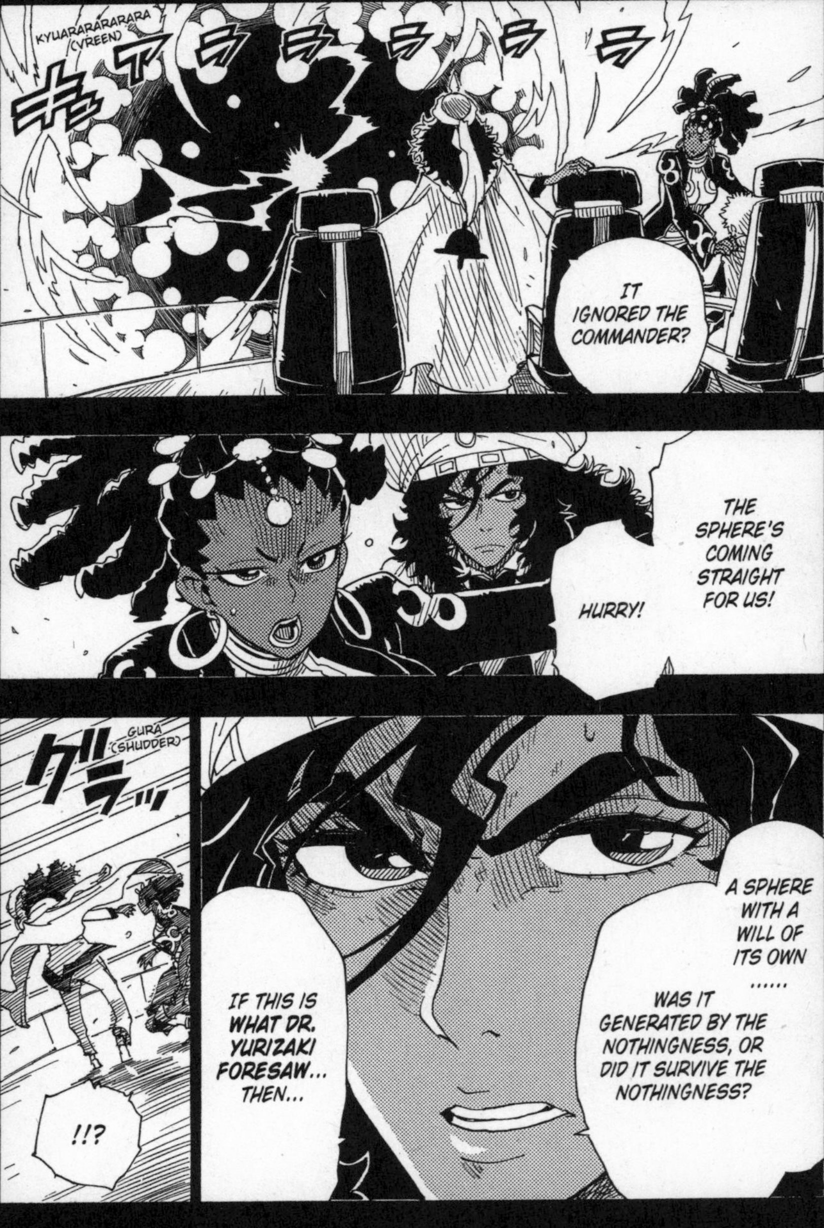
KYUARARARARARA (VREEN)
IT IGNORED THE COMMANDER?
THE SPHERE'S COMING STRAIGHT FOR US!
HURRY!
A SPHERE WITH A WILL OF ITS OWN ......
WAS IT GENERATED BY THE NOTHINGNESS, OR DID IT SURVIVE THE NOTHINGNESS?
IF THIS IS WHAT DR. YURIZAKI FORESAW... THEN...
GURA (SHUDDER)
!!?

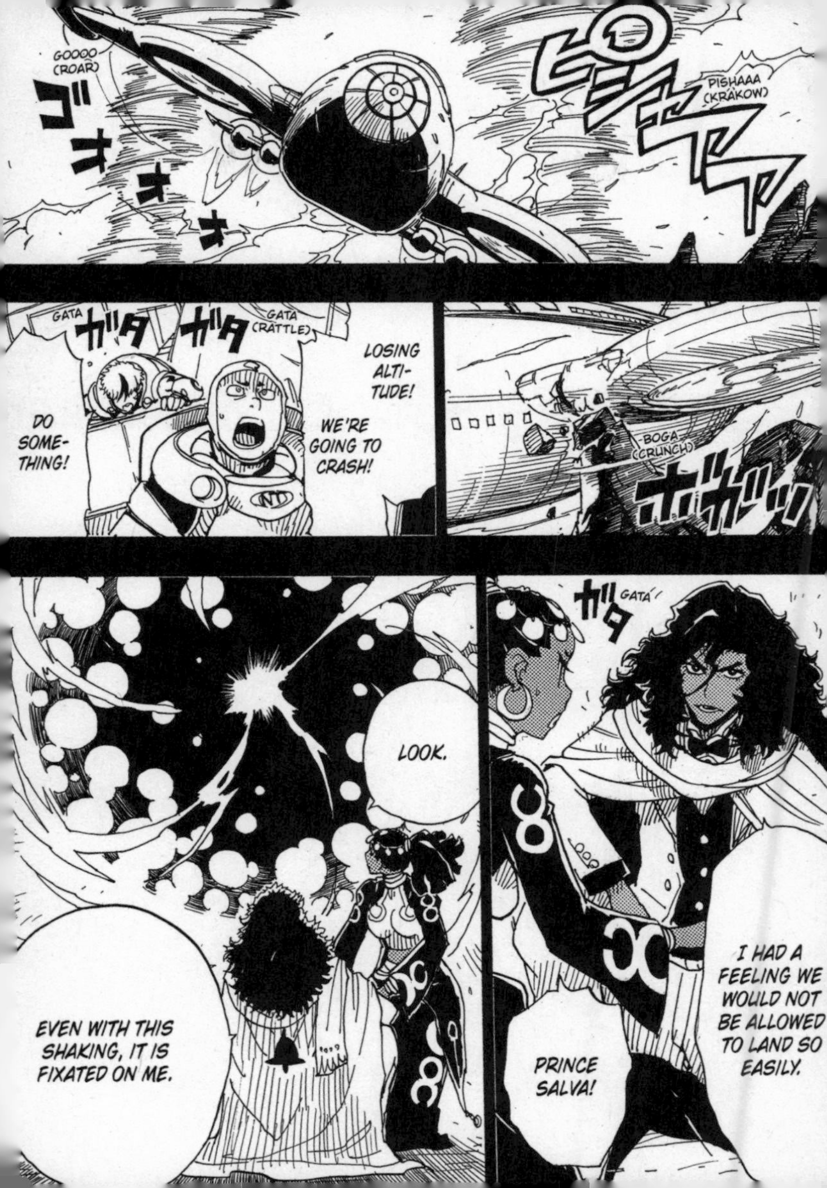
PISHAAA (KRÄKOW)
GOOOO (ROAR)
BOGA (CRUNCH)
GATA (RATTLE)
GATA
LOSING ALTI-TUDE!
WE'RE GOING TO CRASH!
DO SOME-THING!
GATA
I HAD A FEELING WE WOULD NOT BE ALLOWED TO LAND SO EASILY.
PRINCE SALVA!
LOOK.
EVEN WITH THIS SHAKING, IT IS FIXATED ON ME.

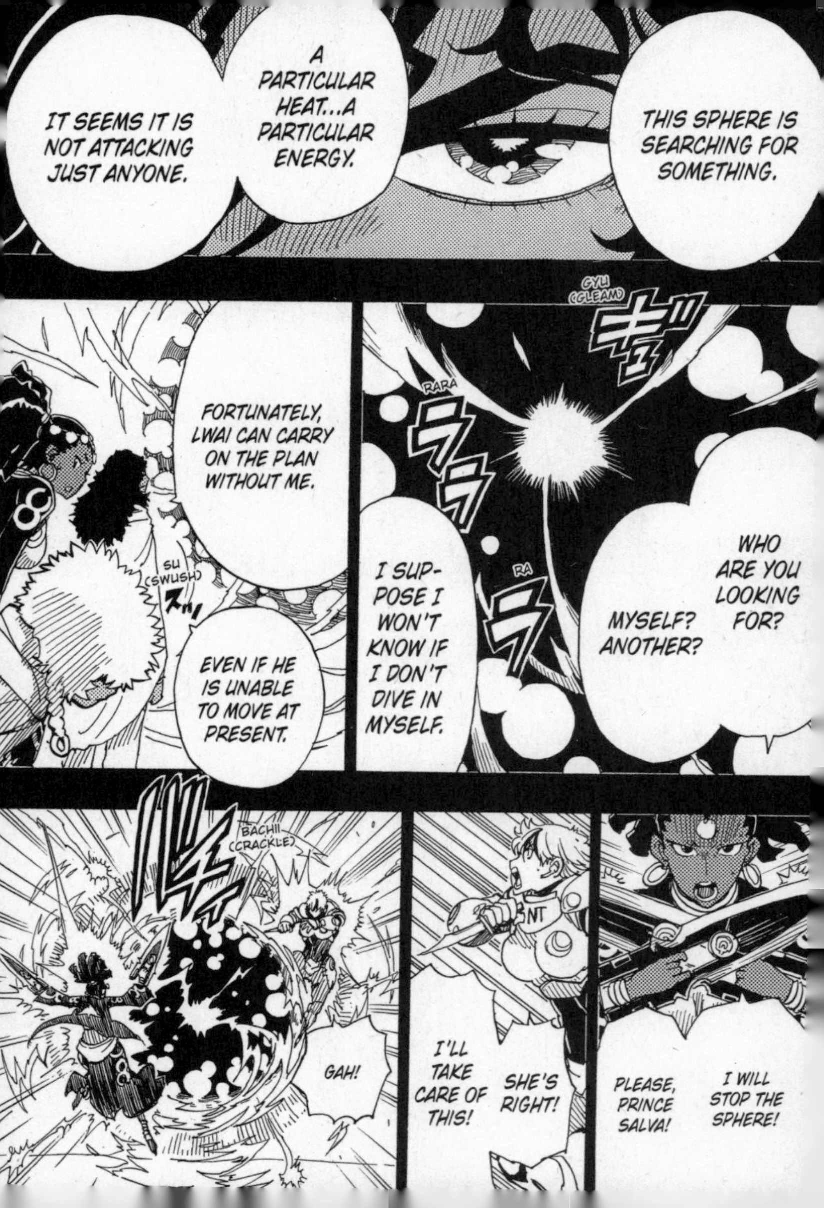
THIS SPHERE IS SEARCHING FOR SOMETHING.
A PARTICULAR HEAT...A PARTICULAR ENERGY.
IT SEEMS IT IS NOT ATTACKING JUST ANYONE.
GYU (GLEAM)
RARA
WHO ARE YOU LOOKING FOR?
MYSELF? ANOTHER?
RA
I SUP-POSE I WON'T KNOW IF I DON'T DIVE IN MYSELF.
FORTUNATELY, LWAI CAN CARRY ON THE PLAN WITHOUT ME.
SU (SWUSH)
EVEN IF HE IS UNABLE TO MOVE AT PRESENT.
I WILL STOP THE SPHERE!
PLEASE, PRINCE SALVA!
SHE'S RIGHT!
I'LL TAKE CARE OF THIS!
BACHII (CRACKLE)
GAH!

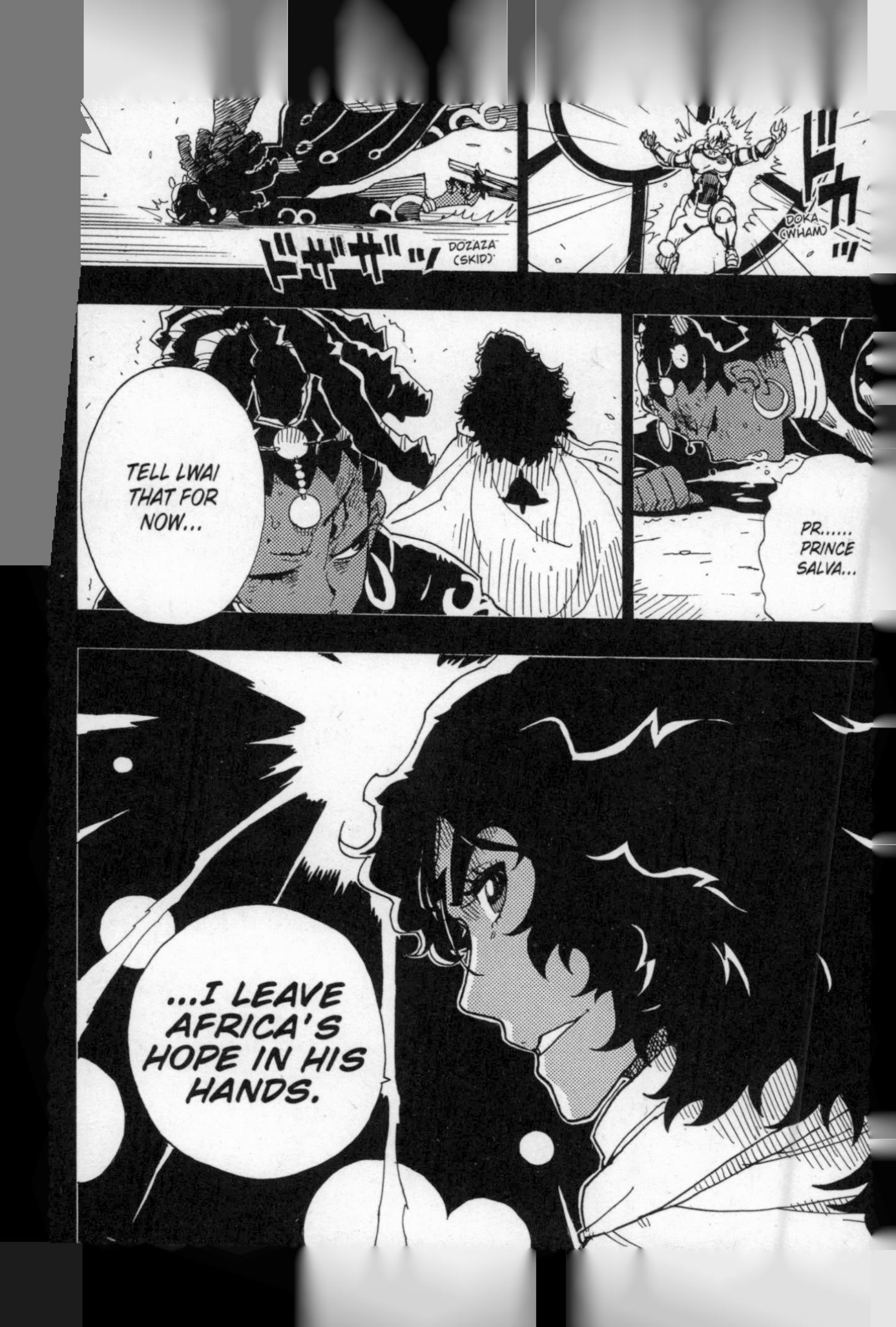
ドカッ
DOKA (WHAM)
ドザザッ
DOZAZA (SKID)
PR...... PRINCE SALVA...
TELL LWAI THAT FOR NOW...
...I LEAVE AFRICA'S HOPE IN HIS HANDS.

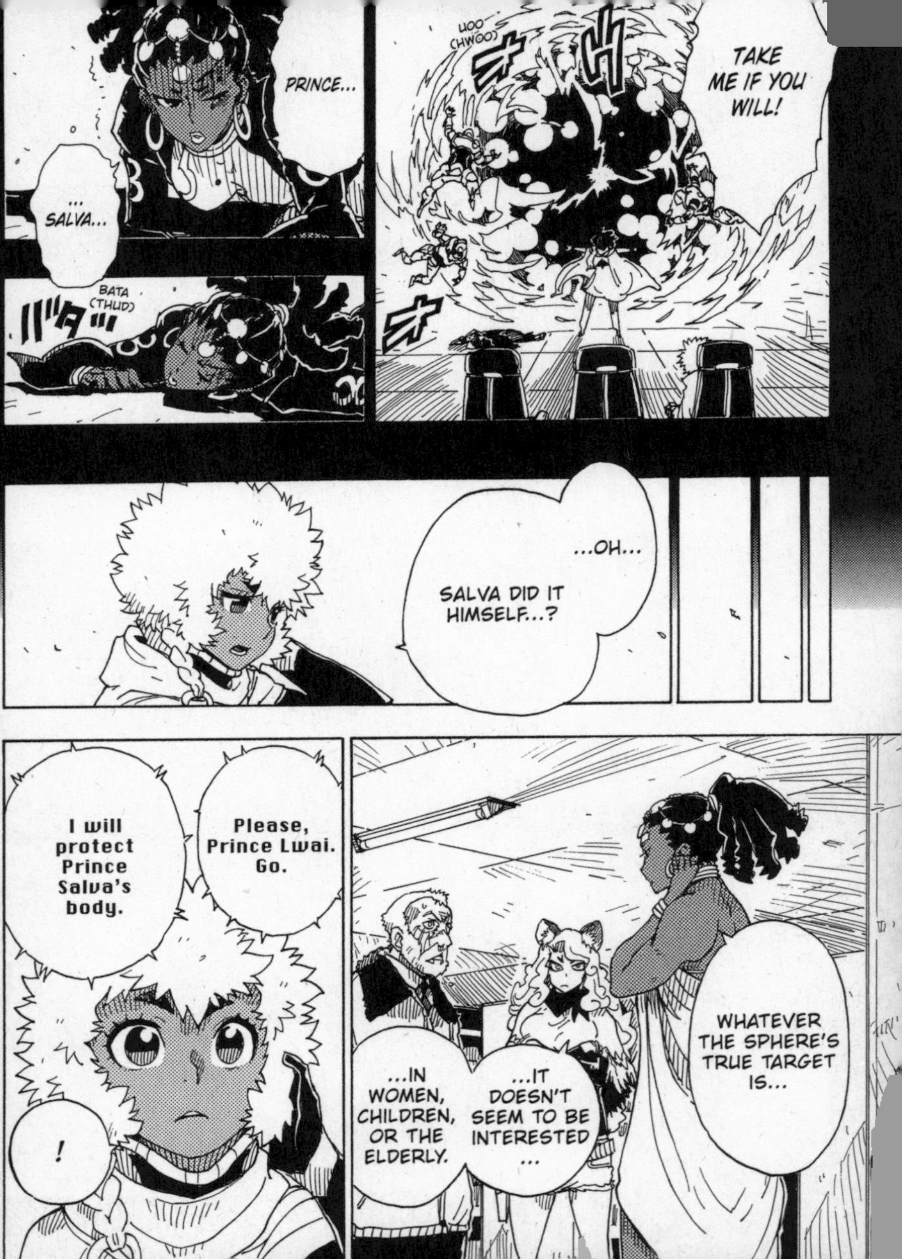
TAKE ME IF YOU WILL!
UOO (HWOO)
PRINCE...
... SALVA...
BATA (THUD)
...OH...
SALVA DID IT HIMSELF...?
WHATEVER THE SPHERE'S TRUE TARGET IS...
...IT DOESN'T SEEM TO BE INTERESTED ...
...IN WOMEN, CHILDREN, OR THE ELDERLY.
Please, Prince Lwai. Go.
I will protect Prince Salva's body.
!

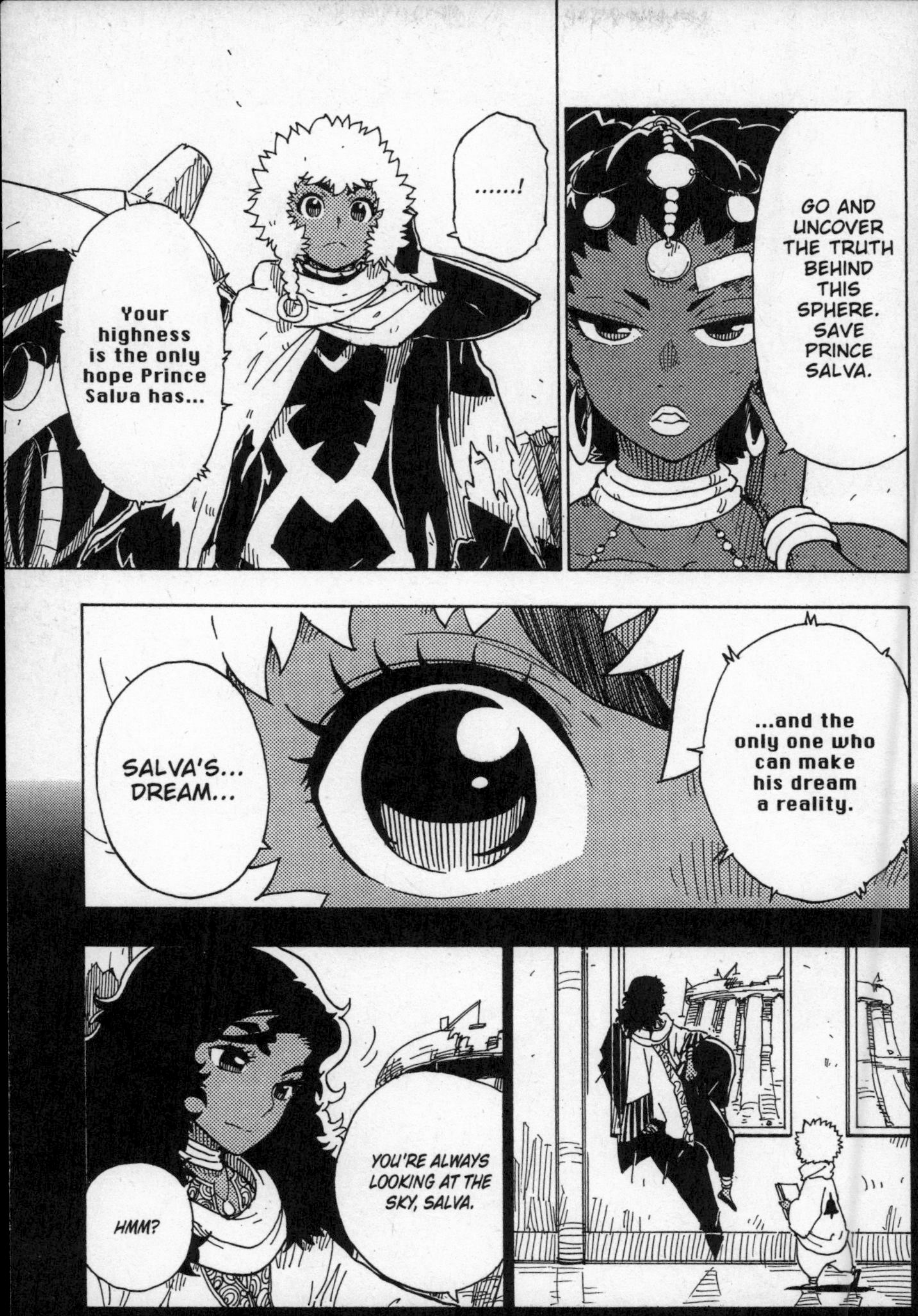
GO AND UNCOVER THE TRUTH BEHIND THIS SPHERE. SAVE PRINCE SALVA.
......!
Your highness is the only hope Prince Salva has...
...and the only one who can make his dream a reality.
SALVA'S... DREAM...
YOU'RE ALWAYS LOOKING AT THE SKY, SALVA.
HMM?

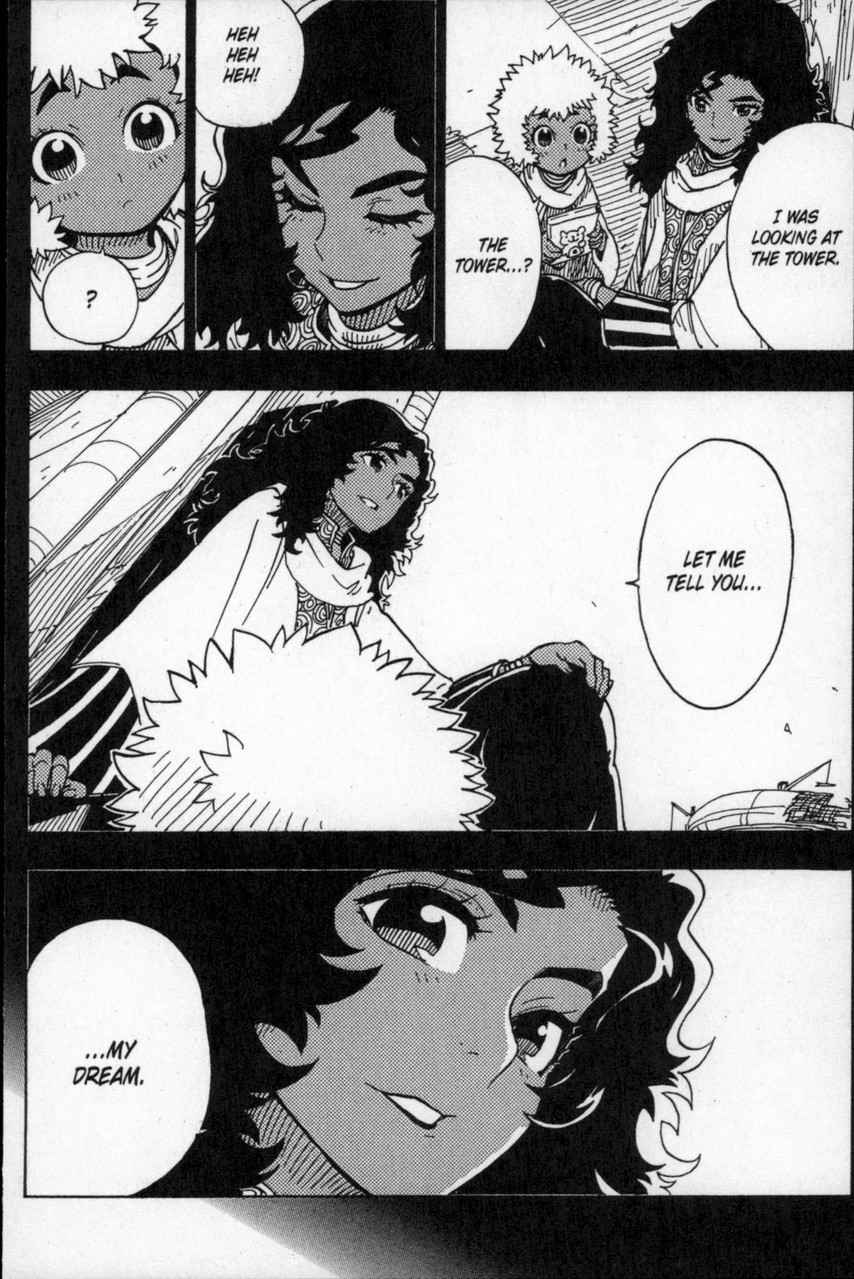
I WAS LOOKING AT THE TOWER.
THE TOWER...?
HEH HEH HEH!
?
LET ME TELL YOU...
...MY DREAM.

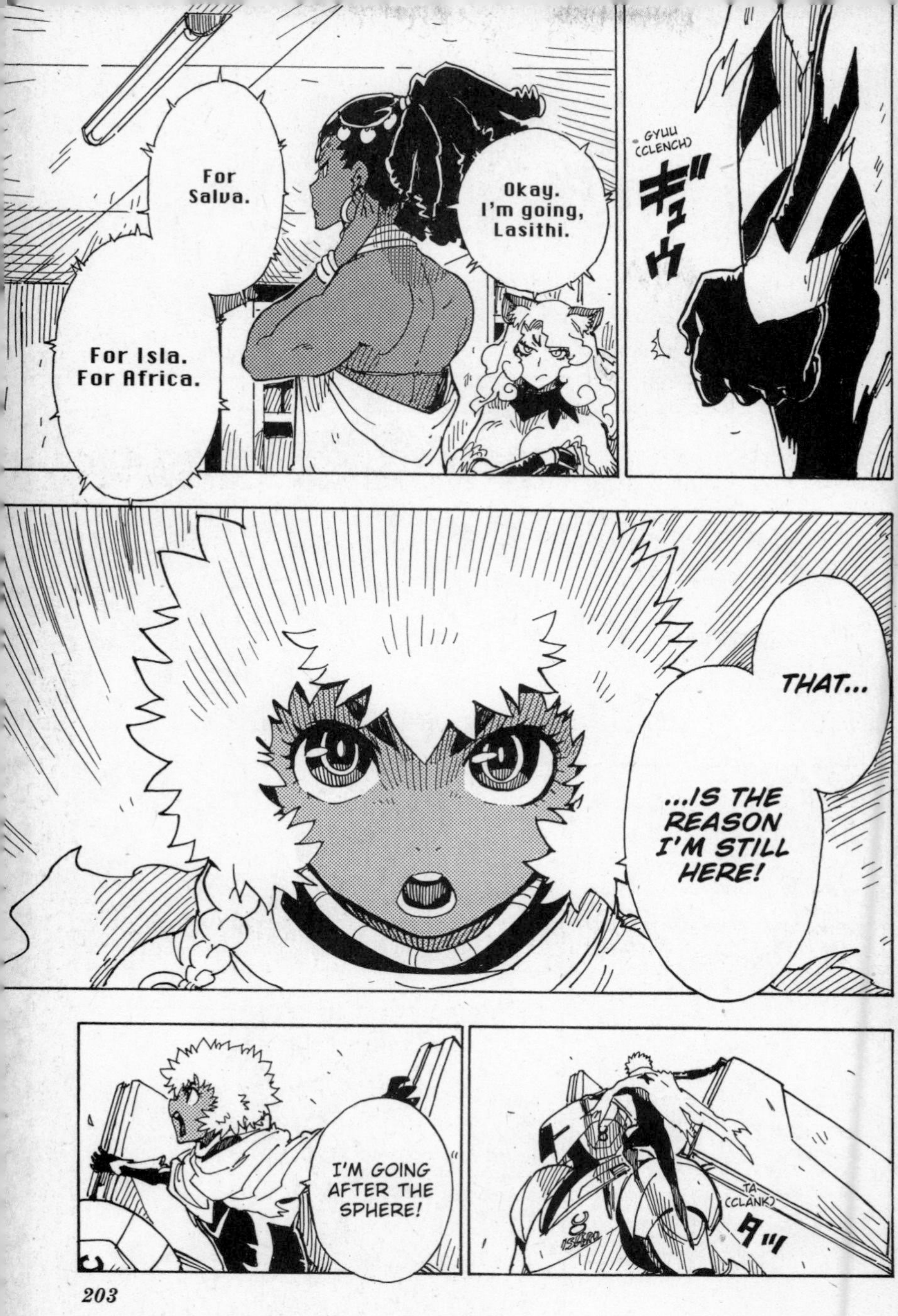
GYUU (CLENCH)
ギュウ
Okay. I'm going, Lasithi.
For Salva.
For Isla. For Africa.
THAT...
...IS THE REASON I'M STILL HERE!
TA (CLANK)
タッ
I'M GOING AFTER THE SPHERE!

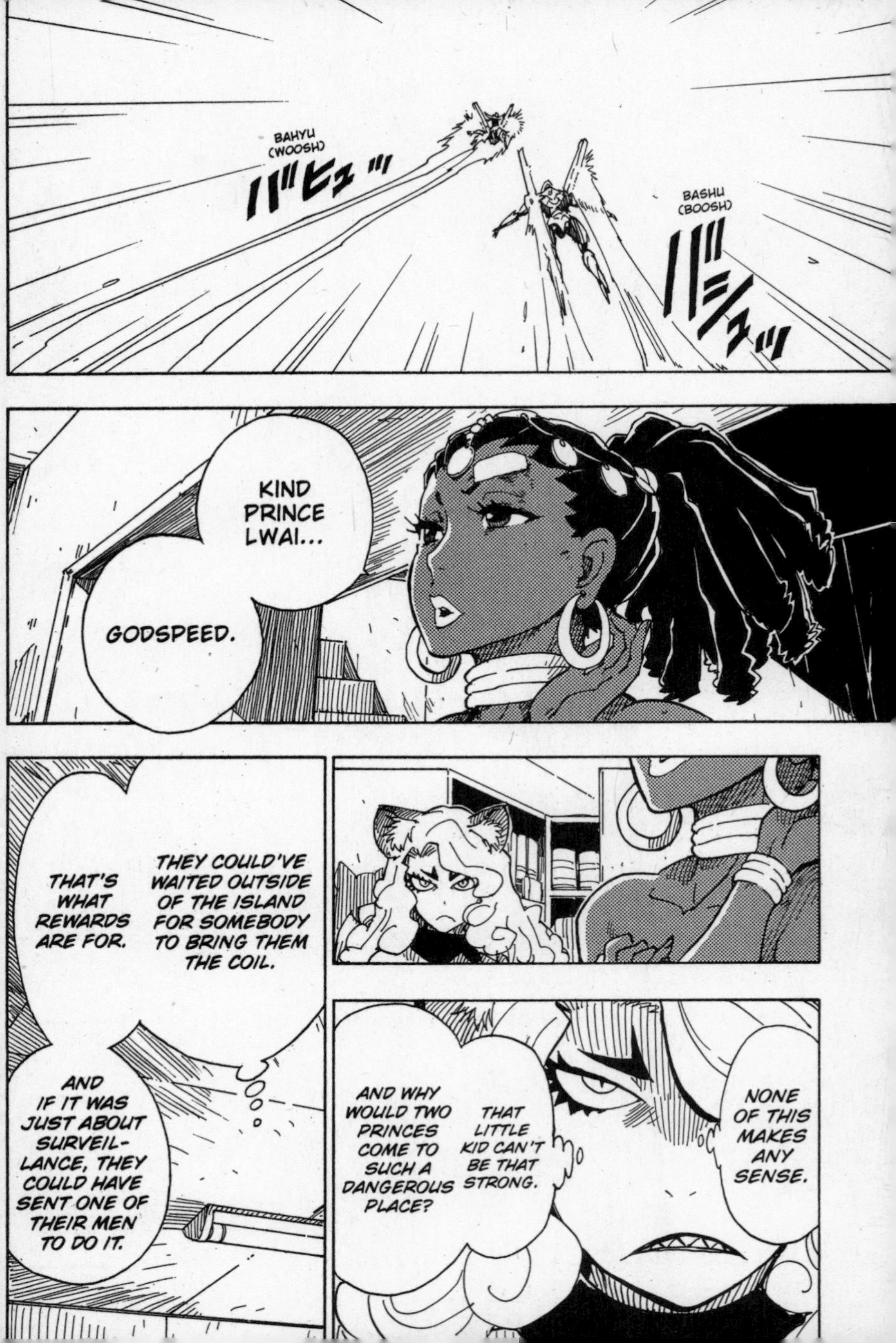
BASHU (BOOSH)
バシュッ
BAHYU (WOOSH)
バヒュッ
KIND PRINCE LWAI...
GODSPEED.
NONE OF THIS MAKES ANY SENSE.
THAT LITTLE KID CAN'T BE THAT STRONG.
AND WHY WOULD TWO PRINCES COME TO SUCH A DANGEROUS PLACE?
THEY COULD'VE WAITED OUTSIDE OF THE ISLAND FOR SOMEBODY TO BRING THEM THE COIL.
THAT'S WHAT REWARDS ARE FOR.
AND IF IT WAS JUST ABOUT SURVEIL-LANCE, THEY COULD HAVE SENT ONE OF THEIR MEN TO DO IT.

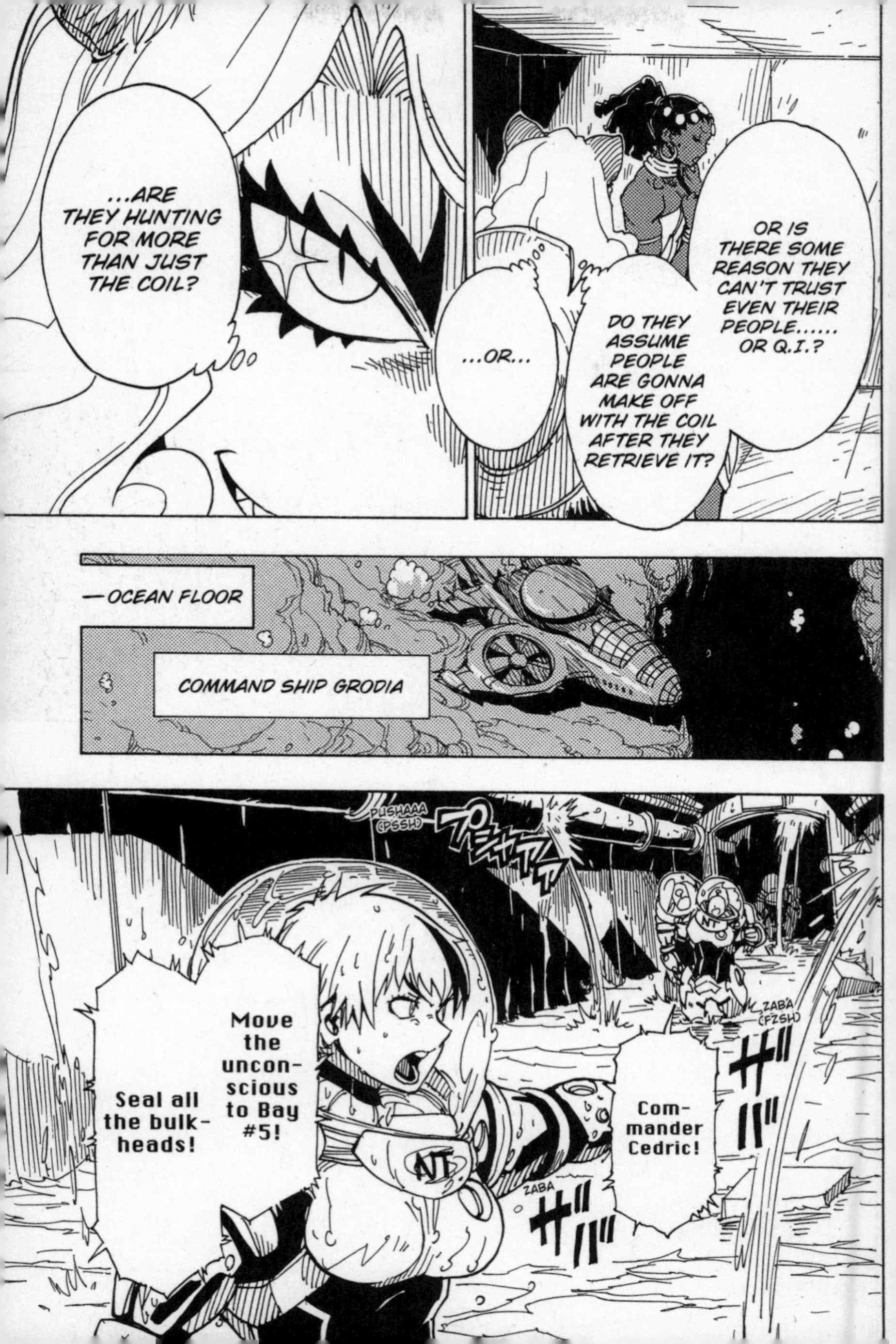

OR IS THERE SOME REASON THEY CAN'T TRUST EVEN THEIR PEOPLE...... OR Q.I.?
DO THEY ASSUME PEOPLE ARE GONNA MAKE OFF WITH THE COIL AFTER THEY RETRIEVE IT?
...OR...
...ARE THEY HUNTING FOR MORE THAN JUST THE COIL?
—OCEAN FLOOR
COMMAND SHIP GRODIA
PUSHAAA (PSSH)
ZABA (FZSH)
Commander Cedric!
Move the unconscious to Bay #5!
ZABA
Seal all the bulkheads!

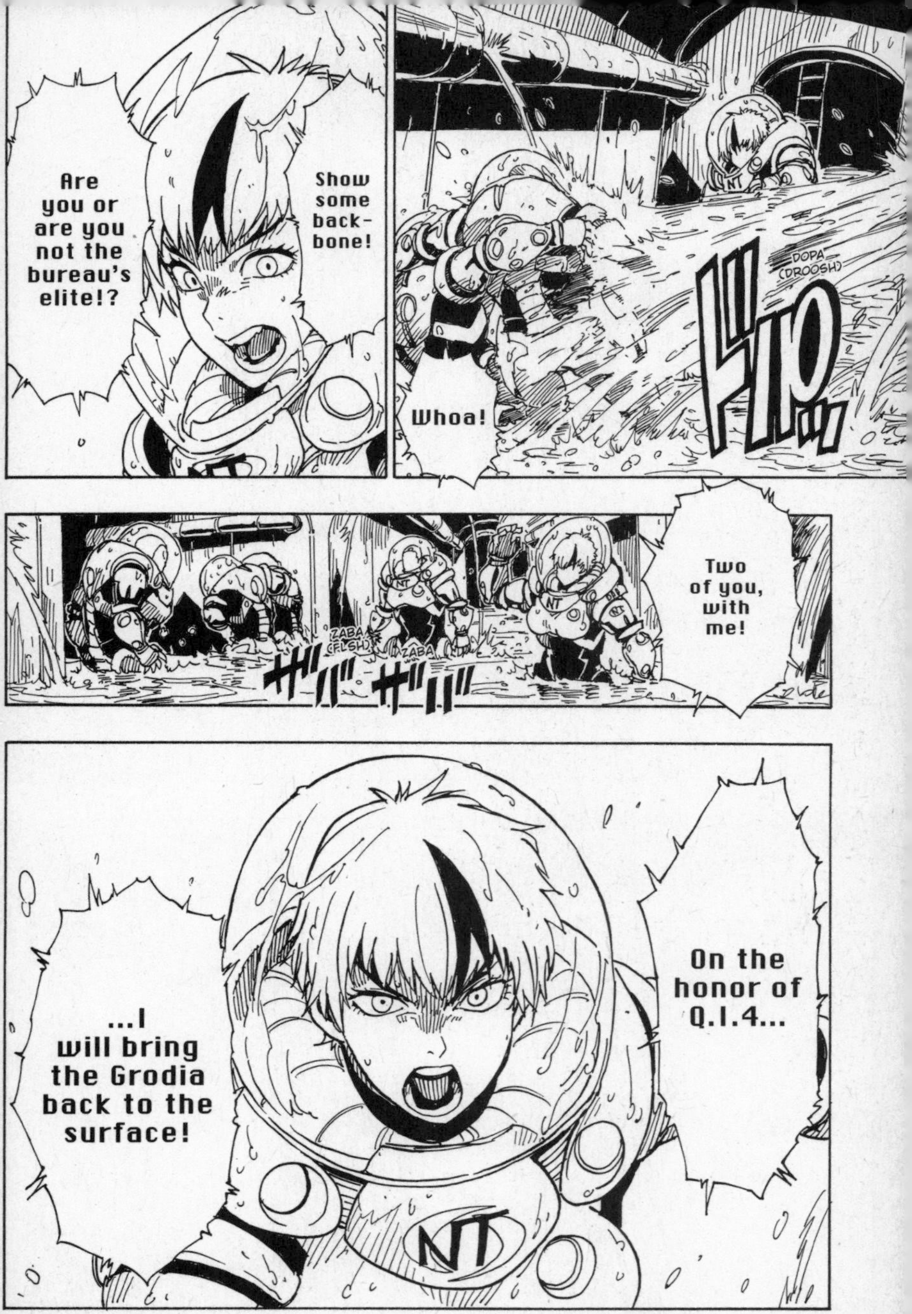
DOPA (DROOSH)
Whoa!
Show some back-bone!
Are you or are you not the bureau's elite!?
Two of you, with me!
ZABA (FLSH)
ZABA
On the honor of Q.I.4...
...I will bring the Grodia back to the surface!

Dimension W

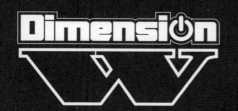

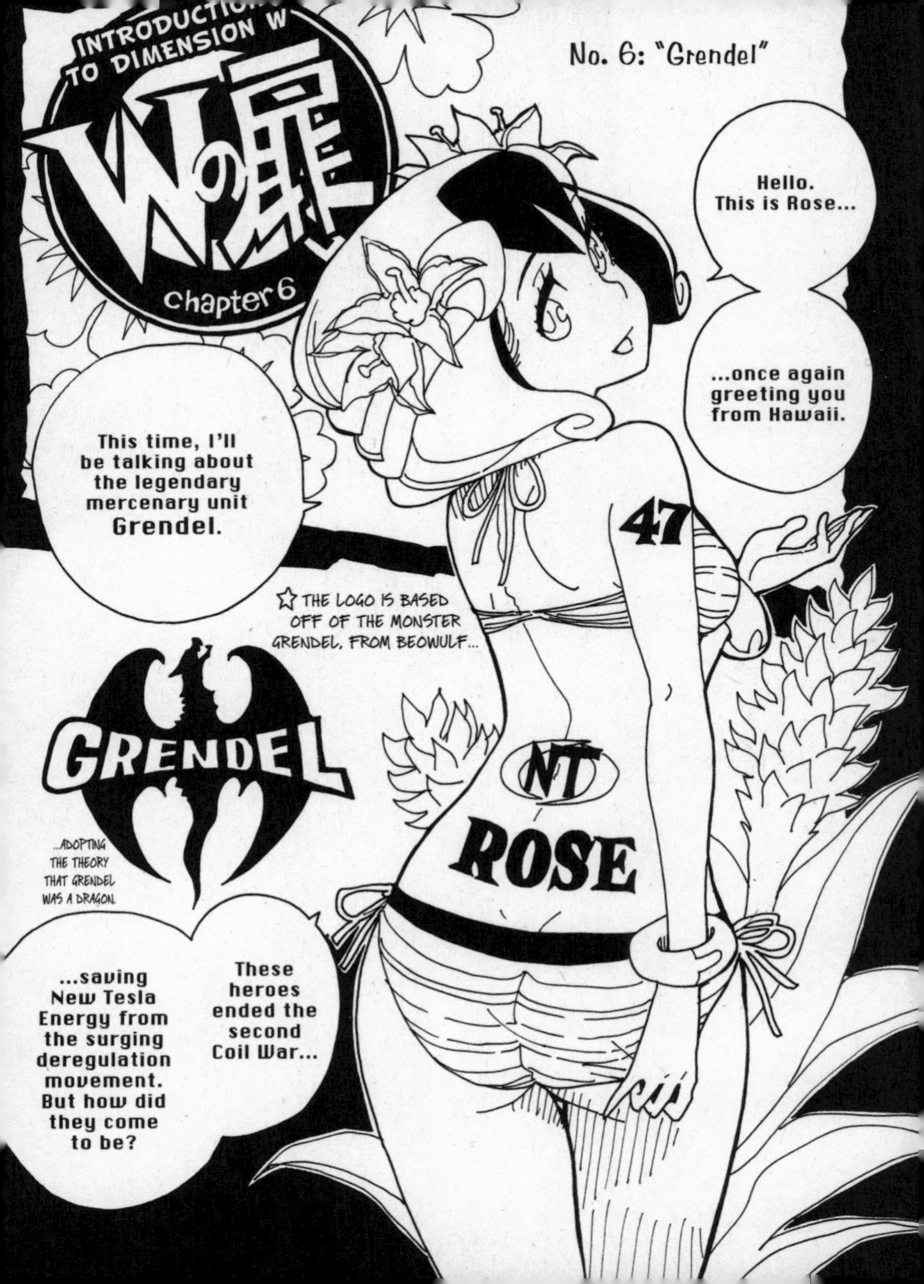
No. 6: "Grendel"
Hello. This is Rose...
...once again greeting you from Hawaii.
INTRODUCTI
TO DIMENSION W
Wの扉
chapter 6
This time, I'll be talking about the legendary mercenary unit Grendel.
☆ THE LOGO IS BASED OFF OF THE MONSTER GRENDEL, FROM BEOWULF...
47
NT
ROSE
GRENDEL
...ADOPTING THE THEORY THAT GRENDEL WAS A DRAGON.
These heroes ended the second Coil War...
...saving New Tesla Energy from the surging deregulation movement. But how did they come to be?

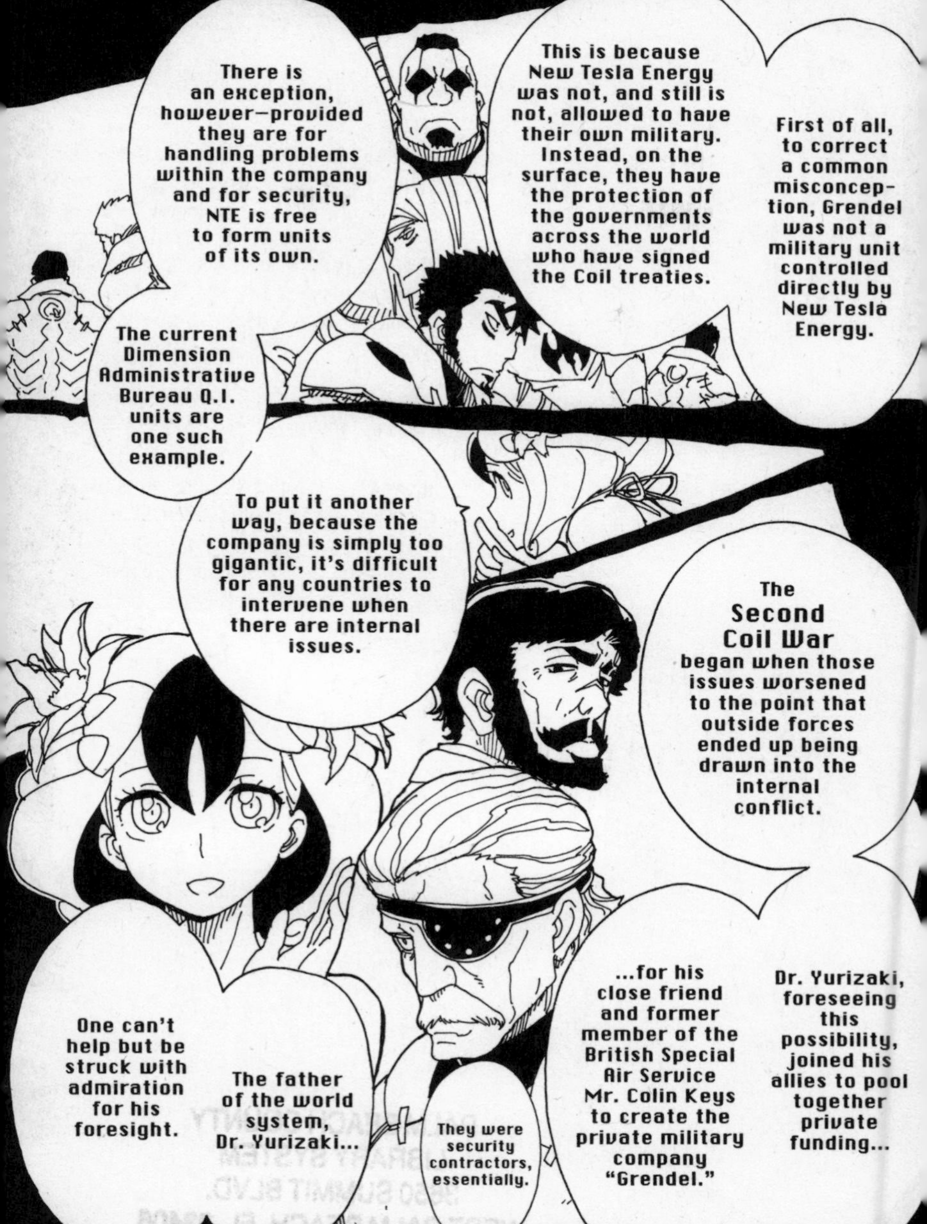
First of all, to correct a common misconception, Grendel was not a military unit controlled directly by New Tesla Energy.
This is because New Tesla Energy was not, and still is not, allowed to have their own military. Instead, on the surface, they have the protection of the governments across the world who have signed the Coil treaties.
There is an exception, however—provided they are for handling problems within the company and for security, NTE is free to form units of its own.
The current Dimension Administrative Bureau Q.I. units are one such example.
To put it another way, because the company is simply too gigantic, it's difficult for any countries to intervene when there are internal issues.
The Second Coil War began when those issues worsened to the point that outside forces ended up being drawn into the internal conflict.
Dr. Yurizaki, foreseeing this possibility, joined his allies to pool together private funding...
...for his close friend and former member of the British Special Air Service Mr. Colin Keys to create the private military company "Grendel."
They were security contractors, essentially.
The father of the world system, Dr. Yurizaki...
One can't help but be struck with admiration for his foresight.

TO BE CONTINUED

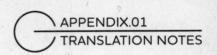
**PAGE 5**
**Bronze Swallow Terrace**: General Jaku likely took the name for his fortress from the historical "Bronze Swallow Terrace," a building from the Three Kingdoms period in Chinese history. It was named for the bronze swallow decoration adorning its roof.

**PAGE 8**
***Ode to Kirihito***: The book Yuri is reading. A manga created by the legendary Osamu Tezuka, it follows Kirihito, a doctor in search of a cure for a mysterious illness that leaves its victims resembling dog people.

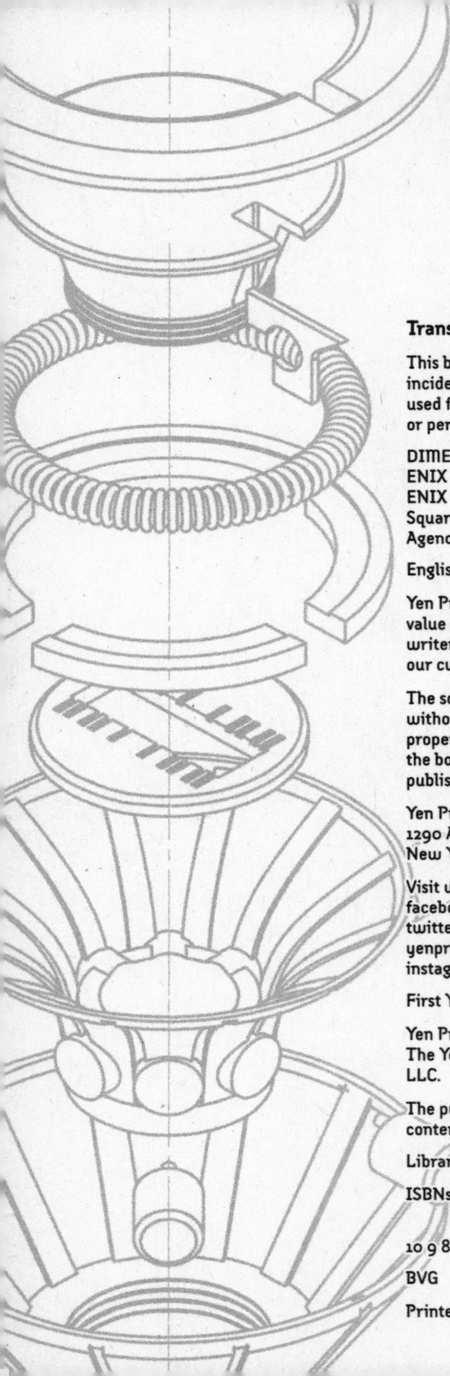

## by YUJI IWAHARA

Translation: Amanda Haley · Lettering: Phil Christie

This book is a work of fiction. Names, characters, places, and incidents are the product of the author's imagination or are used fictitiously. Any resemblance to actual events, locales, or persons, living or dead, is coincidental.

DIMENSION W Volume 6 ©2014 YUJI IWAHARA/SQUARE ENIX CO., LTD. First published in Japan in 2014 by SQUARE ENIX CO., LTD. English translation rights arranged with Square Enix Co., Ltd. and Yen Press, LLC through Tuttle-Mori Agency, Inc.

English translation © 2017 by SQUARE ENIX CO., LTD.

Yen Press
1290 Avenue of the Americas
New York, NY 10104

Visit us at yenpress.com
facebook.com/yenpress
twitter.com/yenpress
yenpress.tumblr.com
instagram.com/yenpress

First Yen Press Edition: May 2017

Yen Press is an imprint of Yen Press, LLC.
The Yen Press name and logo are trademarks of Yen Press, LLC.

The publisher is not responsible for websites (or their content) that are not owned by the publisher.

Library of Congress Control Number: 2015956889

ISBNs: 978-0-316-39779-7 (paperback)
978-0-316-39780-3 (ebook)

10 9 8 7 6 5 4 3 2 1

BVG

Printed in the United States of America